MTEL 47 Math
Middle School Math MTEL Preparation

Mary DeSouza

Table of Contents

I.   Introduction 8
    About the Author 8
    How to Use This Book 8
    About the Test 9
    Test-Taking Strategies 10
    Test Day Preparation 11

1.   Numbers & Operations 13
    Foundations 14
    Numbers & Place Value 20
    Factors, Divisibility, Multiples 26
    Operations 32
    Signed Numbers & Absolute Value 41
    Properties of Numbers 48
    Computation Methods 56
    Module Review 63

2.   Number Sense 77
    Fractions 78
    Decimals 88
    Percents & Conversions 96
    Powers, Roots, Bases 104
    History of Math 112
    Module Review 119

3.   Functions & Equations 133
    Algebraic Expressions 134
    Relations & Functions 141
    Solving Equations 150
    Inequalities 157
    Ratios & Proportions 165
    Operations with Functions 172
    Sequences & Series 181
    Module Review 190

4. Geometry I 203
- Unit Conversions 204
- Circles 209
- Triangles 215
- Perimeter & Area 221
- Coordinate Plane 227
- Module Review 235

5. Algebra & Graphing 249
- Slope & Rate of Change 250
- Graphing Linear Equations & Inequalities 256
- Systems of Equations 262
- Quadratic Equations 271
- Graphing Quadratics 281
- Advanced Functions & Graphing 291
- Algebra Word Problems 300
- Module Review 308

6. Geometry II 325
- Angles, Parallel & Perpendicular Lines 326
- Transformations 333
- Similar & Congruent Polygons 339
- 3-Dimensional Objects & Volume 344
- Surface Area 351
- Geometric Properties & Proofs 358
- Module Review 366

7. Statistics & Probability 377
- Gathering & Visualizing Data 378
- Central Tendency & Dispersion 385
- Sample Space & Probability 391
- Permutations & Combinations 399
- Advanced Statistics 406
- Module Review 414

8. Trigonometry, Calculus, Discrete Math **425**
- Introduction to Trigonometry 426
- Trigonometric Identities & Properties 433
- Trigonometric Graphs 441
- Differential Calculus 448
- Integral Calculus 455
- Discrete Math 461
- Module Review 470

9. Open Response **483**
- Open Response Strategies 484
- Open Response Sample 1 486
- Open Response Sample 2 489
- Open Response Sample 3 492
- Open Response Sample 4 495
- Open Response Sample 5 498

10. Diagnostic Exam **503**
- Diagnostic Questions 504
- Answers & Explanations 514

11. Final Exam **529**
- Final Exam Questions 530
- Answers & Explanations 551

12. Appendix **585**
- Formula Sheet 586
- Glossary 587

I. Introduction

About the Author 8
How to Use This Book 8
About the Test 9
Test-Taking Strategies 10
Test Day Preparation 11

Introduction: About the Author

Mary DeSouza graduated from MIT with a bachelor's degree and a master's degree in Computer Science and Electrical Engineering. She has over 15 years of teaching experience, including designing courses and teaching as an adjunct faculty member at UMASS Boston; TAing discrete math at MIT; and developing curriculum for and teaching classes in high school computer science, LSAT, algebra, geometry, science, humanities, and K-8 math and computers. Outside of teaching, Mary worked in engineering, product management, and strategy for companies including Edusoft and Oracle. In the past few years, she has spoken at international education conferences and has served as Professional Math Consultant at Merrimack College, founder of Omega Teaching, and Research and Development Manager at Houghton Mifflin Harcourt. She currently is the CEO of Dynamite Learning (www.dynamitelearning.com) and MTELprep (www.mtelprep.com) and can be contacted at mary@mtelprep.com.

Introduction: How to Use This Book

This book is designed to help you succeed on the Massachusetts Tests for Educator Licensure (MTEL) Middle School Mathematics (47) Exam. Each test area is given its own separate section in the book so that you can follow a study path that works best for you.

I recommend that you work through all chapters of the book at least once. Each of chapters 1 through 8 is followed by a quiz that will help you to gauge your level of preparedness and see which concepts require further study. Chapter 9 provides guidelines, sample answers, and strategies for the Open Response section. Print out the formula sheet which can be found in the appendix, and get comfortable using it while you work through the problems.

Take the diagnostic exam after you've gone through all nine chapters. Based on your results, go back and review any areas of weakness. Then, take the final exam two weeks before your test date. Make sure to use the test-taking strategies outlined in the book.

Passing the MTEL 47 exam is critical for your future role as a licensed teacher, but understanding the concepts is just as important. With this book and your commitment, you can achieve both goals. Good luck!

Introduction: About the Test

The MTEL Middle School Mathematics (47) exam tests proficiency in the subject areas required to teach math at grades 5–8 in Massachusetts. Prospective middle school math teachers must pass this exam to receive their state teaching license. While this test is challenging, it's also an exciting opportunity to take the next step in your career as a teacher.

Test Structure and Scoring

The MTEL 47 test includes 100 multiple-choice questions and 2 open response questions. Questions are broken down as follows:

Subarea	Number of Questions	Approx. Test Weighting
I. Number Sense and Operations	18–20	15%
II. Patterns, Relations, and Algebra	30–32	25%
III. Geometry and Measurement	21–23	18%
IV. Data Analysis, Statistics, and Probability	14–16	12%
V. Trigonometry, Calculus, and Discrete Math	12–14	10%
VI. Integration of Knowledge & Understanding	2 (Open Response)	20%

The open response question tests your ability to relate concepts from several different areas. You should give yourself about 20 to 30 minutes for each of these two questions.

You will have four hours to complete the test. You might find that you need less time, but be prepared to stay for the entire four hours. Use any remaining time to check your work for accuracy.

Test Objectives

The chapters of this book are mapped to the objectives of the exam. You can download a full list of the objectives from the test-makers' website at **www.mtel.nesinc.com**.

Registering for the MTEL 47

The MTEL 47 exam is held five times per year and can be taken at several test locations throughout Massachusetts. Register for the exam through **www.mtel.nesinc.com** or by calling (866) 565–4894.

The Day of the Test

On test day, bring only your admission ticket, a valid photo ID, a second form of identification (such as a birth certificate or Social Security card), and several sharpened #2 pencils. Cellular phones are prohibited at test sites.

Note that calculators are <u>not allowed</u> on the MTEL 47. You will be provided with a formula sheet, which can be found in the appendix.

Introduction: Test-Taking Strategies

Knowing the subject matter is the best way to prepare for the MTEL exam. But, test-taking strategies can make a difference to your score. Follow these tips to make the most of your performance on the day.

1. Read the Entire Question
Read the entire question carefully before you start solving the problem. Otherwise, there's a chance you will miss some crucial information.

2. Use Your Time Wisely
If you know how to solve the problem, go ahead and do it! But don't waste time on problems that cover material you don't know. Circle these problems and come back to them after you have completed the other problems. Know your strengths and weaknesses, and make decisions based on them.

3. Write It Down
Write out the steps for complex calculations instead of trying to do them in your head. Under test pressure, your ability to perform mental calculations will be put under strain. Writing things down also makes it easier to spot mistakes in your approach.

4. Leave No Blanks
Answer every question, even if that means guessing. You will not be deducted any points for incorrect answers.

5. Eliminate, Then Guess
It's to your advantage to guess on this test, but be clever about it. Eliminate any unreasonable answer choices before guessing.

6. Back Solving
Since the questions are multiple-choice, you can plug the numbers from the answer choices into the question. For example:
Which of the following values for N will make the statement true? $N \times N = N + N$
  A. 1
  B. 2
  C. 3
  D. 4
Try each option in the statement and see which one makes it true.

7. Estimate First
If you quickly estimate the answer before looking at the choices, you are less likely to get thrown off by distractors. It will also help you determine how much work is needed to solve the problem.

8. Plugging In

"Plugging In" can be a useful time-saving strategy when dealing with formula and equation questions. Guess a number; plug it into the original problem; and then plug it into each answer choice to see what works. Make sure to plug in valid numbers. For example, if a problem is dealing with minutes, use 30 or 60, not −143.

Example: If N is an even number, which of the following products is an odd number?

A. $(N + 1)(N - 3)$
B. $(N + 1)(N + 2)$
C. $N(N + 1)$
D. $N(N - 3)$

Think of any even number, such as 4. Then, plug that number into each answer choice to see which option results in an odd number.

9. Open Response Questions

When answering the open response question, remember to address each directive and to write from the perspective of a teacher reviewing a student's work. Answer the question thoroughly to receive as many points as possible. For more on this, see *Chapter 9: Open Response*.

10. Check Your Work

For both the open response and multiple-choice questions, use your remaining time to go back and review your work.

Test Day Preparation

- Before the day of the test, make sure that you know where your test center and its parking facilities are located.

- Check the official MTEL website for a list of items allowed at the test site. Remember, a calculator is not allowed on this test.

- The day before the test, make sure to review the test-taking strategies and open response strategies.

- Try to relax and get a good night's sleep before the test. Performing well in this test requires critical thinking, which is best done when you are fully alert.

- Plan to get to the test center early in case there are unforeseen issues with registration or parking.

1. Numbers & Operations

Foundations..14
Numbers & Place Value...20
Factors, Divisibility, Multiples...................................26
Operations..32
Signed Numbers & Absolute Value.........................41
Properties of Numbers..48
Computation Methods..56
Module Review..63

Numbers & Operations: Foundations

Sets of numbers

Most likely, numbers and counting were the first things you learned about in math. You might have begun by learning about the set of **"natural" or counting numbers:** 1, 2, 3, 4... Later, your knowledge would have expanded to include all **whole numbers**, the set of natural numbers plus zero: 0, 1, 2, 3...

Integers include zero and all the positive and negative numbers that do not need to be represented with fractions or decimals. A number line is a great way of visualizing integers.

If a number can be written as a fraction, it is a **rational** number. Rational numbers include all decimals that either terminate or repeat, since those numbers can be expressed as fractions. Numbers, such as π, whose decimals do not terminate or repeat, are called **irrational** numbers. The **real** numbers include all rational and irrational numbers.

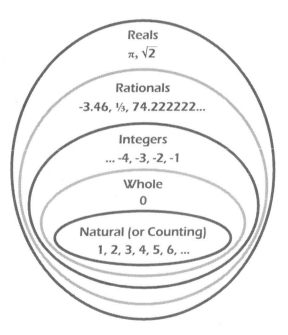

The diagram shows the relationship among the sets of numbers.

For instance, the integers include the negatives and all the whole numbers, while the whole numbers include 0 and the counting numbers.

Each of these sets is infinitely large. In other words, there is not a finite number of whole numbers. You can always keep adding 1 to the largest and get another whole number.

Other common number sets include the **evens** and **odds**. Even numbers include all numbers that equal 2 times an integer, for example –6, 0, 2, 10. Odd numbers are all integers that are not even, such as –5, 1, 9, or 17.

Ordering and Comparing Numbers

The number line helps to show the order of numbers. The farther to the right a number is, the greater its value. For example, when comparing two negative numbers, the one closest to zero will be greater.

The following symbols are used to compare numbers:

= Equal to
> Greater than
< Less than
≥ Greater than or equal to
≤ Less than or equal to

Examples:

28 > 12   (28 is greater than 12)
−12 < −4 (−12 is less than −4)

Foundations: Practice

1. What is the greatest integer smaller than 100?

    A. −99

    B. 99.99

    C. 99½

    D. 99

2. What is a possible value for x if 12 > x > 8?

    A. 9

    B. 20

    C. 7

    D. Not possible

3. What is a possible value for x if 12 < x < 8?

    A. 9

    B. 20

    C. 7

    D. Not possible

4. Identify the properties of the number 3.25.

    I. Integer
    II. Irrational
    III. Real

A. I and III
B. III only
C. II and III
D. I, II, and III

5. Which of the following numbers are irrational?

    I. 1/3
    II. –12.451
    III. π

A. None
B. I and III
C. III only
D. All

6. Which answer is a list of negative integers ordered from least to greatest?

A. –8, –9, –10, –11
B. –8.5, –9.5, –10.5, –11.5
C. 8, 9, 10, 11
D. –11, –10,- 9, –8

7. How many integers are greater than –3 but less than 4?

A. 5
B. 6
C. 7
D. 8

8. How many negative odd integers exist between −10 and 4?

   A. 5
   B. 6
   C. 7
   D. 8

9. How many positive rational numbers are greater than −2 and less than 7?

   A. 6
   B. 7
   C. 9
   D. An infinite number

10. The fraction 1/3 is equal to 0.33333333... (repeats forever). Which of the following number sets does it belong to?

    I. Integers
    II. Rationals
    III. Reals

    A. III only
    B. II and III
    C. I and III
    D. I, II, and III

Foundations: Answer Explanations

1. D An integer is a whole number that can be positive, negative, or zero. Integers do not include decimals or fractions. Answer choices A (−99) and D (99) are the only integers. Answer choice D is the greatest integer smaller than 100.

2. A Let's look at the statement 12 > x > 8.

x must meet two different conditions:

    12 must be greater than x

    x must be greater than 8

Go through each answer choice and eliminate those that don't work. 12 is not greater than 20 (eliminate B). 7 is not greater than 8 (eliminate C). Answer choice A works: 12 is greater than 9, and 9 is greater than 8.

3. D Let's look at the statement 12 < x < 8.

x must meet two different conditions:

    12 must be less than x

    x must be less than 8

No number exists that is both bigger than 12 and less than 8. Answer D is correct.

4. B Let's examine each property against the number 3.25:

    I. Integer – Remember, integers do not include decimals or fractions. Therefore, 3.25 is not an integer.

    II. Irrational – Irrational numbers are numbers that cannot be expressed as fractions. 3.25 can be expressed as $^{325}/_{100}$ or $3¼$, so it is not irrational.

    III. Real – Real numbers include all rational and irrational numbers. Therefore, 3.25 is a real number.

5. C Irrational numbers are numbers that cannot be expressed as fractions.

    I. 1/3: Since this number is a fraction, it is rational.

    II. –12.451: Any number with a terminating decimal can be expressed as a fraction. In this case, –12.451 = –12451/1000. Therefore, it is rational.

    III. π: π cannot be written as a fraction. If π is written in decimal form, it goes on forever and does not repeat. Therefore, it is the only irrational number in the list.

6. D   Negative integers do not include any decimals or fractions. That eliminates option B. Option C only includes positive numbers.

Now, let's examine options A and D.

   A: −8, −9, −10, −11
   D: −11, −10, −9, −8

When comparing two negative numbers, the one closest to zero is greater. So, −10 is greater than −11. Here, the numbers in option D are ordered from least to greatest.

7. B   List all the integers greater than −3 and less than 4. Remember to include 0:

   −2, −1, 0, 1, 2, 3

This gives 6 numbers.

8. A   List all the negative odd integers between −10 and 4:

   −9, −7, −5, −3, −1

This gives 5 numbers.

9. D   There is an infinite number of rational numbers between any two integers. Rationals include any number that can be made into a fraction – for example, 1.1, 1.231, and 1.42347824 are all rational numbers.

10. B   Integers do not include fractions or decimals, so $\frac{1}{3}$ is not an integer.

Rationals are any numbers that can be expressed as fractions, including decimals that repeat forever. So, $\frac{1}{3}$ is rational.

Real numbers include all rationals and irrationals. Therefore, $\frac{1}{3}$ is real.

Numbers & Operations: Numbers & Place Value

Place Value

The number 9,876,543 could be viewed simply as a string of digits. But, with an understanding of place value, you can break the number into its parts. In 9,876,543, the digit 7 stands for 70,000, and the 6 represents 6,000. Each digit is given a specific value by its place in the number. The chart shows some place values.

```
       one millions
          hundred thousands
             ten thousands
                one thousands
                   hundreds
                      tens
                         ones
9 , 8 7 6 , 5 4 3
```

Numbers can be written in expanded form, which shows the value of each digit.

For example: 9,876,543 = 9,000,000 + 800,000 + 70,000 + 6,000 + 500 + 40 + 3

Illustrating Place Value

Pictures or blocks are often used to illustrate the concept of place value. A small block represents one unit. A group of ten small blocks makes a stick used to represent the tens place. This approach makes it easy to see, for instance, that 3 sticks represent 30 blocks or the number 30. The same concept applies to the hundreds and thousands of blocks.

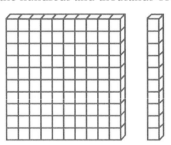

These blocks can also be useful for visualizing redistribution, which is necessary for addition and subtraction. To imagine redistribution, think of a stick of 10 blocks broken into single units or vice versa.

Rounding and Estimation

Imagine that you drove 1,297 miles on a road trip. You would most likely tell your friends you drove 1,300 miles. Approximating numbers to the powers of ten in this way is called rounding. Rounding is useful for quickly estimating the outcome of various operations.

There are specific rules for rounding:

To round a number to a place value, you must look at the value of the digit to the right of the rounding digit. For example, look at the value of the digit in the tens place when rounding to the hundreds place.

If the digit is a number from 0 to 4, round down by keeping the rounded digit the same and make the digits to the right equal to zero. For example, to round 938 to the nearest hundred, look at the digit in the tens place. Because 3 is less than 5, round down to 900.

If the digit is a number from 5 to 9, round up by increasing the digit by 1 and then making all digits to the right equal to zero. For example, to round 217 to the tens place, look at the digit in the ones place. It is 7, which is greater than 5, so you must round up to 220.

If the digit to be rounded up is a 9, then two digits of your number will be affected. For example, if you are rounding 1,296 to the nearest tens, you would first note that the 9 is in the tens place. You would then look to the right of that 9 and see that the 6 is between 5 and 9, and you must round up. First, make the 6 a zero and then round the 9 up by 1 digit to 10. This creates a problem as you can't put a two-digit number in the tens place. So, you must redistribute, giving you 1,300.

$1296 = 1000 + 200 + 90 + 6$

We rounded the 90 to 100 and made the 6 a zero.

$= 1000 + 200 + 100 + 0$
$= 1300$

Numbers & Place Value: Practice

1. What digit is in the ten-thousands place in the following number: 5,609,823

    A. 6

    B. 0

    C. 9

    D. 5

2. Round 72,349 to the nearest hundred.

    A. 72,350

    B. 72,000

    C. 72,300

    D. 72,400

3. Identify the number shown to the right.

    A. 5

    B. 14

    C. 104

    D. 1004

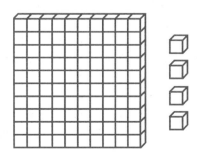

4. Which number is equal to the expanded form 800,000 + 3000 + 600 + 20 + 1?

    A. 83,621

    B. 836,210

    C. 803,621

    D. 830,621

5. Choose the correct symbol to replace the question mark.

    A. >

    B. <

    C. =

    D. ≥

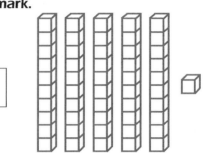

6. Round 28,956 to the nearest hundred.

    A. 28,900

    B. 28,960

    C. 29,000

    D. 29,100

7. Which number has a 6 in the hundreds place but not in the hundredths place?

    A. 632.165

    B. 8642.165

    C. 64.046

    D. 8642.046

8. Order the following from least to greatest: I. 7000 + 6

    II. 800 + 90 + 9

    III. 7000 + 30

    A. I, III, II

    B. III, I, II

    C. II, I, III

    D. II, III, I

Numbers & Operations: Numbers & Place Value

9. What number is equal to 40 + 1000 + 900 + 300000?

   A. 4,193
   B. 3,194
   C. 31,940
   D. 301,940

10. Order the following from least to greatest:

    I. 300,000 + 80,000
    II. 30,000 + 9000 + 900
    III. 300,000 + 70,000 + 900 + 90

    A. I, II, III
    B. II, I, III
    C. III, II, I
    D. II, III, I

Numbers & Place Value: Answer Explanations

1. B   5,609,823 -- Working from the right, the following are the place values:

   3 is in the ones place

   2 is in the tens place

   8 is in the hundreds place

   9 is in the thousands place

   0 is in the ten-thousands place

   6 is in the hundred-thousands place

   5 is in the millions place

2. C   To round 72,349 to the nearest hundred, first determine which digit is in the hundreds place. In this case, it is 3. Now, if the number to the right is 5 or greater, you round the 3 up. In this case, the number is 4, so you leave the 3 the same and add two zeros to the right.

3. **C**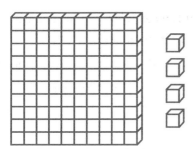

    The large block represents 100. Each small block represents 1.

    There are 1 large block and 4 small blocks to give a total of 104.

4. **C**   This question gives you the expanded form 800,000 + 3000 + 600 + 20 + 1.

    You can either add the numbers or look at the place values:

        8 is positioned in the hundred-thousands place

        There is no value in the ten-thousands place

        3 is in the thousands place

        6 is in the hundreds place

        2 is in the tens place

        1 is in the ones or unit place

5. **B**   First, figure out the value of each image.

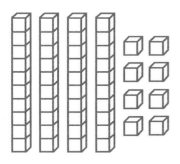 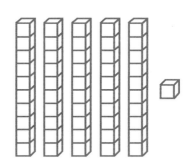

    4 tens and 8 ones = 48.   5 tens and 1 one = 51

    48 is less than 51. This can also be written as 48 < 51.

6. C   To round 28,956 to the nearest hundred, first identify which digit is in the hundreds place. In this case, it is 9. The digit to its right is a 5, so you must round up.

Since the next number after 9 is 10, you must change both the digit in the hundreds place and the digit in the thousands place. Add a 1 to the digit in the thousands place and change the 9 to 0, which gives a rounded number of 29,000.

7. D   The hundreds place is three to the left of the decimal point. The following decimals have a six there:

     A: 632.165

     B: 8642.165

     D: 8642.046

The hundredths place is two to the right of the decimal point. Options A and B both have a 6 in this position, which cancels them out, leaving option D as the answer.

8. C   First, determine the value of each so that they can be ordered:

     I. $7000 + 6 = 7006$

     II. $800 + 90 + 9 = 899$

     III. $7000 + 30 = 7030$

Ordering these values from least to greatest gives us 899; 7006; 7030.

9. D   First, put the numbers in decreasing order:

     $40 + 1000 + 900 + 300000$

     $= 300000 + 1000 + 900 + 40$

Next, convert from expanded form to standard form:

     $300,000 + 1,000 + 900 + 40 = 301,940$

10. D   First, change each number from expanded form to standard form:

     I. $300,000 + 80,000 = 380,000$

     II. $30,000 + 9,000 + 900 = 39,900$

     III. $300,000 + 70,000 + 900 + 90 = 370,990$

Now, order the numbers from least to greatest:

     39,900; 370,990; 380,000

Numbers & Operations: Factors, Divisibility, Multiples

Factors

A factor of a number is an integer that divides evenly into the number with no remainder. For example, 5 is a factor of 50, since 50 divided by 5 is 10 with no remainder. However, 6 is not a factor of 50, since 50 divided by 6 is 8 with a remainder of 2. A number that has only 1 and itself as factors is called a **prime number**. Examples of prime numbers include 5, 17, and 23.

The greatest common factor (GCF) of two numbers is the largest factor that they both share. To explain, let's figure out the GCF of 24 and 18.

Factors of 24: 1, 2, 3, 4, 6, 8, 12, 24

Factors of 18: 1, 2, 3, 6, 9, 18

The largest factor they both share, or GCF, is 6.

Fundamental Theorem of Arithmetic

The fundamental theorem of arithmetic states that every positive integer can be expressed as a product of prime numbers. The theorem also states that it can be expressed in only one way, other than rearrangement. This product of the prime numbers is known as the prime factorization of the number.

Finding the prime factorization of numbers is a critical first step to many arithmetic and algebraic concepts, such as simplifying and factoring numbers, all of which are covered in later lessons. One way to find the prime factorization of a number is by using a factor tree. The "leaves" at the bottom of the two factor trees here are the prime factors of the number 200. It doesn't matter that each level is different; the final prime factorization will always be the same.

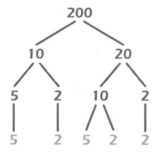 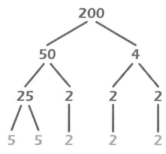

The prime factorization of 200 can be written as 5 x 2 x 5 x 2 x 2 = 5 x 5 x 2 x 2 x 2 = $5^2 \times 2^3$

There is a trick to finding the number of factors of a number. From the prime factorization, add 1 to each exponent and find the product. For 200, the exponents are 2 and 3 ($5^2 \times 2^3$). Add 1 to each and multiply to find the total number of factors. (2 + 1)(3 + 1) = 3 x 4 = 12. There are 12 factors of 200.

Factors, Divisibility, Multiples: Practice

1. Identify factors of 36.

       I. 12

       II. 24

       III. 72

A. I only

B. III only

C. I and II

D. I, II, and III

2. How many factors does 24 have?

A. 4

B. 6

C. 8

D. 9

3. Write 234 as a product of its prime factors.

A. 39 x 6

B. 13 x 2 x 3

C. 13 x 2 x 3^2

D. 13 x 23

4. Find the least common multiple of 12 and 48.

A. 12

B. 24

C. 48

D. 96

5. Find the least common multiple of 15, 25, and 6.

    A. 1

    B. 75

    C. 150

    D. 2250

6. Which of the following numbers is divisible by 9?

    A. 3201

    B. 4050

    C. 3009

    D. 7127

7. Two teams are competing to split all the candy in a jar. If Team A wins, each member will get 6 pieces. If Team B wins, each member will get 5 pieces. Which of the following could be the total amount of candy in the jar?

    A. 65

    B. 36

    C. 11

    D. 60

8. What is the largest prime number less than 70?

    A. 69

    B. 68

    C. 67

    D. 61

9. What is the sum of the least common multiple and greatest common factor of 12 and 24?

    A. 30

    B. 36

    C. 54

    D. 60

10. What is the sum of the prime numbers greater than 1 and less than 20?

    A. 58
    B. 60
    C. 75
    D. 77

Factors, Divisibility, Multiples: Answer Explanations

1. A   A number is a factor of 36 if it divides evenly into 36 with no remainder.

   I. $36 \div 12 = 3$, so 12 is a factor.

   II. $36 \div 24 = 1$ remainder 12, so 24 is not a factor.

   III. 72 does not divide evenly into 36. 72 is a multiple of 36, not a factor.

2. C   The factors of 24 are: 1, 2, 3, 4, 6, 8, 12, and 24.

You could also find the prime factorization of 24 and then use the trick of adding 1 to each exponent and finding the product.

$24 = 3 \times 2 \times 2 \times 2 = 3^1 \times 2^3$

Number of factors $= (1 + 1)(3 + 1) = (2)(4) = 8$

3. C   One way to find the prime factors of a number is to create a factor tree.

The prime factors of 234 are $3 \times 3 \times 2 \times 13$, or $3^2 \times 2 \times 13$.

You could also use the process of elimination on the answer choices. First, eliminate any answer choice that does not have all prime factors. For instance, answer A is not made up of prime numbers. Next, multiply out the remaining answers to see which multiplies to 234.

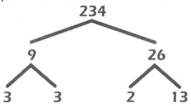

4. C   Remember that the least common multiple (LCM) is the smallest non-zero multiple that a set of numbers share. The LCM can be equal to one of the numbers.

   Multiples of 12: 12, 24, 36, 48...

   Multiples of 48: 48...

48 is the smallest multiple that both numbers share.

5. C One way to find the least common multiple (LCM) is to list out the multiples until you find the smallest one they share.

    Multiples of 25: 25, 50, 75, 100, 125, 150

    Multiples of 15: 15, 30, 45, 60, 75, 90, 105, 120, 135, 150

    Multiples of 6: 6, 12, 18, 24, 30, 36, 42, 48, 54, 60, 66, 72, 78, 84, 90, 96, 102, 108, 114, 120, 126, 132, 138, 144, 150

Another way to find the LCM is to find the prime factors of each number and then multiply the highest powers of each unique prime factor together.

    15 as a product of prime factors = 3 x 5

    25 as a product of prime factors = 5^2

    6 as a product of prime factors = 2 x 3

The highest powers of the prime factors are: 2 x 3 x 5^2 = 150

6. B One way to solve this problem is to divide each number by 9 to see which one leaves no remainder. Another way is to use the shortcut for determining whether a number is divisible by 9. If you add the digits of a number and that sum is divisible by 9, the original number is also divisible by 9.

Answer choice B satisfies this requirement: 4 + 0 + 5 + 0 = 9, which is divisible by 9.

7. D All the candy can be split evenly into either 6 pieces if Team A wins or 5 pieces if Team B wins. This means that the total amount of candy must be divisible by both 5 and 6.

60 is the only answer that is evenly divisible by 5 and 6.

8. C First, no even numbers other than 2 will be prime since they will always have 2 as a factor. This eliminates answer choice B. Next, count backwards from 70 until you find a prime number.

69 is not prime. You can check this by using the divisibility rule for 3. 6 + 9 = 15 and 15 is divisible by 3, therefore 69 is divisible by 3.

67 is a prime number. It has no factors other than 1 and itself.

9. B The least common multiple (LCM) is the smallest number that both 12 and 24 multiply evenly to. Since both 12 and 24 go evenly into 24, it is the LCM.

The greatest common factor (GCF) is the biggest number that divides evenly into both 12 and 24. Since 12 divides evenly into both 12 and 24, and it is the greatest factor of 12, it is the GCF.

The sum of 12 and 24 is 36.

10. D List all the prime numbers greater than 1 and less than 20, and then add them.

2, 3, 5, 7, 11, 13, 17, 19

$2 + 3 + 5 + 7 + 11 + 13 + 17 + 19 = 77$

Numbers & Operations: Operations

Addition

Addition is the process of combining two or more numbers to get a total.

To add large numbers, line the numbers up vertically by place value and add the digits of each column, beginning with the ones place.

For example, 7,325 + 10,644 = ?

$$\begin{array}{r} 7,325 \\ +10,644 \\ \hline 17,969 \end{array}$$

Sometimes, adding numbers will require redistribution (see place values module). Adding 50 + 70 involves redistribution. You have 5 tens and 7 tens, which adds up to 12 tens. Ten of those tens can be combined or redistributed to 1 hundred, with 2 tens remaining. Therefore, the sum of 50 and 70 is 100 + 20 or 120. Here is another sample problem with redistribution. In this question, the 9 ones and the 3 ones added to 12 ones. Those were redistributed to 1 ten, leaving 2 ones.

$$\begin{array}{r} 4563 \\ +1319 \\ \hline 5882 \end{array} \quad 3+9=12$$

Subtraction

Subtraction is the inverse of addition, and the result of a subtraction problem is called the difference of the numbers subtracted. As with addition, line up big numbers by place value to subtract, beginning with the ones place.

$$\begin{array}{r} 97,642 \\ -23,120 \\ \hline 74,522 \end{array}$$

Redistribution is necessary in subtraction when the number subtracted for a certain place value is larger than the number it is subtracted from. In such cases, one from the place value above is broken into ten pieces.

$$\begin{array}{r} {}^{711} \\ 7281 \\ -5137 \\ \hline 2144 \end{array}$$

In the ones place, 1 is smaller than 7, therefore you must redistribute.

From the tens place, you take 1 from the 8 to make it a 7, and you break that into ten ones. Those ten ones are added to the 1 to make 11.

Multiplication

Multiplication, which is repeated addition, results in the product of two or more numbers. Three multiplied by four is the same as adding four three times (3 x 4 = 4 + 4 + 4 = 12) or three four times (3 x 4 = 3 + 3 + 3 + 3 = 12).

In order to multiply large numbers, multiply each digit of one number by each digit of the other number and sum the results.

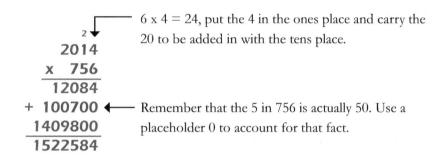

6 x 4 = 24, put the 4 in the ones place and carry the 20 to be added in with the tens place.

Remember that the 5 in 756 is actually 50. Use a placeholder 0 to account for that fact.

Division

Division is the inverse of multiplication, and the result of a division problem is called a quotient. It asks how many groups of a given number can be made out of another number. For example, how many groups of 2 can be made out of 12? 12 ÷ 2 = 6; six groups of 2 can be made out of 12.

Long division is division that shows each step of the process. Unlike all other basic operations, long division starts with the greatest place value and works back to the ones.

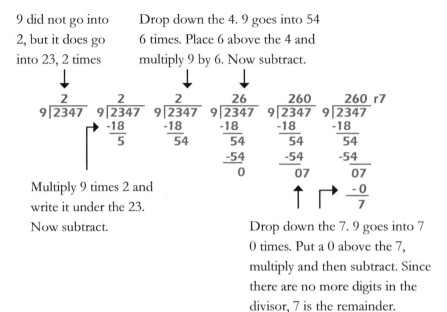

Steps:

1. Determine how many times the divisor (9) goes into the first part of the dividend.

2. Place that number above the line. Mulitply the divisor by that number.

3. Subtract, and bring down the next digit of the divisor.

4. Determine how many times the divisor goes into that number. Repeat steps 1–3.

The problem above had a remainder of 7. It can also be thought of as 7/9. Or, you can add a decimal place and zeros to the dividend and continue the long division process.

Order of Operations

For problems containing multiple operations, there is a standardized order in which these operations must be carried out. Without such an order, a single problem could generate multiple answers. The order is

Parentheses
Exponents
Multiplication and **D**ivision from left to right
Addition and **S**ubtraction from left to right

A common mnemonic device for remembering the order is "Please Excuse My Dear Aunt Sally."

Example: 200 − 7 + 6 x (2 x 3) ÷ 4 =

200 − 7 + 6 x (2 x 3) ÷ 4 =	Parentheses first.
200 − 7 + 6 x 6 ÷ 4 =	No Exponents. Multiply and Divide from left to right.
200 − 7 + 36 ÷ 4 =	Keep multiplying and dividing.
200 − 7 + 9 =	Now Add and Subtract from left to right.
193 + 9 =	The final addition step.
202	Answer.

Averages

The average of a set of numbers is equal to the sum of the numbers divided by the number of numbers.

For example, find the average of 3, 4, and 8.

Average = (3 + 4 + 8) ÷ 3 = 15 ÷ 3 = 5

Averages will be covered in more detail in the Statistics & Probability Module.

Numbers & Operations: Practice

1. **Nadine is totaling her accounts receivable and accounts payable for the month. She owes $496 to one creditor and $736 to another. She receives $1,326 from one source of income and $139 from another. How much has she gained or lost this month?**

   A. Lost $233
   B. Lost $333
   C. Gained $233
   D. Gained $333

2. **Deidre bought 5 notebooks at a cost of $2 each, and 2 bags at $7 each. If she paid $30, how much change should she receive?**

   A. $6
   B. $16
   C. $22
   D. $24

3. Jennifer gave Vanessa half her candy. Vanessa gave David half the candy she received from Jennifer. David ate 6 pieces and gave the remaining 4 pieces to John. How many pieces of candy did Jennifer start with?

   A. 5
   B. 20
   C. 40
   D. 60

4. If Jane's brother is five years older than twice her age when she is eight, how many years older is her brother?

   A. 5
   B. 10
   C. 13
   D. 21

5. If you have an average of 82 after 4 math tests, what do you need on the 5th test to increase your average to an 85?

   A. 88
   B. 92
   C. 95
   D. 97

6. 4 x 9 − 6 ÷ (2 + 1) =

   A. 4
   B. 10
   C. 16
   D. 34

7. 7958 ÷ 25 = ?

   A. 318, remainder 4
   B. 319, remainder 6
   C. 318, remainder 8
   D. 319, remainder 7

8. What number is 32 less than 8 times the quotient of 28 and 4?

   A. 0
   B. 24
   C. 88
   D. 160

9. Calculate:

$$\frac{(12+6) \div 3 \times (18-16)}{16 - 5 \times 2}$$

   A. 2
   B. 1/2
   C. 5/11
   D. 18

10. A jewelry maker manufactures 24 necklaces a week and sells them for $30 each. However, this week she noticed that 8 of them have broken clasps and cannot be sold. If her weekly costs are $64, how much profit will she make this week?

   A. 648
   B. 544
   C. 464
   D. 416

Numbers & Operations: Answer Explanations

1. C   Add the total amount Nadine earned. She received $1326 from one source of income and $139 from another.

$$\begin{array}{r} 1326 \\ + \ 139 \\ \hline 1465 \end{array}$$

Now, find the total amount Nadine owes. She owes one creditor $496 and another $736.

```
   496
 + 736
  1232
```

Nadine earned $1465 and owes $1232.

```
   1465
 - 1232
    233
```

Therefore, she gained $233 this month.

2. A First, figure out the total amount Deidre spent:

She bought 5 notebooks at $2 each. 5 x $2 = $10.

She bought 2 bags at $7 each. 2 x $7 = $14.

Add those two quantities to determine her total spending: $10 + $14 = $24.

Finally, subtract the total from $30 to figure out her change: $30 − $24 = $6.

3. C This problem is best solved by working backward.

John: Got 4 pieces.

David: Ate 6 pieces and gave 4 to John. 6 + 4 = 10.

Vanessa: Gave half to herself and half to David. If 10 is half, then Vanessa must have received 20 pieces.

Jennifer: Gave half to herself and half to Vanessa. If 20 is half, then Jennifer must have started with 40 pieces.

4. C Translate words into numbers.

Jane's age x 2 + 5 = Jane's brother's age when Jane is 8.

8 x 2 + 5 = 16 + 5 = 21

When Jane is 8, her brother is 21. The difference between their ages is 21 − 8 = 13.

5. D In average problems, it is often easier to think of the problem in terms of sums.

First, find the sum of the scores on the first 4 math tests: 82 x 4 = 328.

If you want an average of 85 for all 5 tests, the sum of your scores must be 85 x 5 = 425.

You now know the sum on 4 tests, along with the sum that you need on 5 tests to hit your 85 average. Subtract to find the score required on the 5th test: 425 − 328 = 97.

6. D   Use the order of operations: PEMDAS.

Parentheses first:

$$4 \times 9 - 6 \div (2 + 1) =$$
$$4 \times 9 - 6 \div 3 =$$

Multiply and Divide from left to right:

$$4 \times 9 - 6 \div 3 =$$
$$36 - 6 \div 3 =$$
$$36 - 2 =$$

Finally, Add and Subtract from left to right:

$$36 - 2 =$$
$$34$$

7. C

```
      318 R8
25 ) 7958
    -75
     45
    -25
     208
    -200
       8
```

8. B   Let's take the words and translate them into an equation.

"You have a number that is 32 less than 8 times the quotient of 28 and 4." Remember the quotient is the result of a division problem. Therefore, let's change the final phrase into an equation.

The number is 32 less than 8 times (28 ÷ 4).

"Times" means multiplication, so change that word to a multiplication symbol:

32 less than 8 × (28 ÷ 4)

Numbers & Operations: Operations

Be careful – you don't want 32 minus that product, you want 32 less than that product. Therefore, subtract 32 from the product.

$8 \times (28 \div 4) - 32$

Now, solve the problem following the order of operations:

$8 \times (28 \div 4) - 32 =$

$8 \times (7) - 32 =$

$56 - 32 = 24$

9. A

$$\frac{(12 + 6) \div 3 \times (18 - 16)}{16 - 5 \times 2} =$$

$$\frac{18 \div 3 \times 2}{16 - 5 \times 2} =$$

$$\frac{6 \times 2}{16 - 10} =$$

$$\frac{12}{16 - 10} =$$

$$\frac{12}{6} = 2$$

10. D First, set up an equation for the profit and substitute in the values:

Profit = Revenue – Costs

= (Sold necklaces x Price) – Costs

= (24 – 8) x 30 – 64

Now, solve the equation, following the order of operations:

(24 – 8) x 30 – 64

= 16 x 30 – 64

= 480 – 64

= 416

Numbers&Operations: Signed Numbers & Absolute Value

As discussed in the Foundations module, all numbers greater than zero are positive, and all numbers less than zero are negative. This can be represented on a number line:

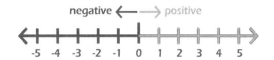

Zero is neither positive nor negative.

To add and subtract positive and negative numbers, use the following techniques:

Add two positive numbers

Add as normal. Example: 23 + 74 = 97.

Add two negative numbers

Add as usual, but place a negative sign in front of the sum. Example: –23 + –74 = –97.

Add one positive and one negative number

Subtract the smaller number from the larger, and then assign the sign of the greater number to the result.

Example: –48 + 32; Subtract: 48 – 32 = 16. Since 48 is greater, and it is negative, the answer is negative.
–48 + 32 = –16

Example: –32 + 48; Subtract: 48 – 32 = 16. Since 48 is greater, and it is positive, the answer is positive.
–32 + 48 = 16

Subtraction of a positive number

When dealing with a combination of positive and negative numbers, treat subtraction as the addition of a negative number.

Example: 25 – 75 is the same as 25 + –75. Now, follow the rules you learned for adding signed numbers. 75 – 25 = 50; 75 is greater, and it is negative, so answer is negative. 25 + –75 = –50

Example: –25 – 75 is the same as –25 + –75. Add the numbers as usual, but keep the negative sign, since they are both negative. –25 + –75 = –100

Subtraction of a negative number

Subtracting a negative number is equivalent to adding a positive number, since two negatives make a positive.

Example: $32 - -45 = 32 + 45 = 77$
Example: $-15 - (-40) = -15 + 40 = 25$

Multiplication or Division of Signed Numbers

To multiply or divide by negative or positive numbers, use the following rules:

A positive times a positive is positive. $(+)(+) = (+)$
A negative times a negative is positive. $(-)(-) = (+)$
A positive times a negative is negative. $(+)(-) = (-)$

Another way to think about that is if there is an even number of negative signs, then you get a positive answer. If there is an odd number of negative signs, the result is negative.

Example: $-2 \times -3 = 6$
Example: $-1 \times -1 \times -1 = -1$

Absolute Value

The absolute value of a number is its magnitude or distance from zero. Absolute value is always expressed in positive terms.

Example: $|42| = 42$
Example: $|-13| = 13$

Signed Numbers & Absolute Value: Practice

1. $-49 - 53 =$

　A. -4
　B. 4
　C. 102
　D. -102

2. Replace the question mark with the correct symbol.

    20 − 70 ? −70 + 20

    A. ≥
    B. >
    C. <
    D. =

3. 32 − 59 =

    A. 27
    B. −27
    C. 91
    D. −91

4. 79 x −1 x −1 =

    A. −79
    B. 97
    C. 79
    D. 77

5. Replace the question mark with the correct symbol. |−7| ? −7

    A. ≤
    B. >
    C. <
    D. =

6. Choose the best answer to replace the question mark:

    0 ? All Positive Numbers

    A. >
    B. <
    C. ≤
    D. ≥

7. Which of the following is true?

   A. The absolute value of a number is always greater than the number.

   B. The absolute value of a number is sometimes negative.

   C. The absolute value of a number is the same as the number times –1.

   D. The absolute value of a number is its distance from zero.

8. –3 x 20 ÷ –4 – 40 =

   A. –55

   B. –25

   C. 25

   D. –104

9. |20 – 33| – 17 + 6(–5) =

   A. –60

   B. –34

   C. –10

   D. 34

10. A math teacher curves all the test scores so that the average score is always 70. Sandra gets a 74 on the first test. On the next test she gets a score 11 below that. On the third test, she gets 15 points higher than her score on the second test. On the fourth test, Sandra gets 22 points below her score on the third test. How does Sandra's score on the fourth test compare to the class average?

    A. 18 below

    B. 14 below

    C. 10 below

    D. Same as class average

Signed Numbers & Absolute Value: Answer Explanations

1. D Subtraction is equivalent to adding a negative number:

$$-49 - 53 = -49 + -53$$

Add the two negative numbers and give the sum a negative sign since they are both negative:

$$-49 + -53 = -102$$

2. D These two expressions are identical. They are simply written in a different order.

You can solve each side to check:

$$20 - 70 = 20 + -70 = -50$$

$$-70 + 20 = -50$$

3. B First, change the subtraction problem into addition of a negative number.

$$32 - 59 = 32 + -59$$

Since the signs of the two numbers are different, subtract the digits and then take the sign of the larger number.

$59 - 32 = 27$. Since $59 > 32$, take the sign of 59, which is negative.

$$32 + -59 = -27$$

4. C $79 \times -1 \times -1$

To multiply signed numbers, first multiply the numbers and then determine the sign.

$$79 \times 1 \times 1 = 79$$

Count the negative signs. There are two, which is an even number, so the answer is positive.

Another way to think about it is to multiply the first two numbers, and then multiply the result by the third number.

$79 \times -1 = -79$ (since positive times negative = negative)

$-79 \times -1 = 79$ (since negative times negative = positive)

5. B Remember, the absolute value is the distance the number is from zero, and it is always expressed as a positive number.

So $|-7|$ has a value of 7.

$7 > -7$.

6. B Positive numbers are all those greater than zero. So:

 0 < All Positive Numbers

7. D Let's analyze each answer.

 A – False. The absolute value of a number will equal the number if it is a positive number. Example: $|3| = 3$

 B – False. The absolute value is always positive.

 C – False. This is only true if you are taking the absolute value of a negative number.

 D – True. The absolute value of a number is its distance from zero.

8. B To solve this question, follow the order of operations and the rules for signed numbers.

 $-3 \times 20 \div -4 - 40 =$

The first step is to multiply: $-3 \times 20 = -60$

 $-60 \div -4 - 40 =$

Next, divide: $-60 \div -4 = 15$

 $15 - 40 =$

To subtract, change the problem into the addition of a negative. $15 - 40 = 15 + -40 = -25$

9. B Following the order of operations, begin by solving what is in parentheses. You can treat the absolute value symbols as parentheses:

 $|20 - 33| - 17 + 6(-5) =$

 $|-13| - 17 + 6(-5) =$

 $13 - 17 + 6(-5)$

Next, perform the multiplication:

 $13 - 17 + 6(-5) =$

 $13 - 17 - 30$

Finally, working from left to right, add or subtract.

 $13 - 17 - 30 =$

 $-4 - 30 =$

 -34

10. B Sandra gets a 74 on her first test.

On the next test, she scores 11 below that: 74 − 11 = 63.

On the third test, she gets 15 points higher than that: 63 + 15 = 78.

She scores 22 points lower on the fourth test: 78 − 22 = 56.

Now, compare 56 to the class average: 70 − 56 = 14.

Numbers & Operations: Properties of Numbers

There are several properties of numbers, most of which you are already aware of — even if you are unfamiliar with the names.

Associative

The associative property says that for problems containing only addition or only multiplication, grouping of numbers does not affect the result. In the cases below, it does not matter whether a and b or b and c are multiplied or added first, the result will always be the same.

$$a + (b + c) = (a + b) + c$$
$$a(bc) = (ab)c$$

Commutative

The commutative property states that for problems containing only multiplication or only addition, order does not matter.

$$a + b = b + a$$
$$ab = ba$$

Distributive

The distributive property states

$$a(b + c) = ab + ac$$

On the left-hand side of the equation, a is multiplied by the sum of b and c, which is equivalent to the sum of a multiplied by b and a multiplied by c.

Example: $5(2 + 3 + 4) = 5(2) + 5(3) + 5(4) = 10 + 15 + 20 = 45$

Additive Identity

The identity of addition is 0. Therefore, any number plus zero equals itself. $17 + 0 = 17$.

In addition, any number minus zero equals itself. $17 - 0 = 17$.

The product of any number and zero is 0. $17 \times 0 = 0$.

Zero divided by any number is 0. $0 \div 17 = 0$.

No number can be divided by 0. 17 ÷ 0 cannot be done. The result is said to be undefined.

Any number raised to the power of zero is 1. $17^0 = 1$.

Multiplicative Identity

The identity of multiplication is 1. Therefore, any number times 1 will equal itself. 17 x 1 = 17.

Any number divided by 1 is itself. 17 ÷ 1 = 17.

Any number raised to the power of 1 is itself. $17^1 = 17$.

Closure

A set is said to be closed under an operation if the operation is performed on members of the set and the result is in the set.

For example, the whole numbers are closed under addition, since if you take any two whole numbers and add them, you will get another whole number. The whole numbers are not closed under subtraction, since if you take two whole numbers and subtract them, you might not get a number that is a whole number. For example, 4 – 9 = –5, which is not a whole number.

Another example would be the set {0, 1}. There are just two elements in this set. Let us think about which operations this set is closed under. It is not closed under subtraction because 0 – 1 = –1, and –1 is not a member of the set. It is not closed under addition, because 1 + 1 = 2, which is not a member of the set. It is not closed under division, as you can't divide by zero. However, it is closed under multiplication, because if you take every combination from members of this set and multiply them, you will always get a product that is also a member of this set. 0 x 0 = 0, 0 x 1 = 0, 1 x 1 = 1. The set {0, 1} is closed under only multiplication.

Properties of Numbers: Practice

1. Which property could you use to calculate the following product more easily?

815 x 100.1

A. Associative

B. Commutative

C. Distributive

D. Identity

2. How would you estimate the sum of 9,178,456 and 97?

    A. 9,178,500 + 100

    B. 9,178,400 + 100

    C. 9,178,000 + 0

    D. 9,178,500 + 95

3. Identify the false statement(s).

        I. $0 \div 7 = 0$

        II. $7 \div 0 = 7$

        III. $7 \div 0 = 0$

    A. I and II

    B. II and III

    C. I and III

    D. I, II, and III

4. Simplify the following expression using the distributive property: $\dfrac{12x + 4y - 16}{4}$

    A. $3x + 4y - 16$

    B. $3x + y - 16$

    C. $12x + 4y - 4$

    D. $3x + y - 4$

5. The associative and commutative properties apply to which of the following operations?

    A. Addition only

    B. Addition and Multiplication

    C. Adding and Subtraction

    D. Addition, Subtraction, Multiplication, and Division

6. **What is the value of $99^1 - 99^0$?**

   A. 0
   B. 1
   C. 98
   D. 99

7. **The even numbers are closed under which of the following operations?**

   A. Only addition and subtraction.
   B. Only addition and multiplication.
   C. Only addition, subtraction, and multiplication.
   D. Addition, subtraction, multiplication, and division.

8. **Choose the best answer to replace the question mark.**

   $p(r - s)$? $pr - ps$

   A. >
   B. <
   C. =
   D. Not enough information.

9. **What is 8(9 + 6)7 the same as?**

   I. 7(9 + 6)8
   II. 8 x 9 + 6 x 7
   III. 8 x 9 x 7 + 8 x 6 x 7

   A. I only
   B. II only
   C. I and III
   D. I and II

10. **Which property would help to solve the following problem quickly in your head?**

    5 x 73 x 2

   A. Associative
   B. Commutative
   C. Inverse
   D. Identity

Properties of Numbers: Answer Explanations

1. C The distributive property would be useful in calculating the product. The property states that $a(b + c) = ab + ac$.

Let's see how it could be applied to this problem.

The number 100.1 can be broken into the sum of two numbers:

815 x 100.1 = 815 x (100 + .1)

The distributive property can then be used:

815(100+.1) = 815(100) + 815(.1)

Both of these products can be calculated in your head:

815(100) + 815(.1) = 81500 + 81.5 = 81581.5

2. A When estimating a sum, first look at the smaller of the two numbers. In this case, 97 is very close to 100. Therefore, you should round both numbers to the nearest hundred:

9,178,456 to the nearest hundred is 9,178,500

97 to the nearest hundred is 100

3. B You can never divide by 0 in math. This can be explained by the rule that division is the inverse of multiplication. For example, if you said that $7 \div 0 = n$, that would mean that n multiplied by 0 would result in 7. Nothing times zero will ever give you 7. Therefore, you can never divide by 0.

4. D First, use the distributive property on the numerator to factor out any like terms.

Numerator: $12x + 4y - 16 = 4(3x + y - 4)$

$(12x + 4y - 16)/4 = 4(3x + y - 4)/4$

Now, you can divide both the numerator and denominator by 4.

Dividing the denominator by 4 results in 1.

Dividing the numerator by 4 leaves $(3x + y - 4)$.

$4(3x + y - 4)/4 = 3x + y - 4$

5. B The associative and commutative properties only hold true for addition and multiplication. Here are some examples:

Associative

Addition: $9 + (4 + 5) = (9 + 4) + 5$

Multiplication: $6 \times (2 \times 5) = (6 \times 2) \times 5$

Subtraction: $9 - (4 + 5) \neq (9 - 4) + 5$

Division: $(12 \div 4) \div 2 \neq 12 \div (4 \div 2)$

Commutative

Addition: $9 + 4 + 5 = 5 + 4 + 9$

Multiplication: $6 \times 2 \times 5 = 2 \times 6 \times 5$

Subtraction: $9 - 4 - 5 \neq 5 - 4 - 9$

Division: $40 \div 4 \div 2 \neq 4 \div 40 \div 2$

6. C Any number raised to the power of 1 is itself.

Any number raised to the power of 0 is 1.

$99^1 = 99$

$99^0 = 1$

$99^1 - 99^0 = 99 - 1 = 98$

7. C Remember that if a set is closed under an operation, the result of any operation to members of the set will also be a member of the set. Let's go through the operations with the even numbers.

Addition

If you add any two even numbers, you will always get another even number. For instance, suppose one number is 2x and another is 2y:

$2x + 2y = 2(x + y)$

Subtraction

Similar to addition, subtracting any two even numbers will always result in another even number. For example:

$2x - 2y = 2(x - y)$

Multiplication

Since an even number has 2 as a factor, multiplying two even numbers will give you a number that still has 2 as its factor.

Division

If you divide an even number by another even number, you don't always end up with an even number. For instance, 12 divided by 4 is 3, which is odd.

8. C This is an example of the distributive property with different variables. Do not get thrown off by the minus sign. Remember that while the original definition of the distributive property refers to addition, subtraction is the same as the addition of the opposite.

$p(r - s)$

The distributive property states that you multiply each term on the outside by each term on the inside.

$p(r - s) = pr - ps$

9. C To solve this problem, you use both the commutative and distributive properties. Let's examine each option.

  I. 7(9 + 6)8

The original problem is the multiplication of three expressions: 8, 9 + 6, and 7. This option differs only in that the positions of 7 and 8 are moved. The commutative property states that you can multiply in any order, and the result will be the same.

  II. 8 x 9 + 6 x 7

To expand our original expression, you start by multiplying the terms inside the parentheses by 8. 8(9 + 6) = 8 x 9 + 8 x 6. Even before multiplying by 7, you can see that option II is not an equivalent expression.

  III. 8 x 9 x 7 + 8 x 6 x 7

To verify this, expand the original expression using the distributive property.

  8(9 + 6)7 = (8 x 9 + 8 x 6)7 = 8 x 9 x 7 + 8 x 6 x 7

10. B Multiplying 5 by 73 in your head would be quite difficult. However, multiplying 5 by 2 first would give you 10. Then, you could multiply 10 by 73 in your head to give you 730.

Changing the order in which you multiply is an example of using the commutative property.

Numbers & Operations: Computation Methods

This lesson reviews the different ways of looking at the four basic operations and highlights the connections among those operations. It also introduces a few additional methods of performing these operations.

Addition and Subtraction

Addition and subtraction are a pair of inverse or opposite operations, meaning that either operation can be undone by the other. For example, $12 - 5 = 7$, $7 + 5 = 12$. Subtracting 5 from a number and then adding 5 to the result will lead back to the original number.

Adding is sometimes taught as "counting forward" from a particular number. For example, $29 + 3$ would be counting forward 3 times: 30, 31, 32. Subtraction can be thought of as counting backward: $32 - 3$: 31, 30, 29.

Multiplication and Division

Multiplication and division make up the other set of inverse operations. Each can be represented in many ways. Here are a few:

Multiplication is generally introduced as repeated addition: adding a number to itself the number of times indicated by the multiplier.

$4 \times 5 = 4 + 4 + 4 + 4 + 4$

Division is often shown as repeated subtraction – subtracting the divisor from the dividend until reaching zero. For repeated subtraction, the number of times the divisor is subtracted from the dividend is equal to the quotient.

$12 \div 3 = ?$; $12 - 3 - 3 - 3 - 3 = 0$; $12 \div 3 = 4$

Rules for Evens and Odds

Anytime two even numbers are added or subtracted, the result will be an even number.
Examples: $4 + 8 = 12$, $22 - 6 = 16$.

Anytime two odd numbers are added or subtracted, the result will be an even number.
Examples: $13 + 5 = 18$, $21 - 7 = 14$.

When one even and one odd number are added or subtracted, the result will always be odd.
Examples: $13 - 2 = 11$, $5 - 8 = -3$, $6 + 9 = 15$.

Whenever an even number is multiplied by an even number or an odd number, the result will be even. Examples: 2 x 4 = 8, 6 x 5 = 30.

When an odd number is multiplied by an odd number, the result will be odd. Examples: 3 x 5 = 15, 7 x 11 = 77.

For division, you might get remainders when dividing even and odd numbers.

Arrays

Arrays are great ways to represent both multiplication and division visually. For multiplication, 6 x 2 could be translated into 6 groups of 2 and drawn as

To calculate the result, you would count the total number of elements. A division problem, such as 12 ÷ 2, could be solved by drawing 12 objects and then circling groups of 2 (as in the image above). The number of groups would be the quotient. 12 ÷ 2 = 6.

Partial Products Method for Multiplication

The concept behind the partial products method is to take the base ten factor of each number, multiply all the terms, and then find their sum. This is easier to illustrate with an example, which is done below.

Multiply 32 x 65:

32 breaks into 30 and 2

65 breaks into 60 and 5

Now, multiply all the possible combinations:

30 x 60 = 1800

30 x 5 = 150

2 x 60 = 120

2 x 5 = 10

Find the sum: 1800 + 150 + 120 + 10 = 2080

32 x 65 = 2080

Lattice Method for Multiplication

This one is also easier to understand by going through an example.

In this problem, we are multiplying 32 by 65.

You put the two numbers you are multiplying on the outside, one along the top, one along the right-hand side.

Then, for each box, you multiply the two integers and put the tens digit above the diagonal and the ones digit below the diagonal. For instance, in the top right box, you multiply 2 by 6, and you get 12. In the top left box, the result is from multiplying 3 and 6.

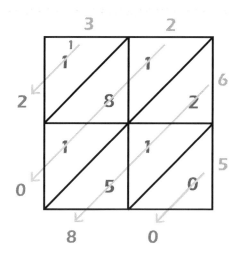

32 x 65 = 2080

Finally, you add along the diagonals, from the right to the left. The first diagonal adds to 0, and then next is 5 + 1 + 2, which gives you 8. The next diagonal is 1 + 8 + 1 = 10. Therefore, put the 0 down and carry the 1. Finally, 1 and 1 = 2.

Now, the product can be read out. 32 x 65 = 2080.

Computation Methods: Practice

1. How many positive integers less than 200 are divisible by both 7 and 3?

   A. 9
   B. 10
   C. 20
   D. 28

2. An even integer divided by an even integer can be

   I. even
   II. odd
   III. fraction

A. I only
B. II only
C. I and III
D. I, II, and III

3. 8 + 8 + 8 + 8 + 8 + 8 =

A. 86
B. 68
C. 6 x 8
D. 6 + 8

4. If you add 17 to a number and then divide the sum by 3, how can you manipulate the result to return to the original number?

A. Subtract 17 and then multiply by 3
B. Add 17 and then divide by 3
C. Multiply by 3 and then subtract 17
D. Subtract 17 and then divide by 3

5. What is one method that can be used to solve 200 ÷ 50?

A. 200 ÷ 5 x 10
B. 200 − 50 − 50 − 50 − 50
C. 200 x 10 ÷ 5
D. 20050

6. Which number line shows how to solve −3 − 4?

A.

B.

C.
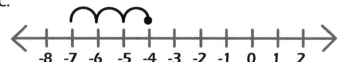

D.
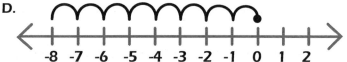

7. If you needed to solve 101 x 73 using mental math, which method would you use to help solve it quickly?

   A. Repeated addition
   B. An array
   C. Distributive property
   D. Counting forward

8. The sum of an even number and an odd number is:

   A. Always odd
   B. Always even
   C. Sometimes odd and sometimes even
   D. Depends on the numbers

9. Identify the two missing numbers.

A. 1 and 2
B. 0 and 4
C. 2 and 3
D. 0 and 3

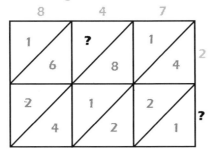

10. The array below could be used to solve which problem?

A. 20 ÷ 5
B. 10 x 2
C. 4 + 5
D. 15 + 5

Computation Methods: Answer Explanations

1. A   If a number is divisible by both 7 and 3, the number is divisible by the lowest common multiple of those numbers. The lowest common multiple of 7 and 3 is 21, since that is the smallest number that both divide evenly into.

We need to figure out how many integers less than 200 are divisible by 21. To figure this out, we divide by 21 to find the number of numbers that are evenly divisible. If you divide 200 by 21, you get 9 11/21. That means that 9 different numbers are multiples of 21 and less than 200.

2. D   An even integer divided by an even can be even. For example: 20 ÷ 2 = 10.

An even divided by an even can be odd. For example: 12 ÷ 4 = 3.

An even divided by an even can be a fraction. For example: 6 ÷ 8 = 3/4

3 C   Multiplication is repeated addition. 8 added to itself 6 times is the same as 8 times 6.

4. C   To "undo" an operation, apply its inverse. Addition is the inverse of subtraction. Multiplication is the inverse of division.

Since division was the last operation performed, you must first do the opposite of this operation. The inverse of divide by 3 is multiply by 3.

The next operation to undo is adding 17, so you must subtract 17.

5. B Repeated subtraction is one way to solve a division problem. Subtract the divisor from the dividend and keep subtracting until you reach zero. The number of times you subtract will be the quotient.

200 − 50 − 50 − 50 − 50 = 0

50 is subtracted 4 times, therefore 200 ÷ 50 = 4

6. B To use a number line to solve a subtraction problem, start at the first number in the problem (−3) and move to the left.

7. C The distributive property is useful when solving complex multiplication problems with mental math:

101 x 73 =

(100 + 1) x 73 =

73 x 100 + 1 x 73 =

7300 + 73

7373

8. A Whenever you add an even and an odd number, you get an odd number.

Examples: 4 + 3 = 7, 12 + 5 = 17, 12 + 11 = 23, 2 + 7 = 9

9. D The lattice method is one way to multiply large numbers. The complete lattice is shown here:

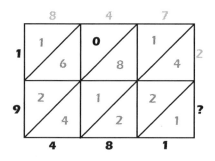

Let's look at the first missing number from the top row. This is the tens digit of the multiplication of the numbers 4 and 2. Since the answer is 8, the tens digit is 0.

The second missing number is the ones digit of the number multiplied. The square in the bottom right shows 21 – the product of 7 and the missing number. 21 divided by 7 gives you 3.

10. A The array shows 20 objects, which are divided into groups of 5 rows and 4 columns.

Numbers & Operations: Module Review

1. Choose which of the following are true about 21,936:

    I. It is divisible by 12.

    II. It is divisible by 8.

    III. It is divisible by 6.

    A. I only
    B. I and II
    C. I and III
    D. I, II, and III

2. Which of the following is a set of four consecutive odd integers?

    A. 1, 2, 3, 4
    B. 0, 1, 3, 5
    C. –9, –11, –13, –17
    D. –3, –1, 1, 3

3. On an extremely cold day in Chicago, the temperature at noon was 3°. By 6 p.m., the temperature had dropped another 5 degrees. If the wind chill factor reduces the temperature by another 10 degrees, what does it feel like outside at 6 p.m., factoring in the wind chill?

    A. –18°
    B. –12°
    C. –8°
    D. 8°

4. Choose all the answers that are true about −4.3:

   I. integer
   II. irrational
   III. real

A. I and III
B. II only
C. III only
D. I, II, and III

5. If the number 720 is written as a product of its prime factors in the form ab^2c^4, then what is the sum of a, b, and c?

A. 10
B. 19
C. 25
D. 27

6. −12 + 3 x −7 + |−4 + 6| x 6 =

A. −45
B. −21
C. 21
D. 27

7. Which of the following is/are false?

   I. Adding a negative number is the same as subtracting the absolute value of that number.
   II. Zero is a negative number.
   III. Any multiplication problem containing a negative number will produce a negative answer.

A. I and II
B. II and III
C. I and III
D. III only

8. What is the product of the least common multiple and greatest common factor of 12, 8, and 6?

   A. 24
   B. 36
   C. 48
   D. 96

9. Four monkeys are stealing bananas from the trees: Monkeys A, B, C, and D. Monkey A steals 9 bananas. Monkey B steals 3 less than 4 times what A stole. C steals the difference of A and B. Monkey D steals 2 more than twice C. How many bananas total did the four monkeys steal?

   A. 80
   B. 82
   C. 116
   D. 118

10. What is the sum of the following 2 numbers in proper expanded form?

    First number: 200,000 + 30,000 + 8,000 + 70 + 6
    Second number: 400,000 + 80,000 + 900 + 10

    A. 700,000 + 10,000 + 8,000 + 900 + 80 + 6
    B. 600,000 + 10,000 + 8000 + 900 + 80 + 6
    C. 600,000 + 110,000 + 8000 + 900 + 80 + 6
    D. 700,000 + 10,000 + 8,000 + 900 + 70 + 16

11. If an even number is multiplied by an odd number and then added to an odd number, the result will be

    A. Even
    B. Odd
    C. Zero
    D. Not enough information

12. Patricia drove the first 120 miles of her trip at 40 mph and the remaining 120 miles at 60 mph. What was her average speed for the entire trip?

    A. 45 mph
    B. 48 mph
    C. 50 mph
    D. 52 mph

13. If you wanted to solve 31 x 101 + 10 quickly in your head, what would you do?

    A. Commutative Property
    B. Associative Property
    C. Distributive Property
    D. Identity Property

14. In the following problem, what properties were used from step 1 to 2 and step 2 to 3, respectively?

    1. 4(16 + 23) + 36 =
    2. 64 + 92 + 36 =
    3. 64 + 36 + 92 =
    4. 100 + 92 = 192

    A. Distributive, Associative
    B. Associative, Commutative
    C. Distributive, Commutative
    D. Commutative, Associative

15. If you subtract 6 from a number and then multiply the difference by 8, how can you manipulate the result to return to the original number?

    A. Add 6. Then, divide by 8.
    B. Subtract 6. Multiply by 8.
    C. Divide by 8. Then, add 6.
    D. Multiply by 8. Subtract 6.

16. You have a string of beads that starts with the following beads: Red, Yellow, Blue, and Green. This sequence continues throughout the entire string. What color is the 49th bead?

   A. Red
   B. Yellow
   C. Blue
   D. Green

17. How many integers between 600 and 700, inclusive, are divisible by both 5 and 3?

   A. 7
   B. 15
   C. 33
   D. 53

18. $(30 + 17) \div 2 =$

   I. $47 \div 2$
   II. $15 + 8½$
   III. $(30 \div 2) + (17 \div 2)$

   A. I only
   B. I and III
   C. II and III
   D. I, II, and III

19. The negative integers are closed under which operations?

   A. Addition only.
   B. Addition and multiplication only.
   C. Addition, subtraction, multiplication, and division.
   D. Not closed under any operations.

20. If you were finding the product of 73 and 24 using the partial products method of multiplication, then you would sum what numbers?

   A. 6 + 12 + 14 + 28
   B. 146 + 292
   C. 72 + 168
   D. 12 + 60 + 280 + 1400

Module Review: Answer Explanations

1. D To figure out whether a number is divisible by 12, you can divide by 12 and see if it goes in evenly. However, the easier way is to check if the number is divisible by both 3 and 4.

To determine divisibility for 3, remember you can add the digits and check if the sum is divisible by 3. 2 + 1 + 9 + 3 + 6 = 21. 21 is divisible by 3; therefore, 21,936 is also divisible by 3.

To determine divisibility for 4, you can check if the last two digits are divisible by 4. In this case, 36 is divisible by 4; therefore, 21,936 is also divisible by 4.

Since, 21,936 is divisible by 3 and 4, it is divisible by 12. I is true.

To determine divisibility by 8, you can check if the last three digits are divisible by 8. In this case, 936 ÷ 8 = 117. Therefore, 21,936 is divisible by 8. II is true.

Since we already determined that 21,936 is divisible by 12, we know that it must also be divisible by 6. III is true.

I, II, and III are all true.

2. D Integers are numbers that can be positive, negative, or zero, but not decimals or fractions. Odd integers are not divisible by 2. We want a list of consecutive odd integers; therefore, each number in the list must be the next biggest odd integer. Let's examine each answer choice:

   A: 1, 2, 3, 4: These are not all odd integers. 2 and 4 are even.

   B: 0, 1, 3, 5: These are not all odd integers. 0 is not odd.

   C: −9, −11, −13, −17: These are all odd integers. However, they are not consecutive. Between −13 and −17, there is another odd integer, −15.

   D: −3, −1, 1, 3: These are consecutive odd integers.

3. B If the temperature was originally 3° and then dropped 5°, you must subtract to find the new temperature.

$$3° - 5° = -2°$$

Now, we must factor in the wind chill effect, which would drop the temperature another 10°, so we must subtract.

$$-2° - 10° = -12°$$

4. C Let's examine each option.

I. Integers – these include positive and negative numbers, but no fractions or decimals. Therefore, –4.3 is not an integer.

II. Irrationals – these are numbers that cannot be expressed as fractions. Numbers that can be expressed as fractions are rational. Since decimals that repeat or terminate can be expressed as fractions, these numbers are rational, not irrational. –4.3 can be expressed as the fraction –43/10 and, therefore, is a rational number. II is not true.

III. Real – all rational and irrational numbers are real. Therefore, –4.3 is real.

III only.

5. A The easiest way to solve this problem is first to make a factor tree.

Then, take the bottom "leaves" of this factor tree.

$$720 = 3 \times 2 \times 3 \times 2 \times 5 \times 2 \times 2$$

Then, write the product of any repeated factors as the factor to a power.

$$720 = 5 \times 3^2 \times 2^4$$

We can now see that a = 5, b = 3, and c = 2.

$$a + b + c = 5 + 3 + 2 = 10$$

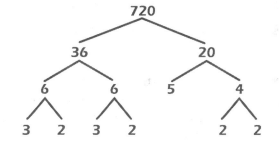

6. B $-12 + 3 \times -7 + |-4 + 6| \times 6 =$

Follow the order of operations (PEMDAS).

P – Parentheses. First, perform what is in the absolute value signs, since the absolute value signs act as parentheses for what is inside.

$$-12 + 3 \times -7 + |-4 + 6| \times 6 =$$
$$-12 + 3 \times -7 + |2| \times 6 =$$
$$-12 + 3 \times -7 + 2 \times 6 =$$

Numbers & Operations: Module Review

E – No exponents.

MD – Multiplication and Division from left to right.

$-12 + 3 \times -7 + 2 \times 6 =$

$-12 + -21 + 2 \times 6 =$

$-12 + -21 + 12 =$

AS – Addition and Subtraction from left to right.

$-12 + -21 + 12 =$

$-33 + 12 =$

-21

7. B The question asks for which statements are false. Let's analyze each option.

I. Adding a negative number is the same as subtracting the absolute value of that number. -- This statement is true. For example: $5 + -3 = 5 - 3 = 2$

II. Zero is a negative number. --This statement is false. Zero is neither positive nor negative.

III. Any multiplication problem containing a negative number will produce a negative answer. --This statement is false. Multiplication problems with an even number of negative numbers will give a positive answer. For example: $-3 \times -2 = 6$.

Therefore, II and III are false.

8. C First, let's find the least common multiple of 12, 8, and 6. You can start listing the multiples of each of them until you find a common one.

12: 12, 24

8: 8, 16, 24

6: 6, 12, 18, 24

24 is the LCM of the three numbers.

Now, let's find the greatest common factor. List the factors of each number.

12: 1, 2, 3, 4, 6, 12

8: 1, 2, 4, 8

6: 1, 2, 3, 6

The GCF is 2.

The product of the LCM and the GCF is $2 \times 24 = 48$.

9. C Let's break this problem down to figure out how many bananas each monkey stole.

Monkey A steals 9 bananas.

    The number A stole has been given, 9.

Monkey B steals 3 less than 4 times what A stole.

    First, find 4 times A and then subtract 3.

    $4(9) - 3 = 36 - 3 = 33$

Monkey C steals the difference of A and B.

    $33 - 9 = 24$

Monkey D steals 2 more than twice C.

    Multiply 24 by 2, and then add 2.

    $24 \times 2 + 2 = 48 + 2 = 50$

Now, find the sum.

    $9 + 33 + 24 + 50 = 116$

    116 total bananas.

10. A There are two ways to approach this problem. Leave the numbers in expanded form and add or convert to standard form, add, and then convert back to expanded form.

Method 1: Convert to standard form and then back.

    First number: $200{,}000 + 30{,}000 + 8{,}000 + 70 + 6 = 238{,}076$

    Second number: $400{,}000 + 80{,}000 + 900 + 10 = 480{,}910$

    Now, add: $238{,}076 + 480{,}910 = 718{,}986$

    Convert back to standard form:

    $718{,}986 = 700{,}000 + 10{,}000 + 8{,}000 + 900 + 80 + 6$

Method 2: Leave in expanded form and add.

When adding numbers in expanded form, it is easiest to start with the smallest place value and work up.

    First number: $200{,}000 + 30{,}000 + 8{,}000 + 70 + 6$

    Second number: $400{,}000 + 80{,}000 + 900 + 10$

    Ones Place: 6.

    Tens Place: $70 + 10 = 80$

    Hundreds Place: 900

Thousands Place: 8,000

Ten-Thousands Place: 30,000 + 80,000 = 110,000

The ten-thousands place went beyond the ten-thousands. Therefore, keep the 10,000 for the ten-thousands place, and bring the 100,000 to the next place.

Hundred-Thousands Place: 100,000 + 200,000 + 400,000 = 700,000

Now, write the number in expanded form:

700,000 + 10,000 + 8,000 + 900 + 80 + 6

11. B An even number multiplied by an odd number will always be even. The reason is that an even number has 2 as a factor, and if you multiply a number with 2 as a factor, the product will also have 2 as a factor. Therefore, the product will be even.

Now, we will take the even number and add it to an odd number. An odd number is just one more than any even number. Therefore, even + odd = even + even + 1.

Two even numbers added will always give you an even number, and since both numbers have 2 as a factor, their sum will also have 2 as a factor. So, even + even = even.

even + odd = even + even + 1

= even + 1

= odd

Result will always be odd.

12. B To find the average speed, divide the total number of miles by the total time.

Patricia drove the first 120 miles at 40 mph. Therefore, divide the distance by the speed to find the time it took.

120 miles ÷ 40 mph = 3 hours

She drove the remaining 120 miles at 60 mph. Divide to find the time this part of the trip took.

120 miles ÷ 60 mph = 2 hours

The total number of miles driven = 120 miles + 120 miles = 240 miles.

The total time for the trip = 3 hours + 2 hours = 5 hours.

Average speed = Total miles ÷ Total time

240 miles ÷ 5 hours = 48 mph

13. C To solve the problem, 31 x 101 + 10, in your head, you would want to make the multiplication easier. The way to accomplish this is to separate the multiplication into two easier multiplication problems, which can be done with the distributive property.

$$31 \times 101 + 10 =$$
$$31(100 + 1) + 10 =$$
$$31(100) + 31(1) + 10 =$$
$$3100 + 31 + 10 =$$
$$3141$$

The commutative property would not work since you can't commute across different operations. The same is true for the associative property. Following the order of operations, you must multiply and then add.

Answer C: Distributive Property

14. C From Step 1 to Step 2:

1. $4(16 + 23) + 36 =$
2. $64 + 92 + 36 =$

In the above steps, the property used was the distributive property. The distributive property states that multiplication distributes to each term over addition.

From Step 2 to Step 3:

2. $64 + 92 + 36 =$
3. $64 + 36 + 92 =$

In the above steps, the 92 and 36 changed their order for addition. The commutative property states that you can change the order without changing the result.

Distributive, Commutative

15. C To "undo" an operation, apply its inverse. Addition is the inverse of subtraction. Multiplication is the inverse of division.

Since multiplication was the last operation performed, you must first undo this operation. The inverse of multiply by 8 is divide by 8.

The next operation to undo is subtracting 6, so you must add 6.

Divide by 8. Then, add 6.

16. A Every four beads, the pattern "Red, Yellow, Blue, Green" repeats. Therefore, the bead in any position that is divisible by 4 will be Green.

Since 48 is divisible by 4, the 48th bead will be green. The 49th bead must be red, since a red bead always comes after a green bead.

17. A If a number is divisible by both 5 and 3, then it must be divisible by 15. Now, we need to find out how many integers between 600 and 700 are divisible by 15.

Starting with 600, since 15 divides evenly into that, count the numbers divisible by 15:

600, 615, 630, 645, 660, 675, 690 --- There are 7 integers

18. D $(30 + 17) \div 2 =$

Let's examine each answer.

I. $47 \div 2$

This is definitely true. Order of operations states that you do what is in parentheses first, which in this case is adding 30 and 17 to get 47.

II. $15 + 8\frac{1}{2}$

As division by 2 is the same as multiplication by $\frac{1}{2}$, this is an example of the use of the distributive property with division. To solve the original problem without first doing the operation in parentheses, you have to divide each term in the parentheses and then find their sum.

$(30 + 17) \div 2 = (30 \div 2) + (17 \div 2) = 15 + 8\frac{1}{2}$

III. $(30 \div 2) + (17 \div 2)$

This is true, and it was a step that was used to calculate II. See above.

I, II, and III are all true.

19. A If a set is closed under an operation, that means that if you perform that operation to any two numbers in that set, you will always end up with another number in that set. In this case, the set we are dealing with is the set of all negative integers. Let's go through a few examples of each operation to get a better idea of whether the negative integers are closed under each.

Addition: We must see that if we take any two negative integers and add them, we always end up with another negative integer. First, an example: $-3 + -5 = -8$. If you add any two negative integers, we will clearly end up with an integer, as no fractions or decimals will be part of the problem. By thinking about the number line, if you start with a negative integer, then you are to the left of zero, and if you add another negative integer, you will get farther to the left, therefore, staying negative. Negative integers, therefore, are closed under addition.

Subtraction: Let's see if we can find two negative integers that when subtracted give you an answer that is not a negative integer. –3 – (–5) = 2. We subtracted two negative integers, and the result was positive. Therefore, negative integers are not closed under subtraction.

Multiplication: A negative integer multiplied by a negative integer will always give you a positive number. Not closed under multiplication.

Division: A negative integer divided by a negative integer will result in a positive number. Not closed under division.

The set of negative integers is only closed under the operation addition.

20. D When solving using the partial products method of multiplication, take the base ten factors of each number, multiply all combinations of the terms, and then find their sum.

$$73 = 70 + 3$$
$$24 = 20 + 4$$

We want to find then the product of each set of terms:

$$70 \times 20 = 1400$$
$$70 \times 4 = 280$$
$$3 \times 20 = 60$$
$$3 \times 4 = 12$$

To find the product of 73 and 24, you would find the sum of the above products.

$$73 \times 24 = 1400 + 280 + 60 + 12 = 1752$$

2. Number Sense

Fractions...78
Decimals..88
Percents & Conversions.......................................96
Powers, Roots, Bases..104
History of Math..112
Module Review...119

Number Sense: Fractions

Fraction Definition

A fraction is simply a number that expresses parts of a whole. The classic way of beginning to work with fractions is to use shapes.

In this example, you see four squares, three of which are shaded. If you think of all four squares as the "whole," then it makes sense to say that three out of four, or three fourths, of the squares are shaded.

When you write in fractional notation, you use a numerator, the number on top of the bar, or division sign (we'll return to the idea of fractions as division later in this lesson), and a denominator, the number on the bottom. Going back to the squares example, you would write three fourths as ¾. The denominator, a 4 in this case, gives the number of parts in the whole. The numerator states the number of parts that satisfy a certain requirement. With regard to the squares, 3 of the 4 total parts meet the requirement of being shaded, so if asked what fraction of the squares is shaded, you answer ¾.

Naming Fractions

Now that you understand the parts of a fraction, you need to be able to name them. The system is simple, use the normal word for the number in the numerator and, for the denominator, use the word for describing someone's place in a line. For example, write $\frac{1}{7}$ as one seventh or write $\frac{82}{95}$ as eighty-two ninety fifths.

Equivalent Fractions

Since the denominator of a fraction describes the total number of parts in the whole, and the numerator states the number of parts that you "have," when does a fraction equal one whole?

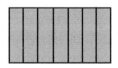

In this picture, all seven rectangles are filled in. You write this fraction as $\frac{7}{7}$, which equals one. Whenever the numerator of a fraction equals the denominator, the fraction equals one. This property of fractions is very useful in mathematics because you can multiply or divide any number or variable by one, or any fraction that equals one, without changing its value.

Here's an example of multiplying a fraction by a fraction equal to one without changing its value:

¼ x 2/2 = 2/8 = ¼

If you look at the shaded areas of the circles below, you will see that the fractions ¼ and 2/8 are equal.

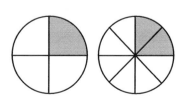

Simplifying Fractions

Manipulating numbers by multiplying and dividing by fractions equal to one is necessary to find the simplest form of a fraction. Simplest form is a way of writing a fraction so that the numerator and denominator have no common factors other than one. If asked to put $^{54}/_{72}$ into simplest form, you should recognize that 54 and 72 share the factor 9. Divide the numerator by 9, and then divide the denominator by 9.

$$^{54}/_{72} \div ^{9}/_{9} = ^{6}/_{8}$$

Now that you have simplified the fraction, see if it can be simplified further. Both 6 and 8 share the factor of 2.

$$^{6}/_{8} \div ^{2}/_{2} = ^{3}/_{4}$$

Since 3 and 4 share no common factors, this fraction is in simplest form. It pays to simplify fractions after adding, subtracting, multiplying, and dividing. The correct answer to a multiple-choice problem will usually be in simplest form.

Comparing Fractions

Another time you will need to manipulate fractions in this way is when you compare them. When comparing fractions, remember that the larger the denominator is, the more parts the whole is divided into. Since the whole is split into more parts, the parts are smaller. Look at the figure to the right, which shows that $^{1}/_{4}$ is greater than $^{1}/_{8}$.

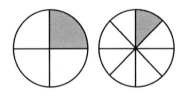

The numerator works in the opposite way. Since the numerator describes the parts of the whole that meet the requirements, a larger numerator includes more parts. Therefore, $^{3}/_{8}$ is smaller than $^{7}/_{8}$.

One easy way to compare fractions is to manipulate them so that they all have the same denominator. Since you know that you can multiply and divide any number by one, that's easy. Look at the following example:

Put the fractions $^{1}/_{4}$, $^{3}/_{32}$, $^{11}/_{64}$, and $^{9}/_{16}$ in order from least to greatest.

By multiplying by fractions equal to one, all the numbers above can be converted to fractions with a denominator of 64.

$$^{1}/_{4} \times ^{16}/_{16} = ^{16}/_{64}$$
$$^{3}/_{32} \times ^{2}/_{2} = ^{6}/_{64}$$
$$^{9}/_{16} \times ^{4}/_{4} = ^{36}/_{64}$$

Now, the problem is easy; with common denominators, the fractions can be ordered by their numerators from least to greatest: $6/64 < 11/64 < 16/64 < 36/64$.

Therefore, $3/32 < 11/64 < 1/4 < 9/16$.

While many people find the concept of fractions intimidating, a deep understanding of the subject is necessary for understanding and expressing probabilities, which will be discussed in Chapter 8. Make sure that you are comfortable manipulating fractions before moving on.

Adding and Subtracting Fractions

The first step when adding or subtracting fractions is to convert them to a common denominator. To make things simple, use the least common denominator, which is the least common multiple of all the denominators to be added or subtracted. After you convert all the fractions to the same denominator, you can add and subtract them by adding and subtracting their numerators and keeping the denominator the same. Remember to simplify the result.

$$9/17 - 17/51 + 6/34$$

The least common multiple for 17, 51, and 34 is 102, so that is the least common denominator for the fractions above. Convert each fraction's denominator to 102 by multiplying by a fraction equal to one.

$$9/17 \times 6/6 = 54/102$$
$$17/51 \times 2/2 = 34/102$$
$$6/34 \times 3/3 = 18/102$$

Add and subtract the numerators left to right, and then simplify the result.

$$54/102 - 34/102 + 18/102 = (54 - 34 + 18)/102 = 38/102 = 19/51$$

Multiplying Fractions

To multiply fractions, simply multiply the numerators to get the new numerator and multiply the denominators to get the new denominator.

$$3/4 \times 7/9 = 3 \times 7 / 4 \times 9 = 21/36$$

Then, simplify if applicable. $21/36 = 7/12$

Often, it is easier to simplify before multiplying. In the same example from above:

¾ x ⁷⁄₉

There is a 3 in the numerator and a 9 in the denominator. Since 3 divides evenly into both of them, you can simplify those numbers by dividing both by 3. The 3 in the numerator becomes 1, and the 9 in the denominator becomes 3. Now, write the simplified problem and multiply.

¼ x ⁷⁄₃ = ⁷⁄₁₂

When multiplying a number by a fraction less than 1, the product will be smaller than the original number. For instance, in the above example, we multiplied ⁷⁄₃ by ¼ which is less than 1, and the resulting number ⁷⁄₁₂ is less than ⁷⁄₃.

Dividing Fractions

To divide fractions, invert the divisor, and then multiply the fractions.

¹⁵⁄₃₂ ÷ ³⁄₂ = ¹⁵⁄₃₂ x ⅔

Now, multiply the fractions. Here, you see the fractions simplified before the multiplication, since 15 and 3 are both divisible by 3, and 32 and 2 are both divisible by 2.

$$\frac{\overset{5}{\cancel{15}}}{32} \times \frac{2}{\underset{1}{\cancel{3}}} = \frac{5}{\underset{16}{\cancel{32}}} \times \frac{\overset{1}{\cancel{2}}}{1} = \frac{5}{16} \times \frac{1}{1} = \frac{5}{16}$$

Mixed Numbers

When a fraction is greater than one, you can write it as a mixed number — a number containing both a fraction and a whole number. In the following example, each square represents 1. We see two whole shaded squares, but a third square has been divided into halves. Only one of those parts is shaded. To name the portion of the squares that are shaded, we use the fraction two and one half or 2½.

Mixed numbers can be useful when adding or subtracting fractions and whole numbers, such as 4½ − 1 = 3½, or fractions with common denominators.

5¾ + 4¼ = 9⁴⁄₄ = 9 + 1 = 10.

Improper Fractions

Mixed numbers can also be written as improper fractions, or fractions with a numerator greater than the denominator, which is useful when multiplying and dividing fractions because improper fractions can be treated the same as proper fractions, those with numerators smaller than their denominators.

$7/2 \times 5/4 = 35/8$

Converting from Mixed Number to Improper Fraction

Often, you will need to convert mixed numbers into improper fractions. To do this, multiply the whole number by the denominator, and then add the numerator to that number. This will give you your new numerator, and the denominator will remain the same. For example:

$5\frac{3}{4} = {}^{(5 \times 4 + 3)}\!/_4 = {}^{23}\!/_4.$

Another way to think of the conversion is that you need to turn the whole number into a fraction with the same denominator as its accompanying fraction and then add the two. To convert $5\frac{3}{4}$, first convert 5 to a fraction with a denominator of 4 and then add that to $\frac{3}{4}$.

$5 \times 4/4 = 20/4$

$20/4 + 3/4 = 23/4$

Converting from an Improper Fraction to a Mixed Number

To convert an improper fraction into a mixed number, divide the numerator by the denominator. The quotient is the whole number, and the remainder is the numerator of the fraction.

$23/4 = 23 \div 4 = 5 \text{ remainder } 3 = 5\frac{3}{4}$

$77/9 = 77 \div 9 = 8 \text{ remainder } 5 = 8\frac{5}{9}$

Remainders as Fractions

When dividing numbers, you can think of the problem as a fraction problem. For instance, $13 \div 5$ is the same as $13/5$, so you can convert the fraction into a mixed number. $13/5 = 2\frac{3}{5}$.

Another way to think of this step is to convert the remainder into a fraction. $13 \div 5 = 2$ remainder 3. That means only 3 out of the 5 were needed to get to the next whole number. Therefore, you can write the remainder as a fraction with the remainder as the numerator and the divisor as the denominator. $13 \div 5 = 2$ remainder $3 = 2\frac{3}{5}$.

Fractions: Practice

1. Which of the following fractions is the greatest?

    A. $7/8$
    B. $8/9$
    C. $9/10$
    D. $10/11$

2. Kate is budgeting her expenses for the next month. She has allotted $2/9$ of her salary for food, $1/5$ for clothing, $7/18$ for rent, and $1/10$ for entertainment. What fraction of her salary will be left over next month?

    A. $11/42$
    B. $4/45$
    C. $31/42$
    D. $41/45$

3. $3/5 \times 8/9 =$

    A. $8/15$
    B. $11/14$
    C. $11/45$
    D. $24/14$

4. $13/9 \times 4\ 3/4 =$

    A. $247/36$
    B. $559/36$
    C. $5\ 1/12$
    D. $4\ 1/3$

5. An elementary school teacher graded $4/7$ of her class papers before lunch and $2/7$ of the papers between lunch and dinner. If she plans to finish her grading by bedtime, what fraction of the papers will she need to grade between dinner and bedtime?

    A. $6/7$
    B. $2/0$
    C. $1/7$
    D. $1/6$

Number Sense: Fractions

6. The Suarez family started filling their new swimming pool yesterday. The pool's capacity is 800 gallons, but they were only able to pump in $400\frac{3}{7}$ gallons. It rained overnight, which added another $3\frac{4}{7}$ gallons to the pool. How many gallons of water will the Suarez family need to fill the pool?

   A. 404 gallons
   B. 399 gallons
   C. 396 gallons
   D. 393 gallons

7. Louise's shoe size is $\frac{17}{24}$ feet. Andrew's shoe size is $\frac{55}{120}$ feet. What is the average of their shoe sizes?

   A. 7 inches
   B. $\frac{7}{6}$ feet
   C. 1 foot
   D. 6 inches

8. In Steve the Magician's 36-card deck, there are 9 spades, 9 diamonds, 9 clubs, and 9 hearts. 12 of the cards in the deck are aces. If the aces are distributed evenly among all the suits, what fraction of the deck are aces of spades?

   A. 3
   B. 1
   C. $\frac{1}{12}$
   D. $\frac{1}{36}$

9. $\frac{19}{20} \div \frac{4}{10} \div \frac{19}{32} =$

   A. $\frac{4}{32}$
   B. 4
   C. $\frac{1}{4}$
   D. $\frac{42}{52}$

84   Number Sense: Fractions

10. A fifth grade after-school club has 14/16 of an extra large pizza to share. If they divide the pizza equally among the students, each child gets 1/8 of the pizza. How many students are in the club?

   A. 7/64
   B. 14
   C. 8
   D. 7

Fractions: Answer Explanations

1. D   Remember that the larger the denominator, the greater the number of pieces into which the whole has been divided. Since each fraction above is missing one piece of the whole, 10/11, the fraction missing the smallest piece, is the greatest.

2. B   First, convert to a common denominator to figure out Kate's total expenses. In this case, the least common denominator is 90:

$$2/9 = 20/90$$
$$1/5 = 18/90$$
$$7/18 = 35/90$$
$$1/10 = 9/90$$

Then, add the numerators:

$$20/90 + 18/90 + 35/90 + 9/90 = (20 + 18 + 35 + 9)/90 = 82/90$$

Kate spent 82/90. To find out what's left over, subtract:

$$90/90 - 82/90 = 8/90$$

Then, simplify:

$$8/90 = 4/45$$

3. A   **Method 1:** Multiply and then Simplify.

Multiply the two numerators to get the new numerator—in this case, 8 x 3 = 24. Then, multiply the two denominators to find the new denominator, 5 x 9 = 45. This gives the fraction 24/45, which simplifies to 8/15.

Method 2: Simplify first.

You can see that 3 in the numerator and 9 in the denominator are both divisible by 3. Simplify by dividing both by 3.

3/5 × 8/9 = 1/5 × 8/3

Then, multiply numerators to get 1 x 8 = 8.
Then, multiply denominators, 5 x 3 = 15.
This gives you the fraction 8/15.

4. A   To multiply mixed numbers, you must first convert to improper fractions. You can NOT multiply the whole numbers and fractions separately.

First, convert 4 3/4 to an improper fraction:

4 3/4 = 19/4

Now, multiply as you would with proper fractions:

13/9 x 19/4 = 247/36

5. C   To solve this problem, you must understand that all the papers can be represented as 1, which can also be written as 7/7. Subtract the completed parts from the whole to find out how much grading the teacher has left to complete:

7/7 − 4/7 − 2/7 = (7 - 4 - 2)/7 = 1/7

6. C   Begin by finding out how much water is in the pool:

400 3/7 + 3 4/7

To add mixed numbers, add the whole numbers separately, add the fractions separately, and then combine the results:

400 + 3 = 403

3/7 + 4/7 = 7/7 = 1

403 + 1 = 404 gallons

Now, subtract the amount of water in the pool from the full capacity to find out how much more water is needed:

800 gallons − 404 gallons = 396 gallons

Number Sense: Fractions

7. A To find the average of numbers, you find their sum and divide by the number of numbers.

Create fractions with the same denominator, use the least common denominator, 120.

$$17/24 \times 5/5 = 85/120$$

Now, add the fractions.

$$17/24 + 55/120 = 85/120 + 55/120 = 140/120 = 7/6$$

Now, divide by 2 to find the average:

$$7/6 \div 2 = 7/6 \times 1/2 = 7/12$$

$7/12$ feet

Since that isn't one of the options, let's convert to inches. Remember, there are 12 inches in one foot.:

$7/12$ feet = 7 inches

8. C The first step is to write the fraction of the deck consisting of aces. There are 12 aces out of the total deck of 36: $12/36$, which can be simplified to $1/3$.

Then, write the fraction that represents the portion of the deck that is spades. There are 9 spades out of the total deck of 36: $9/36$, which equals $1/4$.

To find the portion of the deck that is both aces and spades, multiply the two fractions.

$$1/3 \times 1/4 = 1/12$$

9. B Break this problem into multiple steps. Divide the first two fractions, and then take that result and divide it by the last fraction. Remember, to divide fractions, invert the divisor and multiply:

$$19/20 \div 4/10 = 19/20 \times 10/4 = 19/2 \times 1/4 = 19/8$$

Now, take the result of that division problem and divide it by the last fraction:

$$19/8 \div 19/32 = 19/8 \times 32/19 = 1/8 \times 32/1 = 1/1 \times 4/1 = 4/1 = 4$$

10. D To find the number of students in the club, divide the fraction of the pizza that they have to share, $14/16$, by the fraction that each child receives, which is $1/8$.

$$14/16 \div 1/8 = 14/16 \times 8/1 = 14/2 \times 1/1 = 7$$

7 students

Number Sense: Decimals

Decimals Introduction

Fractions with denominators that are powers of 10 (100, 1000, and so forth) can also be written as numbers called decimals. In a number with a decimal sign, all the numbers to the left of the decimal sign are whole numbers, while all the numbers to the right of it are fractions.

The digit 1 in the tenths place on this place-value chart literally means $^1/_{10}$. The digit 4 in the hundredths place means $^4/_{100}$ and the 3 in the millionths place symbolizes $^3/_{1000000}$. Here are more examples of decimals written as fractions:

.59 = $^{59}/_{100}$ = fifty-nine hundredths

.2222 = $^{2222}/_{10000}$ = two-thousand two-hundred twenty-two ten-thousandths

.30303 = $^{30303}/_{100000}$ = thirty-thousand three-hundred three one-hundred thousandths

Adding & Subtracting Decimals

Adding or subtracting decimal numbers is very similar to adding and subtracting whole numbers. The key is to line up the decimal points in a column. Even if the two numbers have a different number of digits after the decimal point, as long as the decimal places line up, you can add as you normally would.

```
  3.425
+12.2
 15.625
```
↑ Line up the decimal places.

Remember, if you are adding or subtracting a number with no decimal point, the decimal goes after the number.

People often find it easier to add and subtract decimals by putting in placeholder zeros. This can be seen in the following problem.

```
  7.243        7.243
 11.1         11.100
  3            3.000   ← Add placeholder zeros.
+ 8.53       + 8.530
              29.873
```
↑ Line up the decimal places.

88   Number Sense: Decimals

Multiplying Decimals

Like adding and subtracting decimals, multiplying decimals is similar to multiplying whole numbers. Simply multiply the digits as you would with whole numbers, and then count the digits to the right of the decimal in all the multipliers. Place the decimal point so that the product has the total number of digits to the right of the decimal point.

```
      49.83  ←——— two digits to the right of the decimal sign
   x    5.7  ←——— one digit to the right of the decimal sign
      34881
   + 249150
     284.031 ←——— three digits to the right of the decimal sign
```

Dividing Decimals

To divide a decimal by a whole number, simply transfer the decimal sign to the quotient directly above its position in the dividend; then, divide as usual.

$$\begin{array}{r}7.05\\7\overline{)49.35}\end{array}$$

The divisor has no decimal places, so divide as you normally would. But in this case, bring the decimal point from the dividend up to the answer.

To divide any number by a decimal, multiply the divisor and the dividend by the power of ten necessary to turn the divisor into a whole number. Then, divide as usual.

$$0.3\overline{)9.42}$$

First, mulitiply the divisor by a power of ten necessary to make it a whole number, in this case, 10.

Multiply the dividend by the same.

$$\begin{array}{r}31.4\\3\overline{)94.2}\end{array}$$

Then, divide as you normally would, bringing the decimal point up to the quotient.

Decimals: Practice

1. You open a bank account and deposit $150. Over the next month, you withdraw $12.50, $17, and $45.23. How much money is left in the account?

   A. $74.27

   B. $75.27

   C. $76.73

   D. $92.10

2. What number is represented by the letter M on the number line below?

   A. 2.40

   B. 2.405

   C. 2.45

   D. 2.50

3. What is one millionth of 12.97?

   A. 12,970,000

   B. 12.97

   C. 0.000001297

   D. 0.00001297

4. One liter of a solution is .723 water and .178 hydrochloric acid. What part of the solution's composition is unstated?

   A. 0.901

   B. 9.01

   C. 0.99

   D. 0.099

5. A restaurant uses 1.5 pounds of flour every hour it is open. It is open for 5.75 hours per day, 6 days per week. How many pounds of flour does the restaurant use each week?

   A. 5.175

   B. 13.25

   C. 45.75

   D. 51.75

6. 0.003 x 1.24 ÷ 0.05 =

   A. 0.00744

   B. 0.0744

   C. 0.744

   D. 7.44

7. A woman has seven ten-dollar bills, two nickels, seven quarters, and six pennies in her purse. How much money will she have left after buying groceries for $25.72 and lunch for $4.90?

   A. $40.39

   B. $41.29

   C. $71.91

   D. $30.62

8. Chris has $12. He spent $5.47 yesterday, $3.94 before lunch today, and $1.13 between lunch and dinner. How much does Chris have left to spend?

   A. $2.35

   B. $1.79

   C. $1.46

   D. $10.54

Number Sense: Decimals

9. Adam is 3.5 times the age of his son. If Adam is 42, how old is his son?

   A. 7
   B. 12
   C. 14
   D. 21

10. Three students are competing for a prize. In the first phase of the competition, Julie scored 93.67 points, Sophia scored 75.12, and Travis earned 82.53. In the second phase, Julie and Sophia each scored 58.34 points. How many points must Travis score in the second phase to tie with Julie?

    A. 144.6
    B. 101.08
    C. 70
    D. 69.48

Decimals: Answer Explanations

1. B To figure out how much money is left in the account, first find the total amount that was withdrawn. Then, subtract that from the original deposit.

The withdrawal amounts are $12.50, $17, and $45.23. To add, line up the decimal places and add as normal. For $17, put the decimal point after the number and use placeholder zeros, so everything lines up:

$12.50
$17.00
+ $45.23
─────
$74.73

Now, we must subtract the withdrawals from the original deposit:

$150.00
- $74.73
─────
$75.27

2. C

On the number line, the letter M is halfway between 2.4 and 2.5.

Method 1: Convert to fractions.

Adding a zero to the end of a decimal doesn't change the value, so we can think of M as being halfway between 2.40 and 2.50.

2.40 can be written as $^{240}/_{100}$

2.50 can be written as $^{250}/_{100}$

The number halfway between those values is 245/100, which is written as 2.45.

Method 2: Find average.

You can also find the average between 2.4 and 2.5 as M is halfway between them.

First, add 2.4 and 2.5.

2.4 + 2.5 = 4.9

Then, divide by 2 to find the average.

4.9/2 = 2.45

3. D "Of" in math means multiply, so write out one millionth as a decimal and then multiply the two numbers:

```
      12.97   ←——— two digits to the right of the decimal sign
   x .000001  ←——— six digits to the right of the decimal sign
  0.00001297  ←——— eight digits to the right of the decimal sign
```

4. D Add the known or stated fractions of the solution:

```
   0.723
 + 0.178
   0.901
```

Then, subtract that fraction of the solution from the total:

```
   1.000
 - 0.901
   0.099
```

5. D First, calculate the number of hours the restaurant is open per week and then multiply that by the amount of flour used each hour.

To calculate the number of hours the restaurant is open, multiply the hours per day by the days per week:

5.75 x 6 = 34.5

Now, multiply that result by the amount of flour used per hour:

34.5 x 1.5 = 51.75

6. B Following the order of operations, multiply and divide from left to right. First, multiply 0.003 by 1.24. Since there are 3 digits to the right of the decimal point in 0.003 and 2 digits to the right of the decimal point in 1.24, you move the decimal point 5 places in the product:

0.003 x 1.24 = 0.00372

Now, take the result and divide it by 0.05:

0.00372 ÷ 0.05 =

0.372 ÷ 5 = 0.0744

7. B Seven ten dollar bills is $70, two nickels is $0.10, seven quarters is $1.75, and six pennies can be written as $0.06. Add them together to find out how much money she started with:

```
  70.00
   0.10
   1.75
+  0.06
-------
  71.91
```

Now, calculate the total amount she spent:
```
  25.72
+  4.90
-------
  30.62
```

Subtract the amount she spent from what she started with:
```
  71.91
- 30.62
-------
  41.29
```

94   Number Sense: Decimals

8. C Add up what Chris has spent so far and subtract it from the total.

$$\begin{array}{r} 5.47 \\ 3.94 \\ + 1.13 \\ \hline 10.54 \end{array}$$

Now, subtract the amount he spent from the total.

$$\begin{array}{r} 12.00 \\ - 10.54 \\ \hline 1.46 \end{array}$$

$1.46 left.

9. B If we know Adam's age, we can divide to find his son's age:

$$42 \div 3.5 = 12$$

10. D Since Julie and Sophia scored the same number of points in the second phase and Julie scored more in the first phase, Travis will need to beat Julie in the second phase. Calculate Julie's point total:

$$\begin{array}{r} 93.67 \\ + 58.34 \\ \hline 152.01 \end{array}$$

Then, subtract Travis' first-round points from her total:

$$\begin{array}{r} 152.01 \\ - 82.53 \\ \hline 69.48 \end{array}$$

Number Sense: Decimals

Number Sense: Percents & Conversions

Percent Definition

Percents are a way of expressing fractions, where the "whole" is 100%. Therefore, 1 is the same as 100%.

If you have a fraction with a denominator of 100, then the numerator of that fraction is equal to the percent and vice versa.

$3/100 = 3\%$
$17\% = 17/100$
$50\% = 50/100 = 1/2$

Finding Percents

To find the percent when given a fraction, convert the fraction to an equivalent fraction with a denominator of 100, and then the numerator of that fraction is the percent.

$7/25 = 28/100 = 28\%$
$1/20 = 5/100 = 5\%$

Solving Percent Problems

Generally, convert the percent to a fraction or a decimal and then solve as you normally would.

What is 20% of 30?

$= 20\% \times 30$
$= 20/100 \times 30$
$= 1/5 \times 30$
$= 30/5$
$= 6$

Converting Decimals to Fractions

To convert a fraction to a decimal, simply write out the decimal as a fraction with a denominator that is a power of ten. Look at the place value of the last digit to determine what power of ten to use as the denominator. Then simplify.

$.125 = 125/1000 = 1/8$

Converting Fractions to Decimals

Remember that the / in a fraction is actually a division sign. To convert a fraction to a decimal, simply divide the numerator by the denominator.

$855/4 = 855 \div 4 = 213.75$

Converting Decimals to Percents

To convert a decimal to a percent, multiply the decimal by 100%. Another way to think about this process is to move the decimal point two places to the right and add a percent sign.

$0.7345 \times 100\% = 73.45\%$

Converting Percents to Decimals

To convert a percent to a decimal, divide the percent by 100%. Another way to think about it is to move the decimal point two places to the left and remove the percent sign.

$154.9\% \div 100\% = 1.549$

Converting Fractions to Percents

To convert a fraction to a percent, first convert the fraction to a decimal, and then multiply the decimal by 100%.

$3/4 = .75 \times 100\% = 75\%$

Converting Percents to Fractions

To convert a percent to a fraction, convert the percent to a decimal by dividing by 100% and then write the decimal as a fraction with a denominator that is a power of 10. If possible, simplify the fraction.

$40\% \div 100\% = .40 = 40/100 = 2/5$

Percents & Conversions: Practice

1. Write the following words as a decimal:

Eighteen and Thirty-One Fiftieths

A. 18.31

B. 18.62

C. 18.3150

D. 49.50

2. In how many categories in the figure below is the annual budget allotment less than $8,000?

A. One

B. Two

C. Three

D. Four

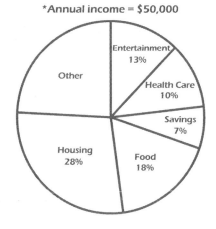

Family annual budget by percents of annual income
*Annual income = $50,000

Entertainment 13%
Health Care 10%
Savings 7%
Food 18%
Housing 28%
Other

3. Write 504.30% as a fraction.

A. 504 3/10

B. 5 43/1000

C. 5043/100

D. 50 43/100

Number Sense: Percents & Conversions

4. Hannah's cat eats pet food that is 2.9% protein. What fraction of her cat's food is not protein?

   A. 971/1000

   B. 9971/10000

   C. 97 1/10

   D. 71/100

5. Which answer choice is the smallest?

   A. 2 1/5

   B. 215%

   C. 2.5

   D. 1 2/5

6. An Internet startup saw its sales increase this quarter by 716%. If its sales last quarter totaled $10,000, what was the sales total for both quarters?

   A. $10,716

   B. $17,160

   C. $71,600

   D. $91,600

7. Two teenagers go to a batting cage. One of them bats .287, and the other bats .345. What is the average percent of balls both players hit?

   A. 0.316%

   B. 0.632%

   C. 31.6%

   D. 63.2%

8. Drew answered all the questions on a test correctly. He also answered one extra credit question. If all questions were counted equally and Drew's final score was 112.5%, how many questions did he answer?

   A. 8

   B. 9

   C. 10

   D. 12.5

Number Sense: Percents & Conversions

9. Four basketball players are comparing their free throw shooting records. These are the fractions of shots made:

Player 1: 42/63

Player 2: 75/94

Player 3: 0.324

Player 4: 0.846

Who has the worst free throw shooting record of the four?

A. Player 1
B. Player 2
C. Player 3
D. Player 4

10. What is 29% of 13%?

A. $377/10$
B. $377/1000$
C. $377/10000$
D. $377/100000$

Percents & Conversions: Answer Explanations

1. B   Eighteen is the whole number, and Thirty-One Fiftieths is the fraction.

$18\ 31/50$

Now, we must take this fraction and convert it to a decimal. There are multiple ways to do this.

Method 1: Divide 31 by 50, and get a decimal, and then put the whole number in front. 31 divided by 50 is 0.62. Therefore, the answer is 18.62.

Method 2: Find an equivalent fraction whose denominator is a multiple of 10. In this case, $31/50$ can be easily converted to a fraction whose denominator is 100. Multiply numerator and denominator by 2, giving you $62/100$. The equivalent mixed number is 18 $62/100$, which is 18 and 62 hundredths, or 18.62.

2. C The percentage for the Other category is not listed. To calculate, add all other categories and subtract the sum from 100.

$$100 - (13 + 10 + 7 + 18 + 28) = 100 - 76 = 24$$

Other = 24%

Method 1: Calculate value of each category.

To calculate the value of a category, convert the percent to a fraction or decimal and multiply that by the annual budget of $50,000.

   Entertainment: 13% x $50,000 = $\frac{13}{100}$ x $50,000 = $6,500.

   Health Care: 10% x $50,000 = 0.10 x $50,000 = $5,000.

   Savings: 7% x $50,000 = 0.07 x $50,000 = $3,500.

   Food: 18% x $50,000 = $\frac{18}{100}$ x $50,000 = $9,000.

   Housing: 28% x $50,000 = $\frac{28}{100}$ x $50,000 = $14,000.

   Other: 24% x $50,000 = $\frac{24}{100}$ x $50,000 = $12,000.

The only categories with a budget below $8,000 are Entertainment, Health Care, and Savings.

Method 2: Determine percentage equal to $8,000.

You could determine the percentage that equates to spending $8,000, and then compare it to the percentage of each category.

To determine what percent of $50,000 is $8,000, divide.

   $\frac{8,000}{50,000} = 0.16 = 16\%$

Now, look through each category to see which is less than 16%.

The categories with a percentage less than 16% are Entertainment, Health Care, and Savings.

3. B First, convert the percent to a decimal, and then convert the decimal to a fraction.

To convert a percent to a decimal, divide by 100%.

   504.30% ÷ 100% = 5.043

To convert a decimal to a fraction, look at the place value of the last digit, and put the number over that power of 10. In this case, the 3 is in the thousandths place, so put the number over 1000.

   $5.043 = \frac{5043}{1000}$

Now, make the fraction a mixed number and reduce if possible.

   $\frac{5043}{1000} = 5\frac{43}{1000}$

4. **A**   Convert the percent that is protein to a decimal and then to a fraction. To convert to a decimal, divide by 100%. To convert to a fraction, look at the place value of the last digit and make a denominator that is a power of 10.

$$2.9\% \div 100\% = 0.029 = 29/1000$$

Subtract the fraction of her cat's food that is protein from 1 (use $1000/1000$ to give the two fractions a common denominator).

$$1000/1000 - 29/1000 = 971/1000$$

5. **B**   Convert each answer choice to a decimal and compare:

A: $2 1/5 = 220/100 = 2.20$

B: $215\% = 2.15$

C: 2.5

D: $1 2/5 = 240/100 = 2.40$

6. **D**   To figure out sales for this quarter, first convert the percent increase to a decimal:

$$716\% \div 100\% = 7.16$$

Multiply the increase by the sales total from last quarter.

$$7.16 \times \$10,000 = \$71,600$$

The sales have increased by $71,600. Add this to the sales total from last quarter to find out the sales total for this quarter:

$$\$71,600 + \$10,000 = \$81,600$$

Sales total last quarter = $10,000.

Sales total this quarter = $81,600.

Total sales for both quarters = $10,000 + $81,600 = $91,600.

7. **C**   Average the decimals by adding them and dividing by two:

$$0.287 + 0.345 = 0.632$$

$$0.632 \div 2 = 0.316$$

Convert the decimal to a percent by multiplying by 100%:

$$0.316 \times 100\% = 31.6\%$$

8. B Answering the regular questions correctly earned Drew 100%. Subtract 100% from his total score to calculate the value of the extra credit question.

$$112.5\% - 100\% = 12.5\%$$

Method 1: Convert to a fraction.

Since the extra credit has the same value as a regular test question, convert the percent of the test that consists of extra credit to a fraction with 1 in the numerator to find the number of regular test questions. Begin by converting the percent to a decimal:

$$12.5\% \div 100\% = 0.125$$

Convert the decimal to a fraction:

$$0.125 = 125/1000 = 1/8$$

There were 8 regular test questions, plus 1 extra credit = 9 questions in total.

Method 2: Divide the percentages.

Since the extra credit has the same value as a regular test question, you know that each question is worth 12.5%. Since you know that the total percent is 112.5%, you can divide to determine the number of questions.

$$112.5\% \div 12.5\% = 112.5 \div 12.5 = 9$$

9 questions in total.

9. C Use estimation here to determine the answer quickly. Player 1 has made about 2/3 of his free throws. Player 2 has made about 7/8, and Player 4 has made about 85/100. All three have easily made more than half their throws. Player 3, however, has made about 1/3 of his free throws. That's less than half, so Player 3 has the worst record.

10. C Convert each percent to a fraction and then multiply:

$$29\% = 29/100$$

$$13\% = 13/100$$

$$29/100 \times 13/100 = 377/10000$$

Number Sense: Percents & Conversions

Number Sense: Powers, Roots, Bases

Powers or Exponents

The terms powers and exponents are interchangeable. The power or exponent represents how many times a number is multiplied by itself. In the expression 2^5, the base number 2 is raised to the 5th power. When a base number is raised to a power, it is multiplied by itself a number of times equal to the power.

$$2^5 = 2 \times 2 \times 2 \times 2 \times 2 = 32$$

$$4^3 = 4 \times 4 \times 4 = 64$$

Multiplying and Dividing Exponents

When multiplying numbers with exponents, if their bases are the same, you can just add the exponents.

For example, $2^3 \times 2^4$ is equal to $(2 \times 2 \times 2) \times (2 \times 2 \times 2 \times 2) = 2^7$

or, since both numbers had a base of 2, you could just add the exponents.

When dividing numbers with exponents, if their bases are the same, you can just subtract the exponents.

For example, $4^7 \div 4^5 = 4^2$

Negative Exponents

Numbers can also be raised to negative exponents, which indicates that the expression is a fraction with 1 as the numerator and the base raised to the power as the denominator. (See Fractions module for help.)

$$2^{-5} = 1/{2 \times 2 \times 2 \times 2 \times 2} = 1/32$$

$$4^{-2} = 1/{4 \times 4} = 1/16$$

Scientific Notation

Scientific Notation is a way of writing numbers (usually very small or very large) as powers of ten. Numbers written in scientific notation take the form of coefficient x 10^{power}. The coefficient must be greater than or equal to 1 and less than 10.

$$63,500,000 = 6.35 \times 10^7$$

$$470,000 = 4.7 \times 10^5$$

$$0.0000348 = 3.48 \times 10^{-5}$$

$$0.0023 = 2.3 \times 10^{-3}$$

As can be seen in the examples above, first find the coefficient, which will be a number between 1 and 10. To figure out the coefficient, place the decimal point after the digit in the greatest place value. Then, determine how many times you moved the decimal places, either in the positive or negative direction.

When multiplying numbers in scientific notation, use the commutative property of multiplication to rearrange the terms and then multiply the coefficients and then the powers of ten.

$$(3 \times 10^8) \times (2 \times 10^{-5}) = (3 \times 2) \times (10^8 \times 10^{-5}) = 6 \times 10^3$$

Roots

A root is the opposite of an exponent. Since the square of a number is a number times itself, for example $9^2 = 81$, the square root of a number is the number that when multiplied by itself equals that number. The square root of 81 is 9.

To find the third root of 64, you need to figure out what number times itself 3 times gives you 64. Since $4 \times 4 \times 4 = 64$, the third root of 64 is 4.

The square root of $25 = \sqrt{25} = 5$. The third root of $27 = 3$.

There are two notations for writing roots. For example, the third root of 64 can be written:
$\sqrt[3]{64}$ or $64^{1/3}$

Fractional Exponents

In the second notation of roots from above, you see that the root is written as a fractional exponent. The denominator is the root, and the numerator should be treated as any exponential power.
For example:

$$81^{1/4} = \text{fourth root of } 81 = 3$$

$$2^{4/2} = \sqrt{(2^4)} = \sqrt{16} = 4$$

$$27^{2/3} = \text{cube root of } 27^2 = (\text{cube root of } 27)^2 = 3^2 = 9$$

Simplifying Radicals

A radical has a root sign (for example, square root, cube root) and a term underneath the radical sign. For example, $\sqrt{432}$ is a radical.

To simplify a radical, begin by finding the prime factors of the number. In this case, the prime factors are: 2x2x2x2x3x3x3=432. There are two "pairs" of prime roots that make perfect squares (4 and 3). We can factor those out:

$$\sqrt{432} = \sqrt{(16 \times 9 \times 3)} = \sqrt{16} \times \sqrt{9} \times \sqrt{3} = 4 \times 3 \times \sqrt{3} = 12\sqrt{3}$$

When you are dealing with expressions with radicals, you can only combine (add or subtract) terms with the same radical. For example, $2\sqrt{3} + \sqrt{3} - \sqrt{2} = 3\sqrt{3} - \sqrt{2}$. In that example, the two terms with $\sqrt{3}$ can be added together.

Bases

A number system has a base to describe the digits. Our typical number system is base 10. For the first digit, we multiply by 10^0. The second digit, we multiply by 10^1. The third digit, we multiply by 10^2...and so on.

In a base 2 number system, we multiply the first digit by 2^0. The second digit, we multiply by 2^1. The third digit, we multiply by 2^2...and so on.

In this fashion, we can use a number system of any integer base.

For example, if the following number was in base 3, we could determine its value in base 10 by determining the value of each digit.

$$201_3 = 1(3^0) + 0(3^1) + 2(3^2) = 1 + 0 + 18 = 19$$

Powers, Roots, Base: Practice

1. $2^5 \times 2^4 \div 2^2 =$

   A. 2^3
   B. 2^7
   C. 2^{10}
   D. 2^{11}

2. $(-3)^4 - (-4)^{-3} =$

   A. 0
   B. –24
   C. 81 1/64
   D. 145

3. **In the following base 10 number, which digit is multiplied by 10^3?**

   5,241,837

   A. 1
   B. 2
   C. 4
   D. 8

4. **Simplify the expression: $\sqrt{48} + \sqrt{27}$.**

   A. $5\sqrt{3}$
   B. $7\sqrt{3}$
   C. $12\sqrt{3}$
   D. $25\sqrt{3}$

5. $100^{1/2} =$

   A. –100
   B. 10
   C. 50
   D. 1/100

6. **Write 9,000,000.00 in scientific notation.**

   A. 9×10^6
   B. 9×10^7
   C. 9×10^8
   D. 9×10^9

7. 2.3×10^{-4} is equal to what number?

   A. 0.0023

   B. 0.00023

   C. 2300

   D. 23000

8. What is the product of (2×10^3) and (4×10^{-7})?

   A. 8×10^{10}

   B. 8×10^{-21}

   C. 8×10^{-4}

   D. 8×10^4

9. Translate the following number to Base 10:

   100101_2

   A. 8

   B. 37

   C. 74

   D. 100,101

10. $36^{3/2}$ is equal to:

    I. $(36^{1/3})^2$

    II. $(36^{1/2})^3$

    III. 216

A. I and II

B. II and III

C. I only

D. III only

Number Sense: Powers, Roots, Bases

Powers, Roots, Base: Answer Explanations

1. B A good approach here is to break the problem into two separate problems. First, find the product, and then take that result and find the quotient.

When multiplying numbers with exponents, you add the exponents if the bases are the same:

$$2^5 \times 2^4 = 2^9$$

Another way to think about it is that 2^5 is 2 times itself 5 times, and 2^4 is 2 times itself 4 times. Therefore, the product will be 2 times itself 9 times: 2^9.

Now, take the 2^9 and divide it by 2^2. To divide numbers with exponents, you subtract the exponents if the bases are the same:

$$2^9 \div 2^2 = 2^7$$

2. C You can break the problem into two separate problems.

A number raised to a power is multiplied by itself the number of times indicated by the power:

$$(-3)^4 = (-3) \times (-3) \times (-3) \times (-3) = 81$$

Notice that there was an even number of negative signs (four), so the answer is positive.

A number raised to a negative power is the same as 1 over that number raised to the positive power:

$$(-4)^{-3} =$$

$$1/(-4)^3$$

$$1/-64$$

$$-1/64$$

Combine the two terms:

$$(-3)^4 - (-4)^{-3} =$$

$$81 - (-1/64) =$$

$$81\,1/64$$

3. A $10^3 = 1000$. We need the digit for the thousands place. In this case, the digit is 1.

4. B To simplify the expression, first find the factors of each number:

$$\sqrt{48} = \sqrt{(4 \times 4 \times 3)} = \sqrt{4} \times \sqrt{4} \times \sqrt{3} = 2 \times 2 \times \sqrt{3} = 4\sqrt{3}$$

$$\sqrt{27} = \sqrt{(9 \times 3)} = \sqrt{9} \times \sqrt{3} = 3 \times \sqrt{3} = 3\sqrt{3}$$

Now, put the terms back together:

$$\sqrt{48} + \sqrt{27} = 4\sqrt{3} + 3\sqrt{3}$$

Since both terms have $\sqrt{3}$, they can be combined:

$$4\sqrt{3} + 3\sqrt{3} = 7\sqrt{3}$$

5. B A number raised to a fractional power is equal to the corresponding root of the number. In this case, $100^{1/2}$ is the same as the second root or square root of 100. Therefore, you need to determine what number times itself equals 100. Since 10 times 10 equals 100, 10 is the square root.

6. A When writing a number in scientific notation, you need to figure out how many times you are moving the decimal point.

To go from 9 to 9,000,000.00, you move the decimal point 6 places in the positive direction. Therefore, 6 is the exponent of the power of 10.

7. B The original number is expressed in scientific notation. The exponent in the power of 10 tells you what direction and how many places to move the decimal point. In this case, you need to move the decimal point 4 places in the negative direction. This gives you 0.00023.

8. C First, multiply the coefficients, and then multiply the powers of ten.

Coefficients:

$$2 \times 4 = 8.$$

To multiply powers when the base number is the same, add the exponents:

$$10^3 \times 10^{-7} = 10^{-4}$$

Now, combine the two products: 8×10^{-4}

9. B The subscript 2 denotes that the number is in base 2. To convert from base 2 to base 10, start from the left, take each digit, and multiply it by consecutive powers of 2, starting with zero.

$$(1 \times 2^0) + (0 \times 2^1) + (1 \times 2^2) + (0 \times 2^3) + (0 \times 2^4) + (1 \times 2^5) =$$

$$1 + 0 + 4 + 0 + 0 + 32 = 37$$

10. B With fractional exponents, the denominator is the root of the number, and the numerator is the power that number is raised to.

Therefore, we want the second or square root of 36. Then we want to raise that to the third power.

I. $(36^{1/3})^2$: This says take the third root of 36 and raise it to the second power. This is not the same thing.

II. $(36^{1/2})^3$: This says take the square root of 36 and raise that to the third power, which is correct.

III. 216: Let's calculate and see if we get 216. The square root of 36 is 6. Raising this number to the third power gives 6 x 6 x 6 = 216.

Number Sense: History of Math

Origins and Development of Math

Mathematics in its earliest forms arose from the need to find a way to count physical objects. From this beginning, various civilizations developed early mathematics for commerce, to create patterns, to measure land, and to measure time.

Early Numeral Systems

Today, we use a base 10 (decimal) numeral system composed of 10 symbols. The Mayans devised one of the earliest recorded numeral systems, which was in base 20. The Mayan math system used 3 symbols: a line to represent 5, a dot to represent 1, and a shell for the concept of 0. These lines, dots, and shells could be used to represent all numbers.

The Babylonian or Mesopotamian numeral system used base 60. It is from this system that we derive modern measurements for time and angles, for example, 60 seconds in a minute and 360 degrees in a circle.

The Egyptian math system was the earliest known development of a base 10 numeral system. The Egyptians also developed methods for fractions, multiplication, and division.

In ancient Rome, a system was adopted based on symbols from the Roman alphabet. The Roman Numeral System is composed of 7 symbols:

$$I = 1, V = 5, X = 10, L = 50, C = 100, D = 500, M = 1000$$

Roman numerals are combined to represent the sum (or difference) in their values. When a lower-value symbol is placed after a higher-value symbol, the numbers are added. When a higher-value symbol is in front of a lower-value one, the numbers are subtracted. For example:

$$XI = 10 + 1 = 11, IX = 10 - 1 = 9, CLXVI = 166$$

Ancient Greece and Beyond

The first civilization to study mathematics in its own right was ancient Greece between 300 and 600 B.C. Whereas previous civilizations used empirical observations to draw conclusions, the ancient Greeks introduced deductive reasoning. Conclusions were derived from axioms and theorems and validated through proofs. Some of Greece's most noteworthy contributions were in geometry, through figures such as Pythagoras, Euclid, and Plato.

Chinese mathematicians' strength was in place value decimal systems, algebra, and algorithms. In 179 AD, the *Nine Chapters on the Mathematical Art* appeared in China, although it is believed that previous versions existed for centuries beforehand. Developed by scholars over several generations, this text included formulas for volume and surface area, taxation, and linear equations.

Indian mathematics made many contributions, including the decimal number system in use today and the binary number system. Trigonometry, having evolved in Greece, was further advanced in India, where the definitions of both sine and cosine were developed.

The Islamic Empire of the eighth century played a key role in bringing the work of Indian mathematicians to the West. The numerals we use today – based on the Hindu numeral system but commonly known as Arabic numbers – were introduced to Europe through the works of Arab scholars in the ninth and tenth centuries. Islamic mathematicians also made significant advances in algebra. The "father of algebra," Al-Khwarizmi, was the first scholar to teach and study algebraic equations for their own sake.

Key Figures in Math History

Math history is best understood through the accomplishments of the great mathematicians. The list of characters is long, however, and their contributions varied. What follows is a brief summary of some characters you might come across in the exam. Follow the links at the end of this lesson for more information on these and other important mathematicians.

Pythagoras (c. 575 – 490 BC)

Pythagoras was a Greek mathematician and philosopher best known for his proof of the Pythagorean Theorem, which states $a^2 + b^2 = c^2$ (where a and b are the lengths of two sides of a right triangle, and c is the hypotenuse). The school of Pythagoras also discovered prime, composite, and perfect numbers.

Euclid (c. 325 – 265 BC)

The Greek mathematician Euclid is best known for his treatise The Elements, which formed the basis of geometry for the next 2,000 years. The Elements also contained other major contributions, such as Euclid's algorithm for finding the greatest common factor.

Archimedes (c. 287 – 212 BC)

Famous for his inventions, the Greek scientist Archimedes also made significant contributions to mathematics. One of Archimedes' accomplishments was developing a remarkably close approximation of π.

Fibonacci (c. 1170 – c. 1250)

The Italian, Leonardo Fibonacci, developed what is now called the Fibonacci sequence – a sequence of numbers that starts with 0 and 1 and proceeds with each term the sum of the previous two numbers. The ratio of the successive terms in this sequence is known as the "golden ratio." This value was widely used in art in the Renaissance Period and later. Intriguingly, Fibonacci sequences have been discovered in nature, for example, in the arrangement of leaf buds on plant stems and in the growth spirals of certain shells.

Descartes (1596 – 1650)

Descartes was a French mathematician and philosopher whose theories formed the basis for modern calculus. Descartes also developed the Cartesian coordinate system – today's coordinate plane – which linked geometry to algebra.

Pascal (1623 – 1662)

The French mathematician and philosopher Blaise Pascal played a key role in developing theories of probability and projective geometry. Pascal is probably best known for his work on what is now called Pascal's triangle. This triangle is an efficient method of listing the coefficients of binomials.

Fermat (1601 – 1665)

Pierre de Fermat was a French lawyer and mathematician who added significantly to calculus, geometry, and probability. He is known for what is called Fermat's Last Theorem, the proof of which eluded mathematicians until the late twentieth century. The theorem states that no three positive integers a, b, and c can satisfy the following equation when n > 2:

$$a^n + b^n = c^n$$

Newton (1643 – 1727)

The great English scientist Isaac Newton is credited, along with Gottfried Liebnitz, with creating differential and integral calculus. Newton used calculus as a tool to push forward the study of nature. His work did much to highlight the interactions between astronomy, physics, and mathematics.

Euler (1707 – 1773)

The Swiss mathematician Leonhard Euler is considered the most important mathematician of the eigthteenth century. Euler invented two new branches of mathematics in the calculus of variations and differential geometry. Some of his contributions include the development of the irrational number e as well as Euler's Formula, which links a trigonometric representation of complex numbers to an exponential representation. Euler also introduced the concept of a function and the notation f(x).

Further Reading:

MacTutor History of Mathematics Archive (University of St. Andrew's Scotland)

http://www-history.mcs.st-andrews.ac.uk/

A comprehensive resource that includes detailed biographies and key developments in the history of math.

History of Mathematics (Wikipedia)

http://en.wikipedia.org/wiki/History_of_mathematics

Summarizes the evolution of math from prehistoric times to the present.

History of Math: Practice

1. Which Italian mathematician was responsible for a number sequence from which the "golden ratio" can be derived?

   A. Euclid

   B. Archimedes

   C. Pythagoras

   D. Fibonacci

2. A number triangle named after which mathematician can be used to find the coefficients in a binomial expansion?

   A. Pythagoras

   B. Descartes

   C. Pascal

   D. Fermat

3. The development of the first base 10 numeral system is attributed to which ancient culture?

   A. Roman

   B. Egyptian

   C. Mayan

   D. Mesopotamian

4. Which French mathematician's "Last Theorem" stated that there is no solution to the equation below when n is greater than 2?

$$a^n + b^n = c^n$$

A. Euler

B. Descartes

C. Pascal

D. Fermat

5. Using the Mayan numeral system, what is the result of the following subtraction of two numbers? The bars are units of 5, and the dots are units of 1.

A. 2

B. 7

C. 19

D. 70

6. Which ancient culture developed a base 60 numeral system, from which many measurements in time and geometry are derived?

A. Roman

B. Mayan

C. Egyptian

D. Mesopotamian

7. Which French mathematician and philosopher is credited with a two-dimensional coordinate system commonly used to plot points and lines?

A. Euler

B. Descartes

C. Pascal

D. Fermat

8. Which Greek mathematician from about 500 B.C. was responsible for developing a theorem relating the sides of a right triangle?

   A. Euclid

   B. Archimedes

   C. Fibonacci

   D. Pythagoras

9. Which culture further advanced the Greek development of trigonometry?

   A. Indian

   B. Chinese

   C. Roman

   D. Mayan

10. Which culture produced the work entitled *Nine Chapters on the Mathematical Art*, which included many geometric applications?

    A. Indians

    B. Egyptians

    C. Greek

    D. Chinese

History of Math: Answer Explanations

1. D In the Fibonacci sequence, each number is the sum of the previous two numbers:

0, 1, 1, 2, 3, 5, 8, 13, 21, 34...

As you move higher in the Fibonacci sequence, the ratio of one number to the number directly before it approaches the golden ratio, which is approximately 1.618.

2. C Blaise Pascal was a French mathematician, scientist, and philosopher. Pascal's triangle is an arrangement of the coefficients of a binomial expansion.

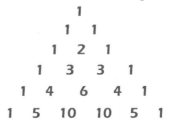

3. B The Egyptians are widely held to have been the first to use a base 10 numeral system. The Egyptians also had symbols for fractions, but not for zero.

4. D Fermat's Last Theorem was first conjectured in 1637 and was not proven until 1995. This is one of the most famous theorems in mathematics, and it became popular because of references in the media, books, and movies.

5. B The Mayans developed one of the earliest numeral systems, based on three symbols: a dot (1), a line (5), and a shell (0).

The first number includes two lines and three dots: 2(5) + 3(1) = 13

The second number includes one line and one dot: 1(5) + 1(1) = 6

$\qquad$ 13 – 6 = 7

6. D The ancient Middle Eastern culture of Mesopotamians or Babylonians used base 60 instead of 10. Measurements in time (60 seconds in a minute, 60 minutes in an hour) and geometry (360 degrees in a circle) come from this system.

7. B Descartes is credited with the Cartesian coordinate system, which provides a link between algebra and geometry.

8. D The Pythagorean Theorem states that in a right triangle, the sides will always be related by the following equation:

$a^2 + b^2 = c^2$

where a and b are the sides of the right triangle, and c is the hypotenuse.

9. A Trigonometry evolved in the ancient Greek culture, but it was brought to ancient India with the translations of Greek text. Indian, or Hindu, mathematics contributed further to trigonometry, including defining sine and cosine.

10. D The *Nine Chapters on the Mathematical Art* is a product of several generations of Chinese scholars. This work included applications of geometry such as calculations of volume and surface area.

Number Sense: Module Review

1. Order the numbers from least to greatest.

   0.81, 9/100, 0.819, 4/5

   A. 9/100, 4/5, 0.81, 0.819
   B. 0.81, 4/5, 9/100, 0.819
   C. 9/100, 0.819, 0.81, 4/5
   D. 4/5, 0.81, 0.819, 9/100

2. $(-1)^6 - (-1)^5 - (-1)^4 =$

   A. −3
   B. −1
   C. 1
   D. 3

3. A cake recipe calls for 2 cups of powdered sugar. It says to use 1/4 of the sugar in the cake batter and the remainder in the frosting. How much sugar, in cups, is needed for the frosting?

   A. 1½
   B. ¾
   C. ⅜
   D. ½

4. The electronics store is holding a sale where everything in the store is 20% off. If the sale price of the stereo is $47.00, what was the original price?

   A. $37.60
   B. $47.20
   C. $56.40
   D. $58.75

5. Steven owns 17,000 shares of stock in a company with 51,000 equal shares. If the annual profits for the company are $270,000 and each stockholder gets a share proportionate to the amount of stock he or she owns, how much should Steven get for the year?

   A. $90,000

   B. $180,000

   C. $200,000

   D. $287,000

6. $(-2)^4 - 3^2 =$

   A. −25

   B. −14

   C. 7

   D. 25

7. A yardwork company cut down a tree that was $98\frac{1}{4}$ feet tall. They must divide the tree into segments no larger than $\frac{13}{16}$ feet for disposal. What is the minimum number of segments into which they can cut the tree for disposal?

   A. 119

   B. 120

   C. 121

   D. 122

8. A sweater is originally $80. It was marked down 10% and still didn't sell, so the store marked it down an additional 25%. What percentage of the original price does the sweater cost?

   A. 35%

   B. 45%

   C. 65%

   D. 67.5%

9. Order the following from least to greatest:

   I. $3 \div \frac{1}{2}$
   II. $3 \times \frac{1}{2}$
   III. $\frac{1}{2} \div 3$

   A. I, II, III
   B. III, II, I
   C. III, I, II
   D. II, III, I

10. Debra worked 4.25 hours on Monday, 5.6 hours on Tuesday, 8 hours on Wednesday, and she took off both Thursday and Friday. What was the average number of hours she worked over the 5 days?

    A. 3.462 hours
    B. 3.57 hours
    C. 5.95 hours
    D. 6.85 hours

11. Matthew was offered 2 possible salaries for the month. Option 1: $10,000 plus 10% of whatever he sold. Option 2: $8,000 plus 15% of whatever he sold. If Matthew sold $35,000 worth of goods, which option should he choose?

    A. Option 1.
    B. Option 2.
    C. Either, they are the same.
    D. Not enough information.

12. Carol bought 6 books for $6.95 each. She was charged an additional $3.34 total on her purchases. She was left with $5.96. How much money did Carol start with?

    A. $39.08
    B. $50.00
    C. $51.00
    D. $67.70

13. The average precipitation for the first 3 months of the year was 12.5mm. If the precipitation for each month had been 1.5mm greater, what would the average have been?

    A. 13mm
    B. 14mm
    C. 17mm
    D. 39mm

14. $12^0 - 12^1 =$

    A. –12
    B. –11
    C. –1
    D. 0

15. Which of the following problems could be solved by finding the product of 3.5 and 6?

    A. You have a 6-foot long string, and you need pieces that are each 3.5 feet. How many pieces can you make from the string?

    B. Six documentaries have an average length of 3.5 hours. How many total hours of film are there?

    C. You have $6 and go to a store to buy $3.50 worth of supplies. How much change do you have?

    D. You are making cookies and put in 6 tablespoons of sugar. The recipe calls for an additional 3.5 tablespoons, how many total tablespoons have you put in?

16. $(-3)^3 - 3(-2)^2 + 25^{1/2} =$

    A. –34
    B. –26.5
    C. –16
    D. –14

17. Two thirds of the students at Sequoia Junior High are female. If 200 students are male, how many females attend Sequoia Junior High?

   A. 100
   B. 200
   C. 400
   D. 600

18. What is the quotient of 3×10^{-4} and 6×10^{7} in scientific notation?

   A. 5×10^{-10}
   B. 2×10^{11}
   C. 5×10^{-12}
   D. 1.8×10^{4}

19. Simplify the following expression:

   $3\sqrt{147} + 4\sqrt{96} - 2\sqrt{150}$.

   A. $21\sqrt{3} + 6\sqrt{6}$
   B. $27\sqrt{6}$
   C. $81\sqrt{2}$
   D. $37\sqrt{3} - 10\sqrt{6}$

20. What is the value of the 4 in the hexadecimal number (base 16 number)?

   2540_{16}

   A. 4
   B. 16
   C. 64
   D. 1024

Number Sense: Module Review

Module Review: Answer Explanations

1. A   The easiest way to compare numbers is to make them all decimals. So, first convert $9/100$ and $4/5$ to decimals.

$$9/100 = \text{nine hundredths} = 0.09$$

$$4/5 = 8/10 = \text{eight tenths} = 0.8$$

Now, your task is to order: 0.81, 0.09, .819, 0.8.

There are two methods for ordering decimals.

Method 1

Line up the decimal places, and compare one digit at a time. So, comparing the first digit of each of those numbers, you see 8, 0, 8, 8. The smallest is 0, so that number (0.09) is the smallest. Now, compare the next digit for the remaining numbers (0.81, 0.819, 0.8). The next digit is 1, 1, and no digit, which can be thought of as 0. Thus, the 0 is the smallest and 0.8 is the next smallest number. Then, compare the third digit, nothing (or zero) and 9. The smallest is again 0, so that is the next smallest number.

Final order: 0.09, 0.8, 0.81, 0.819

Answer A.

Method 2

You can also add zeros so that every number has the same number of decimal places, which might make it easier to compare.

Add zeros so each has 3 decimal places: 0.810, 0.090, 0.819, 0.800.

Now, order by comparing the numbers after the decimal place. 90 is the smallest, then 800, then 810, then 819.

Therefore, the decimal order is 0.090, 0.800, 0.810, 0.819.

2. C $-1 \times -1 = 1$. Therefore, -1 times itself an even number of times will always be positive 1. -1 times itself an odd number of times will always be negative.

$$(-1)^6 - (-1)^5 - (-1)^4 =$$

$$1 - (-1) - 1 =$$

$$1 + 1 - 1 =$$

$$2 - 1 =$$

$$1$$

3. A To determine how much sugar is needed for the frosting, first figure out the fraction of sugar for the frosting. If ¼ is needed for the cake batter, then ¾ is needed for the frosting.

Then multiply the fraction that is needed for the frosting by the total amount of sugar the recipe calls for.

¾ x 2 cups = ¾ x 2/1 = 6/4 = 3/2 = 1½

1½ cups of sugar for the frosting

4. D There are two ways to approach this problem, either solve or work backward using the answer choices.

Method 1:

To solve the equation, we must first take the word problem and translate it into an equation. If $47.00 is 20% off the original price, that means that $47 is 80% of the original price.

$47 = 80% x P   translate into an equation with P as the original price

$47 = 0.80P   convert percent to decimal; 80% is the same as 0.80

$47/0.80=0.80P/0.80   divide both sides by 0.80

$58.75 = P

Answer D. $58.75

Method 2: Work backward.

You know that the sales price is 20% off the original price. Therefore, the sales price is 80% of the original price. Take 80% of each answer choice and see which results in $47.00.

When working backward, it is often easiest to start with one of the middle answer choices. If it does not work and is too high or too low, you can eliminate multiple answer choices right away.

Let's start with answer choice C.

C: $56.40 x 80% = 56.4 x 0.8 = 45.12

This answer is too low. Therefore, you know to eliminate C and all the answer choices less than it. This leaves only answer D, which we will calculate to confirm.

D: $58.75 x 80% = 58.75 x 0.8 = 47

80% of answer choice D gives you $47.00, the sales price.

5. A Break the problem into multiple steps. First, determine what fraction of the total shares Steven owns. Then, determine how much Steven should get.

Steven owns 17,000 shares out of 51,000 shares. Therefore, Steven owns $17000/51000$, which equals $1/3$ of the shares.

To find out how much Steven should get, multiply the fraction he owns by the total annual profits.

$$1/3 \times \$270,000 = \$90,000$$

6. C $(-2)^4 - 3^2$

$(-2)^4 = (-2) \times (-2) \times (-2) \times (-2) = 16$

$3^2 = 3 \times 3 = 9$

$(-2)^4 - 3^2 = 16 - 9 = 7$

7. C Convert the tree height into an improper fraction so that it can be divided by the maximum segment length.

$98\frac{1}{4} = {}^{393}\!/\!_4$ feet

Now, divide the total tree height by the length of each segment.

$\quad\quad {}^{393}\!/\!_4 \div {}^{13}\!/\!_{16} =$

$\quad\quad {}^{393}\!/\!_4 \times {}^{16}\!/\!_{13} =$

$\quad\quad {}^{393}\!/\!_1 \times {}^{4}\!/\!_{13} =$

$\quad\quad {}^{1572}\!/\!_{13} =$

$\quad\quad 120\,{}^{12}\!/\!_{13}$

That means 120 segments with $^{12}\!/\!_{13}$ of a segment left over. Round up to the nearest whole to find the minimum number of segments the yardwork company will need to cut.

8. D This problem has many steps, regardless of which method you use.

Method 1: Determine the price.

First, determine the price of the sweater after the first markdown.

$$\$80 \times 10\% = \$80 \times 0.10 = \$8.$$

Now subtract that discount from the original price.

$$\$80 - \$8 = \$72$$

Second, determine the price of the sweater after the second markdown.

$$\$72 \times 25\% = \$72 \times 0.25 = \$18.$$

Now, subtract to find the new price.

$$\$72 - \$18 = \$54$$

Finally, to find the percentage of the original, you must divide 54 by 80.

$$54 \div 80 = 0.675 = 67.5\%$$

Method 2: Use percentages.

After the first markdown of 10%, the price of the sweater is 90% of the original price.

The next discount is 25% off the marked down price. Therefore, it will be 75% of the marked down price. Multiply to find the percentage of the original price.

$$75\% \times 90\% = 67.5\%$$

9. B Let's solve each expression and then determine the order.

I. $3 \div \frac{1}{2}$
$= 3 \times \frac{2}{1} = 6$

II. $3 \times \frac{1}{2}$
$= \frac{3}{2} = 1\frac{1}{2}$

III. $\frac{1}{2} \div 3$
$= \frac{1}{2} \times \frac{1}{3}$
$= \frac{1}{6}$

Order from least to greatest:

$\frac{1}{6}, 1\frac{1}{2}, 6$

III, II, I

10. B To find the average, add all the numbers and divide by the total number of numbers.

When adding, line up the decimal places.

```
    4.25
    5.6
+   8
    0
    0
　─────
   17.85
```

Now, divide by 5 to find the average.

$17.85 \div 5 = 3.57$

3.57 hours

11. A **Option 1:** $10,000 plus 10% of what he sold.

Matthew sold $35,000, so find 10% of that.

$35,000 x 10% =

$35,000 x 0.10 =

$3,500

Option 1: $10,000 + $3,500 = $13,500

Option 2: $8,000 plus 15% of what he sold.

$35,000 x 15% =

$35,000 x 0.15 =

$5,250

Option 2: $8,000 + $5,250 = $13,250

Option 1 will give Matthew more money.

12. C Break the problem into steps. First, figure out the total cost of the books.

Books: 6 books x $6.95 each = $41.70

Now, add the sales tax.

$41.70 + $3.34 = $45.04

Then, if Carol is left with $4.96, add that back to the $45.04 to see how much she started with.

$45.04 + $5.96 = $51.00

128　　Number Sense: Module Review

13. B There are two ways to approach this problem.

Method 1: Convert to totals.

Instead of dealing with averages, deal with total amount of precipitation. If the average is 12.5mm for 3 months, the total precipitation during those 3 months can be found by multiplying the average by number of months.

Total Precipitation = 12.5 x 3 = 37.5mm

If the precipitation increased by 1.5mm each month, multiply by 3 to find total precipitation increase.

Precipitation increase = 1.5 x 3 = 4.5mm

New total prec. = 37.5mm + 4.5mm = 42mm

To find new average, divide new total by 3 months.

Average = 42mm ÷ 3 = 14mm

Method 2: Keep everything in averages.

If the average was 12.5mm, you can think of each month as having 12.5mm of precipitation. If each month it increased by 1.5mm, you can add 1.5mm to each month to figure out the new amount of precipitation.

12.5mm + 1.5mm = 14mm

If you think of each month as 14mm, then the average across all 3 months is 14mm.

14. B Anything raised to the power of 0 is 1.

$12^0 = 1$

Anything raised to the power of 1 is itself.

$12^1 = 12$
$12^0 - 12^1 = 1 - 12 = -11$

15. B Let's figure out how to solve each answer choice.

A: You have a 6-foot long string, and you need pieces that are each 3.5 feet. How many pieces can you make from the string?

This problem would be found by dividing the total amount of string by the length of each piece. 6 ÷ 3.5. Eliminate A.

B: Six documentaries have an average length of 3.5 hours. How many total hours of film are there?

The average 3.5 is found by dividing the total by 6. Therefore, you can find the total by finding the product of 3.5 and 6. This is the correct answer.

C: You have $6 and go to a store to buy $3.50 worth of supplies. How much change do you have?

To find the change, subtract what you spent from what you had. 6 – 3.5. Eliminate C.

D: You are making cookies and put in 6 tablespoons of sugar. The recipe calls for an additional 3.5 tablespoons, how many total tablespoons have you put in?

To find the total amount of sugar you put in, add the 6 tablespoons to the additional 3.5 tablespoons. 6 + 3.5. Eliminate D.

16. A $(-3)^3 - 3(-2)^2 + 25^{1/2} =$

Let's break this problem up.

$(-3)^3 = (-3)(-3)(-3) = -27$

$3(-2)^2 = 3(-2)(-2) = 12$

$25^{1/2} = 5$

Now, let's solve the entire problem.

$(-3)^3 - 3(-2)2 + 25^{1/2} =$

$-27 - 12 + 5 = -39 + 5 = -34$

17. C If ⅔ of the students are female, then subtract ⅔ from 1 to determine the fraction of males.

$1 - ⅔ = ⅓$

Therefore, ⅓ of the students are males.

Therefore, if ⅓ are males and ⅔ are females, there are twice as many females as males. Therefore, if 200 are male, then 400 are female.

Another way to think of the problem is that if ⅓ of the students are male and that is 200 students, then the total number of students must be 600. Therefore, subtract the number of males from the total to find the number of females. 600 – 200 = 400. 400 females.

18. C $(3 \times 10^{-4}) \div (6 \times 10^7)$

To find the quotient of two numbers in scientific notation, you should break it into smaller problems. First, divide the coefficients, then divide the powers of 10 by subtracting the exponents, and then put those results into scientific notation.

Coefficients: $3 \div 6 = 0.5$

Exponents: $-4 - 7 = -11$

0.5×10^{-11}

Unfortunately, 0.5×10^{-11} is not in proper scientific notation since 0.5 is not between 1 and 10. So, convert 0.5 to scientific notation and multiply by 10^{-11}.

$0.5 \times 10^{-11} =$

$5 \times 10^{-1} \times 10^{-11} =$

5×10^{-12}

19. A To simplify the expression, first simplify each term. Find factors that have perfect square roots.

$3\sqrt{147} = 3 \times \sqrt{(49 \times 3)} = 3 \times \sqrt{49} \times \sqrt{3} = 3 \times 7 \times \sqrt{3} = 21\sqrt{3}$

$4\sqrt{96} = 4 \times \sqrt{(16 \times 6)} = 4 \times \sqrt{16} \times \sqrt{6} = 4 \times 4 \times \sqrt{6} = 16\sqrt{6}$

$2\sqrt{150} = 2 \times \sqrt{(25 \times 6)} = 2 \times \sqrt{25} \times \sqrt{6} = 2 \times 5 \times \sqrt{6} = 10\sqrt{6}$

Now, simplify the expression and combine terms with like radicals.

$3\sqrt{147} + 4\sqrt{96} - 2\sqrt{150}$

$= 21\sqrt{3} + 16\sqrt{6} - 10\sqrt{6}$

$= 21\sqrt{3} + 6\sqrt{6}$

20. C To convert from base 16 to base 10, what we are used to, we take each digit and multiply it by consecutive powers of 16, starting with the exponent 0. In this case, they ask for the value of the 4, which is the second digit. The first digit will be multiplied by 16^0, and the second digit will be multiplied by 16^1.

$4 \times 16^1 = 64$

In case you were curious, the value of each digit in the number 2540_{16} is calculated below.

0: $0 \times 16^0 = 0 \times 1 = 0$

4: $4 \times 16^1 = 4 \times 16 = 64$

5: $5 \times 16^2 = 5 \times 256 = 1280$

2: $2 \times 16^3 = 2 \times 4096 = 8192$

$2540_{16} = 0 + 64 + 1280 + 8192 = 9536$

3. Functions & Equations

Algebraic Expressions 134
Relations & Functions 141
Solving Equations 150
Inequalities 157
Ratios & Proportions 165
Operations with Functions 172
Sequences & Series 181
Module Review 190

Functions & Equations: Algebraic Expressions

Variables

A variable is a letter that represents a value. If you are solving a problem, and you have an unknown value, you could use a variable to represent that value. For example, if you knew that Sam was 5 years older than Andrew was, but you were unsure of how old Andrew was, you could use a variable to represent Andrew's age. Let's use "a," and then Sam's age could be expressed as "a + 5." Once the value for the variable is determined, it could replace the variable in the expression.

Algebraic Expressions

An algebraic expression is a phrase (no equality sign) that contains terms with numbers or variables and one or more operations. For example, 4 + y is an algebraic expression. If there is an equality sign, then it becomes a full statement or equation. For instance, 4 + y = 10 is an algebraic equation. When expressing relationships between numbers or variables, algebraic expressions are used. Algebraic expressions are also conveniently a shorter way to write a long statement.

Add 3 to a number and then multiply the sum by 6 and take the result and subtract 7
= 6(n + 3) − 7.

Patterns

A pattern is a predictable set of elements. The two basic types of patterns are those that repeat and those that are generated based on a model or template. We will briefly examine repeating patterns, but the focus of the lesson is on the second type of pattern, which is a more basic form of algebra. Algebraic expressions are used to represent these patterns.

Repeating Patterns

A repeating pattern is one in which a sequence of elements, called a core, is repeated two or more times. The elements can be anything from shapes to letters to numbers. For instance, the following patterns show several examples of repeated cores. The cores are underlined.

Patterns based on models

The second type of pattern is a much broader category, but it is one that is vital to mathematics. A non-repeating pattern is any predictable set of elements, so anything that uses a template or model to create output for a given input generates a pattern. For mathematical purposes, the input is generally the element number (1st, 2nd, 3rd, 4th, and so on) and the output is the element itself.

Example: 3, 6, 9, 12, 15 ...

For the input 1, there is an output of 3. For the input 2, there is an output of 6. This data is exhibiting a pattern $y = 3x$, where x is the input, and y is the output.

On a multiple-choice test, determining which pattern is exhibited by a set of data is often as simple as plugging in element numbers into the answer choices to find the expression that generates the appropriate outputs.

Example: Which pattern is exhibited by the data below?

–2, –4, –8, –16, –32, –64, –128, ...

A. $y = 2x$, B. $y = -2x$, C. $y = x-3$, D. $y = 4x$

You can see that the 1st input gives you a value of –2. Let's plug in 1 for x in each of the answer choices to see which gives a –2. Answer choice A does not work, and D does not work. Eliminate those, and try plugging in a 2 for x in the remaining equations to see which outputs a 4. Answer choice C gives a –1 ($y = 2 - 3$), so it does not work. Therefore, B is the correct answer, $y = -2x$.

Dependent and Independent Variables

The independent variable is the variable manipulated or changed and the dependent variable is the observed result of the changes in the independent variable. For example, the number of layers of clothing you wear would be the dependent variable, while the temperature outside would be the independent variable. In addition, in the case of standard equations, x is the independent variable and y is the dependent variable.

Tables are often used to show how one variable relates to another variable. For example, the table below shows the relation of $y = x + 3$.

x	y
0	3
1	4
4	7
6	9

Functions & Equations: Algebraic Expressions

Algebraic Expressions: Practice

1. What is the next element in the pattern?

$$-125, 25, -5, 1...$$

    A. 0.5
    B. −0.5
    C. 1/5
    D. −1/5

2. Which pattern is exhibited by the data in the table below?

x	y
1	1
8	2
27	3
125	5

    A. $x = y^3$
    B. $y = x^3$
    C. $y = x \div 4$
    D. $x = y^2 + 4$

3. Sandra is 5 inches shorter than Melissa, whose height is m inches. Write an expression to represent Sandra's height.

    A. m + 5
    B. m − 5
    C. m ÷ 5
    D. 5m

4. Identify the pattern exhibited by:

$$10.5, 20.5, 30.5, 40.5...$$

    A. y = 10.5x
    B. y = 10x + 0.5
    C. y = 0.5x + 10
    D. y = x + 10.5

5. Which of the following equations has the largest value when x = 10?

   A. $y = x + 10{,}000$
   B. $y = x^5 + 100x^4$
   C. $y = 10^x$
   D. $y = 1000x$

6. Which pattern does this data set fit:

   1, 4, 9, 16, 25...

   A. $y = 2x$
   B. $y = x^2$
   C. $y = x + 3$
   D. $y = x$

7. Write "the product of 6 and the sum of 3 and a number n" as an expression.

   A. $6 + 3n$
   B. $6(3n)$
   C. $6(3 + n)$
   D. $6 + 3 + n$

8. Which equation represents the relationship between a and b in the table below?

a	b
2	1
5	−8
7	−14
12	−29

   A. $b = a - 1$
   B. $b = 2a - 3$
   C. $b = -3a + 7$
   D. $b = -4a + 7$

9. What comes next in this series:

    0, 1, 3, 6, 10...

    A. 14
    B. 15
    C. 16
    D. 17

10. Jenna makes a salary of $1000/month plus 10% commission on whatever she sells. If Jenna sold y dollars worth of goods one month, how much did she make that month?

    A. 1010y
    B. 1000 ÷ 10y
    C. 1000 x (0.1y)
    D. 1000 + 0.1y

Algebraic Expressions: Answer Explanations

1. D −125, 25, −5, 1...

In this pattern, you divide by −5 to get from one element to the next. The next number will be 1 divided by −5, which is − 1/5.

2. A Plug the values from the table into each equation and see which equation is true for every set of values.

$x = y^3$ is true for all values.

3. B The question asks you to translate the words into an expression. The unknown quantity is Melissa's height, which is represented by the variable m.

Since Sandra is 5 inches shorter than Melissa, subtract 5 from Melissa's height to get Sandra's.

Sandra's height = Melissa's height − 5

= m − 5

Functions & Equations: Algebraic Expressions

4. B   For each equation, replace x with the element's position in the data set to see which answer works for all elements.

Equation B works for all elements:

1st element: $y = 10(1) + 0.5 = 10.5$

2nd element: $y = 10(2) + 0.5 = 20.5$

3rd element: $y = 10(3) + 0.5 = 30.5$

4th element: $y = 10(4) + 0.5 = 40.5$

5. C   For each answer choice, plug in $x = 10$ and solve for y.

A: $y = x + 10,000$
   $y = 10 + 10,000 = 10,010$

B: $y = x^5 + 100x^4$
   $y = 10^5 + 100(10^4)$
   $y = 100,000 + 100(10,000)$
   $y = 100,000 + 1,000,000$
   $y = 1,100,000$

C: $y = 10^x$
   $y = 10^{10}$
   $y = 10,000,000,000$

D: $y = 1000x$
   $y = 1000(10)$
   $y = 10,000$

6. B   To determine which pattern the data set fits, try each answer.

A: $y = 2x$. The first input of 1 should give you 1 as a result. But if you replace x with 1 in $y = 2x$, you get 2 as the output.

B: $y = x^2$. This equation corresponds to the data set. An input of 1 gives an output of 1; an input of 2 gives an output of 4; an input of 3 gives an output of 9; and so forth.

C: $y = x + 3$. An input of 1 gives 4 with this equation.

D: $y = x$. An input of 1 gives you a 1. But if you try the 2nd element, you get an output of 2 instead of 4.

7. C A product is the result of a multiplication problem. A sum is the result of an addition problem. The "product of 6" and the "sum of 3 and a number" is the same as 6 multiplied by the "sum of 3 and a number."

Let's translate "the sum of 3 and a number" into an expression.

Since we don't know the number, we use n to represent it:

$3 + n$

Now, going back to the product:

6 multiplied by "the sum of 3 and a number" equals 6 multiplied by $(3 + n)$, or $6(3 + n)$.

8.. C

a	b
2	1
5	–8
7	–14
12	–29

The equation $b = -3a + 7$ works for all values.

a = 2, b = 1: $1 = -3(2) + 7 = -6 + 7 = 1$

a = 5, b = –8: $-8 = -3(5) + 7 = -15 + 7 = -8$

a = 7, b = –14: $-14 = -3(7) + 7 = -21 + 7 = -14$

a = 12, b = –29: $-29 = -3(12) + 7 = -36 + 7 = -29$

9. B 0, 1, 3, 6, 10…

Identify the pattern:

To get from the first element to the second element, you add 1. To get from the second to the third, you add 2. You add 3 for the next element, and add 4 for the next after that. Can you see a pattern emerging? Following the pattern, add 5 for the next element: $10 + 5 = 15$.

10. D There are two parts to Jenna's salary: the base salary and the commission. The base salary is $1000. Her commission is 10% on what she sells. If she sells y dollars, multiply by 10% to figure out how much she makes on commission.

Commission = $10\%(y) = 0.1y$

Total Salary = Base plus Commission = $1000 + 0.1y$

Functions & Equations: Relations & Functions

Relations

Relations and functions are closely related to the topics covered in the lesson Algebraic Expressions. A relation is simply a patterned relationship between two variables – by applying an independent variable to a model, it is possible to generate the corresponding dependent variable. Relations are often shown in t-charts, with the input listed in a column on the left side of the "t" and the corresponding output listed on the right.

x	y
2	5
3	7
4	9
5	?
?	15

From a set of data, you might be asked to derive the relationship.

In this case, $y = 2x + 1$.

You might also be asked to use the relationship to fill in missing information. To find the y value that corresponds with x = 5, plug 5 into the equation:

$$y = 2(5) + 1 = 11.$$

To find the x-value that pairs with y = 15, plug 15 into the equation for y, and solve for x:

$$15 = 2x + 1, x = 7$$

Functions

A function is a specific type of relation for which each independent variable produces exactly one dependent variable. So, for each value of x input into the function, there can be only one corresponding y-value. However, multiple x values can produce the same y value.

For example, the following are functions, since each instance of x will produce only one y value:
$y = 2x + 1$
$y = x^2$

The following relation is not a function: $x = |y|$. In this case, if x = 2, y can be 2 or –2.

Function Notation

Functions are sometimes written using f(x), g(x), or other similar notation. The notation does not change the function in any way. Whether the dependent variable is labeled f(x) or y, and whether the independent variable is labeled x or another variable, treat the functions the same. For example, the notations $h(r) = r^2$, $y = x^2$, or $f(x) = x^2$ can all represent the same function.

Vertical Line Test

Functions can be verified graphically through the vertical line test. Since any function will have only one y-value for every x-value, a vertical line drawn through any x-value should hit exactly one y-value and no more. If the vertical line hits more than one point on the graph, then it does not represent a function.

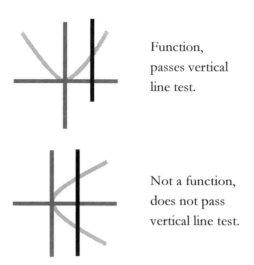

Function, passes vertical line test.

Not a function, does not pass vertical line test.

Domain and Range

The domain is a description of all the inputs or x-values for which the function has a valid output. For example, if we define a function f = {(1, 2), (3, 5), (6, 8), (7, 8)}, the domain is all valid values of x, which are {1, 3, 6, 7}.

While the domain covers all valid values of x, the range covers all valid values of y. Using our same example, the range of f is {2, 5, 8}. Note that we do not repeat any values in the domain or range.

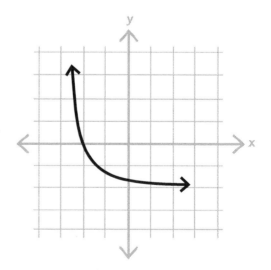

The domain is all possible x-values. In this case, let's look at the graph to the left to see which x-values have a valid y-value. As you can see, there will be no outputs when x is less than −3. Therefore, the domain is x > −3.

One way to write the above is using the ∞ symbol, which stands for infinity. The domain is all possible values between -3 and infinity, written (-3, ∞).

In the graph, the range (all possible y-values) is anything greater than -2, written as y > -2 or (-2, ∞).

Piecewise-Defined Functions

A piecewise-defined function is continuous over certain defined intervals of x. For example, the following is a piecewise-defined function:

$$f(x) = x \text{ if } x < 1$$
$$f(x) = 2x^2 \text{ if } x \geq 1$$

Continuous Functions

A continuous function is one that has no sudden breaks from one value of x to another. For example, $y = 2x$ is a continuous function because there are no breaks in the graph, which is a straight line. A function that is not continuous is said to be discontinuous. For example, a step function is discontinuous because of the sharp breaks at each step.

Inverses

An inverse function is one that reverses another function. For example, a function f(x) transforms the value x = 2 to f(2) = 5; then, another function g(x) transforms x = 5 back to g(5) = 2. Then, f(x) and g(x) are inverses. The inverse of the function f(x) can be written $f^{-1}(x)$.

A more formal way of denoting inverse functions is $f(g(x)) = x$ and $g(f(x)) = x$.

To find the inverse of a relation, you switch the inputs and the outputs. You can also think of it as switching the x and y values in each pair.

Examples:
  relation: {(0, 3), (2, 7), (8, 9)}; inverse: {(3, 0), (7, 2), (9, 8)}
  relation: y = x + 3; inverse: x = y + 3, rearrange y = x – 3

Relations & Functions: Practice

1. Find the inverse of the following relation:

{(2, –4), (11, 5), (–12, 0), (1, 6)}

A. {(–4, 2), (5, 11), (0, –12), (6, 1)}
B. {(–2, 4), (–11, 5), (12, 0), (–1, –6)}
C. {(4, –2), (–5, 11), (0, –12), (–6, –1)}
D. {(½, –¼), (¹⁄₁₁, ⅕), (–¹⁄₁₂, 0), (1, ⅙)}

2. What is the range for the function shown below?

A. all reals
B. y < 1
C. y ≤ 1
D. x > −1

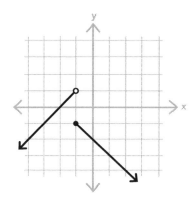

3. A particular function is defined as follows: Take any integer greater than zero. If the integer is odd, multiply it by 2. If the integer is even, add 1 and then multiply the result by 2. What is the domain of the function?

A. The number 2
B. Set of even integers
C. Set of odd integers
D. Set of positive integers

4. Which of the following is not a function?

A. $y = x^2$
B. $y = |x|$
C. $y > x$
D. $x = y$

5. What is the function shown below?

A. $x = -1$
B. $f(x) = -x - 1$
C. $f(x) = -1$
D. $x = -f(x)$

x	f(x)
1	−1
2	−1
5	−1
23	−1

6. Which of the following is not a function?

A.

C.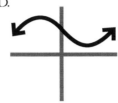

B.

D.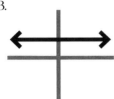

7. What is f(0) − f(3)?

$f(x) = 3x$ if $x < -1$

$f(x) = 5$ if $-1 \leq x < 1$

$f(x) = 2(x + 1)^2$ if $x \geq 1$

A. −27
B. −5
C. −3
D. 5

8. What is the domain of f(x)?

$$f(x) = \frac{\sqrt{x-3}}{2x-5}$$

A. $x > 5/2$
B. $x \geq 5/2$
C. $x \geq 3$
D. $x < 5$

9. What is the range of function f(x)?

$$f(x) = \frac{1}{\sqrt{2x-5}}$$

A. $(0, \infty)$

B. $(-\infty, \infty)$

C. $(5/2, \infty)$

D. $[5/2, \infty)$

10. What is the domain of the function graphed below?

A. $(-\infty, 0]$

B. $[0, \infty)$

C. $[-2, \infty)$

D. All real numbers.

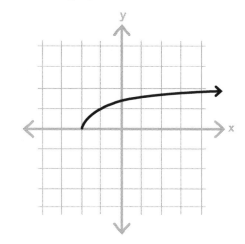

Relations & Functions: Answer Explanations

1. A   To find the inverse of a relation, you switch the inputs and the outputs. You can think of it as switching the x and y values in each pair.

> Original: {(2, –4), (11, 5), (–12, 0), (1, 6)}
>
> Inverse: {(–4, 2), (5, 11), (0, –12), (6, 1)}

2. B   The range of a function is all possible outputs or y values. For the function shown, y is always less than 1.

3. D   The domain of the function is the set of inputs. The definition of this particular function states: "Take any integer greater than zero."

Therefore, the domain is the set of all positive integers.

4. C A function is a set of ordered pairs for which every input x has exactly one output y.

$y = x^2, y = |x|$, and $x = y$

Every time you put a value for x in the above equations, you get exactly one y. It does not matter that for different inputs, you might get the same output.

$y > x$

In this expression, a single value for x gives a range of y values. Therefore, it is not a function.

5. C As can be seen in the t-chart, no matter what x value you put in, the function will output –1. This function is written as $f(x) = -1$.

6. C You can use the vertical line test to determine if the graph represents a function. If you can draw a vertical line through the graph and it crosses more than one point, it is not a function.

7. A To find $f(0) - f(3)$, first evaluate $f(0)$ and then evaluate $f(3)$.

$f(0)$ is the same as saying $x = 0$, which satisfies this piece of the function:

$-1 \leq x < 1$

As stated, when $-1 \leq x < 1$, $f(x) = 5$. So, we can say that $f(0) = 5$.

Next, evaluate $f(3)$. Here, we are saying $x = 3$, which satisfies the condition $x \geq 1$. This falls under the following part of the function:

$f(x) = 2(x + 1)^2$ if $x \geq 1$

Therefore, $f(3) = 2(3 + 1)^2 = 2(4)^2 = 32$

Now, subtract. $f(0) - f(3) = 5 - 32 = -27$

8. C Two conditions must be satisfied for x to be valid in this function.

The denominator must not be zero.

The value under the square root can't be negative.

The first condition states the denominator must not be zero. So, let's find those values of x:

$2x - 5 \neq 0$

$2x \neq 5$

$x \neq 5/2$

$x \neq 5/2$ satisfies the first condition.

The next condition is that the value under the square root must be greater than or equal to 0.

$x - 3 \geq 0$

$x \geq 3$

$x \geq 3$ satisfies the second condition.

$x \geq 3$ supersedes the first condition since it satisfies both the first and second conditions and, therefore, all the conditions necessary for a valid domain.

9. A You can approach this problem by solving for the domain and then plugging that into the function to find the range. Or, you can solve by determining what restrictions are on the function and reasoning about the range.

$$f(x) = \frac{1}{\sqrt{2x-5}}$$

Method 1: Solve for domain, then range.

First, find the domain of the function. There are two restrictions on the domain: can't divide by zero and can't take the square root of a negative number. These can be summed up with the following equation:

$\sqrt{(2x-5)} > 0$

Solve for x:

$\sqrt{(2x-5)} > 0$

Square both sides

$2x - 5 > 0$

$2x > 5$

$x > 5/2$

So, x is between 5/2 and infinity. To find the range, check what happens to x as it gets closer to 5/2 and infinity. As x approaches 5/2, the function approaches $+\infty$, because it is 1 divided by a number that is getting closer and closer to 0. As x approaches ∞, the function approaches zero, as you have 1 divided by a number approaching infinity. However, it does not include 0, as it will never equal 0.

Therefore, the range of the function is $(0, \infty)$, which is all values between 0 and infinity.

Method 2: Reason about the range.

The denominator is the square root of a value. The square root will never be negative. Since both the numerator and denominator are positive, you know that the entire function will be positive. Therefore, eliminate answer B.

There are no other restrictions on the range; however, it is worth looking at the other answer choices to see which can be eliminated. You have one answer that shows values greater than 0 and others greater than 5/2. Therefore, you might want to try a value such as 1. If 1 works as a possible output of the function, then you can eliminate answers C and D.

$$1 = 1/\sqrt{(2x - 5)}$$

Cross-multiply:

$$\sqrt{(2x - 5)} = 1$$
$$2x - 5 = 1$$
$$2x = 6$$
$$x = 3$$

Therefore, eliminate C and D, also, to leave Answer A.

10. C The domain is equal to all the possible inputs, or x-values, to a function. In this case, the function is graphed and valid from −2 to infinity.

Since x can also equal −2, you must make sure to include that value in the domain and, therefore, use a square bracket.

Domain: [−2, ∞)

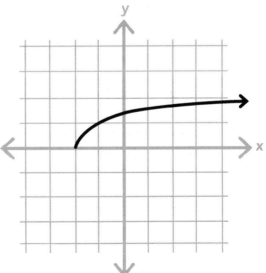

Functions & Equations: Solving Equations

Solving for a Variable

Solving an equation means finding the set of values for the variable in the equation that makes the equation true. For example: $x^2 = 25$ is true when $x = 5$ or $x = -5$.

Plugging In

You can see if a number is a solution to an equation by plugging in the value for the variable and seeing if the equation is true. For example, to check if $x = 5$ is a solution to $x^2 = 25$, plug in 5 for x: $5^2 = 25$. This is true; therefore, 5 is a solution.

Isolate the Variable

To solve for a variable in an equation, you need to isolate the variable on one side of the equal sign, with all the numbers on the other side. This can be done by performing the inverse of whatever operations are performed on the variable on both sides of the equation. In the example above, x was squared in the equation. Taking the square root of both sides gives the two possible x values of 5 and –5.

You must perform the inverse operations in the reverse order of operations.

Example: $6x - 12 = 24$

Perform the inverse operation of the subtraction of 12, which is the addition of 12 to both sides.

$6x - 12 + 12 = 24 + 12$
$6x = 36$

Perform the inverse operation of the multiplication of 6, which is the division of 6 on both sides.

$6x \div 6 = 36 \div 6$
$x = 6$

Absolute Value Equations

To solve for variables inside an absolute value sign, remember that the contents could be positive or negative. Therefore, assign both positive and negative values to the other side of the equal sign, and solve both equations to get all possible values of the variable.

Example: $|x + 2| = 7$
$x + 2 = 7, x = 5$
OR $x + 2 = -7, x = -9$
$x = 5$ OR -9, and you can check both answers in the equation to show that this is true.

Solving Equations: Practice

1. What is the value of n in the following equation?

    $-3n + 6 = 12$

    A. –6
    B. –2
    C. 2
    D. 4

2. What would you do to both sides of the following equation to solve for y?

    $-(3/4) y = 12$

    A. Add ¾
    B. Multiply by – ¾
    C. Multiply by –4/3
    D. Divide by ¾

3. Which of the following is a possible value for c in the following equation:

    $|c + 6| = 14$

    A. 8
    B. –8
    C. 20
    D. –18

4. Solve for y:

    $14y + 27 = 6$

    A. 33/14
    B. –3/2
    C. 3
    D. 26 4/7

5. What should you do to both sides of the following equation to solve for m?

$$m/4 - 6 = 10$$

   A. Add 6, then divide by 4.
   B. Subtract 6, then, divide by 4.
   C. Multiply by 4, then add 6.
   D. Add 6, then multiply by 4.

6. Solve for m:

$$1000m^3 = 1$$

   A. $1/100$
   B. $1/10$
   C. 10
   D. 100

7. Solve for y:

$$|2y| - 1 = y^2$$

   A. –3
   B. –1
   C. 0
   D. 2

8. Solve for n:

$$3n + 4 = 5n + 8$$

   A. –2
   B. $4/3$
   C. 2
   D. –4

Functions & Equations: Solving Equations

9. What is the value of m in the following equation?

$(6m + 3)/3 = 11$

A. $5/3$
B. 4
C. 5
D. 6

10. What does r equal in the following equation?

$-2r + 7 = 8r - 17$

A. $12/5$
B. $-5/3$
C. $5/12$
D. $-3/5$

Solving Equations: Answer Explanations

1. B   Isolate the variable by performing inverse operations on both sides of the equation.

First, subtract 6 from both sides:
$-3n + 6 - 6 = 12 - 6$
$-3n = 6$

Next, divide both sides by -3:
$-3n \div -3 = 6 \div -3$
$n = -2$

2. C $-(3/4)y = 12$

In this case, you are multiplying the variable y by $-3/4$. To isolate the variable, you must perform the inverse operation.

The inverse operation of multiplying by $-3/4$ is dividing by $-3/4$. Since this isn't one of the answer choices, we have to determine if there is another way this operation can be written.

Dividing by $-3/4$ is the same as multiplying by its reciprocal.
Therefore, multiplying both sides by $-4/3$ will solve for y.

$-(3/4)y = 12$
$-(3/4)y \times -4/3 = 12 \times -4/3$
$y = -16$

Functions & Equations: Solving Equations

3. A When dealing with a variable inside an absolute value sign, you have to set up two new equations: one that represents the contents within the absolute value sign as positive and one that represents the contents as negative.

$$|c + 6| = 14$$

Equation 1: $c + 6 = 14$. In this case, $c = 8$.

Equation 2: $c + 6 = -14$. In this case, $c = -20$.

4. B To isolate the variable, first subtract 27 from both sides and then divide by 14:

$$14y + 27 = 6$$
$$14y + 27 - 27 = 6 - 27$$
$$14y = -21$$
$$14y \div 14 = -21 \div 14$$
$$y = -21/14$$
$$y = -3/2$$

5. D To solve for m, you must isolate the variable.

Addition is the inverse of subtraction, so you must add 6 to both sides of the equation:
$$m/4 - 6 = 10$$
$$m/4 - 6 + 6 = 10 + 6$$
$$m/4 = 16$$

Multiplication is the inverse of division, so you must multiply both sides of the equation by 4:
$$m/4 = 16$$
$$m/4 \times 4 = 16 \times 4$$
$$m = 64$$

6. B You must isolate m. First, divide both sides by 1000:

$$1000m^3 = 1$$
$$1000m^3 \div 1000 = 1 \div 1000$$
$$m^3 = 1/1000$$

Next, take the cube root of both sides:
$$m = 1/10$$

7. B This equation is difficult to solve directly; therefore, plug in the answer choices to see which one makes the equation true.

    A: −3

$$|2y| - 1 = y^2$$
$$|2(-3)| - 1 = (-3)^2$$
$$|-6| - 1 = 9$$
$$6 - 1 = 9$$

Not true.

    B: −1

$$|2y| - 1 = y^2$$
$$|2(-1)| - 1 = (-1)^2$$
$$|-2| - 1 = 1$$
$$2 - 1 = 1$$

True. Answer B.

    C: 0

$$|2y| - 1 = y^2$$
$$|2(0)| - 1 = 0^2$$
$$|0| - 1 = 0$$
$$0 - 1 = 0$$

Not true.

    D: 2

$$|2y| - 1 = y^2$$
$$|2(2)| - 1 = 2^2$$
$$|4| - 1 = 4$$
$$4 - 1 = 4$$

Not true.

8. A In this case, there are variables on both sides of the equation. Move all terms with the variable to one side of the equation, and then isolate n.

$$3n + 4 = 5n + 8$$

Subtract 3n from both sides:
$$3n + 4 - 3n = 5n + 8 - 3n$$
$$4 = 2n + 8$$

Subtract 8 from both sides to isolate n:
$$4 - 8 = 2n + 8 - 8$$
$$-4 = 2n$$

Divide both sides by 2:
$$-4 \div 2 = 2n \div 2$$
$$-2 = n$$

9. C Isolate the variable by performing inverse operations on both sides of the equation.

Multiply both sides by 3:
$$(6m + 3)/3 \times 3 = 11 \times 3$$
$$6m + 3 = 33$$

Subtract 3 from both sides:
$$6m + 3 - 3 = 33 - 3$$
$$6m = 30$$

Divide both sides by 6:
$$6m \div 6 = 30 \div 6$$
$$m = 5$$

10. A First, bring all the terms with variables to one side of the equation and all the numbers to the other side. Then, isolate the variable to solve.
$$-2r + 7 = 8r - 17$$

Add 2r to both sides:
$$7 = 10r - 17$$

Add 17 to both sides:
$$24 = 10r$$

Divide by 10:
$$24/10 = r$$
$$12/5 = r$$

Functions & Equations: Inequalities

Definition of Inequalities

An inequality is a statement about the relationship between two values. The greater than >, the less than <, the greater than or equal to ≥, and less than or equal to ≤ signs are used to define the relationship in an inequality. For example, y ≥ 2 means that the value of y is greater than or equal to 2.

Simplifying Inequalities

It is possible to solve for variables in inequalities in a way similar to solving for variables in an equation. Essentially, it is possible to simplify an inequality to generate a range of possible values for a variable. Simplify the inequality in the same way you would approach an equation. You want to isolate the variable on one side of the inequality symbol.

Example: $3x - 6 > 12$

$3x - 6 + 6 > 12 + 6$

$3x > 18$

$x > 6$

Some inequalities are compound, or contain two separate statements. To solve these, follow the same steps of isolating the variable, but make sure to perform the operations on all sides of the inequalities.

Example: $-4 \leq x + 8 < 3$

$-4 - 8 \leq x + 8 - 8 < 3 - 8$

$-12 \leq x < -5$

Multiplying/Dividing by Negative Numbers

When multiplying or dividing an inequality by a negative number, switch the signs. Therefore, < becomes > and ≤ becomes ≥.

Example: $-2x > 8$, divide both sides by -2 and flip the sign

$x < -4$

Example: $12 \geq -2x + 4 > -2$

$8 \geq -2x > -6$

$-4 \leq x < 3$

Graphing Inequalities

The range of values for x can be shown graphically.

A closed circle is used to represent $\leq$ or $\geq$ to show that the end value is included, and an open circle is used for $>$ or $<$ to show that the value is not included.

Absolute Value Inequalities

Just as an equation containing the absolute value of a variable generates two possible values, an inequality with an absolute value generates two ranges of possible values.

$|x| > 2$, Since the absolute value of the variable is greater than a value, this becomes a divergent inequality and can be split into two inequalities with an "or".

$|x| > 2$ can be split into: $x > 2$ or $x < -2$. You can try possible values to show that this is true.

Remember that the absolute value is defined as the distance from zero; therefore, if the distance from zero is greater than 2, it would be all values less than -2 and greater than 2.

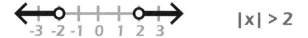

$|x| < 2$, Since the absolute value of the variable is less than a value, this becomes a convergent inequality and can be split into two inequalities with an "and".

$|x| < 2$ can be made into $x < 2$ and $x > -2$. You can also combine these two statements into one compound inequality: $-2 < x < 2$. Therefore, all values between -2 and 2 will make this statement true.

Remember that the absolute value is defined as the distance from zero; therefore, if the distance from zero is less than 2, it would be all the values between –2 and 2.

$|x| < 2$

Inequalities: Practice

1. Write 7 > y in words.

   A. y is greater than 7

   B. 7 is greater than or equal to y

   C. 7 is less than y

   D. 7 is greater than y

2. Simplify the inequality 3r + 4 > 19.

   A. r < 5

   B. r < 3

   C. r > 3

   D. r > 5

3. What are possible solutions to the following inequality?

$$|n| \leq 3$$

   A. –4, 0

   B. –2, 4

   C. –3, –5

   D. 1, –3

4. Which option represents x ≤ 90?

A.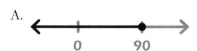

C.

B.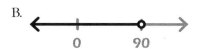

D.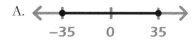

5. Solve the inequality:

$$16 < -2w$$

A. w > −32
B. w < −8
C. w > −8
D. w < 8

6. Separate |x| > 19 into two expressions.

A. |x| > 19 and |x| > −19
B. |x| > 19 or |x| < −19
C. x > 19 or x < −19
D. x > 19 and x < −19

7. Show |r| ≤ 35 on a number line.

A.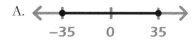

C.

B.

D.

Functions & Equations: Inequalities

8. Give a range of possible values for n if:

$$1 + 9n > 100 \text{ and } 210 > (½)n$$

A. $100 < n < 210$
B. $11 > n > 420$
C. $11 < n < 105$
D. $11 < n < 420$

9. Solve for n in the following inequality:

$$-(⅗)n + 2 \leq 11$$

A. $n \geq -15$
B. $n \geq -27/5$
C. $n \leq -27/5$
D. $n \leq -15$

10. Give a range of possible values for d if:

$$-48 < -3(12d - 4) < 48.$$

A. $-1 < d < 1$
B. $-5/3 < d < 5/3$
C. $5/3 < d < -1$
D. $-1 < d < 5/3$

Inequalities: Answer Explanations

1. D $7 > y$

$>$ is the greater than sign. The wider side of the sign always points to the larger number.

2. D To isolate the variable, the first step is to subtract 4 from all sides:

$3r + 4 - 4 > 19 - 4$

$3r > 15$

Then, divide both sides by 3 to solve for r:

$3r > 15$

$3r \div 3 > 15 \div 3$

$r > 5$

3. D Let's examine each option:

A: −4, 0.

Plug in −4 for n: $|-4| \leq 3, 4 \leq 3$.

Not true.

B: −4, 4.

Plug in 4 for n: $|4| \leq 3, 4 \leq 3$

Not true.

C: −3, −5.

Plug in −5 for n: $|-5| \leq 3, 5 \leq 3$

Not true.

D: 1, −3.

Plug in 1 for n: $|1| \leq 3, 1 \leq 3$

True.

Plug in −3 for n: $|-3| \leq 3, 3 \leq 3$

True.

4. A If x is less than or equal to 90, you need to include 90 (by using a closed circle) and an arrow pointing left toward all smaller numbers.

5. B Remember that when dividing or multiplying sides of an inequality by a negative, you must flip the inequality sign.

From the original equation: $16 < -2w$, you need to divide both sides by -2 and flip the inequality sign:

$16/(-2) > -2w/(-2)$

$-8 > w$

Rearranged as:

$w < -8$.

6. C An absolute value inequality statement can be separated into two inequality statements. Since the absolute value in this inequality is greater than a number, it is split into two divergent inequalities joined by an "or" statement:

$|x| > 19$

$x > 19$ or $x < -19$

You can pick a few numbers to test the answer. Make sure that the numbers work in both the original and the newly separated statements.

Example: 20

$|20| > 19 =$ True

$20 > 19$ or $-20 < -19 =$ True

Example: -33

$|-33| > 19 =$ True, since $|-33| = 33$

$33 > 19$ or $-33 < -19 =$ True

7. A Since the absolute value is ≤ 35, this is a convergent inequality. The two statements that the inequality can be broken into are

$r \leq 35$ and

$r \geq -35$

The circles should be closed since it is $\leq$, not $<$.

8. D Solve both inequalities and then combine them:

$1 + 9n > 100$

$9n > 99$

$n > 11$

$210 > (1/2)n$

$420 > n$

The first inequality states that n is greater than 11. The second inequality states that n is less than 420. We can combine this into one statement:

$11 < n < 420$

9. A Isolate the variable, just as you would if the equation was an equality.

$-(3/5)n + 2 \leq 11$

Subtract 2 from both sides:

$-(3/5)n + 2 - 2 \leq 11 - 2$

$-(3/5)n \leq 9$

Now multiply both sides by $-5/3$. When you multiply both sides of an inequality by a negative, you must flip the inequality sign:

$-(3/5)n \leq 9$

$-(3/5)n \times -5/3 \geq 9 \times -5/3$

$n \geq -15$

10. D Solve for d by isolating the variable. Make sure that what you do to the middle you do to all three sides of the inequality. Remember, also, that when you multiply or divide by a negative, all signs flip.

$-48 < -3(12d - 4) < 48$

Divide all sides by -3 and flip the signs:

$16 > 12d - 4 > -16$

Add 4 to all sides:

$20 > 12d > -12$

Divide by 12 on all sides:

$20/12 > d > -1$

Reduce the fraction and rearrange the inequality:

$-1 < d < 5/3$

Functions & Equations: Ratios & Proportions

Written Forms of Ratios

A ratio is a means of comparing one expression containing numbers or variables to another. In words, ratios are written using "to". For example, in a group of animals containing 3 fish and 2 parakeets, the ratio of fish to parakeets is 3 to 2. This same ratio can be written as 3:2 or $3/2$. Mathematically, the most useful expression of a ratio is a fraction.

Ratios as Rates of Change

In most practical applications, ratios are used to indicate rates of change – the rate at which one variable changes with respect to another. For example, if a student reads 2 pages per minute, then every minute that goes by increases the number of pages by 2. This can be written as $\frac{2 \text{ pages}}{1 \text{ min}}$.

Cross-Multiplication

You can use cross-multiplication to solve for variables easily.

$$\frac{a}{b} = \frac{c}{d}$$

When cross-multiplying, you create a new equation. Take the numerator of one side and multiply it by the denominator of the other side and set that equal to the denominator of the first side times the numerator of the second side.

$$ad = bc$$

In the example, $3/5 = x/20$, you can cross-multiply and get $3(20) = 5x$; $60 = 5x$; $12 = x$.

Direct Variation

If two variables are in direct variation, as one increases the other increases. Rate of change is a case of direct variation, where the value of a variable is equal to a constant multiplied by another variable. The constant is the rate of change. Variable = constant times another variable, $y = kx$, where k is the constant. In the above example, number of pages = 2 x number of minutes. Therefore, as the number of minutes increases, the number of pages goes up by a factor of 2.

Indirect Variation

If two variables vary indirectly, as one increases the other decreases. If two variables vary indirectly, then they are inversely proportional. If y and x vary indirectly, then $y = k/x$, where k is a constant.

For example, volume and pressure vary indirectly for a gas. What happens to the pressure of gas when you double its volume?

$$\text{pressure} = \frac{\text{constant}}{\text{variable}} \; ; \; P = k/V$$

If you double the volume ($k/2V = P/2$), the pressure is halved.

Proportions

By looking at indirect and direct variation as two possible variable relationships, you have been introduced to the concept of proportionality. Generally, a proportion is two equal ratios. For example, if the ratio of red to blue marbles in a bag is 3/5 and the bag has 20 blue marbles, you can determine the number of red marbles.

$$\text{red}/\text{blue} = 3/5 = x/20$$

x must equal 12 for the ratios to be equal; therefore, there are 12 red marbles.

Ratios & Proportions: Practice

1. If a bag contains only red and blue marbles and the ratio of red marbles to blue marbles is 3 to 5, what fraction of the bag is blue marbles?

   A. 3/5

   B. 5/3

   C. 5/8

   D. 3/8

2. What does 2 to 3 represent for a bag containing only 12 blue marbles and 8 red marbles?

   A. Fraction of blue marbles in bag

   B. Fraction of red marbles in bag

   C. Ratio of red to blue marbles

   D. Ratio of blue to red marbles

3. If Georgia bakes 8 cakes for every 4-hour shift she works, how many hours will it take her to bake 96 cakes?

   A. 24 hours

   B. 48 hours

   C. 96 hours

   D. 192 hours

4. Gary has 60 complete outfits for every 25 pairs of shoes. Assuming this proportion stays the same, how many outfits could he make with only 10 pairs of shoes?

   A. 18
   B. 20
   C. 22
   D. 24

5. In which of the following does y vary inversely with x?

   I. $xy = 6$
   II. $y = (½)x$
   III. $y = 4/x$

   A. III only
   B. I and III
   C. II and III
   D. I, II, and III

6. Anita needs 24 pounds of mix for every 120 gallons of concrete she mixes. How many pounds of mix will she need for a driveway that requires 35 gallons of concrete?

   A. 5
   B. 7
   C. 131
   D. 175

7. y is directly proportional to x. If y is 20 when x is 10, what is x when y is 5?

   A. 2.5
   B. 10
   C. 20
   D. 40

Functions & Equations: Ratios & Proportions

8. y is inversely proportional to x. If y is 20 when x is 10, what is x when y is 5?

   A. 2.5
   B. 10
   C. 20
   D. 40

9. At the same moment, two trains leave a station on parallel tracks. Train A travels the 700 miles from Station 1 to Station 3 in the same amount of time that it takes Train B to travel the 500 miles to Station 2. If the total route is 1500 miles long and both trains travel to the very end before turning around and traveling back to Station 1, which of the following proportions shows the total distance Train A has traveled when Train B reaches the end of the route?

   A. $500/700 = x/1000$
   B. $500/700 = 1000/x$
   C. $500/700 = x/1500$
   D. $700/500 = x/1500$

10. In the local college, the ratio of engineering majors to non-engineering majors is 2 to 7. If there are 1260 students in the entire school and all students fall under one of those categories, how many non-engineering majors are at the school?

    A. 140
    B. 180
    C. 630
    D. 980

Ratios & Proportions: Answer Explanations

1. C   For every 3 red marbles in the bag, there are 5 blue marbles, making a total of 8 marbles in each grouping. Therefore, 5 out of every 8 marbles are blue. As a fraction, this is 5/8.

2. C   The ratio of red to blue marbles is 8 to 12. You can reduce this since both are divisible by 4. This gives a ratio of red to blue marbles of 2 to 3.

3. B Set up the ratio between cakes and the hours it takes to bake them.

$$\frac{8 \text{ cakes}}{4 \text{ hours}} = \frac{96 \text{ cakes}}{n \text{ hours}}$$

Cross-multiply to solve for n

$8n = 96(4)$

$n = 48$

48 hours to make 96 cakes.

4. D Set up a proportion between pairs of shoes and complete outfits:

$$\frac{25 \text{ pairs}}{60 \text{ outfits}} = \frac{10 \text{ pairs}}{n \text{ outfits}}$$

Cross-multiply and then solve:

$25n = 60(10)$

$n = {}^{600}\!/_{25} = 24$ outfits

5. B Let's look at each option to check where y varies inversely with x.

I. $xy = 6$

Start by rearranging the equation to isolate y. Divide both sides by x:

$xy \div x = 6 \div x$

$y = {}^{6}\!/_{x}$

As you can see from the equation, as x increases, y decreases. y varies inversely with x in I.

II. $y = (½)x$

As x increases, so does y. For instance, when x = 2, y = 1. When x = 4, y = 2. Therefore, x and y are directly proportional.

III. $y = {}^{4}\!/_{x}$

This is already in the form of an equation where the two variables vary inversely. As x increases, y decreases.

6. B Set up the proportion between mix and concrete:

$$\frac{24 \text{ lbs mix}}{120 \text{ gal concrete}} = \frac{n \text{ lbs}}{35 \text{ gal}}$$

Cross-multiply and then solve for n:

$120n = 24(35)$

$120n = 840$

$n = 7$

7. **A**   **Method 1: Set up direct variation equation.**

    Set up an equation between x and y. If y is directly proportional to x, the equation can be written:

        $y = kx$, where k is the proportionality constant.

    Given the fact that y is 20 when x is 10, let's solve for k. Plug in x and y into the equation:

        $20 = 10k$

        $k = 2$

    Now, plug in y = 5 to solve for x:

        $y = 2x$

        $5 = 2x$

        $x = 2.5$

  Method 2: Set up proportion.

    You can set up a proportion between x and y. Let the unknown value equal n.

        $x/y = 10/20 = n/5$

    Cross-multiply.

        $10(5) = 20(n)$

        $50 = 20n$

        $n = 2.5$

8. **D**   Set up an equation between x and y. If y is inversely proportional to x, the equation can be written:

        $y = k/x$, where k is the proportionality constant.

    Given that y is 20 when x is 10, let's solve for k. Plug x and y into the equation:

        $20 = k/10$

        $k = 200$

    Now, plug in y = 5, to solve for x:

        $y = 200/x$

        $5 = 200/x$

        $x = 200/5$

        $x = 40$

9. D Train A travels 700 miles in the same time it takes Train B to travel 500. This gives you a rate that you can use to set up a proportion.

The other side of the proportion should be x/1500 because you are trying to calculate the distance Train A has traveled in the time it took Train B to travel the 1500-mile track.

Train A/Train B: $700/500 = x/1500$

Another acceptable proportion would be Train B/Train A: $500/700 = 1500/x$.

10. D The ratio of engineering majors to non-engineering majors is 2 to 7. Therefore, the ratio of engineering to non-engineering to total students is 2 to 7 to 9. Therefore, the ratio of non-engineering majors to total students is 7 to 9.

If there are 1260 students in the school, set up a proportion with n representing the number of non-engineering majors at the school.

non-eng majors to total = 7 to 9 = n to 1260

$7/9 = n/1260$

Cross-multiply to solve.
$1260(7) = 9n$
$8820 = 9n$
$n = 980$

Functions & Equations: Ratios & Proportions

Functions & Equations: Operations with Functions

Addition and Subtraction of Functions

The addition and subtraction of functions is similar to addition and subtraction of numbers and variables. The challenge with functions is getting used to the notation of the left-hand side (for example, f(x)).

For example, we can add or subtract f(x) and g(x) as defined below.

$$f(x) = x + 3$$
$$g(x) = 2x^2 - 4x + 5$$

Addition of functions, where sometimes, f(x) + g(x) is written as (f + g)(x)

$$f(x) + g(x) = (x + 3) + (2x^2 - 4x + 5) = 2x^2 - 3x + 8$$

Subtraction of functions (don't forget to distribute the −1), where sometimes, f(x) − g(x) is written as (f − g)(x)

$$f(x) - g(x) = (x + 3) - (2x^2 - 4x + 5) = x + 3 - 2x^2 + 4x - 5 = -2x^2 + 5x - 2$$

Composition of Functions

Sometimes, entire functions can be substituted in place of the variable (for example, x). This is often designated by the form f(g(x)) or g(f(x)).

You always start with the inside parentheses and move out. If we take the above functions f(x) and g(x), we can find the compositions

$$f(g(x)) = f(2x^2 - 4x + 5) = (2x^2 - 4x + 5) + 3 = 2x^2 - 4x + 8$$
$$g(f(x)) = g(x+3) = 2(x+3)^2 - 4(x+3) + 5 = 2x^2 + 12x + 18 - 4x - 12 + 5 = 2x^2 + 8x + 11$$

Graphs and Transformations

Adding or multiplying constants to a function can shift or otherwise transform a graph. This will be covered more extensively in other lessons after you have reviewed graphing. However, it is important to understand the concepts of how functions are shifted and in what direction.

f(x) + k: If you add a constant to the function, then it will shift the graph in the y direction by k units.
　　For instance, f(x) + 2 will shift the entire graph up by 2 units.

f(x + k): If you add a constant to the input of the function, then it will shift the graph in the x direction by -k units. Note the sign.

For instance, f(x + 2) will shift the graph 2 units to the left.

k(f(x)): If you multiply the function by a constant, then it stretches the graph vertically by a factor of k.

For instance, 2f(x) will vertically stretch the graph by 2.

f(kx): If you multiply the input of the function by a constant, then it will shrink the graph horizontally by a factor of k.

For instance, f(2x) will shrink the graph by a factor of 2 horizontally.

In the graphs below, f(x) is represented in gray and the black line is the graph of the transformation.

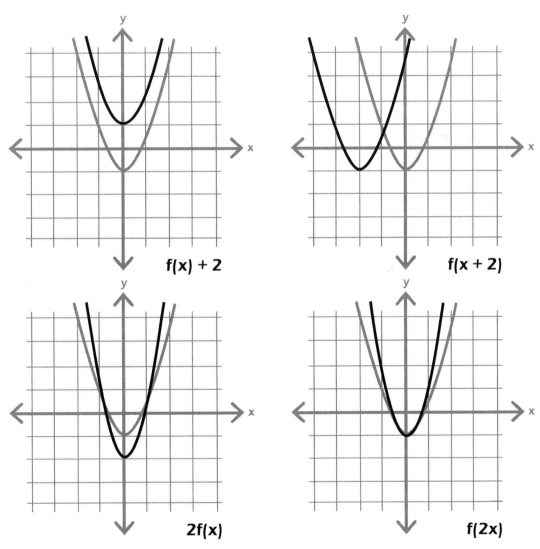

Functions & Equations: Operations with Functions

Operations with Functions: Practice

1. What is $f(x) + g(x)$?

$$f(x) = 2x - 4$$
$$g(x) = x^2 - 3x + 5$$

A. $x^2 + 2x + 5$
B. $x^2 - x + 1$
C. $x^2 + 5x + 9$
D. $2x^2 - 7x + 5$

2. If $f(x) = x + 3$ and $g(x) = 2x^2$, what is the value of $g(f(x))$?

A. $2x^2 + x + 3$
B. $2x^2 + 3$
C. $2(x+3)^2$
D. $2(3)^2$

3. What is $f(x) - g(x)$?

$$f(x) = 2x - 4$$
$$g(x) = x^2 - 3x + 5$$

A. $-x^2 + 5x - 9$
B. $2x^2 - x + 1$
C. $-x + 1$
D. $x^2 - x + 1$

4. How will the graph of $y = (¼)x^2 - 5$ compare with the graph of $y = x^2$?

A. Wider and shifted up.
B. Wider and shifted down.
C. Narrower and shifted up.
D. Narrower and shifted down.

5. What is f(g(−2))?

$f(x) = 2x - 3$

$g(x) = x^2 - 3x + 4$

A. 7
B. 8
C. 25
D. 74

6. What equation is represented by the graphs below?

A. f(g(2))=1
B. g(f(3))=2
C. g(f(4))=3
D. f(g(1))=2

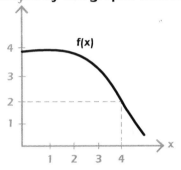
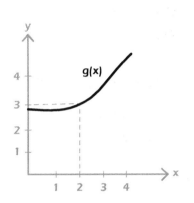

7. What is f(g(x)) + g(f(x))?

$f(x) = 2x - 3$

$g(x) = x^2 - 3x + 4$

A. $2x^2 - 6x + 5$
B. $4x^2 - 12x + 10$
C. $6x^2 - 24x + 27$
D. $10x^2 - 42x + 49$

8. What is f(x) − g(x) − h(x)?

$f(x) = 2x - 4$

$g(x) = x^2 - 3x + 5$

$h(x) = -4x^2 - 1$

A. $-3x^2 - x$
B. $3x^2 + x$
C. $3x^2 + 5x - 8$
D. $3x^2 - 5x + 8$

9. Which graph shows $x^2 + 3$ if the following graph shows x^2?

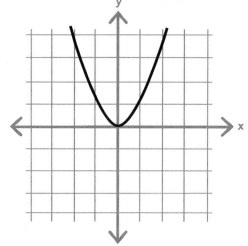

A.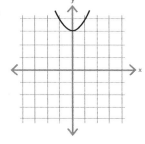

B.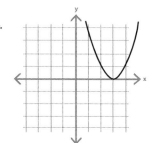

C.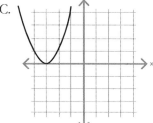

D.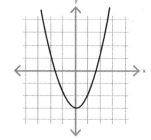

10. Which function is represented by this graph?

A. $g(x) = (x + 2)^2 - 1$
B. $g(x) = (x - 1)^2 - 2$
C. $g(x) = (x - 2)^2 - 1$
D. $g(x) = (x + 1)^2 - 2$

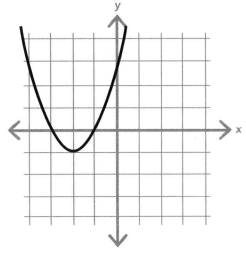

Operations with Functions: Answer Explanations

1. B $f(x) = 2x - 4$
$g(x) = x^2 - 3x + 5$

Adding the functions means adding the expressions. Combine like terms.

$f(x) + g(x) =$
$(2x - 4) + (x^2 - 3x + 5) =$
$x^2 + 2x - 3x - 4 + 5 =$
$x^2 - x + 1$

2. C   To solve a composition of functions, start with the innermost function first:
$f(x) = x + 3, g(x) = 2x^2$
$g(f(x)) = g(x + 3) = 2(x + 3)^2$

3. A $f(x) = 2x - 4$
$g(x) = x^2 - 3x + 5$

To subtract functions, just subtract the expressions. As with other subtraction problems, be careful with the signs.

$f(x) - g(x) =$
$(2x - 4) - (x^2 - 3x + 5) =$
$2x - 4 - x^2 + 3x - 5 =$
$-x^2 + 5x - 9$

4. B Two transformations are performed to the graph of $y = x^2$ to get to the graph of $y = (¼)x^2 - 5$.

Let's first look at the effect of subtracting 5. Remember that when you transform from f(x) to f(x) + k, you are shifting the graph in the vertical direction by k units. In this case, you are taking the output of f(x) and subtracting 5 from it to give you the new output. Therefore, you are shifting the graph down by 5 units. Try plugging in $x = 0$ into both equations – you will see that the original gives you 0, but the new function outputs –5.

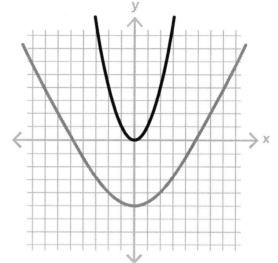

Now, let's look at the effect of multiplying by ¼. If you remember from the lesson, multiplying a function by a factor stretches it vertically. In this case, we are multiplying by a number less than 1; therefore, it will be shrunk vertically. If the entire graph is shrunk vertically, it will get wider.

In the graph to the right, you can see $y = x^2$ in black and $y = (¼)x^2 - 5$ in gray.

5. C There are two ways to approach solving f(g(–2)).

Method 1: Start with calculating f(g(x)).

You can first determine the composition of the two functions f and g and then plug in x as –2.

$$f(g(x))$$
$$= f(x^2 - 3x + 4)$$
$$= 2(x^2 - 3x + 4) - 3$$
$$= 2x^2 - 6x + 5$$

Now, plug in $x = -2$ into this composition:

$$f(g(-2))$$
$$= 2(-2)^2 - 6(-2) + 5$$
$$= 2(4) + 12 + 5 = 25$$

Method 2: Start with plugging –2 into function g.

You can also start by plugging the value of x into the function g and then taking that result and plugging it into the function f.

$$f(g(-2))$$
$$= f((-2)^2 - 3(-2) + 4)$$
$$= f(4 + 6 + 4) = f(14) = 2(14) - 3 = 25$$

6. C There are two approaches.

Method 1: Examine the graphs of the functions.

The first graph shows that an input of 4 gives an output of 2: f(4) = 2

The second graph shows that an input of 2 gives an output of 3: g(2) = 3

To combine these two functions, look for any numbers that overlap. In this case, the only number that overlaps is 2. If you first take 4 as input to f, you will get 2. If you take that output and input it into g, you will get 3.

g(2) = g(f(4)) = 3

Method 2: Plug in each answer choice.

Let's go through each answer choice to see which is true.

A. f(g(2))=1

Start with the inner parentheses. g(2) is 3.

Then, f(g(2)) = f(3) = 3. Not the correct answer.

B. g(f(3))=2

Start with the inner parentheses. f(3) is approximately 3.

Then, g(f(3)) = g(3) = 3.5. Not the correct answer.

C. g(f(4))=3

Start with the inner parentheses. f(4) is approximately 2, as indicated by the dotted lines.

Then, g(f(4)) = g(2) = 3. Correct answer.

D. f(g(1))=2

Start with the inner parentheses. g(1) is approximately 3.

Then, f(g(1)) = f(3) = 3. Not the correct answer.

7. C Let's find each of the compositions of the functions first:

$f(g(x)) = f(x^2 - 3x + 4) = 2(x^2 - 3x + 4) - 3 = 2x^2 - 6x + 8 - 3 = 2x^2 - 6x + 5$

$g(f(x)) = g(2x - 3) = (2x - 3)^2 - 3(2x - 3) + 4 = 4x^2 - 12x + 9 - 6x + 9 + 4 = 4x^2 - 18x + 22$

Now, let's add them together:

$f(g(x)) + g(f(x)) = 2x^2 - 6x + 5 + 4x^2 - 18x + 22 = 6x^2 - 24x + 27$

8. C Subtract functions just as you would subtract expressions. Be sure to distribute the negative sign when subtracting. Then, combine like terms.

$$f(x) - g(x) - h(x) =$$
$$(2x - 4) - (x^2 - 3x + 5) - (-4x^2 - 1) =$$
$$2x - 4 - x^2 + 3x - 5 + 4x^2 + 1 =$$
$$3x^2 + 5x - 8$$

9. A In this case, you are transforming the original function $f(x) = x^2$ and adding 3 to the output.

If you transform a graph by adding a constant k to it, then it will shift the graph vertically by k units. Therefore, in this case, we are adding 3 and, therefore, shifting the graph up by 3 units. You could have also plugged in a value for x to see which graph yielded the correct points.

10. A The graph is a transformation of the function $f(x) = x^2$. The graph is shifted down by 1 unit and to the left by 2 units.

When shifting down by 1 unit, you are taking a function f(x) and subtracting 1 from the output. $f(x) - 1$.

Remember that when you are adding a constant to the input, it shifts the graph horizontally by –k units. Therefore, since you are shifting to the left by 2 units, you add 2 to the input. $f(x + 2)$

Putting the two transformations together: $f(x + 2) - 1 = (x + 2)^2 - 1$

Another way to solve this question is to plug in a few points and see which function fits the points.

Functions & Equations: Sequences & Series

Sequences and Series

A sequence is the result of a function at each consecutive input, with the inputs starting at x = 1, then x = 2, x = 3, and so on.

For example, the function f(x) = 2x. A sequence is 2, 4, 6, 8, 10...

When the terms of a sequence are summed, the result is called a series.

Arithmetic Series

For an arithmetic series, there is a constant difference from one term to the next in the sequence. In the sequence, 1, 2, 3, 4, 5..., you can see that the difference between each term is 1. This series is written below:

$$\sum_{i=1}^{10} i = 1 + 2 + 3 + 4 + 5 + 6 + 7 + 8 + 9 + 10 = 55$$

The example above is written using sigma notation. Sigma notation is a concise way of representing a finite series, as in the above example. In sigma notation, you look at the variable below the sigma sign and the starting value, and then above the sigma sign is the end value. You find the sum of the expression with each consecutive value of the variable from the starting to ending value.

The formula for the sum of an arithmetic series is given on the exam.

$$S_n = \frac{n}{2}[2a + (n-1)d] = n\left(\frac{a + a_n}{2}\right)$$

When we manually add the above series, we get a sum of 55. We can also use the above formulas. Here, a = 1; n = 10; d = 1 where a is the first number in the series; n is the count of the number of this series; and d is the difference between each pair of numbers. See calculations below.

$S_{10} = {}^{10}\!/_2[2(1) + 9(1)] = 55$

$S_{10} = {}^{10(11)}\!/_2 = 55$

Geometric Series

In a geometric series, the quotient is constant between consecutive terms. For example, 2, 4, 8, 16, 32... is a sequence where the ratio between terms is always 2.

$$\sum_{i=1}^{5} 2^i = 2 + 4 + 8 + 16 + 32 = 62$$

As you can see in the above example, if you divide each term by the term in front of it, you will always get 2. A geometric series is based on a constant raised to incremental exponents.

The formula for the sum of a finite geometric series is given on the formula sheet on the exam:

$$S_n = \frac{a(1-r^n)}{1-r}$$

where a is the first element in the series; r is the ratio of the terms; n is the count of the number of this series. For the above finite geometric series, a = 2, r = 2, n = 5.

$$S_5 = 2(1 - 2^5)/(1 - 2) = 2(1 - 32)/(-1) = 62$$

There is also a finite sum for an infinite geometric series. The formula for the sum of an infinite geometric series is given on the formula sheet but is also repeated below. As can be seen in the notation below, this is an infinite series as the variable n goes from 0 to ∞. It is also a geometric series, as the ratio is raised to the power of n, and therefore, each successive term will be multiplied by r.

$$\sum_{n=0}^{\infty} ar^n = \frac{a}{1-r}, \ |r| < 1$$

The sum can only be calculated for an infinite geometric series when the ratio between the terms is less than 1; otherwise, the sum would grow to infinity. For example, if a = 1 and r = 2, then the series would be = 1 + 2 + 4 + 8 + ... and as you can see, this will continue to grow, and therefore, you can't find the sum of this series.

Fibonacci Sequence

The Fibonacci sequence is 1, 1, 2, 3, 5, 8, 13, 21..., where each successive number is equal to the sum of the two previous numbers. The Fibonacci numbers are said to appear commonly in nature.

Analyzing Sequences and Series

Series can grow infinitely large or small, or they can approach a certain value. A series is said to be convergent if the sequence of numbers tends toward zero over time. For example, an infinite geometric series with r < 1 is convergent since taking a fraction to a high power is close to zero. One example of a convergent geometric series is if each term is equal to 1/n: 1, 1/2, 1/3, 1/4... As you can see, as n gets higher, each term will get closer to zero, and thus the series converges.

A convergent series can be demonstrated by limits. In a convergent series, the limit of a function as x approaches infinity is equal to a constant. You will learn more about limits in a later module.

Sequences & Series: Practice

1. Which of the following series is a geometric series?

    A. 8, 12, 18, 27, 40.5…

    B. 6, 9, 12, 15, 18…

    C. ½, ⅓, ¼, ⅕, ⅙…

    D. 25, 20, 15, 10, 5…

2. What is the sum of the first 12 terms of the following series? 7, 3, −1, −5…

    A. −180

    B. −48

    C. 12

    D. 348

3. Find the sum of the infinite geometric series: 4800, 1200, 300, 75…

    A. 3,600

    B. 6,375

    C. 6,400

    D. 19,200

4. Find the sum of all the terms of the following series: 9, 3, 1, 1/3, 1/9, 1/27 ...

   A. 13.5
   B. 14
   C. 26
   D. ∞

5. The 12th term in the Fibonacci sequence is 89, and the 13th term is 144. What is the 10th term?

   A. 21
   B. 34
   C. 55
   D. 233

6. What is the sum of the following series?

   $$\sum_{i=1}^{99} i$$

   A. 4,950
   B. 5,000
   C. 9,900
   D. 10,000

7. Which word could be used to describe the following series?

   $$\sum_{k=0}^{\infty} 8\left(\frac{3}{4}\right)^k$$

   A. Finite
   B. Fibonacci
   C. Convergent
   D. Arithmetic

8. What is the sum of the following series?

   $$\sum_{k=1}^{20} (3k + 1)$$

   A. 450
   B. 650
   C. 900
   D. 1300

Functions & Equations: Sequences & Series

9. What is the sum of the following series?

   A. 65/81
   B. 130/81
   C. 65/27
   D. 130/27

   $$\sum_{k=1}^{4} \left(\frac{2}{3}\right)^k$$

10. What is the sum of the following series?

    A. 3/10
    B. 8/5
    C. 2
    D. 4

    $$\sum_{k=0}^{\infty} \frac{2}{5}\left(\frac{3}{4}\right)^k$$

Sequences & Series: Answer Explanations

1. A   A geometric series has the same ratio from term to term. You can quickly test to see if a series is geometric by dividing each consecutive term by the term before it to see if the ratio is consistent. Let's go through each answer choice.

A. 8, 12, 18, 27, 40.5 …

    12/8 = 1.5

    18/12 = 1.5

    27/18 = 1.5

    40.5/27 = 1.5

This is a geometric series, as the ratio from term to term is always 1.5.

B. 6, 9, 12, 15, 18 …

    9/6 = 3/2

    12/9 = 4/3

The ratio between the terms is not the same. This is an arithmetic series, as the difference between the terms is the same.

C. ½, ⅓, ¼, ⅕, ⅙…

    ⅓ ÷ ½ = ⅓ x 2 = ⅔

    ¼ ÷ ⅓ = ¼ x 3 = ¾

Not a geometric series, as the ratio is not the same.

D. 25, 20, 15, 10, 5…

20/25 = 4/5

15/20 = 3/4

Not a geometric series, as the ratio is not the same. This one is an arithmetic series, as the difference between the terms is always 5.

2. A To determine the sum of the series, you must first determine whether it is an arithmetic or geometric series. Remember that if the difference from term to term stays the same, then it is an arithmetic series. If the ratio from term to term stays the same, then it is a geometric series.

For this series: 7, 3, –1, –5…

The difference between the terms is always the same.

3 – 7 = –4; (–1) – 3 = –4; (–5) – (–1) = –4

Therefore, this is an arithmetic series. You should now know to refer to the formula sheet to find the appropriate formula to use.

$$S_n = \frac{n}{2}[2a + (n-1)d] = n\left(\frac{a + a_n}{2}\right)$$

Let's make sure it is clear what each variable represents.

S_n is the sum of the first n terms.

n is the number of terms

a is the first term

d is the difference to go from one term to the next

a_n is the nth term

In this case, we don't yet know what a_n equals, so let's use the first equation.

n = 12, a = 7, d = –4

S_n = n/2[2a + (n – 1)d]
= 12/2[2 × 7 + (12 – 1)(–4)]
= 6[14 + 11(–4)]
= 6[14 + (–44)]
= 6[–30] = –180

3. C   The formula is provided. To find the sum of the infinite geometric series, you need "a" and "r". a is the first number in the series, and r is the growth rate.

$$\sum_{n=0}^{\infty} ar^n = \frac{a}{1-r}, \ |r| < 1$$

In this case, a = 4800, and the growth rate is ¼.

Sum = a/(1 − r)

= 4800/(1 − ¼)

= 4800/(¾)

= 6400

4. A   When given a question such as this, you must first determine whether the series is geometric or arithmetic. Find the pattern by looking at how you get from one term to the next.

9, 3, 1/3, 1/9, 1/27...

As you can see, to get from one term to the next you are multiplying by 1/3. Since there is the same ratio from one term to the next, you are dealing with a geometric series. And since the ratio is less than 1, this is an infinite geometric series. Refer to the formula sheet to find the formula:

$$\sum_{n=0}^{\infty} ar^n = \frac{a}{1-r}, \ |r| < 1$$

Make sure you understand what each variable represents. "a" is the first term in the series and "r" is the ratio.

In this case, the first term, a, is 9. The ratio, r, is ⅓. Therefore, the sum of all the terms is equal to

= 9/(1 − ⅓) = 9/(⅔) = 9 ÷ 2/3 = 9 × 3/2 = 27/2 = 13.5

5. B   In the Fibonacci sequence, each number is the sum of the previous two terms. As opposed to starting at the beginning of the sequence and finding the 10th term, we are given the 12th and 13th terms and can work backward.

12th term = 89

13th term = 144

Functions & Equations: Sequences & Series

We know that the 13th term was found by adding the 11th and 12th terms. Therefore, to find the 11th term, subtract

11th term = 144 − 89 = 55

Now, follow the same process to find the 10th term:

10th term = 12th term − 11th term = 89 − 55 = 34

6. A Before finding the sum of the series, you must first determine whether the series is arithmetic or geometric.

The series is 1, 2, 3, 4... 99 and, therefore, is an arithmetic series that increases by 1 for each term. Look at the formula sheet to find the formula for a finite arithmetic series:

n = 99 – there are 99 terms

a = 1 – the first term

a_{99} = 99 – the last term

S_{99} = 99[(1 + 99)/2] = 99(100/2) = 99(50) = 4950

7. C This is an infinite geometric series, since the ratio from one term to the next is 3/4, which is less than 1. Each term will be less than the term before it. This means that it is a convergent series. If the ratio, r, was greater than 1, it would be a divergent series, as each term would continue to get larger than the previous term without approaching a value.

This is not an arithmetic series, since the differences between each pair of numbers are not constant.

8. B First, figure out if it is an arithmetic or geometric series. In this case, it is arithmetic – as you can see, the difference between one term and the next stays constant at 3.

4 + 7 + 10 + ... + 61

Now, look at the formula sheet to find the formula for the sum of an arithmetic series.

$$S_n = \frac{n}{2}[2a + (n-1)d] = n\left(\frac{a + a_n}{2}\right)$$

For this series, let's find the value of each of the variables:

n = 20, as you are finding the sum from 1 to 20.

a = 4, as it is the first term.

d = 3, as it is the difference between each term.

Now, plug in these values to find the sum:

$$S_{20} = (20/2)[2(4) + (20 - 1)3]$$
$$= 10[8 + 19(3)]$$
$$= 10[8 + 57]$$
$$= 10[65]$$
$$= 650$$

9. B This is a finite geometric series: $(2/3) + (2/3)^2 + (2/3)^3 + (2/3)^4$

Use the formula for finding the sum of a finite geometric series, which can be found on the formula sheet:

$$S_n = \frac{a(1 - r^n)}{1 - r}$$

$a = 2/3$, which is the first term

$r = 2/3$, as it is the ratio from one term to the next

$n = 4$, as there are four terms

$$S_4 = (2/3)(1 - (2/3)^4)/(1 - 2/3)$$
$$= (2/3)(1 - 16/81)/(1/3)$$
$$= (2/3)(65/81)/(1/3)$$
$$= (130/243)/(1/3)$$
$$= 130/81$$

As there were only 4 terms to be summed, this could also have been done manually without using the formula.

10. B First thing to note is that this is an infinite geometric series, and the ratio between terms is 3/4. Since r is less than 1, we know that we can find the sum of this series. Use the formula on the formula sheet:

$$\sum_{n=0}^{\infty} ar^n = \frac{a}{1 - r}, \ |r| < 1$$

$a = 2/5$, as it is the first term when $k = 0$

$r = 3/4$

$$\text{Sum} = (2/5)/(1 - 3/4) = (2/5)/(1/4) = 8/5$$

Functions & Equations: Sequences & Series

Functions & Equations: Module Review

1. A tree that is 18 feet tall casts a shadow 8 feet long. If the height of an object and its shadow length are proportional, how long a shadow will a 6 foot tall man cast?

  A. 2 ft
  B. 2⅓ ft
  C. 2⅔ ft
  D. 3 ft

2. What piecewise function is represented by the graph to the right?

  A. when $x < -1$, $y = x + 2$
  when $x \geq -1$, $y = -x - 2$

  B. when $x < -1$, $y = x + 1$
  when $x \geq -1$, $y = -x - 1$

  C. when $x \leq -1$, $y = x + 2$
  when $x > -1$, $y = -x - 2$

  D. when $x \leq -1$, $y = -x + 1$
  when $x > -1$, $y = -x - 1$

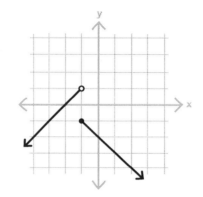

3. The sum of 4 times a number y and 21 is greater than 45 and less than 73. What are all possible values for that number?

  A. $6 < y < 13$
  B. $y > 6$ or $y < 13$
  C. 8, 9, and 10
  D. $y > 6$

4. What does r equal in the following equation? $(2r - 12)/6 = 4$

  A. 3
  B. 12
  C. 18
  D. 48

Functions & Equations: Module Review

5. If 3y − 2 = 7, what does (2/3)y + 5 equal?

   A. 11/3
   B. 11
   C. 7
   D. 8 2/3

6. Jennifer types at an average rate of 12 pages per hour. At that rate, how long will it take Jennifer to type 100 pages?

   A. 8 hours and 3 minutes
   B. 8 hours and 4 minutes
   C. 8 hours and 20 minutes
   D. 8 hours and 33 1/3 minutes

7. What is the sum of the following series?

   A. 1/3
   B. 2/3
   C. 3/2
   D. 4/3

   $$\sum_{k=0}^{\infty} \left(\frac{1}{3}\right)^k$$

8. Why is the horizontal line test not used to determine whether a relation is a function?

   A. It could also be used; we just generally use the vertical line test.
   B. All relations are functions, so no test is needed.
   C. Horizontal lines have an undefined slope.
   D. A function can have the same y-value for different x-values.

9. What is the sum of the two missing values in the table to the right?

   A. 31
   B. 32
   C. 33
   D. 34

x	y
5	8
7	10
?	13
12	15
17	20
21	?

Functions & Equations: Module Review

10. Write the following equation with variables.

The sum of the opposite of a number and 7 is equal to the quotient of the number and 3.

A. $-7n = n - 3$
B. $-n + 7 = n/3$
C. $1/n + 7 = n/3$
D. $-7 + n = 3n$

11. What is the domain of the function $y = \sqrt{x}$?

A. All reals.
B. $x \geq 0$
C. $x > 0$
D. Positive integers

12. What are all possible values for y in the following equation, $|y - 12| = |-15|$?

A. -3
B. 27
C. 30
D. -3 or 27

13. A particular function is defined as follows: Take any negative integer and multiply it by -2. What is the range of the function?

A. Negative integers
B. Positive integers
C. All real numbers.
D. Positive even integers

14. If a is inversely proportional to b and a is 16 when b is 4, what is b when a is 8?

A. 2
B. 8
C. 16
D. 64

15. Find the 21st partial sum of $a_n = (2/3)n - 1$.

   A. 67
   B. 100
   C. 133
   D. 266

16. What is the range of possible values for m if $-14 \leq 2(-3m + 5) < 28$?

   A. $-3 < m \leq 4$
   B. $-3 > m \geq 4$
   C. $3 \leq m < -4$
   D. $-3 \geq m > 4$

17. Phone plan T costs $25/month plus $0.10/minute and plan R is $10/month plus $0.25/minute. How many minutes of talking in one month would cost the same on either plan?

   A. 10 minutes
   B. 25 minutes
   C. 100 minutes
   D. 250 minutes

18. Which of the following graphs represents the inequality:

   $-3n + 5 < -4$

   A.

   C.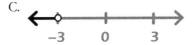

   B.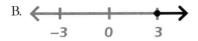

   D.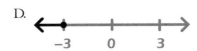

19. What is the value of $f^{-1}(g(3))$?

$f(x) = 2x + 4$
$g(x) = x^2 - 5$

A. 0
B. 2
C. 12
D. 95

20. How does the graph of $g(x) = (x + 1)^3 - 4$ compare to the graph of $f(x) = x^3$?

A. Shifted 1 unit to the right and 4 units down.
B. Shifted 1 unit to the left and 4 units down.
C. Shifted 1 unit to the right and 4 units up.
D. Shifted 1 unit to the left and 4 units up.

Module Review: Answer Explanations

1. C Draw a picture to help you understand the problem.

The sun shines on both the tree and the man at the same angle, meaning that the triangles formed by the tree, the shadow, and the light will be similar to the triangle formed with the man, his shadow, and the light.

Use a proportion to solve for the shadow length.
$6/18 = n/8$
Cross multiply to solve.
$18n = 6(8)$
$n = 48/18$
$n = 2\frac{2}{3}$ feet

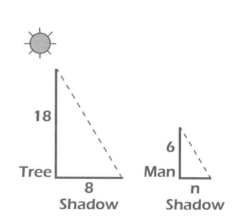

194 Functions & Equations: Module Review

2. A In the graph, you can see that the function changes when x = –1. First, let's find the equation of the line when x < –1. That line has a slope of 1 and intersects the y-axis at 2. The equation is y = x + 2. This is true when x < –1 because there is an open circle at –1. When x ≥ –1, the line has a slope of –1 and an intercept of –2. y = –x – 2.

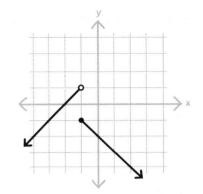

    When x < –1, y = x + 2

    When x ≥ –1, y = –x – 2

3. A Take the words and translate them into an inequality.

The sum of 4 times a number and 21 is greater than 45.

    4y + 21 > 45

The sum of 4 times a number and 21 is less than 73.

    4y + 21 < 73

Combine the two inequalities into one statement.

    4y + 21 > 45 and 4y + 21 < 73

    45 < 4y + 21 < 73

Now, solve by isolating the variable.

    45 < 4y + 21 < 73

Subtract 21 from all sides.

    24 < 4y < 52

Divide by 4 on all sides.

    6 < y < 13

4. C Isolate the variable. $(2r - 12)/6 = 4$

Multiply both sides by 6.

    $(2r - 12)/6 \times 6 = 4 \times 6$

    2r – 12 = 24

Add 12 to both sides.

    2r – 12 + 12 = 24 + 12

    2r = 36

Divide both sides by 2.

    2r ÷ 2 = 36 ÷ 2

    r = 18

Functions & Equations: Module Review

5. C   This problem has multiple steps. First, solve the first equation for y.

$$3y - 2 = 7$$
$$3y - 2 + 2 = 7 + 2$$
$$3y = 9$$
$$3y \div 3 = 9 \div 3$$
$$y = 3$$

Plug into the second expression.

$$(2/3)y + 5$$
$$(2/3)(3) + 5$$
$$2 + 5$$
$$7$$

6. C   If Jennifer types 12 pages per hour, set up a proportion to find out how long it will take her to type 100 pages.

$$\frac{12 \text{ pages}}{1 \text{ hour}} = \frac{100 \text{ pages}}{y \text{ hours}}$$

Now, cross-multiply to solve this proportion.

$$12y = 100$$
$$y = 100/12 = 8\,1/3$$
$$8\,1/3 \text{ hours}$$

All the answer choices have minutes, so let's convert the 1/3 hour to minutes.

$$1/3 \text{ hour} \times \frac{60 \text{ minutes}}{1 \text{ hour}} = 20 \text{ minutes}$$

8 hours 20 minutes, Answer C

7. C   As the variable for the summation is the exponent, and finding the first few terms will confirm it, this is a geometric series. Since k goes from 0 to infinity, it is an infinite geometric series with the ratio r = 1/3. Since r is less than 1, we can find the sum of this infinite geometric series.

On the formula sheet is the formula for the sum of an infinite geometric series.

$$\sum_{n=0}^{\infty} ar^n = \frac{a}{1-r}, \; |r| < 1$$

In this problem, a = 1 and r = 1/3.

$$\text{Sum} = 1/(1 - 1/3) = 1/(2/3) = 3/2.$$

8. D Let's go through each answer.

A: It could also be used; we just generally use the vertical line test.

This is not true. Only the vertical line test is used to determine whether a relation is a function.

B: All relations are functions, so no test is needed.

This is not true. All functions are relations, but not all relations are functions. Therefore, a test is needed.

C: Horizontal lines have an undefined slope.

This is not true. A horizontal line has a zero slope. This is also irrelevant to testing for functions.

D: A function can have the same y-value for different x-values.

This is true. A function is a set of ordered pairs where for each x-value, there is only one y-value. Therefore, the vertical line test would find any x-value that has two y-values. However, it is permissible that different x-values produce the same y-value, so a horizontal line test would demonstrate nothing.

9. D First, figure out the pattern between x and y. Then, determine the missing values, and find their sum.

The y-value is always 3 greater than the x-value; you can write this as

$y = x + 3$

The first question mark represents 3 less than 13, which is 10.

The second question mark represents 3 more than 21, which is 24.

Sum = 10 + 24 = 34

x	y
5	8
7	10
?	13
12	15
17	20
21	?

10. B Take the words, and translate the expression into an equation.

"The sum of the opposite of a number and 7"

Sum is the result of addition.

Opposite of a number is –1 times that number; for example, the opposite of 3 is –3.

Let n represent the number

$-n + 7$

"is equal to the quotient of the number and 3."

Quotient is the result of division.

$= n/3$

$-n + 7 = n/3$

Functions & Equations: Module Review

11. B The domain of a function is all the possible inputs or all possible x-values. You cannot take the square root of a negative number; therefore, x cannot be negative. Eliminate answer choice A.

x does not have to be just an integer. For example, if x = ¼, then y = ½. Eliminate answer D.

x could equal 0. If so, y = 0. Therefore, eliminate answer C.

x can be any real number greater than or equal to 0.
x ≥ 0

12. D Simplifying the right side of the equation, |y − 12| = |−15| is the same as |y − 12| = 15.

To solve |y − 12| = 15, set up two equations.

Equation 1: y − 12 = 15. In this case, y = 27

Equation 2: y − 12 = −15. In this case, y = −3.

For questions such as this one, you can also plug in each answer choice to see which is true.

13. D The range of a function is the output, or all possible y-values. Let's try a few inputs to see what this function does.

Function: Take any negative integer and multiply it by −2.

x = −1, y = −1(−2) = 2
x = −2, y = −2(−2) = 4
x = −3, y = −3(−2) = 6

Multiplying a negative integer by a negative will always result in a positive.

Multiplying any number by an even will always result in an even number.

Therefore, multiplying a negative integer by −2 will result in a positive even integer.

Range = Positive Even Integers

14. B If a is inversely proportional to b, then you can set up an equation between them:
a = k/b, where k is a constant.

We know that a = 16 when b = 4, and so we can solve for k.
a = k/b
16 = k/4
k = 64
a = 64/b

Functions & Equations: Module Review

Now, plug in a = 8 to solve for b.
$$a = 64/b$$
$$8 = 64/b$$
$$b = 64/8$$
$$b = 8$$

15. C The 21st partial sum is the sum of the first 21 elements in the series. Check the first few numbers to see if this is an arithmetic series.

$$a_1 = (2/3)1 - 1 = -1/3$$
$$a_2 = (2/3)2 - 1 = 1/3$$
$$a_3 = (2/3)3 - 1 = 1$$

The difference between the terms stays constant at 2/3. Since the differences are the same, it is an arithmetic series. You can use the formula on the formula sheet for the sum of an arithmetic series.

$$S_n = \frac{n}{2}[2a + (n-1)d] = n\left(\frac{a + a_n}{2}\right)$$

In this problem, n = 21, a = –1/3, d = 2/3.

$$S_{21} = (21/2)[2(-1/3) + (21-1)(2/3)]$$
$$= (21/2)[-2/3 + 40/3]$$
$$= (21/2)[38/3]$$
$$= 133$$

16. A Isolate the variable by performing inverse operations to all sides of the inequality.

$$-14 \leq 2(-3m + 5) < 28$$

Distribute
$$-14 \leq -6m + 10 < 28$$

Subtract 10 from all sides
$$-24 \leq -6m < 18$$

Divide all sides by –6. When dividing by a negative, you must flip all the inequality signs.

$$4 \geq m > -3$$

Rearrange
$$-3 < m \leq 4$$

17. C The unknown variable in this case is the number of minutes of talking. Let's call that m.

Cost for Plan T: $25 + 0.10m$

Cost for Plan R: $10 + 0.25m$

Set the costs equal to solve for m, the number of minutes.

$$25 + 0.10m = 10 + 0.25m$$
$$15 + 0.10m = 0.25m$$
$$15 = 0.15m$$
$$100 = m$$

100 minutes

18. A $-3n + 5 < -4$

Subtract 5 from both sides.

$$-3n < -9$$

Divide by –3. When dividing by a negative, flip the inequality sign.

$$n > 3$$

To determine which graph correctly represents the equation, note that the inequality is >, so the circle on the 3 should be open. Also, n is greater than 3, so all values that are larger than 3 should be shaded.

19. A $f^{-1}(g(3))$
$f(x) = 2x + 4$
$g(x) = x^2 - 5$

There are multiple steps in solving this problem. You will need to work from inside the parentheses out. Therefore, you can first find g(3). Then, find the inverse of function f(x). Finally, plug the result of g(3) into the inverse function $f^{-1}(x)$.

$$g(x) = x^2 - 5$$
$$g(3) = 3^2 - 5$$
$$g(3) = 4$$
$$f^{-1}(g(3)) = f^{-1}(4)$$

Now, find the inverse of f(x). Easiest way is to replace f(x) with y, switch the x's and y's, and then solve for y.

$$f(x) = 2x + 4$$
$$y = 2x + 4$$

Switch x's and y's.

$x = 2y + 4$

$x - 4 = 2y$

$y = (x - 4)/2$

$f^{-1}(x) = (x - 4)/2$

$f^{-1}(x) = (x - 4)/2$

$f^{-1}(4) = (4 - 4)/2 = 0$

$f^{-1}(g(3)) = f^{-1}(4) = 0$

20. B There were two major transformations to go from the graph of f(x) to the graph of g(x). Let's see what the effect of each transformation is.

$g(x) = (x + 1)^3 - 4$

The subtraction of 4 will affect the graph in the y-direction. This happens when you change f(x) to f(x) + k; it will move the graph by k in the y-direction. After the input is cubed, the result is subtracted by 4 to give the output, meaning that the output is reduced by 4, and so the graph will shift down in the y-direction.

The adding of 1 to the input before the cube will affect the graph in the x-direction. Instead of cubing x, the function g(x) is cubing x + 1. The effect of the transformation of f(x) to f(x + k) will move the graph by –k in the x-direction, meaning that the graph will shift –1 in the x-direction.

Total transformation will shift down by 4 units and left by 1 unit.

4. Geometry I

Unit Conversions 204
Circles 209
Triangles 215
Perimeter & Area 221
Coordinate Plane 227
Module Review 235

Geometry I: Unit Conversions

Conversion Methods

To convert measurements from one type of unit into another type of unit, multiply the number by the appropriate conversion factor. You can determine which the appropriate conversion factor is when the units you want to change are cancelled and the units you want are the only ones left. For example, to convert 17 yards into feet, you know that you want to find a conversion factor where the units of yards cancel and you are left with only feet. We know that 1 yard equals 3 feet, and the conversion factor is a fraction with different units in the numerator and denominator. Since we want the yards to cancel, leaving us with feet, we put the yards in the denominator and feet in the numerator.

$$17 \text{ yards} \times \frac{3 \text{ feet}}{1 \text{ yard}} = 51 \text{ feet}$$

Try converting 64 ounces into pounds (1 pound = 16 ounces):

$$64 \text{ ounces} \times \frac{1 \text{ pound}}{16 \text{ ounces}} = 4 \text{ pounds}$$

Some unit conversions will appear repeatedly in word problems and other types of problems. Some should be familiar to you from everyday life, but try to commit as many to memory as possible.

Weight and Mass
16 ounces (oz) = 1 pound (lb.)
1 kilogram (kg) = 2.20 pounds (lb.)
1000 grams (g) = 1 kilogram (kg)
1 ton = 2000 pounds (lb.)

Volume
2 cups (cp.) = 1 pint (pt.)
2 pints (pt.) = 1 quart (qt.)
4 quarts (qt.) = 1 gallon (gal.)
1 gallon (gal.) = 3.79 liters (L)
1 Liter (L) = 1000 milliliters (mL)
1 milliliter (mL) = 1 centimeter cubed (cm^3)

Length
1 inch (in.) = 2.54 centimeters (cm)
1 meter (m) = 3.28 feet (ft.)
100 centimeters (cm) = 1 meter (m)
1000 millimeters (mm) = 1 meter (m)
1000 meters (m) = 1 kilometer (km)
1 kilometer (km) = 0.62 miles
1 foot (ft.) = 12 inches (in.)
5280 feet (ft.) = 1 mile
3 feet (ft.) = 1 yard (yd.)

Temperature
degrees Fahrenheit = 32 + 9/5 x degrees Celsius
degrees Celsius = 5/9 x (degrees Fahrenheit − 32)

Metric System

Looking at the units above, a pattern is evident among the meters, grams, and liters. That is because they are the base units of the metric system. The metric system uses the following pattern of prefixes:

1000 = kilo-
100 = hecto-
10 = deka-

.1 = deci-
.01 = centi-
.001 = milli-

Example 1: Convert 1.2 kilometers to meters.
$$1.2 \text{ km} \times \frac{1000 \text{ m}}{1 \text{ km}} = 1200 \text{ m}$$

Example 2: Convert 340 meters to kilometers.
$$340 \text{ m} \times \frac{1 \text{ km}}{1000 \text{ m}} = 0.34 \text{ km}$$

Unit Conversions: Practice

1. Convert 212 degrees Fahrenheit into degrees Celsius.

A. 100° C

B. 324° C

C. 136° C

D. 439° C

2. What is 27 grams in kilograms?

A. 0.00027 kilograms

B. 0.027 kilograms

C. 0.27 kilograms

D. 27000 kilograms

3. If there are 5,280 feet in 1 mile, which of the following is the longest?

A. 3 miles

B. 4,000 yards

C. 15,500 feet

D. 180,000 inches

4. How many square inches are equal to 10 square yards?

A. 360 sq. in.

B. 720 sq. in.

C. 1,080 sq. in.

D. 12,960 sq. in.

5. If the volume of a box is 8 cubic meters, what is the volume in cubic centimeters?

   A. 0.08 cubic cm

   B. 800 cubic cm

   C. 80,000 cubic cm

   D. 8,000,000 cubic cm

6. A man is painting one wall in his dining room. He uses 1 gallon of paint to cover 14 square yards of wall space. If the wall is 12 feet high and 21 feet long, how many gallons of paint will he need?

   A. 1 gallon

   B. 2 gallons

   C. 6 gallons

   D. 18 gallons

7. Baking a chocolate cake requires 2 cups of flour. If you have 3 quarts of flour, how many cakes can you make?

   A. 3 cakes

   B. 6 cakes

   C. 12 cakes

   D. 24 cakes

8. If 1 inch = 2.54 centimeters, 200 inches is equal to how many meters?

   A. 0.508 m

   B. 5.08 m

   C. 50.8 m

   D. 50,800 m

9. Suppose you are in Europe, and the exchange rate between Euros and dollars is 1 Euro = $1.54. How many Euros would you have to pay for a book that is $10.78?

   A. 7 Euros

   B. 9.24 Euros

   C. 12.32 Euros

   D. 16.60 Euros

10. **Julian is 6 feet 3 inches tall. Barbara is $1\frac{4}{8}$ yards tall, and Sandra is 70 inches tall. Order them from shortest to tallest.**

   A. Julian, Sandra, Barbara

   B. Julian, Barbara, Sandra

   C. Barbara, Julian, Sandra

   D. Barbara, Sandra, Julian

Unit Conversions: Answer Explanations

1. A The formula for converting from Fahrenheit to Celsius is

degrees Celsius = $\frac{5}{9}$ x (degrees Fahrenheit − 32).

Plug 212 degrees F into the formula. Then, solve for degrees C.

degrees Celsius = $\frac{5}{9}$ x (212 − 32) = $\frac{5}{9}$ x 180 = 100

2. B To convert grams to kilograms, first note that 1000 grams = 1 kilogram. Now, multiply by the appropriate unit conversion. You want to make sure that the grams cancel, leaving you with kilograms in the numerator.

27 grams x $\frac{1 \text{ kilogram}}{1000 \text{ grams}}$ = $\frac{27 \text{ kilograms}}{1000}$ = 0.027 kilograms

3. A Convert each answer choice to the same dimensions and then compare. Let's choose to convert each answer to feet.

A: 3 miles x $\frac{5280 \text{ ft}}{1 \text{ mile}}$ = 15,840 feet

B: 4,000 yards x $\frac{3 \text{ feet}}{1 \text{ yard}}$ = 12,000 feet

C: 15,500 feet

D: 180,000 inches x $\frac{1 \text{ foot}}{12 \text{ in}}$ = 15,000 feet

4. D First, convert square yards to square feet, then convert from square feet to square inches.

To convert from square yards to square feet, you will need to use the unit conversion factor twice since the units are each squared:

10 square yards x $\frac{3 \text{ feet}}{1 \text{ yard}}$ x $\frac{3 \text{ feet}}{1 \text{ yard}}$ = 90 square feet

Now, convert from sq. ft. to sq. in. (remember to use the conversion factor twice):

90 square feet x $\frac{12 \text{ inches}}{1 \text{ foot}}$ x $\frac{12 \text{ inches}}{1 \text{ foot}}$ = 12,960 sq. in.

Another way to solve this problem is to note that 1 yard = 3 feet = 36 inches, and then convert from square yards directly to square inches:

10 square yards x $\frac{36 \text{ inches}}{1 \text{ yard}}$ x $\frac{36 \text{ inches}}{1 \text{ yard}}$ = 12,960 sq. in.

5. D   Use three unit conversions to convert each dimension of meters to centimeters.

$$8 \text{ cubic meters} \times \frac{100 \text{ cm}}{1 \text{ m}} \times \frac{100 \text{ cm}}{1 \text{ m}} \times \frac{100 \text{ cm}}{1 \text{ m}} = 8{,}000{,}000 \text{ cubic centimeters}$$

6. B   This problem has many steps:

       1 – Convert wall dimensions from feet to yards.
       2 – Find the area of the wall.
       3 – Determine how many gallons of paint are needed to cover that wall.

Convert wall dimensions from feet to yards:

$$12 \text{ feet} \times \frac{1 \text{ yard}}{3 \text{ feet}} = 4 \text{ yards}$$
$$21 \text{ feet} \times \frac{1 \text{ yard}}{3 \text{ feet}} = 7 \text{ yards}$$

Find the area of the wall:

$$4 \text{ yards} \times 7 \text{ yards} = 28 \text{ square yards}$$

Find the number of gallons of paint needed:

$$28 \text{ sq. yd.} \times \frac{1 \text{ gallon}}{14 \text{ sq. yds}} = 2 \text{ gallons}$$

7. B   Convert 3 quarts to pints to cups and then figure out how many cakes can be made:

$$3 \text{ quarts} \times \frac{2 \text{ pints}}{1 \text{ quart}} = 6 \text{ pints}$$
$$6 \text{ pints} \times \frac{2 \text{ cups}}{1 \text{ pint}} = 12 \text{ cups}$$
$$12 \text{ cups} \times \frac{1 \text{ cake}}{2 \text{ cups}} = 6 \text{ cakes}$$

8. B   First, convert from inches to centimeters, then from centimeters to meters:

$$200 \text{ inches} \times \frac{2.54 \text{ cm}}{1 \text{ in}} = 508 \text{ cm}$$
$$508 \text{ cm} \times \frac{1 \text{ m}}{100 \text{ cm}} = 5.08 \text{ m}$$

9. A   You are given a quantity in dollars, and you want to convert it to Euros. Multiply by a unit conversion of Euros to dollars so that the dollars cancel, and you are left with Euros:

$$\$10.78 \times \frac{1 \text{ Euro}}{\$1.54} = 7 \text{ Euros}$$

10. D   Convert all the heights to mixed numbers with a common denominator. Remember that 1 foot equals 12 inches, and 1 yard equals 3 feet.

     Julian: 6 feet 3 inches = $6\frac{3}{12}$ feet

     Barbara: $1\frac{4}{8}$ yards $\times \frac{3 \text{ ft}}{1 \text{ yd}} = 4\frac{2}{8}$ feet $= 2\frac{1}{4}$ feet $= 5\frac{1}{4}$ feet $= 5\frac{3}{12}$ feet

     Sandra: 70 inches = $\frac{70}{12}$ feet $= 5\frac{10}{12}$ feet

Geometry I: Circles

Points and Circles

A circle is a set of points equidistant (the same distance) from a center point. Imagine picking a point on the x-y coordinate plane. If you were to mark every possible point 4 units away from the center point, you would create a continuous line around that point called a circle.

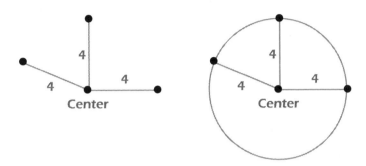

Circle Measurements

An important measurement for a circle is its radius (r). The radius is the distance between the center of a circle and any point on the circle itself. In the previous example, each point was 4 units from the center. Therefore, the circle's radius is 4.

The diameter of a circle is any line beginning at one point on a circle, passing through the center, and ending at another point on the circle. The diameter of a circle is always twice as long as its radius. When working with circles, you will often need to use the diameter to find the radius so that you can calculate perimeter, arc length, or area.

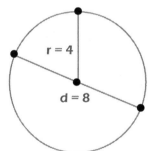

In the diagram to the right, the radius is 4, and the diameter is 8.

Circumference and Area

The number pi, also represented by the Greek letter π, equals approximately 3.14. Pi is an irrational number (an unending decimal), but 3.14 is accurate enough for most purposes. Pi gives the ratio of a circle's perimeter – the distance around the outside of the circle – to its diameter (d). The perimeter of a circle is also called its circumference (c). The equation can be expressed as

$\pi = c/d$ $c = \pi d$ $c = 2\pi r$

The last of these equations probably looks most familiar to you, but keep in mind that it can be manipulated to generate the other two.

The area of a circle is also calculated using pi. The formula is

Area = π x r x r = πr^2

So, for a circle of radius 7 yards, the area is 49π square yards.

Arcs and Wedges

There are 360 degrees in a circle. You can use this information to calculate the distance around a section of the circle, known as **arc length**. Formulate the angle of the arc as a fraction of 360, and then multiply that fraction by the perimeter of the whole circle. The equation is

arc length = (degrees/360) x 2πr

For example, suppose you want to find the arc length around 30 degrees of a circle with a radius of 3 inches. 30/360 is equal to 1/12, so you can plug this into the formula to simplify your calculations:

arc length = (1/12) 2π x 3 = π/2 = 1.57 inches

Just as arc length is a fraction of the perimeter of a circle, a wedge is a fraction of the area of a circle. The formula is analogous to that for arc length— it involves multiplying the angle of the arc in fractional form by the area of the entire circle. The formula is

area of a wedge = (degrees/360) x π x r^2

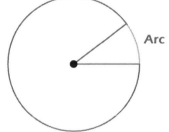

To find the area of 50 degrees of a circle with a 4-meter radius, plug the values into the formula

(50/360) x π x 16 = 20/9 x π = 6.98 square meters

Tangents and Chords

Two other types of lines are commonly seen in problems involving circles.

Chords are lines that begin at one point on the circle and end at another but do not necessarily pass through the center. The diameter is the longest possible chord in a circle.

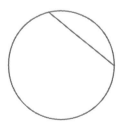

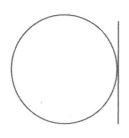

Tangents are lines on the outside of a circle that touch the circle at only one point.

Tangents and chords are useful for calculating radii of circles when they are part of a known shape (such as a triangle) or for finding the measure of angles within the circle (see "Angles and Parallel Lines"). When chords are present in a test problem, look for a familiar shape that might help you calculate the length of the radius.

Circles: Practice

1. What is the radius of the following circle?

A. 30
B. 15
C. 7.5
D. 225

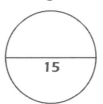

2. Find the perimeter of the following circle:

A. 46 π
B. 23 π
C. 46
D. 529 π

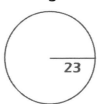

3. In the circle below, which is the longest?

A. Radius
B. Chord (line in diagram)
C. Diameter
D. Not enough information

4. What is the area of a circle with a diameter of 20?

A. 20π
B. 40π
C. 100π
D. 400π

Geometry I: Circles

5. The perimeter of Circle A is ? times the perimeter of Circle B?

   A. 1/2
   B. 2
   C. 4
   D. 15/4

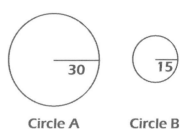

Circle A   Circle B

6. The area of Circle A is ? times the area of Circle B?

   A. 2
   B. 4
   C. 8
   D. 15

7. A dartboard has a red bull's-eye 6 inches in diameter. No other part of the dartboard is red. If the dartboard is 30 inches in diameter, what area of the dartboard is not red?

   A. 576π sq. in.
   B. 396π sq. in.
   C. 216π sq. in.
   D. 144π sq. in.

8. What is the perimeter of the 45 degree wedge of the circle if its radius is 4 meters?

   A. 8 + π
   B. 2π
   C. 4 + 2π
   D. 8 + 8π

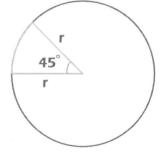

9. What is the area of the wedge from question #8 above?

   A. 2π sq. m
   B. 4π sq. m
   C. 8π sq. m
   D. 16π sq. m

212   Geometry I: Circles

10. A circular track is 63 meters long. Approximately how long is the diameter of the circle formed by the track?

  A. 8m

  B. 15m

  C. 20m

  D. 30m

Circles: Answer Explanations

1. C The circle has a diameter of length 15. The radius is one half the diameter.

2. A Remember that the perimeter of the circle is the same as the circumference of the circle.
Circumference = 2 x pi x r

Circumference = 2 x π x 23 = 46π

3. C A chord is a line going from one point on a circle to another point. The diameter of a circle is the longest possible chord, since it goes from a point to the farthest point from it. Therefore, the diameter will be longer than the chord in the image.

4. C The area of a circle is found by multiplying π x radius^2

  Radius = half of diameter = 10

  Area = π x radius^2

  = π x 10^2

  = 100π

5. B You can solve this problem by finding the perimeter of each circle and then creating a ratio.

Perimeter or circumference of Circle A = 2 x π x r = 2 x π x 30 = 60π

Perimeter or circumference of Circle B = 2 x π x r = 2 x π x 15 = 30π

Now, create a ratio with the perimeter of Circle A over the perimeter of Circle B.

  60π/30π = 2

Geometry I: Circles

6. B The radius of Circle A is 30, and the radius of Circle B is 15. Let's find the area of each and then create a ratio:

$$\text{Area of Circle A} = \pi \times r^2 = \pi \times 30^2 = 900\pi$$

$$\text{Area of Circle B} = \pi \times r^2 = \pi \times 15^2 = 225\pi$$

Now, create a ratio with the area of Circle A over the area of Circle B:

$$900\pi \div 225\pi = 4$$

7. C Find area of the dartboard and subtract area of the bull's-eye to find area that is not red.

$$\text{Area of dartboard} = \pi 15^2 = 225\pi$$

$$\text{Area of bull's-eye} = \pi 3^2 = 9\pi$$

$$\text{Area of dartboard} - \text{area of bull's-eye} = (225 - 9)\pi = 216\pi$$

8. A There are 3 pieces to the perimeter of the wedge: 2 radii and a fraction of the circumference (arc length).

The fraction of the circumference:

The wedge is 45 degrees and the entire circle has 360 degrees.

The entire circumference is $= 2\pi r = 2\pi \times 4 = 8\pi$

The fraction of the circumference (arc length) $= \frac{45}{360} \times 8\pi = \pi$

Perimeter of the wedge = radius + radius + fraction of circumference

$$= 4 + 4 + \pi = 8 + \pi$$

9. A To find the area of the wedge, first find the area of the entire circle. Area is calculated by multiplying $\pi \times \text{radius}^2$.

$$\text{Area of circle} = \pi \times 4^2 = 16\pi$$

A circle has 360 degrees, and the wedge has 45 degrees. Determine what fraction of the circle the wedge is and multiply that by the area of the whole circle to find area of the wedge:

$$\frac{45}{360} \times 16\pi = \frac{1}{8} \times 16\pi = 2\pi$$

10. C A distance around the track of 63m means the circumference or perimeter is 63m.

The circumference is equal to $2 \times \pi \times \text{radius} = \pi \times \text{diameter}$.

$$63 = \pi \times \text{diameter} = 3.14 \times \text{diameter}$$

$$\text{diameter} = 63 \div 3.14$$

The diameter is approximately 20 meters.

Geometry I: Triangles

Properties of Triangles

A triangle is a closed polygon with three sides. In a triangle, all angles must add up to 180 degrees. The angles of a triangle are always proportionate to the sides opposite them, meaning that the longest side of a triangle will be opposite the largest angle, and the shortest side will be opposite the smallest angle. The relationship between sides and angles is shown by using a letter for an angle and the same letter for the corresponding side, with either all the angles with lowercase letters and sides with uppercase letters, or vice versa.

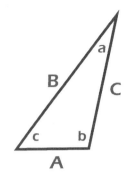

When any two sides of a triangle are added together, their sum is always greater than the third side. In the image to the right, A + B > C, A + C > B, and B + C > A.

Types of Triangles

A triangle with two equal sides is called an isosceles triangle. Because angles are proportionate to the sides opposite them, the two angles opposite the two equal sides are also equal. In the isosceles triangle shown here, A = B and a = b.

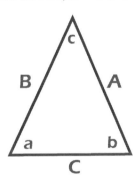

An equilateral triangle has three equal sides and three equal angles. Because 180/3 = 60, the angles of an equilateral triangle will always equal 60 degrees. In the equilateral triangle to the right, A = B = C and a = b = c.

An **equilateral** triangle has three equal sides and three equal angles. Because 180/3 = 60, the angles of an equilateral triangle will always equal 60 degrees. In the equilateral triangle to the right, A = B = C and a = b = c.

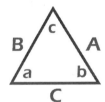

A **right triangle** is any triangle with a 90-degree angle, which is usually represented by a small square. In a right triangle, the side opposite the 90-degree angle, which will always be the longest side, is called the hypotenuse (C). The other two sides are labeled A and B, interchangeably.

Right triangles are the only triangles for which the **Pythagorean Theorem** can be used to calculate missing side lengths. The Pythagorean Theorem states that the square of the hypotenuse is equal to the sum of the square of the other two sides. Or,

$A^2 + B^2 = C^2$

There are two special types of right triangles.

Geometry I: Triangles   215

30–60–90 Triangle

A triangle with angles measuring 30, 60, and 90 degrees will always have sides with a specific ratio. The hypotenuse will always be twice as long as the shortest side, and the side of middle length will always be the length of the shortest side times the square root of 3.

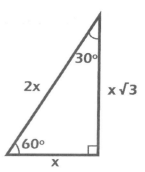

45–45–90 Triangle

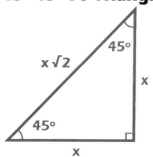

This special triangle is known as the right isosceles. It has one 90-degree angle and two 45-degree angles. The right isosceles triangle will always follow the pattern shown below. The hypotenuse will always be the length of one side times the square root of 2.

Triangles: Practice

1. How many degrees is Angle b?

A. 242

B. 180

C. 142

D. 62

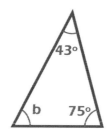

2. In degrees, what are the measurements of the three angles in an isosceles right triangle?

A. 30, 60, 90

B. 45, 45, 90

C. 45, 90, 90

D. 60, 60, 60

3. In the diagram below, Side A ? Side B?

A. >

B. <

C. ≥

D. =

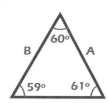

216   Geometry I: Triangles

4. Which of the following CANNOT be the length of side C in the triangle?

   A. 10
   B. 12
   C. 15
   D. 19

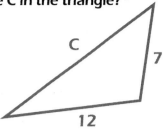

5. Ken leans a 13-foot ladder against a wall. If the base of the ladder is 5 feet from the wall, at what height on the wall does the top of the ladder rest?

   A. 9 feet
   B. 10 feet
   C. 11 feet
   D. 12 feet

6. What is the area of the circle?

   A. 13π
   B. 144π
   C. 169π
   D. 225π

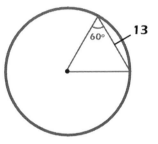

7. What is the perimeter of the outer triangle?

   A. 36m
   B. 72m
   C. 144m
   D. 288m

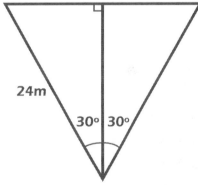

8. Todd and Anne are making their way home from school. Todd walks 2 miles due north to get home. Anne walks 1.5 miles due east to get home. How far apart are their houses?

   A. 1 mile
   B. 2.5 miles
   C. 3.5 miles
   D. 5 miles

9. If the hypotenuse of a right triangle is 25m and another side of the triangle is 20m, what is the length of the third side?

   A. 15m

   B. 20m

   C. 22.5m

   D. 25m

10. How long is Side C?

    A. 10

    B. 12.1

    C. 13

    D. 14

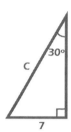

Triangles: Answer Explanations

1. D   The angles of a triangle always add up to 180 degrees. Add the other two angles, and subtract their sum from 180 to find the measure of Angle b.

$180 - (75 + 43) = 180 - 118 = 62$

2. B   Even if you can't recall the exact definition of an isosceles right triangle, the name of the triangle gives you enough clues to work out the answer.

Remember:
- An isosceles triangle has two sides and two angles that are equal.
- A right triangle has a 90-degree angle.
- The angles in a triangle add up to 180 degrees.

Angle y + Angle y + 90° = 180°

2 x Angle y = 90°

Angle y = 45°

3. B   The angle opposite side A is smaller than the angle opposite side B. Therefore, side A is smaller than side B.

4. D   Remember that the sum of any two sides of a triangle must be greater than the length of the third side.

12 + 7 > C

19 > C

Therefore, C has to be less than 19 and cannot equal 19.

5. D   The easiest way to solve this problem is to first draw a picture. The wall, the ground, and the ladder create a right triangle as in the diagram below.

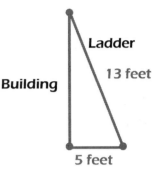

To find the point at which the top of the ladder rests against the wall, use the Pythagorean Theorem.

$5^2 + x^2 = 13^2$

$25 + x^2 = 169$

$x^2 = 144$

$x = 12$

6. C   Two sides of the triangle are radii of the circle. Therefore, they are equal. One of those sides is opposite a 60-degree angle, so the other side must also be opposite a 60-degree angle. Since the angles of a triangle must add up to 180 degrees, and two of the angles add up to 120, the third angle must also be 60 degrees, making this an equilateral triangle. Equilateral triangles have three equal sides, so each side of this triangle is 13 units long.

Now, we know that the radius is 13, so we can calculate the area by squaring the radius and multiplying by pi:

Area of circle = $\pi r^2 = \pi \times 13^2 = 169\pi$

7. B   One angle of the outer triangle was cut in half to create two 30–60–90 triangles. If you add the halves of that angle together, they equal 60 degrees. Therefore, each angle of the outer triangle is 60 degrees, making the triangle equilateral.

Since it is equilateral, all sides are equal. To find the perimeter, add the lengths of the three sides:

24m + 24m + 24m = 72m.

Geometry I: Triangles

8. B Draw a picture to help solve the problem. Todd and Anne began their respective trips at the school. If Todd went north while Anne went east, their trips would look like this right angle:

Use the Pythagorean Theorem to find the distance between their houses, which will be the hypotenuse of the right triangle.

$(1.5)^2 + 2^2 = c^2$
$2.25 + 4 = c^2$
$6.25 = c^2$
$c = 2.5$ miles

9. A If you know two sides of a right triangle, you can always calculate the third side of the triangle using the Pythagorean Theorem. In this case, they have given you the hypotenuse (or the longest side) and one of the sides. Plug those values into the Pythagorean Theorem to calculate the third side.

$a^2 + b^2 = \text{hypotenuse}^2$
$20^2 + b^2 = 25^2$
$400 + b^2 = 625$
$b^2 = 225$
$b = 15$

10. D The side with length 7 is the shortest side in a 30–60–90 triangle, since it is opposite the 30° angle. The longest side in a 30–60–90 triangle is the hypotenuse, which is always twice as long as the shortest side. Side C is the hypotenuse here, so Side C is 14.

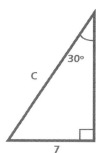

220   Geometry I: Triangles

Geometry I: Perimeter & Area

Perimeter

The perimeter of an object is the distance around its edge. Calculating the perimeter of any polygon simply requires finding the length of each side and then adding the lengths of all sides together.

```
        60 feet
    ┌─────────────┐
    │             │ 30 feet
    └─────────────┘
```

For example, the perimeter of the rectangle is 30 + 30 + 60 + 60 = 180 feet.

```
┌───┐
│   │
└───┘
20 yards
```

Since all sides of a square are of equal length, the perimeter of a square is the length of 1 side times 4. The perimeter of the square shown here is 20 yards x 4, or 80 yards.

Finding the perimeter of a triangle sometimes requires you to use what you know about the properties of triangles. For example, based on the information shown, you should recognize that the triangle to the right is equilateral – in other words, all sides are the same length (see the lesson "Triangles" in this module). The perimeter is therefore 9 + 9 + 9, or 27 units.

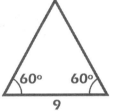

Area – Triangles

The formula for the area of a triangle is
½ x base x height

The height of a triangle is the length of a line from the base, or bottom, of the triangle to the opposite angle.

The line representing the height will always be perpendicular to the base. For example, in the triangle, the base length is 14, and the height is 6. Therefore, the area is ½ x 14 x 6 = 42 sq. units.

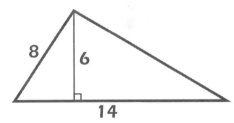

At times, you will have to use what you know about the angles and side lengths of triangles to calculate their heights. The equilateral triangle to the left has sides of length 18, so the base is 18. To find the height, draw a line down from the topmost angle to the base, this creates two right right triangles.

Geometry I: Perimeter & Area   221

You can use the Pythagorean Theorem to calculate the height because you already know two sides of the right triangle (the hypotenuse is 18, and half the base is 9). You can calculate the height by plugging these values into the theorem:

$$18^2 = 9^2 + height^2$$
$$324 = 81 + height^2$$
$$324 - 81 = height^2$$
$$243 = height^2$$
$$\sqrt{243} = height$$
$$15.59 = height$$

Now that we know the height of the original triangle and the base, we can calculate the area:

½ x 18 x 15.59 = 140.31 square units

Perimeter & Area: Practice

1. If the perimeter of the rectangle is 78, what is the value of x?

A. 14.5
B. 17
C. 24.5
D. 34

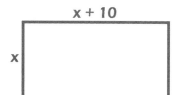

2. A backdrop for a play is a triangle 9 meters tall. If the total area of the backdrop is 45 square meters, how wide is the base?

A. 4.5 m
B. 5 m
C. 9 m
D. 10 m

3. What is the perimeter of the figure below?

A. 40
B. 42
C. 44
D. 46

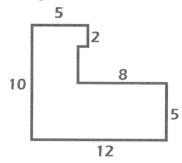

Geometry I: Perimeter & Area

4. What is the area of the figure?

   A. 46
   B. 82
   C. 100
   D. 120

5. If you double all the sides of a rectangle, by how much does the area change?

   A. Doubles
   B. Increases by 2
   C. Quadruples
   D. Increases by 8

6. Daniel is painting a square wall with 9-foot sides. If he uses ⅓ gallon of paint per square foot, how many gallons of paint will he need?

   A. 14 gal
   B. 27 gal
   C. 54 gal
   D. 81 gal

7. You have a picture that is 8 inches by 10 inches. You place it in a frame 2 inches wide all around. How much wall space will the framed picture cover up?

   A. 96 sq. in.
   B. 100 sq. in.
   C. 120 sq. in.
   D. 168 sq. in.

8. The area of Triangle T is how many times larger than the area of Triangle S?

   A. 2
   B. 4
   C. 6
   D. 8

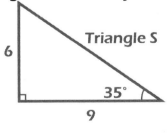
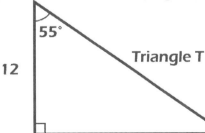

Geometry I: Perimeter & Area   223

9. **What is the area of the figure?**

    A. 34
    B. 74
    C. 90
    D. 98

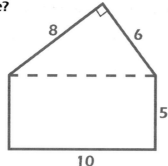

10. **Find the perimeter of the shape.**

    A. 28m
    B. 30m
    C. 32m
    D. 34m

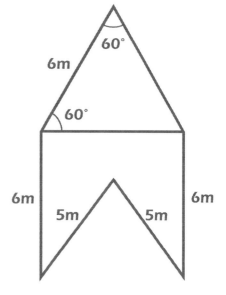

Perimeter & Area: Answer Explanations

1. A   Perimeter = width + width + length + length
    = 2(width) + 2(length)
    = 2x + 2(x + 10)
    = 2x + 2x + 20
    = 4x + 20

The perimeter equals 78, so set the equation equal to 78 and solve for x:

    4x + 20 = 78
    4x = 58
    x = 14.5

2. D   Use the area of a triangle formula to calculate the length of the base:

    Area = ½ x base x height
    45 = ½ x b x 9
    45 = 4.5 x b
    b = 10 m

3. D To determine the perimeter, you first need to find the lengths of the missing sides.

Let's first find the missing vertical side. Since the total height of the shape is 10, and you know that the three vertical edges make up the height and two of them are 5 and 2, the missing vertical side must be 10 − 5 − 2 = 3.

Now, to find the missing horizontal side. The total width of the shape is 12, and two sides are 8 and 5. Therefore, they overlap by 13 − 12 = 1 unit.

To find the perimeter, add the lengths of all the sides:
5 + 2 + 1 + 3 + 8 + 5 + 12 + 10 = 46

4. B First, the lengths of the missing sides need to be filled in.
The missing vertical side must be 3, since the total vertical height is 10, and you know that two sides add up to 7. The missing horizontal side is 1, since the total horizontal width is 12, and the two overlapping sides add to 13. Now, you must divide the figure into shapes for which you can calculate area. In this case, let's divide it into 3 rectangles.

The top rectangle has a length of 5 and a width of 2, so its area = 5 x 2 = 10.

The second rectangle has a width of 4 and a height of 3, so its area = 12.

The third rectangle's dimensions are 12 by 5 for an area of 60.

Total area = 12 + 10 + 60 = 82.

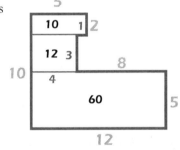

5. C Let's say that the original rectangle has a width of w and a height of h. Therefore, the area of the original rectangle is wh.

If all sides are doubled, the new rectangle has a width of 2w and a height of 2h. Therefore, the area of the new rectangle is (2w)(2h) = 4wh.

Divide the new area by the original area to see how many times bigger the new area is
4wh ÷ wh = 4

6. B Calculate the area of the wall:
9 ft x 9 ft = 81 sq ft

Then, multiply by the ratio of gallons to square feet:
81 sq ft x $\frac{1 \text{ gal}}{3 \text{ sq ft}}$ = 27 gal

Geometry I: Perimeter & Area

7. D Let's figure out the dimensions of the frame and of the picture.

The width of the picture is 8 inches, and the frame is 2 inches wide. That adds 2 inches to the left side of the picture and 2 inches to the right side. The total width is now $8 + 2 + 2 = 12$ inches.

The length of the picture is 10 inches, and the frame adds 2 inches to top and bottom. Total length $= 10 + 2 + 2 = 14$ inches.

Area = 12 inches x 14 inches = 168 sq. in.

8. B First, calculate the area of each triangle using the formula, area = ½ x base x height

Triangle T's Area = ½ x 12 x 18 = 108

Triangle S's Area = ½ x 6 x 9 = 27

Divide the area of triangle S into the area of Triangle T:
$108 \div 27 = 4$

9. B To find the area of the entire shape, find the area of the triangle and add that to the area of the rectangle.

Area of triangle = ½ x base x height
= ½ x 6 x 8
= 24

Area of rectangle = length x width
= 5 x 10
= 50

Area of shape = 50 + 24 = 74

10. D For any shape, the perimeter involves adding the lengths of all the outside edges. You must determine the lengths of all the sides.

Since two angles of the triangle are 60 degrees, the third angle is also 60 degrees, making it an equilateral triangle. An equilateral triangle has all sides of equal length, so the missing side of the shape is 6 m.

Perimeter = 6 m + 6 m + 6 m + 6 m + 5 m + 5 m = 34 m

Geometry I: Coordinate Plane

x-axis and y-axis

Graphs are useful for showing the relationships between variables. The coordinate plane on which graphs are shown is simply a two-dimensional variation of the number line.

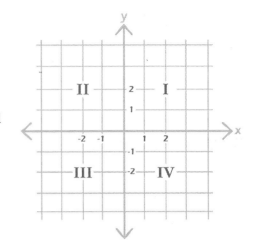

The horizontal number line, labeled the **x-axis**, represents all possible values of the x-variable. The vertical number line, called the **y-axis**, serves the same function for the y-values. Any pair of possible x and y coordinates is called a **coordinate pair** (also known as an ordered pair). Coordinate pairs are always written in the order (x, y). The point at which the x-axis and y-axis intersect (0, 0) is called the **origin**.

Quadrants

The Roman numerals on the graph show the four quadrants of the coordinate plane.

Quadrant I: all x and y values are positive.
Quadrant II: x is negative; y is positive.
Quadrant III: x and y are negative.
Quadrant IV: x is positive; y is negative.

Plotting Coordinate Pairs

The graph below shows a few points and their coordinate pairs. The coordinate pair for Point A is (1, 2). To plot Point A, you start at the origin (0, 0) and move 1 space to the right along the x-axis. From there, move 2 spaces upward along the y-axis.

Now, check to see that you understand how to plot the rest of the coordinate pairs shown.

A = (1, 2)
B = (−2, 3)
C = (−3, −1)
D = (4, −3)
E = (0, 0)
F = (0, −4)

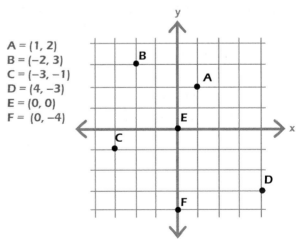

Geometry I: Coordinate Plane   227

Midpoint

When asked to find the midpoint between two points on the coordinate plane, use the following formula:

$$\text{Midpoint} = \left(\frac{x_1 + x_2}{2}, \frac{y_1 + y_2}{2} \right)$$

This formula is provided for you on the formula sheet for the exam. To find the x-coordinate halfway between the two points, add the two x-values and divide by 2. The same process can be used to find the y-coordinate.

Example:
Find the midpoint of the two points (2, 6) and (4, 8).

$x_1 + x_2 = 2 + 4 = 6$
$y_1 + y_2 = 6 + 8 = 14$

Midpoint = (6/2, 14/2)
Midpoint = (3, 7)

Distance

The distance between two points can be found using a formula also provided on the formula sheet:

$$\text{Distance} = \sqrt{(x_2 - x_1)^2 + (y_2 - y_1)^2}$$

This formula is derived from the Pythagorean Theorem. The distance between the two points forms the hypotenuse of a right triangle. You can determine the vertical side of the triangle by taking the difference between y_1 and y_2. The horizontal side is found by taking the difference between x_1 and x_2. You then use the Pythagorean Theorem to find the hypotenuse, or distance.

Hypotenuse² = horizontal side² + vertical side²
Distance² = $(x_2 - x_1)^2 + (y_2 - y_1)^2$
Distance = $\sqrt{(x_2 - x_1)^2 + (y_2 - y_1)^2}$

Example: Find the distance between (2, 4) and (5, 8).

$$\text{Distance}^2 = (5 - 2)^2 + (8 - 4)^2$$
$$\text{Distance}^2 = 3^2 + 4^2$$
$$\text{Distance}^2 = 9 + 16$$
$$\text{Distance} = \sqrt{(9 + 16)}$$
$$= \sqrt{25}$$
$$= 5$$

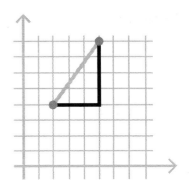

Three-Dimensional Coordinate Plane

It is possible to show the relationship among 3 variables using a 3-D graph, in which the third axis is labeled z, and the coordinates are written (x, y, z).

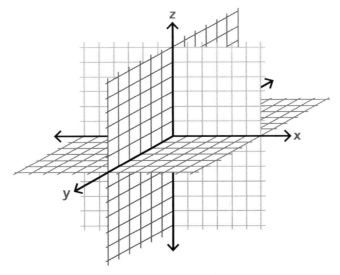

Coordinate Plane: Practice

1. In which quadrant is the point (−3, 2)?

  A. I
  B. II
  C. III
  D. IV

Geometry I: Coordinate Plane 229

2. Identify the coordinate pair.

    A. (−3, 1)
    B. (1, −3)
    C. (1, −4)
    D. (−1, −3)

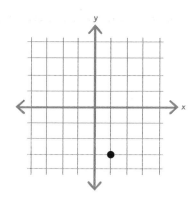

3. All points in quadrant III

    I. Have negative x-values
    II. Have negative y-values
    III. Can be described by a coordinate pair

A. I and III
B. I and II
C. II and III
D. I, II, and III

4. The graph below shows a circle with its center at the origin. What are the coordinates of point A?

    A. (−3, 0)
    B. (0, −3)
    C. (0, 3)
    D. (3, 0)

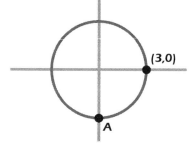

5. What is the distance between Point A and Point B?

    A. 3
    B. 4
    C. 5
    D. 6

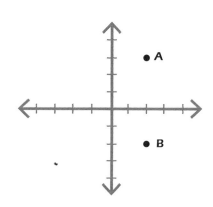

230   Geometry I: Coordinate Plane

6. What is the midpoint of the line segment that connects Point R at (−4, 6) and Point S at (2, −1)?

    A. (−2, 3.5)
    B. (−2, 5)
    C. (−1, 2.5)
    D. (−1, 3)

7. If the first three corners of a rectangle are at (−2, −3), (−2, 4), and (4, 4), what is the coordinate pair for the last corner?

    A. (−2, −2)
    B. (−2, 3)
    C. (4, −3)
    D. (−4, −3)

8. What is the distance between (−3, 4) and (3, −4)?

    A. 7
    B. 8
    C. 10
    D. 14

9. Point M is the midpoint of the line PQ. If the coordinates of P are (9, 11) and M is at (4, 7.5), find the coordinates of Q.

    A. (−1, 4)
    B. (5, 3.5)
    C. (6.5, 9)
    D. (−1, 3)

10. If the distance between (−2, 12) and (n, 32) is 25, what is n?

    A. 3
    B. 7
    C. 13
    D. 23

Coordinate Plane: Answer Explanations

1. B As the graph shows, (–3, 2) is in Quadrant II.

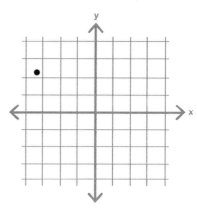

2. B To determine the coordinate pair, start at the origin (0, 0), and count along each axis. The first value in a coordinate pair is the x-value, so you begin by counting along the horizontal x-axis. Values to the right of the origin are negative, and values to the left are positive. This point is 1 to the right of the origin, so its x-value is 1.

The y-value is the second value in the coordinate pair. Count along the vertical y-axis: points above the origin are positive; points below are negative. This point is 3 below the origin, so the y-value is –3.

3. D A coordinate pair can describe any point in the coordinate plane; therefore, III is true.

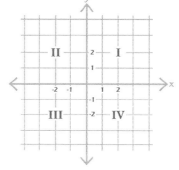

Any point in Quadrant III will have negative x and y values. Therefore, I and II are also true.

4. B All points on a circle are the same distance from the center; therefore, each point is 3 away from the origin. In a coordinate pair, the first element listed is the x-coordinate. In this case, Point A is on the y-axis, and it did not move horizontally. Therefore, the x-coordinate is 0.

The y-coordinate of point A is –3, since it is 3 away from the origin in the negative direction.

5. C Points A and B have the same x-coordinate. They only differ in y-coordinates. Point A is 3 units above the x-axis, and Point B is 2 units below. That makes 5 units separating the points.

You could also solve this by determining the coordinate pair of each point and then subtracting. Point A = (2, 3) and Point B = (2, –2). Therefore, the difference between the y-coordinates is $3 - (-2) = 3 + 2 = 5$.

6. C To find the midpoint of a line segment between (–4, 6) and (2, –1), find the average of the x-coordinates and the average of the y-coordinates.

The x-coordinates are –4 and 2. The average can be found by adding and dividing by 2.
Average of x-coordinates = (-4 + 2)/2 = –1

The y-coordinates are 6 and –1. The average can be found by adding and dividing by 2.
Average of y-coordinates = (6 + – 1)/2 = 2.5

7. C Graphing the coordinate pairs will help you find the last corner of the rectangle.

The coordinates (–2, –3), (–2, 4), and (5, 4) are graphed, and the last corner to complete the rectangle has been included in black.

The last corner is at (4, –3).

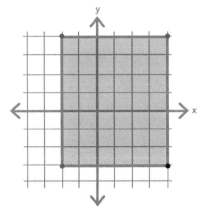

8. C There are two methods to solving this question. You could plug the points into the distance formula, which can be found on the formula sheet, or you could draw a right triangle and find the hypotenuse.

Distance Formula: distance = $\sqrt{[(x_2 - x_1)^2 + (y_2 - y_1)^2]}$

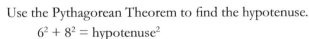

In this case, the points are (–3, 4) and (3, –4). So, $x_2 = 3$, $x_1 = -3$, $y_2 = -4$, $y_1 = 4$.

distance = $\sqrt{[6^2 + (-8)^2]} = \sqrt{[36 + 64]} = \sqrt{100} = 10$

Pythagorean Theorem:
In the image, you can see the two points have been graphed on the coordinate plane. Then, a right triangle is drawn with the hypotenuse representing the distance between the points.

The vertical side of the right triangle has a length of 8, as this is the difference between the y-coordinates of the two points.

The horizontal side of the right triangle has a length of 6, which is the difference between the x-coordinates of the two points.

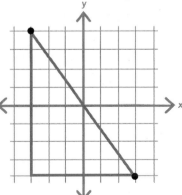

Use the Pythagorean Theorem to find the hypotenuse.
$6^2 + 8^2 = hypotenuse^2$
$36 + 64 = hypotenuse^2$
$100 = hypotenuse^2$
$hypotenuse = 10$

Geometry I: Coordinate Plane

9. A To find the coordinates of a midpoint, you find the average of the x-coordinates of the endpoints and the average of the y-coordinates of the endpoints.

In this problem, you have been given one endpoint and the midpoint, and you need to find the other endpoint.

Let's first look at the x-coordinates. The x-coordinate of the endpoint is 9, and the x-coordinate of the midpoint is 4. Therefore, 4 equals the average of 9 and Q's x-coordinate:

$$4 = (9 + x)/2$$
$$8 = 9 + x$$
$$-1 = x$$

Now, do the same for the y-coordinate:

$$7.5 = (11 + y)/2$$
$$15 = 11 + y$$
$$4 = y$$

10. C When asked to find the distance between two coordinate pairs, you can either use the distance formula or draw a right triangle and use the Pythagorean Theorem. In this case, let's use the formula:

$$\text{Distance} = \sqrt{(x_2 - x_1)^2 + (y_2 - y_1)^2}$$

Since the two points are (–2, 12) and (n, 32), the values for the variables are

$x_2 = n$, $x_1 = -2$, $y_2 = 32$, $y_1 = 12$.

$$25 = \sqrt{(n - (-2))^2 + (32 - 12)^2}$$
$$25 = \sqrt{(n + 2)^2 + 20^2}$$
$$625 = [(n + 2)^2 + 20^2]$$
$$625 = (n + 2)^2 + 400$$
$$225 = (n + 2)^2$$
$$15 = n + 2$$
$$n = 13$$

Geometry I: Module Review

1. You need to paint a huge outside wall that is 36 ft by 25 ft. If every 2 gal of paint cover 50 sq yd, how many gallons of paint do you need?

    A. 2
    B. 4
    C. 12
    D. 36

2. If you have a circle with radius r, the area of the circle is equal to how many times the circle's circumference?

    A. 2r
    B. 4r
    C. r/2
    D. r/4

3. Victor ran 30 degrees around a circular park. If the diameter of the park is 12 miles, how many miles did he run?

    A. 10π
    B. 6π
    C. 3π
    D. π

4. Selena wants to draw a line around the edge of the triangle shown below. If the triangle has two sides of 4 cm each, then approximately how many centimeters will she need to color to draw a line that goes completely around the triangle?

    A. 8 cm
    B. 12 cm
    C. 5.66 cm
    D. 13.66 cm

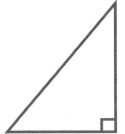

5. Triangle PQR is an isosceles triangle. If Angle P = 70°, which of the following is not a possible measure for Angle Q?

    A. 20°
    B. 40°
    C. 55°
    D. 70°

6. If a quilting club uses rolls of fabric measuring 6 ft by 3 ft to construct a quilt of 4 in. squares, how many squares of fabric will it take to create a quilt measuring 3 yd by 3 yd?

    A. 729
    B. 162
    C. 27
    D. 11664

7. Find the perimeter of the following triangle.

    A. 20
    B. 40
    C. 55
    D. 60

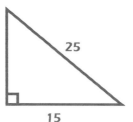

8. The field below is made of two half-circles on either end with a straight line of 50 meters connecting them. If the height of the field is 20 m, what is the perimeter of the entire field?

    A. 120 m
    B. 140 m
    C. 162.8 m
    D. 414 m

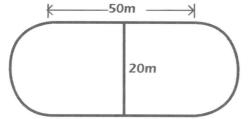

236   Geometry I: Module Review

9. The field below is made of two half-circles on either end with a straight line of 50 m connecting them. If the height of the field is 20 m, what is the area of the entire field?

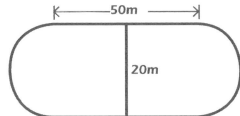

A. 3140 sq m

B. 1000 sq m

C. 1062.8 sq m

D. 1314 sq m

10. If 1 kilogram is equal to approximately 2.2 lb, how many ounces are there in 20 kg?

A. 44 oz

B. 11¼ oz

C. 96.8 oz

D. 704 oz

11. What is the distance between Point A with coordinates (−1, −2) and Point B with coordinates (6, −2)?

A. 5

B. 6

C. 7

D. 8

12. Choose the best answer to replace the question mark:

Perimeter of Circle A ? Perimeter of Square B

A. >

B. <

C. =

D. Not enough information.

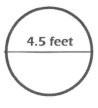

Circle A

Square B

Geometry I: Module Review   237

13. **Which of the following is the largest?**

    A. 1 sq yd

    B. 9 sq ft

    C. 1296 sq in

    D. All the above are the same.

14. **If a rectangle has corners at the origin, (0, 4), and (2, 4), where is the fourth corner of the rectangle?**

    A. (0, 2)

    B. (2, 0)

    C. (4, 4)

    D. (4, 0)

15. **Jordan took a shortcut when walking around her circular neighborhood. She walked halfway around the circumference and then cut straight across the middle to return to her starting point. If the distance around the circular path of the neighborhood is 7 km, approximately how much walking did she save by taking the shortcut?**

    A. 1.27 km

    B. 2.52 km

    C. 3.5 km

    D. 5.73 km

16. **If you have one point in Quadrant III and another point in Quadrant IV, and you found the product of their x-coordinates, what would you get?**

    A. Positive Number

    B. Negative Number

    C. Zero

    D. Not enough information.

17. George is a kindergartener coloring in wedges of circles for a project on fractions. If the diameter of a circle is 6 in., and the circle is divided evenly into 6 wedges, what is the area that George colored if he carefully colored in 1 wedge?

    A. π
    B. 1.5π
    C. 2π
    D. 3π

18. If the width of a rectangle is w and the length is 4 less than 3 times the width, what is the perimeter of the rectangle in terms of w?

    A. $8 - 4w$
    B. $3w^2 - 4w$
    C. $4w - 4$
    D. $8w - 8$

19. Choose the best answer to replace the question mark.

    The area of the circle below is ? times that of the triangle inscribed in it.

    A. π
    B. 2π
    C. 5π
    D. 10π

    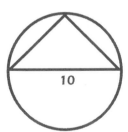

20. What is the perimeter of a right triangle that has a 45-degree angle, and the side opposite the 45-degree angle is equal to 3?

    A. 9
    B. $6 + 3\sqrt{2}$
    C. $6\sqrt{2}$
    D. 18

Module Review: Answer Explanations

1. B This problem involves several steps. First, find the area of the wall. Second, convert the units to square yards. Then, determine the gallons of paints needed.

Area of a rectangular wall is length x width = 36 ft x 25 ft = 900 sq ft

To convert from square feet to square yards, two unit conversions are necessary.

900 sq ft x $\frac{1 \text{ yd}}{3 \text{ ft}}$ x $\frac{1 \text{ yd}}{3 \text{ ft}}$ = 100 sq yd

You could also convert the dimensions from feet to yards first, and then find the area. Either way, you end up with 100 sq yd.

$\frac{2 \text{ gal}}{50 \text{ sq yd}} = \frac{x \text{ gal}}{100 \text{ sq yd}}$	set up a ratio to find gallons
50x = 2(100)	cross-multiply and set them equal
50x = 200	multiply
x = 4	divide both sides by 50

Answer B. 4 gal

2. C The area of the circle = πr^2

The circumference of the circle = $2\pi r$

Now, you must use algebra to solve this question. Let y represent the answer to this question, which asks how many times the circumference the area is. This can be set up as

Area = y x Circumference.

πr^2 = y x $2\pi r$

Divide both sides by π.

r^2 = y x 2r

Divide both sides by r.

r = y x 2

Divide both sides by 2.

r/2 = y

Geometry I: Module Review

3. D To find the arc length, multiply the fraction of the circle Victor ran around by the circumference of the circle.

Since there are 360 degrees in a circle, Victor ran 30/360 = 1/12 of the circle.

The total circumference of the circle is π x diameter = 12π.

Therefore, multiply the fraction of the circle times the total circumference.

(1/12) x 12π = π miles

4. D The triangle has a right angle and two equal sides; therefore, it must be a right isosceles triangle. The side remaining to be figured out is the hypotenuse. You can use the Pythagorean Theorem to find the length of the hypotenuse.

Pythagorean Theorem says that one side squared plus second side squared = hypotenuse squared, or more commonly written as: $a^2 + b^2 = c^2$.

$4^2 + 4^2$ = hypotenuse^2
16 + 16 = hypotenuse^2
32 = hypotenuse^2

If you take the square root of both sides, you find that the hypotenuse is approximately 5.66 cm.

The question asks for the perimeter of the triangle: 4 cm + 4 cm + 5.66 cm = 13.66 cm.

5. A If Triangle PQR is an isosceles triangle, then two angles must be equal. The question tells you one angle. Therefore, that angle is equal to a second angle, or it is the one different angle. Remember, in a triangle, all angles add to 180°.

One possible triangle: Angle P equals another angle. Therefore, two angles equal 70°. To find the third angle, subtract the sum of the two angles from 180.

180 − (70 + 70) = 180 − 140 = 40.

Another possible triangle: Angle P is the different angle. Therefore, the other two angles, Q and R, must be equal. Let the variable y represent the measure of Angle Q, which also equals the measure of Angle R.

70 + y + y = 180
70 + 2y = 180
2y = 110
y = 55

The diagram at the top of the next page shows the two possible isosceles triangles.

Here are the two possible isosceles triangles.

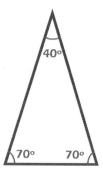
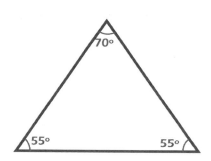

Angle Q cannot equal 20°.

6. A   To calculate the number of squares needed to create the quilt, find the length of one side of the quilt, which is 3 yd, in inches.

   3 yd x 3 ft/yd = 9 ft
   9 ft x 12 in/ft = 108 in

Now, let us convert the number of inches to quilt squares.

   108 in x 1 square/4 in = 27 squares long

Since the quilt is 3 yd by 3 yd, it is 27 squares by 27 squares. Therefore, to find the number of squares needed, find the area by multiplying the length of the two sides.

   27 x 27 = 729
   Answer A

Notice that the information about the rolls of fabric is not important for solving the problem.

7. D   To find the perimeter, you need to add the length of all the sides. Unfortunately, only two sides of the triangle were given. But, since the triangle is a right triangle, you can use the Pythagorean Theorem to find the length of the other side.

   $15^2 + b^2 = 25^2$
   $225 + b^2 = 625$
   $b^2 = 400$
   $b = 20$

Now, add all the sides.

   15 + 20 + 25 = 60

8. C The perimeter of the field is the total distance around the outside. First, let's find the perimeter around the two half-circles, and then we can add in the two straight lines.

Since the two half-circles will equal one total circle, we need to find the perimeter of one circle. Perimeter of a circle, often called circumference, is found by multiplying π by the diameter. In this case, you can see that the height of the field, 20 m, is equal to the diameter of the circle.

    Perimeter of Circle = π x 20 m = 62.8 m

Now, there are two straight edges: the top and bottom. Each is 50 m.

    Total Perimeter = 62.8 m + 50 m + 50 m = 162.8 m

9. D

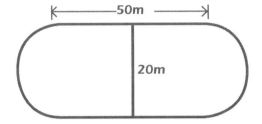

To find the area of the entire field, first find the area of the two half-circles, and add in the area of the rectangular middle of the field.

The two half-circles will add up to one complete circle. The area of a circle = π x radius². The diameter of the circle is the same as the height of the field, 20 m. Therefore, the radius = 10 m.

    Area of Circle = π x 10^2 = 314 sq m.

The area of the middle rectangular portion can be found by multiplying the base by the height. The base is 50 m, and height is 20 m.

    Area of Rectangle = 50 m x 20 m = 1000 sq m

    Total Area = 1000 + 314 = 1314 sq m

10. D The question asks you to convert from kilograms to ounces. First, convert from kilograms to pounds, and then convert that result to ounces.

    20 kg x $\frac{2.2 \text{ lb}}{1 \text{ kg}}$
    = 44 lb

Note that the kilogram units canceled, and you were left with pounds.

Now, convert from pounds to ounces. There are 16 ounces in 1 pound.

    44 lb x $\frac{16 \text{ oz}}{1 \text{ lb}}$
    = 704 oz

11. C Points A and B are graphed on the coordinate plane. As you can see from the graph and their coordinates, Points A and B have the same y-coordinate. Therefore, we must find the difference in their x-coordinates to figure out the distance between the points.

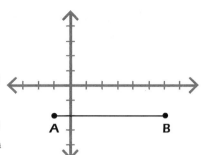

Point A's x-coordinate is at –1, and Point B's x-coordinate is at 6. Subtract to find the difference or distance between them.
6 – (–1) = 6 + 1 = 7

12. B Don't forget to convert the units first so that they are the same.

Square B: First, convert the units from yards to feet. There are 3 ft in each yard; therefore, the length of the side is 6 ft. To find the perimeter of the square, multiply the length of the side times 4. Therefore, the perimeter is 4 x 6 ft = 24 ft.

Circle A: The formula for calculating the perimeter or circumference of a circle is π x diameter. The diameter is 4.5 ft and pi is a little more than 3. A quick estimate will show that this is definitely less than the perimeter of the square.

Perimeter of Circle A < Perimeter of Square B

13. D Convert each answer choice to the same units and compare. Since the units are squared, use two unit conversions.

A: 1 sq yd x $^{3 \text{ ft}}/_{1 \text{ yd}}$ x $^{3 \text{ ft}}/_{1 \text{ yd}}$ = 9 sq ft

B: 9 sq ft

C: 1296 sq in x $^{1 \text{ ft}}/_{12 \text{ in}}$ x $^{1 \text{ ft}}/_{12 \text{ in}}$ = 9 sq ft

Answer D: All the same.

14. B This problem gives you three of the coordinates of the rectangle and asks you to find the fourth. It is easy to see the solution to this problem when you graph the coordinates.

The last corner is at (2, 0).

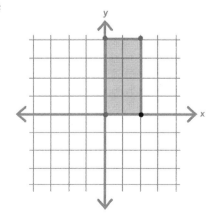

Geometry I: Module Review

15. A To calculate the distance she walked, find the diameter of her neighborhood, and add it to half the circumference.

Circumference = 7 km. Therefore, half the circumference is 7 km ÷ 2 = 3.5 km.

To find the diameter, use the circumference. The circumference can be found by multiplying the diameter times π. Therefore, divide the circumference by π to find the diameter.
Circumference ÷ π =
   7 km ÷ 3.14 = 2.23 km

Therefore, Jordan walked 3.5 km + 2.23 km = 5.73 km.

Subtract the distance she walked from the circumference to find the amount of walking she saved.
   7 km – 5.73 km = 1.27 km

16. B If a point is in Quadrant III, then its x-coordinate is negative. If a point is in Quadrant IV, its x-coordinate is positive.

If you multiply a negative and a positive, you get a negative.
Therefore, the product of their x-coordinates will be negative.

17. B Find the area of the entire circle. Then, find ⅙ of the area since George colored in 1 of the 6 evenly sized wedges.

Area of the circle = πradius^2
Since the diameter is 6 in., the radius is 3 in.
   Area = $\pi 3^2$
   Area = 9π

Now, find ⅙ of the area of the circle.
   ⅙ x 9π = 1.5π

18. D Let's first find the length of the rectangle in terms of w. The length is 4 less than 3 times the width, and the width is w.
   Length = 4 less than 3 times width
   Length = 4 less than 3w
   Length = 3w – 4

There are four sides on a rectangle: two widths and two lengths.
   perimeter = width + width + length + length
   perimeter = (2 x width) + (2 x length)
   perimeter = 2w + 2(3w – 4)
   = 2w + 6w – 8
   = 8w – 8

19. A Calculate the area of the circle and the area of the triangle.

Circle: Area of a circle = π x r².
The radius of the circle is half the diameter; therefore, the radius = 5.
  Area of Circle = π x 5² = 25π.

Triangle: Area of a triangle = ½ x base x height.
The base of the triangle is 10. The height of the triangle equals the radius of the circle = 5.
  Area of Triangle = ½ x 10 x 5 = 25.

To find how many times bigger the area of the circle is divide the areas.
Area of Circle ÷ Area of Triangle = 25π ÷ 25 = π.

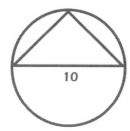

20. B If you have a right triangle, one angle is 90 degrees. They tell you that another angle is 45 degrees, so you can easily calculate that the third angle will also be 45 degrees. Therefore, you have an isosceles right triangle with angles of 45, 45, and 90 degrees. They tell you that the side opposite the 45-degree angle is equal to 3; well, we know that this will be the case for both 45-degree angles. Therefore, you have a right triangle with both sides equal to 3, and we need to find the third side, the hypotenuse, to calculate the perimeter around all the sides.

You should memorize the patterns for 45–45–90 triangles and 30–60–90 triangles. However, in this instance, I'll calculate the hypotenuse in case you haven't memorized these values.

Using Pythagorean Theorem: $3^2 + 3^2 = hypotenuse^2$
  $9 + 9 = hypotenuse^2$
  $18 = hypotenuse^2$
Hypotenuse = √18 = √9 x √2 = 3 x √2 = 3√2

Therefore, perimeter = 3 + 3 + 3√2 = 6 + 3√2

5. Algebra & Graphing

Slope & Rate of Change...250
Graphing Linear Equations & Inequalities..................256
Systems of Equations..262
Quadratic Equations..271
Graphing Quadratics...281
Advanced Functions & Graphing................................291
Algebra Word Problems...300
Module Review...308

Algebra & Graphing: Slope & Rate of Change

Rate of Change

In the previous module, you learned to set up proportions based on the concept of equivalent ratios or rates of change – the relative change in one variable with respect to another. You can use the fact that two variables interact in a predictable way to determine what the value of one variable would be for a given value of the other.

Let's use an example. Maria is reading a book. For every minute Maria reads, the number of pages she has read will increase by 2. The rate of change can be written as

$$\frac{2 \text{ pages}}{1 \text{ min}}$$

You can use this information to calculate, for example, how many pages she will read in 1 hour:

$$\frac{2 \text{ pages}}{1 \text{ min}} \times 60 \text{ mins} = 120 \text{ pages}$$

This rate of change can also be shown as the **slope** of a line on a graph:

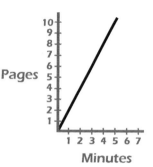

Calculating Slope

In graphing, the slope of a line is the change in the y-coordinate divided by the change in the x-coordinate, which is often referred to as "rise over run."

If you have two points on a graph (x_1, y_1) and (x_2, y_2), you can use the following formula to find the slope of the straight line connecting them:

$$\text{Slope} = \frac{y_2 - y_1}{x_2 - x_1} \quad \text{or} \quad \text{Slope} = \frac{y_1 - y_2}{x_1 - x_2}$$

If you were to calculate the slope of the line, which would be the number of pages per minute that could be read, you would pick two points along the line – in this case, (1, 2) and (2, 4), and then, you could calculate the slope.

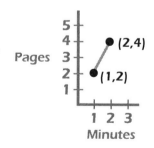

The slope between (1, 2) and (2, 4)

$= (4 - 2)/(2 - 1) = 2/1 = 2.$

To travel between these two points, a line must rise 2 units and run 1 unit to the right.

The above formula for calculating slope only works if you choose two points along the same line. If the slope changes, known as a variable slope, throughout the graph or if the graph is not a straight line, then the above formula is invalid.

Negative Slope

The slope of a line is negative if its y-coordinate decreases as you move to the right. In other words, the slope is negative if the rise is negative, as the run stays positive. For example, the graph to the right has a slope of –3/5:

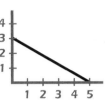

Zero Slope

A horizontal line has a slope of 0. There is no rise as you move to the right.

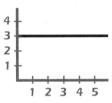

Undefined Slope

A vertical line's slope cannot be defined. It continually rises but has a run of zero, and it is impossible to divide a number by zero.

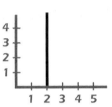

Slope & Rate of Change: Practice

1. **What is the slope of the line that passes through Points A and B?**

   A. –3/5
   B. –5/3
   C. 3/5
   D. 5/3

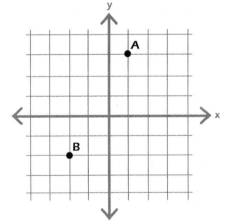

2. **What is the slope of the line?**

   A. 3
   B. –3
   C. 1
   D. 1/3

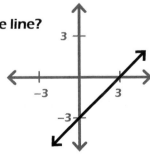

3. **What is the slope of the line that passes through the origin and (−3, −4)?**

   A. 4/3

   B. 3/4

   C. − 3/4

   D. − 4/3

4. **Which of the following graphs has a variable slope?**

   A.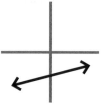

   C.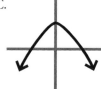

   B.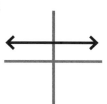

   D.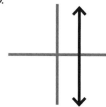

5. **Choose the best option to replace the question mark.**

   The slope from Point A to Point B ? the slope from Point B to Point C.

   A. >

   B. <

   C. =

   D. One slope is undefined, so it can't be determined.

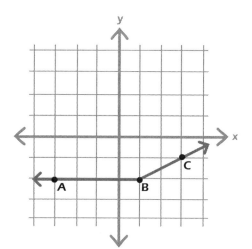

6. Melissa can type 80 words every 3 minutes. How long will it take her to type 6 pages with 1,000 words on each page?

   A. 37.5 mins

   B. 1 hour, 15 mins

   C. 3 hours, 45 mins

   D. 4 hours

7. A line with a slope of −12 passing through the origin has what y-value when x is 5?

   A. 60

   B. −60

   C. −7

   D. 17

8. Which of the following lines has an undefined slope?

   A.

   C.

   B.
   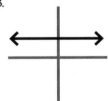

   D.
   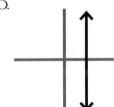

9. What is the slope of the line that passes through (−2, 4) and (5, 3)?

   A. −1/7

   B. 3/7

   C. −7

   D. −5/6

Algebra & Graphing: Slope & Rate of Change

10. How many times does the slope of the line below change?

A. 2
B. 3
C. 4
D. 5

Slope & Rate of Change: Answer Explanations

1. D   Slope is rise over run. From Point B to Point A, the rise is 5 and the run is 3.

2. C   To determine slope, figure out how much the line rises over how much it runs. In other words, find the change in the y-coordinates and divide by the change in the x-coordinates.

For this line, let us start at (0, –3) and go to (3, 0). From the first point to the second point, the line rises 3 and goes across 3. Therefore, the slope is equal to $3/3 = 1$.

3. A   The slope is rise over run. Therefore, the slope is the change in the y-coordinates over the change in the x-coordinates. You need to find the change between the 2 coordinate pairs (0, 0) and (–3, –4).

$$\text{Slope} = (-4 - 0)/(-3 - 0) = -4/-3 = 4/3$$

4. C   Any straight line will have a slope that does not change. Answer C starts with a positive slope, but then it changes to a negative slope.

5. B   The slope from Point A to Point B is zero since it is a horizontal line. The slope from Point B to Point C is positive since the line is increasing. Therefore, the slope from Point A to B is less than the slope from B to C.

6. C   Since we assume that Melissa's typing rate remains the same, set up a ratio between words and minutes.

$$\frac{80 \text{ words}}{3 \text{ min}} = \frac{6000 \text{ words}}{y \text{ min}}$$

Cross-multiply and solve:

$80y = 6000(3)$
$80y = 18000$
$y = 225$
$225 \text{ minutes} = 3 \text{ hours } 45 \text{ min}$

7. B   The formula to find slope is:

$$\text{Slope} = \frac{\text{change in y}}{\text{change in x}}$$

Plug in the values you know, and solve for y:

$$\text{Slope} = \frac{\text{change in y}}{\text{change in x}} = \frac{(y-0)}{(5-0)} = -12$$

$y/5 = -12$
$y = -60$

8. D   Answer A has a positive slope, since the line is increasing.
Answer B has a slope of zero, since it is a horizontal line.
Answer C has a slope that keeps changing, but it is always defined.
Answer D has an undefined slope, since it is a vertical line.

9. A   The slope of a line is rise over run. Or, slope is the change in y over the change in x.

The change in y-values is $4 - 3 = 1$.
The change in x-values is $-2 - 5 = -7$.

$$\text{Slope} = \frac{\text{change in y}}{\text{change in x}}$$

$= 1/-7 = -1/7$

10. B   The image has 4 different slopes, therefore the slope changes 3 times. The black dots in the image below show the places where the slope changes.

Algebra & Graphing: Slope & Rate of Change

Algebra & Graphing: Graphing Linear Equations & Inequalities

Linear Equations

A linear equation is one that results in a straight line when graphed. The equation of a straight line typically takes the form:

$$y = mx + b$$

In this equation, m is the slope and b is the **y-intercept**. The y-intercept is the point at which the line crosses the y-axis – in other words, the y-value when x = 0. The x and y represent the x and y values of any coordinate pair on the line.

Let's graph the following linear equation:

$$y = (3/2)x - 2$$

You can see from the equation that the y-intercept is –2. This point is plotted on the graph as (0, –2). The equation also tells us that the slope is 3/2. Starting at (0, –2), draw a second point up 3 and 2 to the right. Now, connect those points to create the graph of the line:

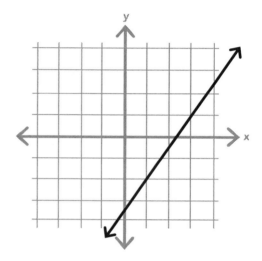

Determining Equations

If you are given two coordinate pairs, you can calculate the slope using the formula you learned in the lesson "Slope & Rate of Change". Once you have the slope, plug in either pair to solve for the y-intercept.

Example: Find the equation for the line through the two pairs of points (–4, 6) and (–2, –8).
Slope = $(-8 - 6)/(-2 - (-4)) = -14/2 = -7$

Use the slope and one point to calculate the y-intercept:
y = mx + b
y = –7x + b
6 = –7(–4) + b
6 = 28 + b
–22 = b
y = –7x – 22

Graphing Inequalities

You've seen inequalities graphed on a number line, but how would you visually represent an inequality with multiple variables? If you have an inequality with two variables, you can graph it on a coordinate plane.

First, you determine the boundary line and graph it. Then, you shade one side of the line.

Boundary Line

To determine the boundary line, treat the inequality as if it were an equation. For example, to graph $y > x + 2$, the boundary line would be the graph of $y = x + 2$. Plug some values for x into the equation, and use the resulting coordinate pairs to plot your line. For example, let's plug in the values 2 and 4 for x:

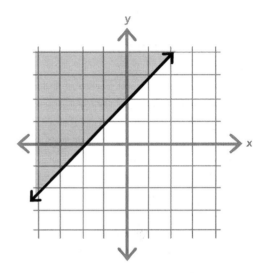

When $x = 2$
$y = 2 + 2 = 4$

When $x = 4$
$y = 4 + 2 = 6$

Now, we have two pairs to plot the line with: (2, 4) and (4, 6).

If the inequality contains the symbols ≥ or ≤, the boundary line should be included as part of the inequality. This is indicated by drawing a solid line. If the inequality contains the symbols > or <, the boundary line is not included and so should be drawn as a dashed line.

Shading

Now, you need to shade one side of the line or the other to represent the range of values that correspond to the inequality. In this case, we want to graph $y > x + 2$, so we shade the part above the boundary line. As you can see, the shaded part of the graph shows all values for y that are greater than $x + 2$.

A good way to determine what side of the line to shade is to test a point. Pick any point that is not on the line; usually, the origin is the easiest. Then, test that point in the equation. If it holds true, shade the side of the graph that includes that point. If it is not true in the equation, then shade the opposite side of the line.

For example, in the equation above, $y > x + 2$, we can plug in the origin (0, 0). $0 > 0 + 2$ is not true. Therefore, we shade the side of the line that does not contain the origin.

Graphing Linear Equations & Inequalities: Practice

1. What is the equation of the line?

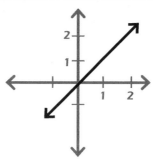

A. $y = (½)x + 1$

B. $y = x$

C. $y = x + 1$

D. $(½)y = x + 1$

2. What is the slope of the line represented by this equation? $1 - (¾)y = (⅓)x - 2$

A. $¾$

B. $⅓$

C. -2

D. $-4/9$

3. What is the y-intercept of the line represented by $-7x + 14 = 2y - 19$

A. -19

B. 14

C. 33

D. $16½$

4. What is the equation of the line that passes through the points (4, −3) and (2, 7)?

A. $y = 6x + 4$

B. $y = -5x + 17$

C. $y = -(⅕)x - 3$

D. $y = -5x + 4$

5. Which graph represents the inequality? $80 - 20y > -15x + 40$

A. 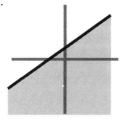   B. 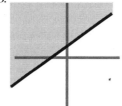   C. 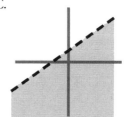   D.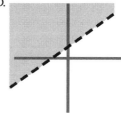

258   Algebra & Graphing: Graphing Linear Equations & Inequalities

6. A scientist is growing bacteria in a petri dish. He measures growth every minute. Initially, there are 20 bacteria. By the end of the first minute, there are 60. By the end of the second minute, there are 100. If the scientist represents these results with a graph, what would be the y-intercept?

   A. 20
   B. 40
   C. 60
   D. 100

7. What is the x-intercept of the line y = 4x – 9?

   A. 4
   B. –9
   C. 9/4
   D. 4/9

8. Which represents the graph of –x – 19 ≤ y?

   A.

   C.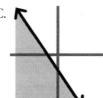

   B.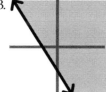

   D.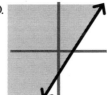

9. What is the equation of the line in the graph?

   A. y = –2x – 1
   B. y = 2x – 1
   C. y = (½)x – 1
   D. y = –2x + 1

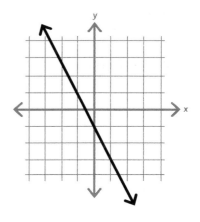

Algebra & Graphing: Graphing Linear Equations & Inequalities   259

10. A line with a slope of −3 that passes through (−2, 4) has what y-value when x is 3?

   A. −11
   B. −9
   C. 6
   D. 9

Graphing Linear Equations & Inequalities: Answer Explanations

1. B Use the following format for a linear equation: y = mx + b, where m is the slope and b is the y-intercept.

The y-intercept is where the line crosses the y-axis. In this case, the line crosses at 0. Therefore, b = 0.

The slope is the rise over the run. In this case, the line goes up 1 every time it goes across 1. Therefore, slope is 1.

$$y = mx + b$$
$$y = 1(x) + 0$$
$$y = x$$

2. D Manipulate the equation to isolate y and get the equation in the form y = mx + b. Once in that form, you can see that the coefficient in front of the x (represented by m) will be the slope.

$$1 - (3/4)y = (1/3)x - 2$$
$$-(3/4)y = (1/3)x - 3$$
$$(-4/3)(-3/4)y = (-4/3)(1/3\,x - 3)$$
$$y = -(4/9)x + 4$$

Slope is −4/9.

3. D Manipulate the equation to isolate y and get the equation in the form: y = mx + b, where the b represents the y-intercept.

$$-7x + 14 = 2y - 19$$
$$-7x + 33 = 2y$$
$$-(7/2)x + 33/2 = y$$
$$y = -(7/2)x + 33/2$$

The y-intercept is 33/2 = 16½

260   Algebra & Graphing: Graphing Linear Equations & Inequalities

4. B   The form of the equation is y = mx+b, where m is the slope and b is the y-intercept.

First, find the slope of the line between the two points. Slope is rise over run, or the change in y over the change in x.

$$\text{Slope} = \frac{(-3 - 7)}{(4 - 2)} = \frac{-10}{2} = -5$$

Now, find the y-intercept:

y = −5x + b

Plug either point into the equation and solve for b. Let's use the first point (4, −3):

y = −5x + b
−3 = −5(4) + b
−3 = −20 + b
b = 17

Equation: y = −5x + 17

5. C   First, isolate y.

80 − 20y > −15x + 40

Subtract 80 from both sides:

−20y > −15x − 40

Divide everything by −20:

$y < \frac{-15x}{-20} - \frac{40}{-20}$

$y < \frac{3x}{4} + 2$

Now, graph the equation. The line should not be solid since the equation is y <, not y ≤. Finally, shade all the values less than the dashed line. You can test a point to confirm which side of the line should be shaded. Test the origin (0, 0).

$0 < \frac{3(0)}{4} + 2$

0 < 2

True. Therefore, shade the side that includes the origin.

6 A.   The scientist graphs the data with time on the x-axis and the number of bacteria on the y-axis, because time is the independent variable, which is always graphed on the x-axis.

The y-intercept is the point where the line crosses the y-axis. If a point is crossing the y-axis, its x-value is 0. If the x-value is 0, then we want the value when the scientist started his experiment. He starts with 20, so that is the y-intercept.

7. C The x-intercept is where a line crosses the x-axis. When something crosses the x-axis, the y-value of that point is y = 0. Plug in y = 0 and solve for x:

$$y = 4x - 9$$
$$0 = 4x - 9$$
$$9 = 4x$$
$$x = 9/4$$

8. B First, rewrite the inequality with the y on the left side:

$$-x - 19 \leq y$$
$$y \geq -x - 19$$

The line should be solid, since it is ≥, and not >. Now, graph the line y = –x – 19, and then decide which side of the line to shade.

The graph of the line y = –x – 19 has a negative slope, which only happens in answers B and C.

You want to graph y ≥ –x – 19. To see which side should be shaded, try plugging in a point. In this case, it's the section above the line.

9. A When finding the equation of a line, find the slope and y-intercept to represent y = mx + b. This line crosses the y-axis at –1. Therefore, b = –1.
The slope is rise over run. Pick any two points on the line, and then figure out how much from one point to the next the line rises and runs. This line goes down 2 for every 1 across.

$$\text{Slope} = -2/1 = -2$$
$$y = -2x - 1$$

10. A First, find the equation of the line, then plug in x = 3 to solve for y.
The line has a slope of –3. Therefore, the basic form of an equation is y = mx + b. Plug in –3 for m.

$$y = -3x + b$$

Now, plug in the point (–2, 4) to solve for b.

$$4 = -3(-2) + b$$
$$4 = 6 + b$$
$$-2 = b$$

Equation: y = –3x – 2
Plug in x = 3 to solve for y.

$$y = -3(3) - 2$$
$$y = -9 - 2$$
$$y = -11$$

Algebra & Graphing: Systems of Equations

Introduction

A system of equations is a set of equations that can be used to find possible values for multiple variables. Generally, you will be given two equations with two unknowns, and you will solve for the values that make both equations true. Systems of equations can have zero, one, multiple, or an infinite number of solutions. Systems of equations can be solved in four ways.

1. Graphing

To find the possible values of a set of variables for two equations, find the point or points where the graphs of the equations intersect. A graph of an equation represents all the points that make the equation true. Therefore, the point where two graphs intersect is the point that makes both equations true.

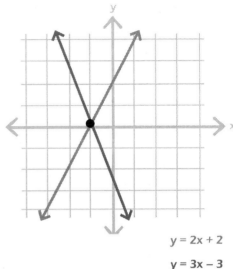

$y = 2x + 2$

$y = 3x - 3$

For example, if you were asked to solve the following system of equations; $y = 2x + 2$ and $y = -3x - 3$, you could graph both equations. The point where they intersect, $(-1, 0)$, represents the solution ($x = -1$, and $y = 0$).

Another example is if you were asked to solve the following system of equation, $y = 2x + 1$ and $y = 2x + 3$, you would graph two parallel lines that never intersect, and therefore there are no solutions to these equations as no values of x and y make both statements true.

2. Substitution

Another way to solve a system of equations is by substitution. This involves isolating a variable in one equation, and then substituting the value of that variable into the other equation.

Example: $3x + y = -5$, $2x + 3y = -1$
Using the first equation, solve for y: $3x + y = -5$, $y = -5 - 3x$

Now, plug that value for y into the second equation:
$2x + 3(-5 - 3x) = -1$
$2x - 15 - 9x = -1$
$-7x = 14$, $x = -2$

Now, plug the value of x back into any equation to solve for y:
$y = -5 - 3x = -5 - 3(-2) = 1$
Solution: $x = -2$, $y = 1$

Algebra & Graphing: Systems of Equations   263

3. Elimination

You can also solve a system of equations with elimination. Manipulate the equations so that you can add them to eliminate all but one variable. After solving for that variable, plug it into one of the original equations to solve for the other variable.

Example: $3x + y = -5$, $2x + 3y = -1$.

Choose which variable to eliminate – in this case, let's choose y. You want the y's to cancel when the equations are added, so multiply the first equation by -3:
$$-9x - 3y = 15$$

Now, add the two equations:
$$-9x - 3y = 15$$
$$2x + 3y = -1$$
$$-7x = 14$$
$$x = -2$$

Now, plug in $x = -2$ to solve for y:
$$y = -5 - 3x = -5 - 3(-2) = 1$$

Solution: $x = -2$, $y = 1$

4. Plugging In

The final option works when you are given a multiple-choice question with a set of possible answers. You can plug each set into the original equations and see which solution makes both equations true.

Systems of Equations: Practice

1. What is the solution to the following system of equations?

$$4x + 2y = 6$$
$$3x - y = 7$$

A. (−2, 1)
B. (3, 3)
C. (2, −1)
D. (1, −4)

264   Algebra & Graphing: Systems of Equations

2. Solve for j in the following system of equations: $5j + 3 = x - 2$
   $j + 45 = x$

   A. 10
   B. 15
   C. 40
   D. 55

3. Which statement is true about the solution to a system of equations?

   A. It is always a coordinate pair.
   B. It makes just one of the equations true.
   C. It never has the same x and y values.
   D. It is true for all the equations in the system.

4. Which of the following are solutions to the system of equations, $y = x^2$ and $y = 2x^2 - 1$? Both equations are graphed below.

   I. (−1, −1)
   II. (−1, 1)
   III. (1, 1)

   A. I and II
   B. III only
   C. II and III
   D. I, II, and III

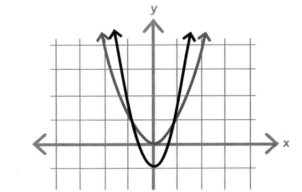

5. What is the solution to this system of equations?

   A. (0, 1)
   B. (1, −2)
   C. (1, 2)
   D. (−2, 1)

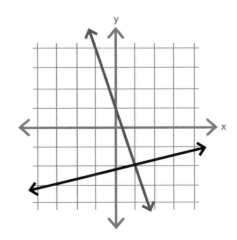

6. What is the solution to the system of equations graphed below?

A. (0, 0)
B. (1, 0)
C. (1, 1)
D. No solution

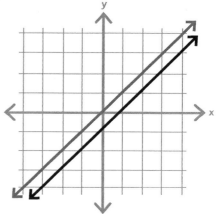

7. Solve for y in the following equations:

$$2y - 3x = 8$$
$$x = 3y + 2$$

A. –4
B. –2
C. 3
D. 6

8. Solve for x in the following system of equations:

$$-3x + 2y = -13$$
$$3x = y + 11$$

A. –2
B. 3
C. 9
D. 11

9. Admission to a baseball game is $2 for general admission and $3.50 for reserved seats. If 12,500 people paid a total of $36,250 to attend the game, how many general admission tickets were sold?

A. 3,500
B. 5,000
C. 7,250
D. 18,125

10. You have 16 coins in your pocket that are all pennies and nickels. If the coins are worth 32 cents, how many pennies do you have?

   A. 4
   B. 8
   C. 10
   D. 12

Systems of Equations: Answer Explanations

1. C There are multiple ways to solve questions of this type. The easiest method is to plug each answer into both equations and see which answer makes them both true. Another method is to solve using elimination.

Method 1: Plugging in
Take each answer, and plug in the first value for x and the second value for y.
Answer A (–2, 1): $4(-2) + 2(1) = -8 + 2 = -6$; False.
Answer B (3, 3): $4(3) + 2(3) = 12 + 6 = 18$; False.
Answer C (2, –1): $4(2) + 2(-1) = 8 - 2 = 6$. Works in the first equation.
  $3(2) - (-1) = 6 + 1 = 7$. Works in the second equation.
Answer D (1, –4): $4(1) + 2(-4) = 4 - 8 = -4$. False.

Method 2: Elimination
Choose a variable to eliminate. In this case, let's eliminate y. Therefore, multiply the entire second equation by 2:
  $2(3x - y = 7)$
  $6x - 2y = 14$

Now, line up the two equations, and add them to eliminate y.
  $4x + 2y = 6$
  $6x - 2y = 14$
  $10x = 20$
  $x = 2$

Now, plug the value for x into either equation to solve for y:
  $4(2) + 2y = 6$
  $8 + 2y = 6$
  $2y = -2$
  $y = -1$

2. A Let's use substitution to solve for j, since one variable is already isolated in one of the equations.

Substitute $j + 45$ for x in the first equation:
$5j + 3 = x - 2$
$5j + 3 = (j + 45) - 2$

Now solve for j.
$5j + 3 = j + 45 - 2$
$5j + 3 = j + 43$
$4j + 3 = 43$
$4j = 40$
$j = 10$

3. D Let's examine each answer choice:

A: It is always a coordinate pair.
This is false. There can be any number of solutions to a system of equations. You can have a solution that is a coordinate pair, or you can have no solutions, infinite solutions, and so on.

B: It makes just one of the equations true.
The solution to a system of equations makes all the equations true, not just one.

C: It never has the same x and y values.
This is also false. For instance, $x + y = 2$ and $x - y = 0$ has the solution $x = 1$ and $y = 1$.

D: Is true for all the equations in the system.
This is the definition of a solution to a system of equations.

4. C When solving a system of equations using graphs, the points of intersection are the solutions. In this case, the lines cross twice, once at (−1, 1) and another time at (1, 1).

You could have also plugged each set of points into both equations and seen which solutions make both true.

5. B If the equations are already graphed, simply look for the point where the two lines intersect.

6. D The solution to a graphed system of equations is the point where the two lines intersect. In this case, the lines never intersect. Therefore, no x and y pairs makes both equations true.

7. B Use substitution to solve this system of equations. Plug the value for x from the second equation into the first equation:

$$2y - 3x = 8$$
$$2y - 3(3y + 2) = 8$$
$$2y - 9y - 6 = 8$$
$$-7y - 6 = 8$$
$$-7y = 14$$
$$y = -2$$

8. B **Method 1: Substitution**

Rearrange the second equation to solve for y: $y = 3x - 11$

Plug in the value for y into the first equation:

$$-3x + 2y = -13$$
$$-3x + 2(3x - 11) = -13$$
$$-3x + 6x - 22 = -13$$
$$3x = 9$$
$$x = 3$$

Method 2: Elimination

Rearrange the equations so that the variables are in the same order and on the same side of the equations.

$$-3x + 2y = -13$$
$$3x - y = 11$$

If you add the equations, you see that the x's will be eliminated.

$$0x + 1y = -2$$
$$y = -2$$

Now, plug the value for y into either equation and solve for x:

$$3x = y + 11$$
$$3x = -2 + 11$$
$$3x = 9$$
$$x = 3$$

9. B Create a variable for each unknown:

g for the number of general admission tickets sold

r for the number of reserved seat tickets sold

Now, set up equations:

12,500 total tickets were sold; therefore, $g + r = 12{,}500$

Algebra & Graphing: Systems of Equations

$36,250 was brought in: $2 for general admission and $3.50 for reserved seats.

The amount of money generated for the general admission tickets: 2g

Amount of money for reserved tickets: 3.50r

$2g + 3.5r = 36,250$

Now, solve for the system of equations:

$g + r = 12,500$
$2g + 3.5r = 36,250$

You can use any method, but let's try substitution in this case.

Take the first equation, and solve for r:

$g + r = 12500, r = 12500 - g$

Substitute r into the second equation:

$2g + 3.5r = 36,250$
$2g + 3.5(12500 - g) = 36,250$
$2g + 43750 - 3.5g = 36,250$
$-1.5g = -7500$
$g = 5000$

5,000 tickets sold

10. D There are two unknowns in this equation. Set up a variable for each:

p = number of pennies

n = number of nickels

Now, set up equations:

The total number of pennies and nickels equals 16; therefore, $p + n = 16$.

The total value of the pennies and nickels is 32; therefore, $1p + 5n = 32$.

Now, solve the system of equations.

Use substitution, and isolate a variable in the first equation:

$p + n = 16$
$n = 16 - p$

Plug the value for n into the second equation:

$1p + 5n = 32$
$1p + 5(16 - p) = 32$
$p + 80 - 5p = 32$
$-4p + 80 = 32$
$-4p = -48$
$p = 12$

Algebra & Graphing: Systems of Equations

Algebra & Graphing: Quadratic Equations

Quadratic Expressions

A simplified quadratic expression takes the form:

$$ax^2 + bx + c$$

One way to generate a quadratic expression is by multiplying two binomials, for example, $(x - 2)(2x + 3)$. The method of multiplication follows the acronym FOIL:

1. First terms of each binomial
2. Outer terms
3. Inner terms
4. Last terms

The sum of these multiplications forms the quadratic expression.

Example:

$$(x - 2)(2x + 3) =$$
$$(2x)(x) + (x)(3) + (-2)(2x) + (-2)(3) =$$
$$2x^2 + 3x - 4x - 6 =$$
$$2x^2 - x - 6$$

Solving Quadratic Equations and Inequalities

A quadratic equation has a quadratic expression on the left-hand side and $= 0$ on the right. For example:

$$5x^2 + 3x + 7 = 0$$

Factoring

One way to solve quadratic equations is to factor, although factoring is not always possible. Here is one systematic method of factoring, sometimes called the ac-method:

Find the coefficients a, b, and c in $ax^2 + bx + c$.
Calculate ac.
Find two integers that multiply to equal ac and add to equal b.
Split the bx term into the sum of the two integers found in step 3, both times x.
Factor the resulting four terms by grouping two at a time to the final factored form.
Use FOIL to check.

Example 1: $2x^2 - x - 6$

    1. Find the coefficients: a = 2, b = −1, c = −6
    2. Calculate ac: ac = −12
    3. Find integers that multiply to −12 and add to equal −1: −4 and 3
    4. Split bx term: $2x^2 - 4x + 3x - 6$
    5. Factor: $2x(x - 2) + 3(x - 2) = (2x + 3)(x - 2)$

Example 2: $x^2 - 11x + 30$

    1. Find the coefficients: a = 1, b = −11, c = 30
    2. Calculate ac: ac = 30
    3. Find integers that multiply to 30 and add to equal −11: −6 and −5
    4. Split bx term: $x^2 - 6x - 5x + 30$
    5. Factor: $x(x - 6) - 5(x - 6) = (x - 5)(x - 6)$

Once the quadratic expression is factored, you need to set each binomial equal to zero and solve for x. This is because you have two terms that when multiplied equal zero, and thus one of them must equal zero. Using the two examples from above:

$x^2 - 11x + 30 = 0$
$(x - 5)(x - 6) = 0$
$x - 5 = 0, x - 6 = 0$
$x = 5, x = 6$

$2x^2 - x - 6 = 0$
$(2x + 3)(x - 2) = 0$
$2x + 3 = 0, x - 2 = 0$
$x = -3/2, x = 2$

Completing the Square

The Completing the Square method works when solving for x in any quadratic equation. This method is difficult and rarely used, however it is important to understand. In fact, the quadratic equation (which you will review next) is derived from completing the square.

    1. Find the coefficients a, b, and c in $ax^2 + bx + c$.
    2. Divide the entire equation by a. This creates a new a, b, and c.
    3. Subtract c from both sides.
    4. Add $(b/2)^2$ to both sides.
    5. Factor the left-hand side and simplify the coefficients on the right-hand side.
    6. Take the square root of both sides.
    7. Solve for x.

Example 1:

$x^2 - 11x + 30 = 0$

1. Find coefficients: $a = 1, b = -11, c = 30$
2. Divide entire equation by 1. Because it's 1, the a, b, and c values remain the same.
3. Subtract c from both sides: $x^2 - 11x = -30$
4. Add $(b/2)^2$ to both sides: $x^2 - 11x + 121/4 = -30 + 121/4$
5. Factor and simplify: $(x - 11/2)^2 = 1/4$
6. Square root both sides: $x - 11/2 = \pm\sqrt{1/4} = \pm 1/2$
7. Solve: $x - 11/2 = 1/2, x = 6$ OR $x - 11/2 = -1/2, x = 5$

Example 2:

$2x^2 - x - 6 = 0$

1. Find coefficients: $a = 2, b = -1, c = -6$
2. Divide entire equation by 2: $x^2 - x/2 - 3 = 0, a = 1, b = -1/2, c = -3$
3. Subtract c from both sides: $x^2 - x/2 = 3$
4. Add $(b/2)^2$ to both sides: $x^2 - x/2 + 1/16 = 3 + 1/16$
5. Factor and simplify: $(x - 1/4)^2 = 49/16$
6. Square root both sides: $x - 1/4 = \pm\sqrt{49/16} = \pm 7/4$
7. Solve: $x - 1/4 = 7/4, x = 2$ OR $x - 1/4 = = -7/4, x = -3/2$

Quadratic Formula

Like Completing the Square, the Quadratic Formula can be used to solve for x in any quadratic equation. Plug in the values for a, b, and c, and then solve for x. This equation is listed on the formula sheet for the exam – but make sure you know how to use it.

Example: $x^2 - 11x + 30 = 0$
$a = 1, b = -11, c = 30$

$$x = \frac{-b \pm \sqrt{b^2 - 4ac}}{2a}$$

$x = [11 \pm \sqrt{121 - 120}]/2$
$x = (11 \pm 1)/2$
$x = 12/2 = 6$ OR $x = 10/2 = 5$

Real and Complex Roots of Quadratic Equations

The roots (solutions) to a quadratic equation can be either real or complex numbers. See the section below for more on complex numbers. One way to tell whether the roots will be real or complex is to calculate the discriminant, which is $b^2 - 4ac$.

If $b^2 - 4ac > 0$, there are two real roots (as in examples above).
If $b^2 - 4ac < 0$, there are two complex, or imaginary roots (taking square root of negative).
If $b^2 - 4ac = 0$, there is one real root repeated (just $-b/2a$).

Graphing

The values for x can also be found by graphing, although this is a difficult method to use in practice. The points where the graph intersects the x-axis (that is, the x-intercepts) are the solutions. See the next lesson "Graphing Quadratic Equations" for more information on graphing.

Complex Numbers

Most problems you encounter will use real numbers, but complex numbers are also important in math. A complex number is represented by "i", which is defined as the square root of –1.

$$i = \sqrt{-1}$$

As you know, you cannot take the square root of a negative, which is why a complex number is not a real number.

You can perform operations on complex numbers, as you would with real numbers. Treat the complex number as a variable. For example:

addition: $i + i = 2i$
multiplication: $3i \times 4 = 12i$

Now, what happens when you multiply two complex numbers by each other?

$$i \times i = i^2$$

Again, if you think of the complex number as a variable, you can see that a variable times a variable is equal to a variable squared. Instead of leaving the answer as i^2, let's substitute the value of i back into the equation:

$$i \times i = i^2 = (\sqrt{-1})^2 = -1$$

Remember, if you square the square root of a number, it is equal to the original number.

Let's go through a few more examples:

$i^3 = i \times i^2 = i \times -1 = -i$
$i^4 = i^2 \times i^2 = -1 \times -1 = 1$
$i^{18} = (i^2)^9 = (-1)^9 = -1$

Quadratic Equations: Practice

1. Simplify the following quadratic expression to standard form:

$$2x^2 - 5x + 7 - (5x^2 - 4)$$

A. $-3x^2 - 5x + 3$

B. $-3x^2 - 5x + 11$

C. $7x^2 - 5x + 3$

D. $7x^2 - 5x + 11$

2. Simplify: $(3x^2 - 9x)/(x - 3)$

A. 0

B. $3x$

C. $6x$

D. $3x - 3$

3. What are all the possible values for x in the quadratic equation $x^2 - 10x + 24 = 0$?

A. $-2, 12$

B. $-4, 6$

C. $-12, 2$

D. $4, 6$

4. What is $(i + 3)(i - 2)$?

A. -8

B. -6

C. $i - 5$

D. $i - 7$

5. Solve the following equation for x: $x^2 - 5x + 6 = 0$

A. $x = 1$ or $x = 6$

B. $x = -1$ or $x = -6$

C. $x = 3$ or $x = 2$

D. $x = -3$ or $x = -2$

Algebra & Graphing: Quadratic Equations

6. **What is the nature of the solution for $2x^2 + 5x + 6 = 0$?**

    A. Two real roots

    B. One real root

    C. One real and one complex root

    D. Two complex roots

7. **Solve the equation: $2x^2 + 7x + 6 = 0$**

    A. $x = 2$ or $x = 6$

    B. $x = -7/4$ or $x = -9/4$

    C. $x = -3/2$ or $x = -2$

    D. $x = -7$ or $x = -4$

8. **If solving this problem by completing the square, what is the first thing you should do to both sides?**

    $$x^2 - 8x = -10$$

    A. add 16

    B. add 64

    C. subtract 16

    D. subtract 100

9. **Find the zeros of the following function:** $y = 2x^2 + x - 6$

    A. $(3/2, 0); (-2, 0)$

    B. $(0, 3/2); (0, -2)$

    C. $(-3, 0); (2, 0)$

    D. $(3, 0); (-2, 0)$

10. **What are the roots of the following equation?** $4x^2 - 4x + 2$

    A. $-2, 4$

    B. $1/2, -1/4$

    C. $0.5 \pm 2i$

    D. $0.5 \pm 0.5i$

Quadratic Equations: Answer Explanations

1. B To simplify the expression, combine like terms. Be careful to distribute the negative sign to each term in the parentheses.

$$2x^2 - 5x + 7 - (5x^2 - 4)$$
$$= 2x^2 - 5x + 7 - 5x^2 + 4$$
$$= -3x^2 - 5x + 11$$

2. B First, factor both the numerator and denominator so that you can see if any terms can cancel.

Numerator: $3x^2 - 9x = 3x(x - 3)$
Denominator $= x - 3$

Therefore, $(3x^2 - 9x)/(x - 3) = 3x(x - 3)/(x - 3)$
You can see that the term $(x - 3)$ is common to both numerator and denominator and can be cancelled.

$$3x(x - 3)/(x - 3) = 3x/1 = 3x$$

3. D There are several ways to solve this problem.

Method 1:

The easiest way to solve this problem is to plug in each answer choice to see which values make the equation true.

A: −2, 12
$(-2)^2 - 10(-2) + 24 = 4 + 20 + 24 = 48$
This does not equal zero. Eliminate A.

B: −4, 6
$(-4)^2 - 10(-4) + 24 = 16 + 40 + 24 = 80$
This does not equal zero. Eliminate B.

C: −12, 2
$(-12)^2 - 10(-12) + 24 = 144 + 120 + 24 = 288$
This does not equal zero. Eliminate C.

D: 4, 6
$(4)^2 - 10(4) + 24 = 16 - 40 + 24 = 0$
$(6)^2 - 10(6) + 24 = 36 - 60 + 24 = 0$
Both values for x in this answer choice make the equation true.

Answer D is correct.

Method 2:

Another way to solve this problem is to first factor the equation, which can be thought of as reversing the FOIL operation.

$$x^2 - 10x + 24 = 0$$
$$(x - 6)(x - 4) = 0$$

Now, we know that if the product of two terms is zero, one of those terms must equal zero. Set both terms equal to zero to find the possible values for x:

$$x - 6 = 0, x = 6$$
$$x - 4 = 0, x = 4$$
$$x = 6 \text{ or } 4$$

4. D When solving this equation, remember that i is the complex number equal to the square root of −1. $i = \sqrt{(-1)}$

The easiest way to solve this problem is to treat i as a variable, and then plug in its value at the end to simplify.

$$(i + 3)(i - 2) = i^2 - 2i + 3i - 6 = i^2 + i - 6$$

Now, let's see what i^2 equals. Since i is $\sqrt{(-1)}$, $i^2 = (\sqrt{(-1)})^2 = -1$.
Replace i^2 with −1:

$$i^2 + i - 6 = -1 + i - 6 = -7 + i = i - 7$$

5. C Often, the easiest way to solve quadratic equations is by factoring, so it is worthwhile to check if factoring is possible before trying other methods.

$$x^2 - 5x + 6 = 0$$
$$a = 1, b = -5, c = 6$$

We want to find two integers that multiply to 6 and add to −5. Think about the factors of 6 to see which combination add to −5. In this case, −3 and −2 multiply to 6 and add to −5:

$$(x - 3)(x - 2) = 0$$

Set each equation to zero to solve for x:

$$x - 3 = 0, x = 3$$
$$x - 2 = 0, x = 2$$

6. D To find the nature of the solution for the equation, find the discriminant. Remember, the discriminant is equal to $b^2 - 4ac$.

$$2x^2 + 5x + 6 = 0$$
$$a = 2, b = 5, c = 6$$

Discriminant: $b^2 - 4ac = 5^2 - 4(2)(6) = 25 - 48 = -23$

Since the discriminant is negative, the solution has two complex roots. You can see that if you were solving this equation using the quadratic formula, you would be taking the square root of a negative, and therefore, the result would be a complex number.

7. C Factoring quadratic equations when the coefficient of the x^2 term is not 1 is generally harder. Therefore, to solve this equation, let's use the quadratic formula.

$$x = \frac{-b \pm \sqrt{b^2 - 4ac}}{2a}$$

$2x^2 + 7x + 6 = 0$

$a = 2, b = 7, c = 6$

$x = [-7 \pm \sqrt{(49 - 48)}]/4$

$= [-7 \pm 1]/4$

$= (-7 + 1)/4 = -3/2$ or $= (-7 - 1)/4 = -2$

$x = -3/2$ or -2

8. A To complete the square, you can think of taking half of "b" and squaring that.

$x^2 - 8x = -10$

$x^2 - 8x + (-4)^2 = -10 + (-4)^2$

$x^2 - 8x + 16 = -10 + 16$

$(x - 4)^2 = 6$

If you add 16 to both sides, you can create a perfect square polynomial on the left side.

9. A The question is essentially asking you to solve the quadratic equation. The zeros of the equation are where the graph will cross the x-axis, and this is where the quadratic equation will equal zero. Therefore, set y to zero and solve the quadratic.

There are several ways to solve this quadratic equation. Here are two methods.

Method 1: Factoring

In this case, we won't divide by 2, since it will cause fractions and more confusion. Therefore, we want to find two integers that multiply to –12 (which is equal to ac) and add to 1 (which is equal to b). –3 and 4 satisfy these criteria.

$2x^2 + x - 6 = 0$

$2x^2 + 4x - 3x - 6 = 0$

$2x(x + 2) - 3(x + 2) = 0$

$(2x - 3)(x + 2) = 0$

Now, set each binomial to zero, and solve for x:

$2x - 3 = 0, x = 3/2$

$x + 2 = 0, x = -2$

Method 2: Quadratic Formula

Sometimes it is hard to factor when the coefficient of the x^2 term does not equal 1. The quadratic formula is the next easiest way to solve the quadratic equation. Remember that the quadratic formula is on the formula sheet, so refer to that if you forget it.

$$x = \frac{-b \pm \sqrt{b^2 - 4ac}}{2a}$$

$2x^2 + x - 6 = 0$

$a = 2, b = 1, c = -6$

$x = [-1 \pm \sqrt{(1 + 48)}]/4$

$= (-1 \pm 7)/4$

$x = (-1 + 7)/4 = 3/2$ OR $x = (-1 - 7)/4 = -2$

$(3/2, 0); (-2, 0)$

10. D Since the quadratic equation has a coefficient in front of the x^2 term, it might be difficult to factor. Use the quadratic equation to solve. Remember that this formula is also included on the formula sheet if you have trouble memorizing it.

$$x = \frac{-b \pm \sqrt{b^2 - 4ac}}{2a}$$

$4x^2 - 4x + 2$

$a = 4, b = -4, c = 2$

$x = [4 \pm \sqrt{(16 - 32)}]/8$

$x = [4 \pm \sqrt{-16}]/8$

Note that we are taking the square root of a negative number. We know the roots will be complex and not real.

$x = [4 \pm 4i]/8$

$x = 0.5 \pm 0.5i$

Algebra & Graphing: Graphing Quadratics

Graphs of Quadratic Functions

The graph of a quadratic function is a parabola. One typical form for quadratic functions is $y = ax^2 + bx + c$, where a, b, and c are coefficients, and x and y are variables.

All quadratic functions are symmetric along a line called the axis of symmetry. The parabola intersects its axis of symmetry at a point called the vertex.

Vertex

The first step in graphing quadratic functions is to find the vertex:

1. The x-coordinate of the vertex follows the formula $x = -b/2a$.

2. Find the y-coordinate of the vertex by plugging x from step 1 into the quadratic function and solving for y.

Plot the vertex on the coordinate plane.

Up or Down Shape

Next, check whether a is positive or negative. If a is positive, the graph opens upward. If a is negative, the graph opens downward. Note that a cannot be zero. Often, you can eliminate one or more options from a multiple-choice question by checking a for the direction of the graph.

Axis of Symmetry

Next, find the axis of symmetry by using the x-coordinate of the vertex. The equation for the axis of symmetry is

x = x-coordinate of the vertex

A point on one side of this line will also have a mirror point on the other side.

Intercepts

The y-intercept can be found by plugging in zero for x and solving for y. The x-intercepts can be found by plugging in zero for y and solving for x. Note that not every quadratic function will intercept the x-axis. The x-intercepts are also known as the zeros or roots of the quadratic equation.

Vertex Form

Another representation of quadratic functions is $a(x - h)^2 + k$. In this form, the vertex can be found by inspection:

vertex = (h, k), where h is the x-coordinate, and k is the y-coordinate of the vertex.

Note that the a coefficient is the same in both forms of the quadratic function.

Maximum and Minimum

The graphs of quadratic equations are parabola-shaped (U-shaped) either up or down. If it opens upward, then it will have a minimum point, which will be the vertex of the graph. If it opens downward, then it will have a maximum, which will also be the vertex of the parabola. Therefore, to determine whether there is a maximum or minimum, simply determine whether the graph opens up or down.

When asked to find the maximum or minimum point of a quadratic function, find the vertex and take the value of the y-coordinate.

Example: Let's graph the quadratic $y = 2x^2 - 4x - 2$.

First, note that a, the coefficient of the x^2 term, is equal to 2, which is positive. Therefore, we know that the graph will open upward and that the vertex will be the minimum point on the graph.

Next, let's find the vertex. The x-coordinate of the vertex equals $-b/2a$.
Here, a = 2, b = –4.

x-coordinate of vertex = $-(-4)/2(2) = 1$

Find the y-coordinate by plugging in the x-coordinate:
$y = 2(1)^2 - 4(1) - 2 = 2 - 4 - 2 = -4$
Vertex = (1, –4)

The axis of symmetry is the vertical line over which the graph is symmetric. It goes through the vertex. Since it is a vertical line, the x-coordinate remains constant. Here, the x-coordinate of the vertex is 1.
Axis of Symmetry: x = 1.

Next, let's find the intercepts. The y-intercept is where the graph crosses the y-axis and x = 0.
$y = 2(0)^2 - 4(0) - 2 = -2$
y-intercept = (0, –2)

You know that the graph is symmetric about the line x = 1. You also know that one point on the graph is (0, –2), which is one unit to the left of the axis of symmetry in the x direction.

So, if you move one unit to the right of the axis of symmetry (when x = 2), you will also have a y-coordinate on the graph that is at –2. You now have a third coordinate point, (2, –2).

This gives you enough information to sketch the graph.

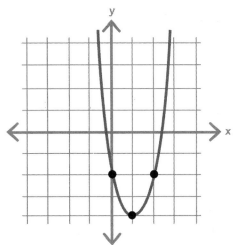

Graphing Quadratics: Practice

1. If the equation y = –3x² – 7x + 8 was graphed, what would the y-intercept be?

   A. –7

   B. –3

   C. –2

   D. 8

2. Where is the vertex of the following equation?

   $-5x^2 + 7x + 4 = 0$

   A. Minimum, below x-axis

   B. Maximum, below x-axis

   C. Minimum, above x-axis

   D. Maximum, above x-axis

3. Which quadratic function has no real solutions?

A.
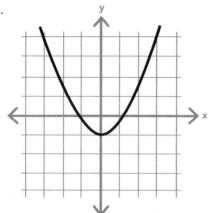

C.
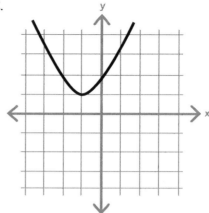

B.
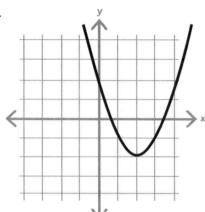

D.
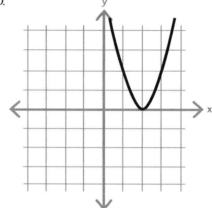

4. Find the vertex of the following function:

$$y = x^2 - 6x + 8$$

A. $(3, -1)$

B. $(1, -6)$

C. $(-2, -4)$

D. $(2, -6)$

5. What are the x-intercepts of the following function?

$$y = x^2 - 6x + 8$$

A. (4, 0) and (2, 0)
B. (8, 0) and (1, 0)
C. (0, 8) and (0, 1)
D. (−8, 0) and (1, 0)

6. A person standing on the side of a cliff throws a stone toward the ocean. The height of the stone is a function of time, which is represented by the following equation:

$$h(t) = -16t^2 + 96t + 112$$

When does the stone reach a height of 192 feet?

A. t = 6
B. t = 2 and t = 10
C. t = 7
D. t = 5 and t = 1

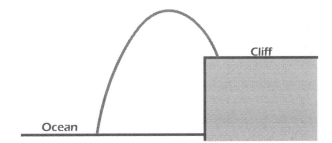

7. A person standing on the side of a cliff throws a stone toward the ocean. The height of the stone is a function of time, which is represented by this equation:
$$h(t) = -16t^2 + 96t + 112$$

When does the stone hit the ocean?

A. t = 1
B. t = 5
C. t = 7
D. t = 8

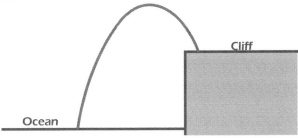

8. A parabola has a vertex (4, 3) and a vertical axis of symmetry. The parabola passes through points (5, 5) and (7, p). What is the value of p?

   A. 9
   B. 18
   C. 21
   D. 28

9. What is the y-intercept of the following equation?

   $$y = x^2 - 6x + 8$$

   A. (3, –1)
   B. (6, –1)
   C. (0, 8)
   D. (8, 0)

10. Which quadratic function is represented by this equation?

    $$y = -x^2 - 4x + 3$$

A.

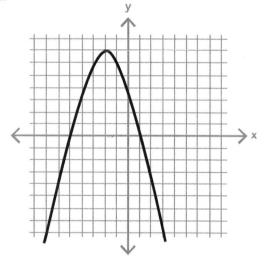

B.

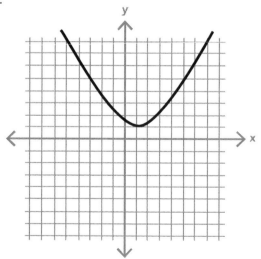

C.
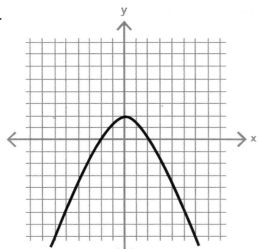

D.
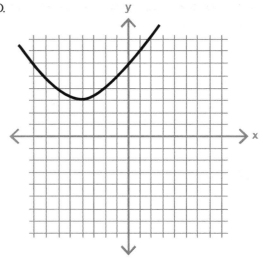

Graphing Quadratics: Answer Explanations

1. D The y-intercept on a graph is where it crosses the y-axis and, therefore, when x is equal to 0. Plug x = 0 into the equation and solve for y:
$$y = -3x^2 - 7x + 8$$
$$y = -3(0)^2 - 7(0) + 8$$
$$y = 8$$

2. D The first step would be to find the number of real roots of this equation to see how many times it crosses the x-axis. The easiest way to do this is to use the discriminant.
$$-5x^2 + 7x + 4 = 0$$
$$a = -5, b = 7, c = 4$$

Discriminant: $b^2 - 4ac = (7)^2 - 4(-5)(4) = 49 + 80 = 129$

Remember, if the discriminant is positive, there will be 2 real roots to the quadratic equation.

Also, from the equation, since a is negative, we can tell that the parabola opens downward. If it opens downward and there are 2 roots, it means the parabola will cross the x-axis twice, the vertex must be a maximum, and it must be above the x-axis.

3. C When looking at the graph of a quadratic equation, the solutions can be found by looking for the zeros. The zeros are the places where the graph crosses the x-axis. Another way to think about it is that the zeros are the x-intercepts. This question is asking which quadratic equation has no real solutions; in other words, which graph does not cross the x-axis.

4. A A simple formula can be used to find the vertex of a quadratic graph when the quadratic equation is in the standard form $y = ax^2 + bx + c$.

The coefficients for this quadratic function are $a = 1$; $b = -6$; $c = 8$.

The x-coordinate of the vertex is equal to $-b/2a$. You can remember this easily, as it is derived from the quadratic formula.
The x-coordinate of the vertex: $-b/2a = -(-6)/2 = 3$.

If you know the x-coordinate of any point on a graph, you can plug it into the equation and solve for y to find the y-coordinate. Therefore, plug 3 into the function:
$$y = x^2 - 6x + 8$$
$$= 3^2 - 6(3) + 8$$
$$= 9 - 18 + 8$$
$$= -1$$

The vertex is $(3, -1)$.

5. A Remember that regardless of the type of equation (linear, quadratic, and so on), if a question is asking you for the x-intercepts, it is asking for the points where the graph hits the x-axis. This happens when $y = 0$, so plug in 0 for y to solve:
$$x^2 - 6x + 8 = y$$
$$x^2 - 6x + 8 = 0$$

To solve this quadratic equation, first check if the quadratic can be factored. You want to find two integers that multiply to 8 and add to -6. The two integers that satisfy this condition are -4 and -2:
$$x^2 - 6x + 8 = 0$$
$$(x - 4)(x - 2) = 0$$

Now, set each binomial equal to zero, and solve for x:
$$x - 4 = 0, x = 4$$
$$x - 2 = 0, x = 2$$

The x-intercepts are $(4, 0)$ and $(2, 0)$.

6. D Plug the height into the equation and solve for t: $192 = -16t^2 + 96t + 112$

Rearrange into a standard quadratic equation with all terms on one side: $0 = -16t^2 + 96t - 80$

Divide all terms by -16, so the coefficient of t^2 is 1: $0 = t^2 - 6t + 5$

Factor the quadratic equation: $0 = (t - 5)(t - 1)$

Set each binomial to zero, and solve:
$t - 5 = 0, t = 5$
$t - 1 = 0, t = 1$

7. C The question asks when the stone hits the ocean. At that point, the height will be zero. Therefore, plug in 0 for the height, and solve for the time:
$0 = -16t^2 + 96t + 112$

Divide all terms by -16, so the coefficient of t^2 is 1:
$0 = t^2 - 6t - 7$

Factor the quadratic equation:
$0 = (t - 7)(t + 1)$

Set each binomial to zero, and solve:
$t - 7 = 0, t = 7$
$t + 1 = 0, t = -1$

Since time must be positive, the only valid answer is $t = 7$.

8. C Since you have been given the vertex of the parabola, it is best to use the following form of the quadratic equation:
$y = a(x - h)^2 + k$

Remember that in this form, the vertex = (h, k).

In this problem, the vertex is given as $(4, 3)$ so $h = 4$ and $k = 3$. We have two of the three coefficients needed to find this quadratic equation. We must still solve for a.
$y = a(x - 4)^2 + 3$

We are given the point $(5, 5)$, so we can plug it in to find the value of a:
$5 = a(5 - 4)^2 + 3$
$5 = a + 3$
$a = 2$

The full form of the quadratic equation is $y = 2(x - 4)^2 + 3$.

Now, plug in the point $(7, p)$:
$y = 2(x - 4)^2 + 3$
$p = 2(7 - 4)^2 + 3$
$p = 18 + 3 = 21$

9. C Any time a question asks you to find the y-intercept, it is asking you to find out where the graph will cross the y-axis. For anything to cross the y-axis, the x-coordinate of the point must be 0. Therefore, plug 0 for x into the equation and solve for y to find the y-intercept.

$$y = x^2 - 6x + 8$$
$$y = 0^2 - 6(0) + 8$$
$$y = 8$$

Therefore, $x = 0$, $y = 8$.

10. A When analyzing the graphs of quadratic functions, follow the steps:

Step 1. Determine whether the graph opens up or down. Check this by looking at the coefficient of the x^2 term.

Step 2. Find the y-intercept by plugging 0 for x into the quadratic equation.

Step 3. Find the vertex or line of symmetry.

Step 4. If you have yet to find the graph, determine the zeros or solutions of the quadratic to find the y-intercepts.

For this problem, you are given the quadratic equation $y = -x^2 - 4x + 3$.

The coefficient a, which is the coefficient of the x^2 term, is –1. Whenever the coefficient a is negative, the graph will open downward. The only graphs that open down are answers A and C. Eliminate B and D.

Next, find the y-intercept. The y-intercept crosses the y-axis when $x = 0$. Plug in $x = 0$, and solve for y:

$$y = -x^2 - 4x + 3$$
$$y = -0^2 - 4(0) + 3 = 3$$

Graph A has a y-intercept of 3, while graph C does not.

Algebra & Graphing: Advanced Functions & Graphing

Graphing Absolute Value Equations

When graphing equations involving absolute values, the key is to remember that absolute value operations always return positive values. The graph to the right shows the following function:

$$f(x) = |x|.$$

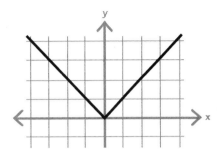

As you can see, when x is positive, the graph follows the line y = x. When x is negative, y is still positive; therefore, you get a mirror image of the graph.

To graph absolute value equations that are not of the standard form, (for example, graphing $f(x) = |x + 2| - 3$), use the rules of graph transformations you learned in the Lesson: Functions & Equations, Operations with Functions.

Graphing Multiple Inequalities

You might be asked to graph a system of inequalities on the same graph. Just follow the standard method for graphing each inequality, but plot the results on the same coordinate plane. If the system has an "or," leave everything shaded. If the system of inequalities has an "and," only shade the region of overlap.

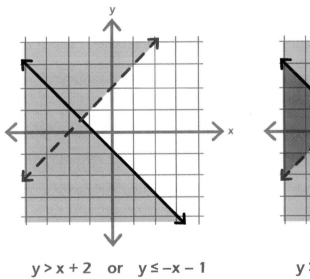

y > x + 2   or   y ≤ −x − 1

The entire shaded region is the solution to this set of inequalities.

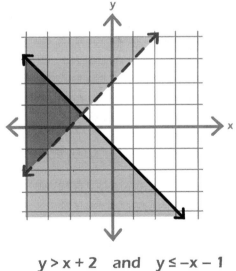

y > x + 2   and   y ≤ −x − 1

The overlapped darker region is the solution to this set of inequalities.

Exponential Growth and Decay

Exponential functions can either grow extremely quickly or decline at a rapid rate. Whereas the rate of change for a straight line is the same, the rate of change for an exponential function increases or decreases along the graph.

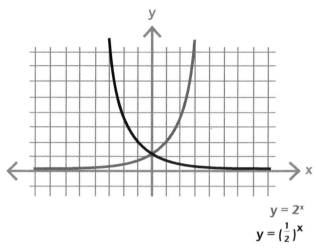

The graph to the right shows two exponential functions: a growth and a decay. As you can see, the rate of change quickly increases for the exponential growth graph in gray and quickly decreases for the exponential decay graph in black.

$y = 2^x$

$y = (\frac{1}{2})^x$

The general forms for exponential growth or decay formulas are

>Exponential Growth: $y = a(1 + r)^x$
>Exponential Decay: $y = a(1 - r)^x$

where a is the initial amount, r is the rate of growth/decay, and x is the number of time intervals.

For example, if you had a petri dish that started with 10 bacteria and doubled every hour, how many bacteria would there be after 6 hours?

>a = 10 bacteria (initial amount in petri dish)
>r = 1 (since it doubles, the rate of increase is 100%)
>x = 6 hours
>
>$y = a(1 + r)^x = 10(1 + 1)^6 = 10(2)^6 = 640$

Compound Interest

Compound interest is a common example of exponential growth. When money is invested at a fixed interest rate over a period, that money grows by compound interest. The word "compound" means that the interest earned in one period also earns interest in subsequent periods.

Compound interest uses the same formula as an exponential growth problem, though it is often written using the following variables:

$$A = P(1 + r/n)^{nt}$$

Where:
A = accumulated amount
P = principal (amount invested or initial amount)
r = interest rate
n = number of periods that interest compounds
t = time of the investment

For example, suppose you put $100 in the bank with a 2% interest rate that compounds quarterly. You can use the formula to calculate how much money you will have after 3 years.
In this case, P = 100, r = 0.02, n = 4, t = 3:

$$A = 100(1 + 0.02/4)^{4 \times 3} = 100(1.005)^{12} = 106.17$$

There is a special case of compound interest called continuous compounding, which is expressed using the number *e*. The number e, which equals approximately 2.718, is an important constant used in advanced math topics such as logarithms. The formula for continuous compound interest is

$$A = Pe^{rt}$$

where A is accumulated amount, P is principal, e is the mathematical constant, r is the interest rate, and t is the time of investment.

Graphing Nonlinear Equations

A straight line will not represent nonlinear equations that are graphed. These equations might have variables raised to powers or the roots of variables. For example $y = 3x^2$, $y = 5x^{1/2}$

If you are familiar with the standard graphs of that nonlinear equation – for example, the graphs of quadratic equations – then proceed with your usual methods of graphing those equations. For other nonlinear equations, plugging in points will be your best approach.

Be sure also to look out for any limits or restrictions on the domain of the function. For example, you cannot take the square root of a negative number or divide by zero.

Algebra & Graphing: Advanced Functions & Graphing

Advanced Functions & Graphing: Practice

1. A person invests $1,000 in a savings account at an interest rate of 2%, compounded semiannually. How much will have accumulated in the savings account at the end of 5 years?

    A. $1000(0.01)^{10}$

    B. $1000(1.02)^5$

    C. $1000(1.01)^{10}$

    D. $1000(1.01)^{20}$

2. Which equations does the graph below represent?

    A. $y \leq x$ or $y \geq -x$

    B. $y \geq x$ or $y \leq -x$

    C. $y \leq x$ and $y \geq -x$

    D. $y \geq x$ and $y \leq -x$

    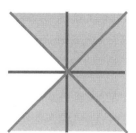

3. You have two different types of bacteria in petri dishes. Both start with the same number of bacteria. Bacteria A doubles every 2 days, and Bacteria B triples every 3 days. After 12 days, which bacteria will have increased the most?

    A. Bacteria A

    B. Bacteria B

    C. Equal

    D. Not enough information

4. Which of the following represents a population (P) that starts with 100 and increases by 10% each year (t)?

    A. $P = 100 + 0.10t$

    B. $P = 100(0.10)^t$

    C. $P = 100(1.1)^t$

    D. $P = 100(1.1)t$

5. The following is the graph of which inequalities?

A. $y \leq -2x$ or $y \geq 4x$
B. $y \leq -2x$ and $y \geq 4x$
C. $y \geq -2x$ or $y \leq 4x$
D. $y \geq -2x$ and $y \leq 4x$

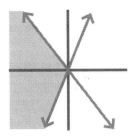

6. What is the equation for the graph below?

A. $f(x) = |x - 3|$
B. $f(x) = |x + 3|$
C. $f(x) = |x| - 3$
D. $f(x) = |x| + 3$

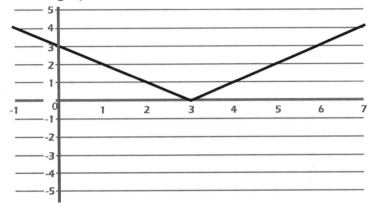

7. What equation does the graph below represent?

A. $y = x^3$
B. $y = (-x)^3$
C. $y = -3^x$
D. $y = x^{-3}$

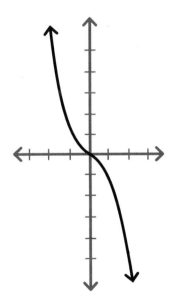

8. What is the equation for the graph below?

A. $f(x) = 2\sqrt{(x-2)}$
B. $f(x) = 2\sqrt{(x+2)}$
C. $f(x) = 3/(x-2)$
D. $f(x) = 3/(x+2)$

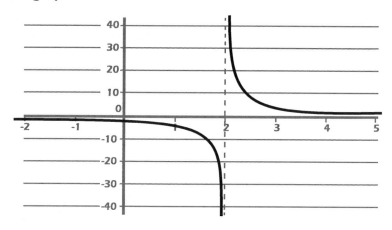

9. The graph below is of an ellipse. What is the equation for the graph?

A. $(x-4)^2/2 + (y-2)^2 = 1$
B. $(x-4)^2/4 + (y-2)^2 = 1$
C. $(x-4)^2/8 + (y-2)^2/2 = 1$
D. $(x-4)^2/8 + (y-2)^2/2 = 1$

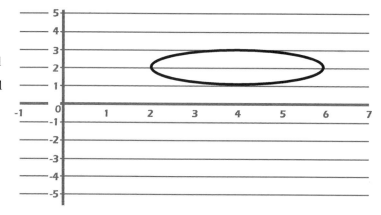

10. You have 200 grams of a radioactive substance with a half-life of 5 years. How much of the substance is left after 20 years?

A. 12.5 g
B. 25 g
C. 50 g
D. 100 g

Advanced Functions & Graphing: Answer Explanations

1. C   This question is a straightforward testing of the formula for compound interest.

$$A = P(1+r/n)^{nt}$$

where the principal is 1000, the rate is 2%, the number of times per year is 2, and the time 5 years.

$P = 1000$
$r = 0.02$ (2% written as a decimal)
$n = 2$ (for semiannual compounding)
$t = 5$

$$A = 1000(1 + 0.02/2)^{2 \times 5}$$
$$= 1000(1 + 0.01)^{10}$$
$$1000(1.01)^{10}$$

2. A   First, you can tell that the graph represents an OR statement because all the areas that satisfy either inequality have been shaded.

Let's look at the line $y = x$, which has the positive slope. All the points below that are shaded. Therefore, $y \leq x$ has been shaded.

Now, let's look at the line $y = -x$, which has the negative slope. All the points greater than that are shaded. Therefore, $y \geq -x$ has been shaded.

$$y \leq x \text{ OR } y \geq -x$$

3. B   Assume both start with y as the initial value.

Bacteria A doubles every 2 days. This can be modeled as $y(2)^{t/2}$
Bacteria B triples every 3 days. This can be modeled as $y(3)^{t/3}$

Now, t is 12 days, so plug 12 in and compare.
Bacteria A: $y(2)^{12/2} = y(2)^6 = 64y$
Bacteria B: $y(3)^{12/3} = y(3)^4 = 81y$

4. C   This is a classic exponential growth question. The problem gives you both the initial value and the growth rate.

$$P = \text{Initial Value } (1 + \text{Growth Rate})^t$$
$$P = 100(1 + 0.10)^t$$
$$P = 100(1.1)^t$$

5. B Let's start by looking at the line y = –2x. This is the line with the negative slope. The shaded section of the graph represents all y-values less than –2x. Therefore, look for answers that include the line y ≤ –2x, which are answers A and B.

The next thing to look at is whether you want "and" or "or". In this case, it is clear that only the overlap has been graphed, so look for "and".

6. A The easiest way to approach questions such as this is to plug in points to see which make the equations true. You can also look at the transformation of the standard absolute value graph.

You can see that the graph passes through (3, 0). Plug x = 3 into each answer choice, and see which results in f(x) = 0.
Answers A and C are the only choices that satisfy this coordinate pair.

Now, choose any other point on the graph, such as (2, 1).
In this case, answer A is the only answer that works.

Another way to approach this question is to think about how the graph shifts from the standard absolute value equation. The graph of f(x) = |x| is a v-shaped graph that goes through the origin. Now, let's look at the shift of each answer choice:

  A: f(x) = |x – 3| will shift the graph 3 units to the right. This is correct.
  B: f(x) = |x + 3| will shift the graph 3 units to the left.
  C: f(x) = |x| – 3 will shift the graph 3 units down.
  D: f(x) = |x| + 3 will shift the graph 3 units up.

7. B Plug values from the graph into the options to see which equation is true. On the graph, when x = 1, y = –1.

  Option A. When x = 1, y = x^3 = 1
  Option B: When x = 1, y = $(-x)^3$ = –1 (Correct)
  Option C. When x = 1, y = -3^1 = –3
  Option D. When x = 1, y = x^{-3} = 1

8. C Approach questions such as this by examining the type of graph to see which type of equation it represents. You can plug points from the graph into each answer choice to see which one is valid.

In this case, you can see that the graph represents a function that never hits the line, x = 2. When a function approaches a line but never reaches it, it is called an asymptote. Therefore, x=2 is known as the vertical asymptote, which is covered more in Module 8. In answers A and B, you have functions with square roots. You know that these will have a wide range of x-values that are invalid, as you cannot take the square root of a negative number. Eliminate these answer choices.

Now, let's think more about the implication of the vertical asymptote. At x = 2, the equation cannot have a valid answer. Plug x = 2 into the remaining equations, and see which one gives an invalid answer with a division by zero error.

For answer C: f(x) = 3/(x – 2), when x = 2, f(x) = 3/0; therefore, at x = 2, this function would have an asymptote.

9. B If you are unfamiliar with the general form of the equation of an ellipse, the easiest way is to plug in points from the graph to see which make the equations true.

Method 1: Plugging in Points
Choose coordinate pairs on the graph, and plug them into the answer choices to see which give valid answers.
The only equations that work for the point (4, 1) are in answers A and B.
If you also try the coordinate pair (2, 2), answer B is the only answer choice that works.

Method 2: Standard Equation for Ellipse
The center of the ellipse is (4, 2). In the x-direction, the radius of the ellipse is 2. In the y-direction, the radius of the ellipse is 1.

The equation of a general ellipse is $(x - h)^2/r_x^2 + (y - k)^2/r_y^2 = 1$

In this problem, the center is at (4, 2) = (h, k); h = 4, k = 2.
The radius in x-direction = r_x = 2.
The radius in y-direction = r_y = 1.

Plug those values into the standard form of the ellipse equation:
$(x - 4)^2/4 + (y - 2)^2 = 1$.

10. A This is a classic exponential decay problem. The half-life of a substance is the time it takes for half the substance to decay. Let's use the formula for exponential decay:

$y = a(1 - r)^x$

a = 200g (the initial amount of the substance)
r = 1/2 (the amount decreases by 1/2)
x = 4 (there are 4 time intervals, since it decays by 1/2 every 5 years)

$y = 200(1 - 1/2)^4$
$= 200(1/2)^4$
$= 200(1/16)$
$= 12.5$

Algebra & Graphing: Algebra Word Problems

Translating Word Problems into Equations

Algebraic word problems are similar to the word problems you encountered involving basic operations, and the same strategies are applicable. However, they require you to form an equation containing a variable, and that adds a level of difficulty.

Let's begin with a simple example of translating a given situation into a mathematical expression:

Nadine has only red shirts and blue shirts. She has 29 red shirts and 43 shirts total. How many blue shirts does she have?

Use key words such as "total" to determine the function that needs to be performed. Then, use a variable to represent any unknown quantities.

Red shirts + Blue shirts = Total shirts
$$29 + b = 43$$

In the equation above, b represents the number of blue shirts Nadine has. Solve for the variable b by subtracting 29 from both sides:
$$29 + b - 29 = 43 - 29$$
$$b = 14, \text{ Nadine has 14 blue shirts.}$$

The most complex algebra word problems involve multiple unknown quantities. Whenever possible, represent all unknown quantities in terms of a single variable. This is easy to do when a specific relationship is given for two or more unknowns.

Example: Colleen bought twice as many oranges as apples at the grocery store. If she bought 45 apples and oranges, how many apples did Colleen buy?

Choose as the variable the quantity the question asks you to find, then define the relationship between that variable and any other unknown quantities.

Let x represent the number of apples Colleen buys.
Therefore, the number of oranges is 2x.

Then, write and solve an equation using only 1 variable:
$$\text{Apples} + \text{Oranges} = 45$$
$$x + 2x = 45$$
$$3x = 45$$
$$x = 15, \text{ Colleen buys 15 apples.}$$

Algebra Word Problems: Practice

1. Andrew has pennies, dimes, and quarters. He has a total of $8.70. There are two times as many pennies as quarters. There are six times as many dimes as quarters. How many dimes does he have?

   A. 6
   B. 10
   C. 60
   D. 87

2. Find three consecutive odd integers, such that the sum of the third and twice the first is 7 more than twice the third. What is the largest number of the three?

   A. 7
   B. 11
   C. 13
   D. 15

3. An airplane takes 5 hours to fly from San Francisco to Boston, but 6 hours to return. The wind velocity is 50 mph and increases the plane's speed from San Francisco to Boston but decreases the plane's speed from Boston to San Francisco. What is the average speed of the airplane? (hint: rate x time = distance)

   A. 450 mph
   B. 500 mph
   C. 550 mph
   D. 600 mph

4. Two trains leave Chicago and New York at the same time. They move toward each other with constant speeds. The train from Chicago is moving at a speed of 40 miles per hour. The train from New York is moving at a speed of 60 miles per hour. The distance between Chicago and New York is 1000 miles. How long after their departure will they meet?

   A. 10
   B. 15
   C. 17
   D. 20

5. Christine's father is 3 times her age. Four years ago, he was 4 times older than she was then. How old is Christine now?

   A. 4
   B. 12
   C. 15
   D. 18

6. A woman on a bike and a man in a car leave a restaurant at the same time. The woman heads due east, and the man goes due west. If the woman is biking at 15 mph and the car is traveling at 35 mph, in how many hours will they be 300 miles apart?

   A. 2
   B. 4
   C. 6
   D. 8

7. A door is 3 times as long as it is wide. If the area is 108 square feet when the length and width are each doubled, how wide was the door originally?

   A. 2
   B. 3
   C. 4
   D. 5

8. How much pure water (with no saline) would you need to add to 4 liters (L) of an 80% saline solution to make it a 20% saline solution?

   A. 1 L
   B. 8 L
   C. 12 L
   D. 16 L

9. Two trains, A & B, are 540 km apart and traveling toward each other on parallel tracks. Train A travels 40 km per hour. Train B travels 10 km per hour faster than A. In how many hours will they meet?

   A. 6 hours

   B. 7 hours

   C. 8 hours

   D. 9 hours

10. The sum of the digits of a two-digit number is 10. When the digits are reversed, the number decreases by 36. Find the original two-digit number.

    A. 84

    B. 73

    C. 64

    D. 53

Algebra Word Problems: Answer Explanations

1. C   You need to assign a variable to one of your unknowns. In this case, let's choose the number of quarters and set that equal to q. Now, relate all the unknowns in terms of that variable:

Number of quarters: q

Number of pennies: 2q

Number of dimes: 6q

Now, make an equation. Since you know the total amount of money and the value of each coin, you can write the following equation:

(0.25)(Number of Quarters) + (0.10)(Number of dimes) + (0.01)(Number of pennies) = $8.70

(0.25)(q) + (0.10)(6q) + (0.01)(2q) = $8.70

0.25q + 0.6q + 0.02q = $8.70

0.87q = 8.70

q = 10

The number of dimes is 6q = 6(10) = 60.

2. D For algebra word problems, you need to assign a variable to the unknown. You could set the smallest integer to x. Then, you can find out what the other two numbers are in terms of x.

Since we are dealing with consecutive odd integers, the second number will be two more than the first, and the third number will be two more than the second.

Therefore, the three unknowns are x, x + 2, and x + 4.

The sum of the third and twice the first is 7 more than twice the third. Take each word and translate it into an equation:

Sum = addition, third = x + 4, twice = multiply by 2, first = x, more = add

(x + 4) + 2(x) = 7 + 2(x + 4)	Translate words into equation.
x + 4 + 2x = 7 + 2x + 8	Distribute.
3x + 4 = 15 + 2x	Combine like terms on each side.
3x = 11 + 2x	Subtract 4 from each side.
x = 11	Subtract 2x from each side.
Integers are 11, 13, 15	You solved for x, the first. So find the next 2 consecutive odd integers.

3. C The one formula to remember when dealing with travel problems is that Distance = Rate x Time.

For any algebra word problem, assign a variable to the unknown. In this case, the unknown is the average speed of the airplane. Let's assign r to represent this value.

Now, set up equations. For the trip from San Francisco to Boston, the airplane was flying at a rate of r, but the wind was helping the plane fly faster; therefore, the rate was (r + 50). The distance the plane flew is then the rate x time = (r + 50) x 5.

For the return trip, the airplane was flying at a rate of r. The wind was going against the plane; therefore, the rate was (r − 50). The distance the plane flew back was then the rate x time = (r − 50) x 6

The distances were the same in each case, so we can set the two equations equal to each other.

6(r − 50) = 5(r + 50)	Set distances equal to each other
6r − 300 = 5r + 250	Distribute on both sides
6r = 5r + 550	Add 300 to both sides
r = 550	Subtract 5r from both sides

4. A The classic train problem. This is a travel word problem, where the important equation to remember is that distance = rate x time.

First, let us assign a variable to the unknown. In this case, we want to find out how long it is after they departed that they meet. So, let's assign t to represent this time.

The distance the train that left Chicago travels is the rate x time = 40(t)
The distance the train that left New York travels is the rate x time = 60(t)

If the distance between the two cities is 1000 miles, the total distance the trains travel is 1000. Therefore, add the distances, and set them equal to 1000:

$40t + 60t = 1000$

$100t = 1000$

$t = 10$

Time = 10 hours

5. B Let's choose the variable c to represent Christine's age now and f to represent her father's age. Now, set up equations with the two variables. Translating the words into equations:

Christine's father is 3 times as old as she is:
$\quad f = 3c$

4 years ago, he was 4 times older than she was then:
$\quad f - 4 = 4(c - 4)$

Now, we have two equations and can solve. You can use any appropriate method to solve. Here, we will use substitution. Substitute 3c for f in the second equation:

$\quad f = 3c$
$\quad f - 4 = 4(c - 4)$
$\quad 3c - 4 = 4(c - 4)$

Now, solve for c:
$\quad 3c - 4 = 4(c - 4)$
$\quad 3c - 4 = 4c - 16$
$\quad -4 = c - 16$
$\quad c = 12$

Christine's age is 12, making her father 36.

Algebra & Graphing: Algebra Word Problems

6. C Since the man and woman are traveling in exactly opposite directions, the distances they travel can be added together to find out how far apart they are at a given time.

The distance traveled can be calculated by multiplying the rate of travel by the time traveled. You know the rate and the total distance for both the man and woman, so use a variable such as t to represent the time they have traveled. Since they have both traveled for the same amount of time, you can use one variable for both people.

15 (the speed of the woman on the bike) x t + 35 (the speed of the man on the bike) x t = 300 (the total distance they have gone in opposite directions)

Then, solve for time:
$15t + 35t = 300$
$50t = 300$
$t = 6$ hours

7. B The trickiest part of this problem is visualizing the door's dimensions. Draw a diagram to help with this.

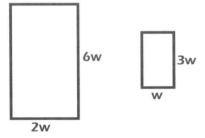

Label all the dimensions in terms of the original width because that is the quantity for which you are asked to solve.

The original width should be labeled with a variable. We'll use w.
The original length is equal to 3 times the width: 3w.
The new width is doubled: 2w.
The new length is doubled: 2 x 3w = 6w.

The area of a rectangle is determined by length times width, so the formula is

$2w \times 6w = 108$ sq ft
$12w^2 = 108$ sq ft
$w^2 = 9$ sq ft
$w = 3$ ft

8. C You need to solve for the amount of water to add. Let's create a variable for this, called w.

The amount of saline in a solution can be found by multiplying the amount of solution by its concentration. Since adding pure water does not change the amount of saline, you can set up the following equation:

Amount of saline in water + amount of saline in 80% solution = amount of saline in 20% solution.

$$0(w) + (0.80)(4) = (0.20)(4 + w)$$
$$3.2 = 0.8 + 0.2w$$
$$2.4 = 0.2w$$
$$w = 12$$

9. A When solving a traveling problem, keep in mind the three aspects: rate, time, and distance, where rate x time = distance.

Rate:
    Train A: 40 km per hour
    Train B: 10 km per hour faster than Train A = 50 km per hour

Time:
    This is unknown but is the same for both trains, so let's create a variable to represent the time, t.

Distance:
    The total distance they travel is 540 km.
    Train A travels 40 km per hour x t hours = 40t.
    Train B travels 50 km per hour x t hours = 50t.

Set up an equation to relate the distances:

$$40t + 50t = 540$$
$$90t = 540$$
$$t = 6$$

6 hours

10. B There are two unknowns in this problem: the digit in the tens place and the digit in the ones place for the two-digit number. Let t represent the digit in the tens place and y represent the digit in the ones place. Now, set up equations.

"The sum of the digits is 10"

$t + y = 10$

"When the digits are reversed, the number decreases by 36."
First, determine the value of the original number in terms of t and y. Since the t is in the tens place and the y is in the ones place, the original number equals $10t + y$.
Similarly, the number with its digits reversed will have a value of $10y + t$.

$(10t + y) - (10y + t) = 36$
$9t - 9y = 36$

Now, you have two equations with two unknowns. You can use any appropriate method to solve this system of equations. Let's use substitution:

$t + y = 10$
$t = 10 - y$

Substitute the value of t in the second equation:

$9t - 9y = 36$
$9(10 - y) - 9y = 36$
$90 - 9y - 9y = 36$
$90 - 18y = 36$
$-18y = -54$
$y = 3$

Plug back in and solve for t:

$t + y = 10$
$t + 3 = 10$
$t = 7$

The original number has a 7 in the tens place and a 3 in the ones place = 73.

Algebra & Graphing: Module Review

1. Which of the following decreases as x increases, if $x \geq 2$?

   A. $3x^2 - 2x$
   B. $-3x + x^2$
   C. $2x^2 - x^3$
   D. $x^4 - x^2$

2. $|2y| \leq 6$ is graphed as

   A.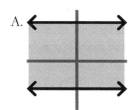

   C.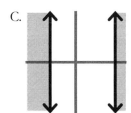

   B.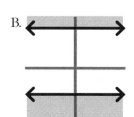

   D.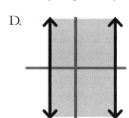

3. What does y equal in the following system of equations?

   $$3x + 5y = -20$$
   $$-2x - 3y = 11$$

   A. -9
   B. -7
   C. 5
   D. 7

4. If the determinant of a quadratic equation equals 1, how many times will the graph cross the x-axis?

   A. 0
   B. 1
   C. 2
   D. Not enough information.

5. What is the equation of the line that passes through (12, 16) and (−4, 8)?

   A. $y = -(1/2)x + 22$
   B. $y = -2x + 40$
   C. $y = 2x - 8$
   D. $y = (1/2)x + 10$

6. If you were solving the following equation by completing the square, what would be the next step?

   Solve: $2x^2 + 7x + 6 = 0$
   1. $x^2 + (7/2)x + 3 = 0$
   2. $x^2 + (7/2)x = -3$

   A. Add 7/2 to both sides.
   B. Add 49/4 to both sides.
   C. Add (49/16)x to both sides.
   D. Add 49/16 to both sides.

7. You have coins in your pocket that are all dimes and quarters. If the number of dimes is four less than 3 times the number of quarters, and the total value of the coins is $1.80, how many quarters do you have?

   A. 2
   B. 4
   C. 6
   D. 8

8. Which of the following equations is represented by the graph below?

    A. $y = x^2$
    B. $y = 2^x$
    C. $y = x^3$
    D. $y = 4x$

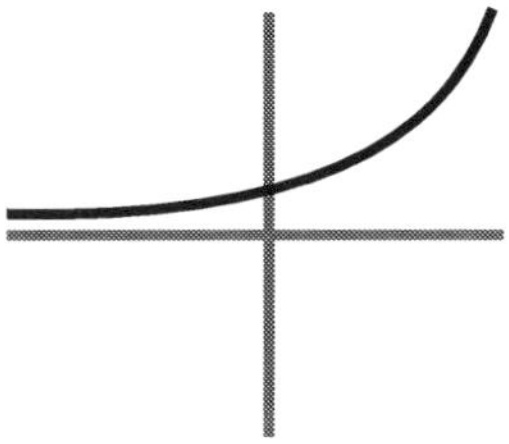

9. Which inequalities would represent a graph with just Quadrant II shaded?

    A. $x \leq 0$ or $y \geq 0$
    B. $x \leq 0$ and $y \leq 0$
    C. $x \geq 0$ or $y \leq 0$
    D. $x \leq 0$ and $y \geq 0$

10. The slope of a line is −3. If you wanted to find the equation of the line, which of these pieces of information would be enough on its own?

    I. a coordinate pair on the line
    II. the y-intercept
    III. the x-intercept

    A. II only
    B. I and II
    C. II and III
    D. I, II, and III

11. Belmont Middle School is headed on a field trip to the museum. Adult tickets are $5, and student tickets are $3. If 50 people are going to the museum, and they pay a total of $162, how many adults are on the trip?

    A. 10
    B. 8
    C. 6
    D. 4

12. **Which of the following could be an explanation of why some lines have undefined slopes?**

    A. Horizontal lines have undefined slopes, since slope is change in y over change in x, and the change in x can be any value, depending on which two points you pick on the line.

    B. Horizontal lines have undefined slopes, since slope is rise over run, and there is no rise for horizontal lines.

    C. Vertical lines have undefined slopes, since slope is rise over run, and you can't determine the rise because you don't know which two points on the vertical line to test.

    D. Vertical lines have undefined slopes. Slope is change in y divided by change in x, but any two points on a vertical line have a 0 change in x, and dividing by 0 is undefined in math.

13. **Simplify the rational expression.**

    $$(x^2 - 5x + 6)/(x^2 + 2x - 15)$$

    A. $(x - 3)(x - 2)/(x - 5)(x + 3)$
    B. $(-5x + 6)/(2x - 15)$
    C. $x + 2$
    D. $(x - 2)/(x + 5)$

14. **What are the solutions for x in the following equation?**

    $$(x - 3)(2x - 1) = 0$$

    A. $3, -\frac{1}{2}$
    B. $-3, -2$
    C. $3, \frac{1}{2}$
    D. $-3, -1$

15. A manufacturer needs 24 tons of a 60% copper alloy. He has tons of 80% copper alloy and 50% copper alloy. How much of the 80% copper alloy does he need to use?

   A. 8 tons
   B. 12 tons
   C. 16 tons
   D. 20 tons

16. When you graph y = –4x² + 3x, what is the y-intercept?

   A. –4
   B. –1
   C. 0
   D. 3

17. An old machine can put 240 caps on bottles every 2 minutes. If the newer model can work at twice the rate of the old machine, how long will it take the new machine to cap 72,000 bottles?

   A. 2.5 hours
   B. 5 hours
   C. 10 hours
   D. 20 hours

18. Which quadratic function has a range of (–∞, 2] ?

   A. y = x² – 4x + 2
   B. y = –x² + 2x + 2
   C. y = –x² + 4x – 2
   D. y = x² + 6x – 4

19. Bob is buying supplies for his office. He has $60 to spend on pens and pencils. Each pen costs $3, and each pencil costs $1. Which graph represents his buying options?

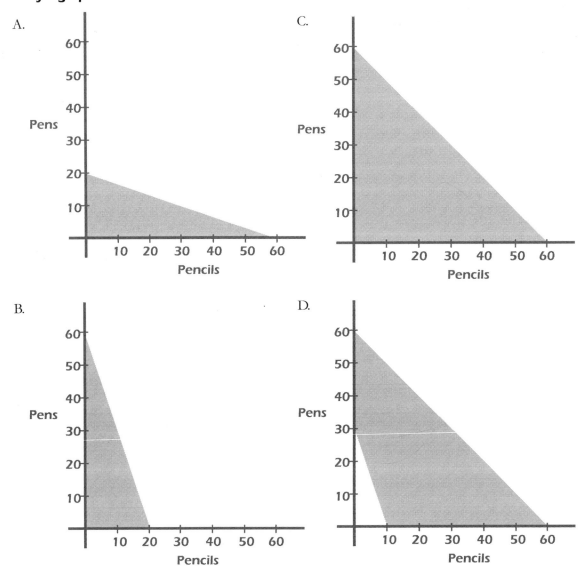

20. A person invests $2000 in a CD at an interest rate of 4% compounded quarterly. How much will the individual have after 10 years?

   A. $2000(1.01)^{10}$

   B. $2000(1.04)^{10}$

   C. $2000(1.01)^{40}$

   D. $2000(1.04^{10} - 1)$

Module Review: Answer Explanations

1. C Let's go through each answer and see what happens as x increases.

A. $3x^2 - 2x$: As x increases, $3x^2$ will increase faster than 2x. Therefore, the difference will increase. You can also try picking numbers and plugging in to see what happens.
   $x = 2, 3(2^2) - 2(2) = 12 - 4 = 8$
   $x = 3, 3(3^2) - 2(3) = 27 - 6 = 21$
As x increases, answer A increases. Eliminate answer A.

B. $-3x + x^2$: As x increases, x^2 will increase faster than 3x, so the overall expression will increase. Let's pick numbers to see.
   $x = 2, -3(2) + 2^2 = -6 + 4 = -2$
   $x = 3, -3(3) + 3^2 = -9 + 9 = 0$.
As x increases, answer B increases. Eliminate answer B.

C. $2x^2 - x^3$: As x increases, x^3 will increase faster than $2x^2$. Therefore, the difference will decrease. Let's pick numbers to see.
   $x = 2, 2(2^2) - 2^3 = 8 - 8 = 0$
   $x = 3, 2(3^2) - 3^3 = 18 - 27 = -9$.
As x increases, answer C decreases. Answer C is correct.

D. $x^4 - x^2$: As x increases, x^4 increases faster than x^2, and the overall expression will increase. Let's pick numbers to see.
   $x = 2, 2^4 - 2^2 = 16 - 4 = 12$
   $x = 3, 3^4 - 3^2 = 81 - 9 = 72$
As x increases, answer D increases. Eliminate answer D.

2. A First, write the absolute value as two separate inequalities connected with *and*. Then, isolate y in each equation.
   $|2y| \leq 6$
   $2y \leq 6, y \leq 3$
   $2y \geq -6, y \geq -3$

Now, graph the two boundary lines, and shade the part that overlaps.
$y \leq 3$ is graphed as a horizontal line at $y = 3$, and you should shade the part below the line.
$y \geq -3$ is graphed as a horizontal line at $y = -3$, and you should shade the part above the line.
The shaded part that overlaps is between the two lines.

Algebra & Graphing: Module Review   315

3. B **Method 1: Elimination:** To solve this system of equations, the easiest method is to use elimination. In this case, since the question only asks you to solve for y, eliminate x.

Therefore, you have to multiply the equations so that the x's will cancel.

$3x + 5y = -20$ --- multiply equation by 2: $6x + 10y = -40$
$-2x - 3y = 11$ --- multiply equation by 3: $-6x - 9y = 33$

Now, line up the two equations, and add them to eliminate the x's.

$$\begin{aligned} 6x + 10y &= -40 \\ -6x - 9y &= 33 \\ \hline 0x + y &= -7 \\ y &= -7 \end{aligned}$$

Method 2: Substitution: You could first add the equations as is, and then use substitution.

$3x + 5y = -20$
$-2x - 3y = 11$
$x + 2y = -9$

Rearrange to get the variable x alone.
$x = -2y - 9$

Now, substitute into either equation and solve for y. Let's use the first equation.
$3x + 5y = -20$
$3(-2y - 9) + 5y = -20$
$-6y - 27 + 5y = -20$
$-y - 27 = -20$
$-y = 7$
$y = -7$

4. C The determinant of a quadratic equation is $b^2 - 4ac$. Note that the determinant is the part of the quadratic equation under the square root.

$$x = \frac{-b \pm \sqrt{b^2 - 4ac}}{2a}$$

If the determinant is equal to a positive number, in this case 1, then there are two possible x values, both of which will be real:

$x = (-b + 1)/2a$
$x = (-b - 1)/2a$

A determinant of 1 has two real roots. Each real root will have a zero in the graph, which means that the graph will cross the x-axis at each of those solutions. The graph will cross the x-axis twice.

Algebra & Graphing: Module Review

5. D To find the equation of the line through the two coordinate pairs, first find the slope.

The slope is rise over run, so find the difference in y-coordinates and divide by the difference in x-coordinates.

$(12, 16)$ and $(-4, 8)$

slope = $(8 - 16)/(-4 - 12) = -8/-16 = 1/2$

Therefore, the equation $y = mx + b$ is now $y = (1/2)x + b$

Plug in either coordinate pair to solve for b.

$y = (1/2)x + b$
$16 = (1/2)(12) + b$
$16 = 6 + b$
$b = 10$
$y = (1/2)x + 10$

6. D Completing the square is usually the last method people choose to use when solving quadratic equations, as it is the most complicated. However, the quadratic formula is derived from it, and it is important that you understand how to use it. Let's completely solve this equation using the method of completing the square, and you can see which step is the next one.

Solve $2x^2 + 7x + 6 = 0$

1. First, divide both sides by a, so that the coefficient in front of the x^2 term is 1.
   $x^2 + 7/2x + 3 = 0$

2. Next, subtract c from both sides.
   $x^2 + 7/2x = -3$

3. Then, add $(b/2)^2$ to both sides. $b = 7/2$ (remember to use b from the new equation generated after step 1). Therefore, $b/2 = 7/4$, and $(b/2)^2 = (7/4)^2 = 49/16$.
   $x^2 + 7/2x + 49/16 = -3 + 49/16$

4. Now, factor and simplify. The left-hand side will factor to $(x + b/2)^2$.
   $(x + 7/4)^2 = 1/16$

5. Take the square root of both sides. Don't forget $\pm$.
   $x + 7/4 = \pm 1/4$

6. Solve.
   $x = -7/4 \pm 1/4$
   $x = -7/4 + 1/4 = -6/4 = -3/2$ OR $x = -7/4 - 1/4 = -8/4 = -2$
   $x = -3/2$ OR -2

The next step would be the third step above.

7. B You have two unknowns: the number of quarters and the number of dimes. Use variables to represent each.

q = number of quarters
d = number of dimes

Now, set up two equations. The first equation can be set up knowing "the number of dimes is four less than 3 times the number of quarters."

$d = 3q - 4$

The second equation can be set up from: "the total value of the coins is $1.80." Think in terms of cents instead of dollars so that the equation does not have decimals.

$10d + 25q = 180$

Now, solve the system of equations. You can use substitution and plug the value from d in the first equation into the second equation.

$d = 3q - 4$
$10d + 25q = 180$
$10(3q - 4) + 25q = 180$
$30q - 40 + 25q = 180$
$55q - 40 = 180$
$55q = 220$
$q = 4$

The number of quarters is 4.

8. B Let's examine each answer choice.

A: $y = x^2$

The graph of this answer choice looks like a parabola. For instance, as x goes from –1 to –2, y should go from 1 to 4. Eliminate answer A.

B: $y = 2^x$

This is the correct graph. As x increases, y increases quickly. As x decreases, y gets closer to 0 without ever being negative.
Answer B

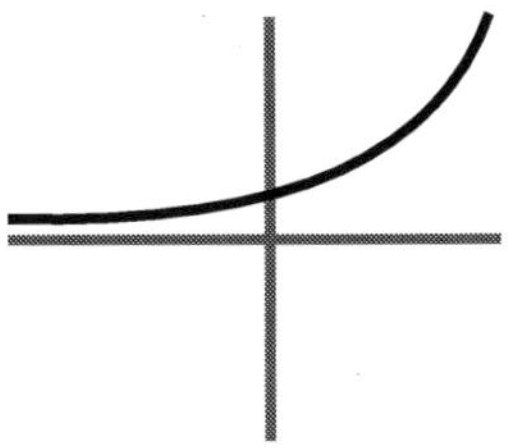

C: $y = x^3$

This cannot be the correct equation, since when x is negative, $y = x^3$ is also negative, but this is not the case in the graph.

D: $y = 4x$

This is the graph of a straight line with a slope of 4. Eliminate D.

9. D As can be seen in the graph, Quadrant II is in the top left corner.

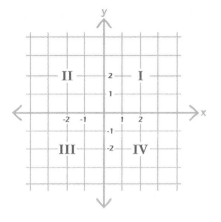

The x-values of any point in Quadrant II are negative. Therefore, x is less than or equal to 0. $x \leq 0$

The y-values of any point in Quadrant II are positive. Therefore, y is greater than or equal to 0. $y \geq 0$

Since only Quadrant II is shaded, we want to use AND to restrict the area to just the overlap of the two equations.
$x \leq 0$ and $y \geq 0$

10. D Throughout the lesson, you saw methods for finding the equation of a line by knowing the slope and a coordinate pair. Remember, the y-intercept is just a coordinate pair with the x-value of 0. Also, the x-intercept is a coordinate pair with the y-value of 0. With a coordinate pair and a slope, you can plug it into the equation $y = -3x + b$ and solve for b.

I, II, and III

11. C Use variables to represent the unknowns:
$\quad$ a = number of adult tickets
$\quad$ s = number of student tickets

Now, set up equations with the variables.
"50 people are going to the museum"
$\quad a + s = 50$
"they pay a total of $162"
$\quad 5a + 3s = 162$

Now, solve the system of equations. In this case, let's use elimination. Multiply the first by –3, so that the s's will cancel.
$\quad a + s = 50$
$\quad -3a - 3s = -150$

Now, add the two equations.
$\quad -3a - 3s = -150$
$\quad \underline{5a + 3s = 162}$
$\quad 2a = 12$

$a = 6$
6 adult tickets were sold.

Algebra & Graphing: Module Review

12. D Horizontal lines have a slope of zero, and vertical lines have an undefined slope. Therefore, eliminate answers A and B.

Now, let's look at the explanations for answers C and D.
C: Vertical lines have undefined slopes, since slope is rise over run, and you can't determine the rise because you don't know which two points on the vertical line to test.
The first part of the statement is true. Vertical lines do have undefined slopes, and slope is rise over run. However, when finding the slope of any straight line, you can pick any two points, and you will always find the same slope. Eliminate answer C.

D: Vertical lines have undefined slopes. Slope is change in y divided by change in x, but any two points on a vertical line have a 0 change in x, and dividing by 0 is undefined in math.
This is a valid explanation for the fact that vertical lines have undefined slopes. Slope is change in y divided by change in x, and on a vertical line, the change will always be 0. You can never divide by 0 in math.

13. D When simplifying a rational expression, first factor the numerator and the denominator.

Numerator: $x^2 - 5x + 6$
To factor this expression, you need to find two integers that add to -5 and multiply to 6. This is true for -2 and -3.
$$x^2 - 5x + 6 = (x - 2)(x - 3)$$
Denominator: $x^2 + 2x - 15$
You must find integers that add to 2 and multiply to -15. 5 and -3 work.
$$x^2 + 2x - 15 = (x + 5)(x - 3)$$

Now, recombine the expression and see if anything cancels.
$$(x^2 - 5x + 6)/(x^2 + 2x - 15)$$
$$= (x - 2)(x - 3)/(x + 5)(x - 3)$$
Since the numerator and denominator both have the term $(x - 3)$, these can be cancelled.
$$= (x - 2)/(x + 5)$$

14. C $(x - 3)(2x - 1) = 0$
In this problem, you have two expressions that multiply to 0. The only way a product can equal zero is if one of the terms being multiplied equals zero. Therefore, set each expression to zero to find all possible solutions to this equation.

$x - 3 = 0$, $x = 3$
$2x - 1 = 0$, $2x = 1$, $x = ½$
$x = 3$ or $x = ½$

You can also plug in each answer choice and see which values make the equation true. Solutions are 3, ½.

15. A There are two unknowns in this problem: how many tons of the 80% copper alloy and how many tons of the 50% copper alloy. Let's create variables to represent the unknowns.

a = tons of 80% alloy
b = tons of 50% alloy

Now, let us set up equations with the two unknowns.
The manufacturer needs 24 tons. Therefore, the sum of tons of alloy a and alloy b must equal 24.

$a + b = 24$

Now, with 2 unknowns, you need two equations. The second equation can come from how much copper the manufacturer needs. The amount of copper in the tons of 80% copper alloy = 80% x a = 0.8a. The other alloy has 0.5b. The manufacturer needs 0.6(24).

$0.8a + 0.5b = 0.6(24)$

Now, solve the system of equations.

$0.8a + 0.5b = 0.6(24)$
$a + b = 24$

Multiply the first equation by 10 to remove all the decimals. Multiply the second equation by −5 so that b cancels. Then, add the two equations.

$8a + 5b = 144$
$-5a - 5b = -120$
$3a = 24$
$a = 8$

You have solved for the unknown a, which represents the number of tons of 80% copper alloy needed.

8 tons

16. C The y-intercept is the point on the graph that crosses the y-axis. The point that crosses the y-axis has an x-coordinate of 0. Plug x = 0 into the equation to solve for y.

$y = -4x^2 + 3x$
$y = -4(0)^2 + 3(0)$
$y = 0 + 0$
$y = 0$

y-intercept = 0

17. B The rate of the old machine is 240 caps per 2 minutes, which reduces to 120 caps per minute. The newer model works at twice the rate of the old machine. Therefore, the newer model can cap 240 caps per minute.

If the newer machine can cap 240 caps per minute, and there are 72,000 bottles to cap, divide 72,000 by 240 to figure out how long it will take this machine.

$$72000 \div 240 = 300$$

300 minutes

All the answers are in hours, so convert 300 minutes to hours.

$$300 \text{ minutes} \times \frac{1 \text{ hour}}{60 \text{ min}} = 5 \text{ hr}$$

18. C This question provides the range of the function. Remember that the range is the output or y-value. We know that the range can be anything from $-\infty$ to 2; therefore, 2 is the maximum value for y. If we have a maximum, then we know that the graph opens downward. Therefore, the coefficient of the x^2 term must be negative, which leaves only answers B and C. To find which has a maximum of 2, find the vertex of each equation.

When a quadratic equation is in the form: $y = ax^2 + bx + c$, then the x-coordinate of the vertex is equal to $-b/2a$. To find the y-coordinate, just plug x into the equation.

Answer B: $y = -x^2 + 2x + 2$
  $a = -1, b = 2, c = 2$
  x-coordinate of vertex $= -b/2a = -2/-2 = 1$
  y-coordinate $= -x^2 + 2x + 2 = -(1)^2 + 2(1) + 2 = 3$
  Vertex $= (1, 3)$
  The range is from $(-\infty, 3]$

Answer C: $y = -x^2 + 4x - 2$
  $a = -1, b = 4, c = -2$
  x-coordinate of vertex $= -b/2a = -4/-2 = 2$
  y-coordinate $= -x^2 + 4x - 2 = -(2)^2 + 4(2) - 2 = 2$
  Vertex $= (2, 2)$
  The range is from $(-\infty, 2]$

19. A First, use the variables x and y to represent the two unknown quantities.

  Let x = number of pencils Bob purchases.
  Let y = number of pens Bob purchases.

Set up an equation to represent the amount Bob can spend.
Each pen costs $3, so the total cost of pens = 3y.
Each pencil costs $1, so the total cost of pencils = 1x.
Bob has only $60 to spend.

  $3y + 1x \leq 60$

Isolate y, and then graph.

  $3y + x \leq 60$
  $3y \leq -x + 60$
  $y \leq -x/3 + 20$

The graph of that inequality will have a y-intercept of 20 and a slope of $-1/3$. You want to shade below the line. Also, since x and y cannot be negative, only shade in Quadrant I.

20. C This question is a simple application of the compound interest formula, which is based on exponential growth.

  $A = P(1 + r/n)^{nt}$

  P = principal or initial amount = $2000
  r = interest rate = 4% = 0.04
  n = number of times compounded = quarterly = 4
  t = time = 10 years

  $A = 2000(1 + 0.04/4)^{4 \times 10}$

  $A = 2000(1.01)^{40}$

Algebra & Graphing: Module Review

6. Geometry II

Angles, Parallel & Perpendicular Lines 326
Transformations 333
Similar & Congruent Polygons 339
3-Dimensional Objects & Volume 344
Surface Area 351
Geometric Properties & Proofs 358
Module Review 366

Geometry II: Angles, Parallel & Perpendicular Lines

Parallel Lines

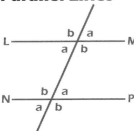

Lines are considered parallel if they have the same slope. Any line that intersects two parallel lines will create identical sets of angles with each line. The Lines LM and NP in the diagram are parallel, and the intersecting line has created equal sets of Angles a and b.

Perpendicular Lines

Perpendicular lines intersect to form four 90-degree angles. Lines C and D in the diagram shown here are perpendicular.

Perpendicular lines will have slopes that are opposite reciprocals of each other. Another way to think about it is that if you multiple the slopes of perpendicular lines, the product will always equal –1. For instance, if you had one line with a slope of ½, a line perpendicular to it will have a slope of –2.

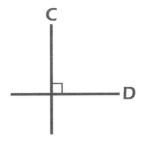

Supplementary Angles

Just as triangles and circles have a set number of degrees that all their angles contain, a straight line always contains 180 degrees. Angles that add up to 180 degrees are called supplementary angles.

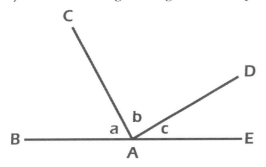

The picture to the left contains three supplementary angles, a, b, and c. Each of those angles can also be named by referencing the three points that form the angle – for example, Angle c could also be called Angle DAE or EAD. When angles are referenced in this way, the point that forms the apex of the angle – in this case A – will always be in the middle.

Complementary Angles

Two angles adding to 90 degrees are known as complementary angles.

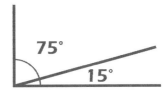

Angles in Polygons

A triangle contains 180 degrees. To determine the number of degrees in any other polygon, divide the polygon into triangles and multiply the number of triangles by 180°. The following diagram shows a few common polygons and the sum of the degree measure of their angles.

 Triangle = 180°

 Rectangle = 2 Triangles
= 2 x 180°
= 360°

 Pentagon = 3 Triangles
= 3 x 180°
= 540°

 Hexagon = 4 Triangles
= 4 x 180°
= 720°

The sum of the measures of the interior angles in a polygon is one of the formulas included on your formula sheet. It states that S = (n - 2) x 180, where S is the sum and n is the number of sides. For instance, the hexagon above has 6 sides, so n = 6 and S = (6 - 2) x 180 = 4 x 180 = 720°. The method above demonstrates how the formula is derived.

Bisectors

A line that cuts an angle in half is a bisector. Since the bisected angle is cut into halves, each angle created by the line is equal to one half the measure of the whole angle. In the figure below, Line LN is bisecting Angle MNO:

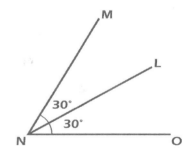

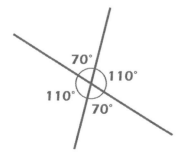

Opposite Angles

Angles adding to 180 degrees are supplementary, so any two intersecting lines create two sets of supplementary angles. In addition, angles on opposite sides of the intersecting lines are equal.

Geometry II: Angles, Parallel & Perpendicular Lines

Angles, Parallel & Perpendicular Lines: Practice

1. In the picture below, y is how many degrees?

    A. 53
    B. 127
    C. 153
    D. 180

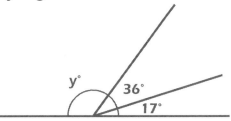

2. In the diagram below, Lines L and M are parallel. Choose the best answer to replace the question mark:

a b

    A. >
    B. <
    C. =
    D. Not enough information.

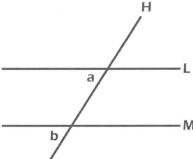

3. Choose the best answer to fill in the blank.
In a regular hexagon, each angle equals ___ degrees.

    A. 30
    B. 60
    C. 90
    D. 120

4. Which of the following lines are parallel?

    I. $2x + 3y = 7$
    II. $y = (2/3)x - 12$
    III. $-6y = 4x + 12$

    A. I and II
    B. I and III
    C. II and III
    D. I, II, and III

5. If Triangle ABC is equilateral, what is the measure of Angle BCA?

   A. 45

   B. 60

   C. 90

   D. 180

6. If Angle CAB = 65°, what is the measure of Angle ACD?

   A. 25°

   B. 65°

   C. 115°

   D. 155°

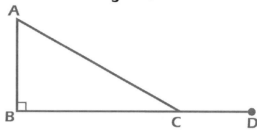

7. In Parallelogram ABCD, Angle BAC = 70°. What is the measure of Angle ACD?

   A. 20°

   B. 70°

   C. 110°

   D. 170°

8. What is the equation of a line perpendicular to $y = -3x + 5$ and passing through the point $(6, -2)$?

   A. $y = 3x - 20$

   B. $y = (1/3)x - 4$

   C. $y = -(1/3)x$

   D. $y = -(7/6)x + 5$

9. What does one interior angle of a regular octagon measure?

   A. 1080

   B. 135

   C. 180

   D. 45

10. Which of the following is parallel to the line in the graph?

   A. y = 2x + 2
   B. y = (½)x – 2
   C. y = –2x + 4
   D. y = –(½)x + 2

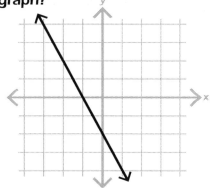

Angles, Parallel & Perpendicular Lines: Answer Explanations

1. B There are 180 degrees on each side of a straight line. To find y, add the measures of the two angles and subtract their sum from 180.

180 – (36 + 17) = 127 degrees

2. C Any line that passes through two parallel lines will create equal sets of angles with each line. Therefore, Angle a = Angle b.

3. D A regular hexagon has six equal sides and six equal angles. A hexagon can be divided into 4 triangles, so it has 4 x 180, or 720 degrees. See tutorial for more information on determining the total measure of interior angles in a polygon.

A hexagon contains 720 degrees for the 6 angles, so divide 720 by 6 to find the measure of each angle.

720° ÷ 6 = 120°

4. B Parallel lines have the same slopes. Therefore, let's find the slope of each line and compare.

I. 2x + 3y = 7
Rearrange the equation first, isolating y.
2x + 3y = 7 (subtract 2x from each side)
3y = –2x + 7 (divide both sides by 3)
y = –(2/3)x + 7/3
If the equation is in the above form, it is easy to find the slope. It is the coefficient of the variable x. Therefore, the slope of the line is –2/3.

II. y = (2/3)x – 12
This equation is already in the right format to easily find the slope. The slope is 2/3.

330 Geometry II: Angles, Parallel & Perpendicular Lines

III. $-6y = 4x + 12$

Isolate the y to find the slope. Divide both sides by –6.
$-6y = 4x + 12$
$y = -(2/3)x - 2$
The slope of the line is $-2/3$.

Now, compare the slopes to find out which lines are parallel. Equations I and III have the same slope.

5. B If a triangle is equilateral, then all its sides and angles are equal. Let y represent the measure of Angle BCA. Since all the angles are equal, each angle in this triangle will equal y.

The angles in a triangle add to 180°. Set up an equation to solve for y.
$y + y + y = 180$
$3y = 180$
$y = 60$

All angles in the equilateral triangle are equal to 60°.

6. D First, calculate Angle BCA, the third angle in the triangle. We know two angles in the triangle are 65° (given in problem) and 90° (right angle), and we know that all the angles in a triangle add to 180°.

$90° + 65° + $ Angle BCA $= 180°$
$155° + $ Angle BCA $= 180°$
Angle BCA $= 25°$

Now, find the measure of Angle ACD. We know that Angle BCA and Angle ACD form a straight line, and the sum of the measures of angles forming a straight line is 180°.
Angle BCA + Angle ACD $= 180°$
$25° + $ Angle ACD $= 180°$
Angle ACD $= 155°$

7. C Since we know that the quadrilateral is a parallelogram, the opposite sides of the polygon are parallel. Therefore, AB is parallel to CD. If you extend line CD, as seen in the diagram below, you can see that line segment AC cuts across the parallel lines.

Since the lines are parallel, the two angles marked in the diagram must be equal. They are both equal to 70°. Angle ACD and the 70° angle form a straight line where the measures add to 180°.

Angle ACD $+ 70° = 180°$

Angle ACD $= 110°$

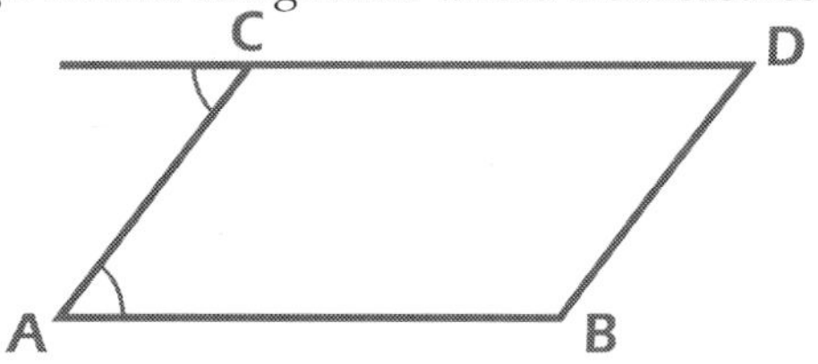

Geometry II: Angles, Parallel & Perpendicular Lines

8. B Perpendicular lines have slopes that are negative reciprocals. Since the slope of the given equation is –3, the slope of the line perpendicular to that will be ⅓.

y = (⅓)x + b. Now, plug in the point (6, –2) to solve for b.

–2 = (⅓)(6) + b
–2 = 2 + b
–4 = b
y = (⅓)x – 4.

9. B This problem is extremely easy when you again use the formula sheet. Remember to be completely familiar with the content on the formula sheet so that you don't have to struggle with problems, and you can instantly know when to refer back to it. In this case, the formula is

Sum of the Measures of the Interior Angles in a Polygon: S = (n – 12) x 180

Before you start using any formula, make sure you know what each variable represents. In this formula, S is the sum of the measures of the interior angles in a polygon. n is the number of sides of the polygon.

Since we are dealing with an octagon, we know that it has 8 sides. n = 8.

S = (n – 2) x 180 = (8 – 2)x 180 = 6 x 180 = 1080

Now be careful, the question doesn't ask what the sum of the measures of the interior angles is; it asks what one interior angle measures. Since we are dealing with an octagon, we know that it has 8 interior angles, so therefore, divide the sum of the measures by 8 to find out what each angle equals.

One interior angle = 1080/8 = 135.

10. C To find out which line is parallel to the line in the graph, first calculate the slope of the line, and then find out which equation has a line with the same slope.

To calculate the slope of the line in the graph, take any two points on the line. It doesn't matter which points you choose, the slope will always be the same. Let's choose (0, –2) and (1, –4). Remember, to find the slope, it is the change in y over the change in x.

Slope = (change in y)/(change in x)
      = (–2 – (–4))/(0 – 1)
      = (–2 + 4)/(0 – 1)
      = 2/–1
      = –2

Now, let's look at each answer choice to see which has a slope of –2. All the equations are in the form: y = mx + b, where m is the slope. The only equation with a slope of –2 is C.

Geometry II: Transformations

Types of Transformations

Transformations are ways of manipulating a line, point, or shape on the coordinate plane. There are four basic types of transformations:

> Translation (shifting position)
> Reflection (flipping)
> Rotation (turning)
> Dilation (increasing or decreasing scale)

This lesson will cover these basic types of transformations and their effect on the graphs and formulas of equations.

Translation

Imagine translation as picking up a graph and moving it without changing it in any other way. Graphs can be translated up, down, right, left, or some combination.

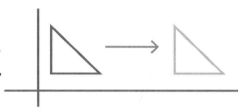

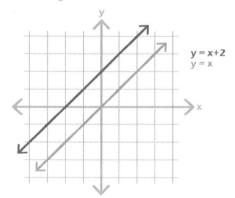

Graphs of equations can be moved up or down by changing the y-intercept. For example, $y = x + 2$ is up 2 units from $y = x$.

Reflection

You can reflect an object over any straight line, but the most common types of flips are over the x-axis and y-axis. Flipping all the coordinates around an axis is called reflection, since the objects before and after are mirror images of each other.

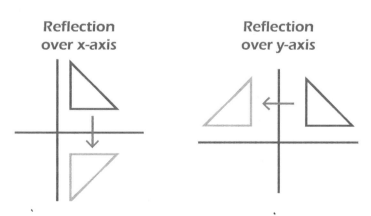

Reflection over x-axis

Reflection over y-axis

Rotation

A graph can be rotated by any number of degrees and about any pivot point. The rotation can be clockwise or counter-clockwise. The examples below are all rotated clockwise.

Rotation 180 degrees about pivot point A

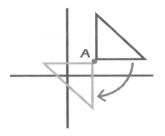

Rotation 45 degrees about pivot point A

Rotation 90 degrees about pivot point A, origin

Dilation

A graph of an object is dilated by increasing or decreasing all the coordinates of the object proportionately to make the object bigger or smaller on the coordinate system.

Symmetry

Lines of symmetry in gray

Symmetry about a line is the ability to flip an object across the line without changing it.

Tessellations

A tessellation or tiling is a collection of figures that completely fills a plane with no overlaps and no gaps. The image on the right is an example of a tessellation made up of hexagons and quadrilaterals.

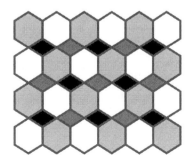

Transformations: Practice

1. Which of the following transformations was used on the shape below from the image on the left to the image on the right?

   A. translation
   B. dilation
   C. rotation
   D. reflection

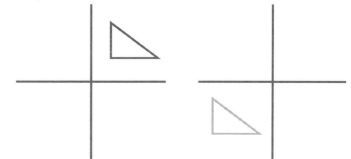

2. Which of the following shapes is symmetric about the x-axis?

A.    B.    C.    D.

3. How many lines of symmetry does the following object have?

   A. 0
   B. 1
   C. 2
   D. 3

4. Which of the following transformations has been performed on the shape below?

   A. translation
   B. dilation
   C. reflection
   D. rotation

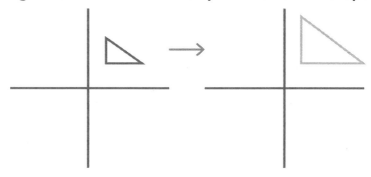

Geometry II: Transformations   335

5. **Which of the following transformations were performed on the object below?**

I. translation
II. reflection
III. dilation

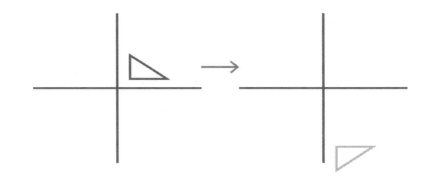

   A. I
   B. I and II
   C. II and III
   D. I, II, and III

6. **To transform the graph of y = 3x into y = 3x + 2, what transformation would you perform?**

   A. translation
   B. rotation
   C. reflection
   D. dilation

7. **By how many degrees and in what direction has the following object been rotated about the origin?**

   A. 90° clockwise
   B. 90° counterclockwise
   C. 45° clockwise
   D. 180° clockwise

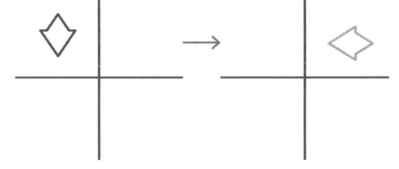

8. **If a square with corners at (0, 0), (0, 4), (4, 0), and (4, 4) is dilated by a factor of 3, where are its new corners?**

   A. (3, 3), (3, 7), (7, 3), (7, 7)
   B. (0, 0), (0, 12), (12, 0), (12, 12)
   C. (3, 3), (3, 12), (12, 3), (12, 12)
   D. (0, 0), (0, 4), (4, 0), (4, 4)

9. What transformation(s) was/were performed on the shape below?

A. reflection
B. dilation and translation
C. dilation and rotation
D. translation and rotation

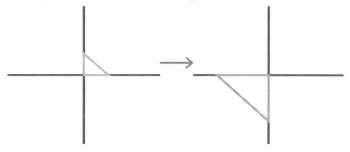

10. If the lengths of all sides of a triangle are tripled, what happens to its perimeter?

A. Increase by 3
B. Triple
C. Multiply by 6
D. Multiply by 9

Transformations: Answer Explanations

1. A   To translate an object is to move it without changing its shape, size, or orientation. The shape moved down and to the left without any other changes, so the shape was translated.
Dilation involves changing the size of a shape. Rotation would have changed the orientation of the shape. Reflection would have also changed the orientation.

2. D   Symmetry about an axis means that you can flip the shape over that axis without changing it.

Answer A shows a shape symmetric about the y-axis.
Answer B shows a shape that is symmetric, but not about either axis.
Answer C also shows a shape symmetric about the y-axis.
Answer D shows a shape symmetric about the x-axis.

3. A   There are no lines of symmetry in the shape.
No matter what lines you draw, you cannot flip the object over that line to make it identical.

4. B   An object is dilated by increasing or decreasing all its x and y values proportionately. In this case, the shape has changed size proportionately, which means dilation was performed.

5. B   Multiple transformations were performed on the shape. The object was reflected about the x-axis, which means it was flipped over the x-axis. In addition, the shape was translated downward. The shape was not dilated since the size of the shape didn't change.

I and II, Translation and Reflection.

6. A Both equations are graphed to the right. As can be seen, the graph has been translated, or moved, by 2 units.

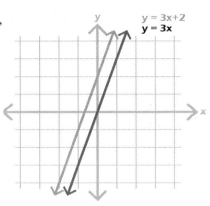

7. A The object has been rotated in a clockwise diretion. You can tell that, since it has moved one full quadrant, it has moved 90°. If you draw a line from any point on the object to the origin and then draw a line perpendicular to that, you will see it will touch the same point on the new object.

90° clockwise.

8. B Dilation is a type of transformation where the object is resized. Each coordinate is multiplied by the factor of dilation; in this case, the factor is 3. Therefore, to solve this question, take each original coordinate pair of the corners and multiply the x-value and y-value by 3.

(0, 0) becomes (0, 0)
(0, 4) becomes (0, 12)
(4, 0) becomes (12, 0)
(4, 4) becomes (12, 12)

9. C This shape had more than one transformation performed on it. The first one to notice is that the shape is now a different size. The only transformation where the size of an object changes is dilation.

The next transformation to note is that the shape now faces the other direction. This shape has been rotated around the origin so that it is now facing the other way.
Dilation and Rotation

10. B Let the sides of the original triangle equal X, Y, and Z. Then the sides of the new triangle will equal 3X, 3Y, and 3Z.

Original perimeter = X + Y + Z
New perimeter = 3X + 3Y + 3Z = 3(X + Y + Z) = 3(Original perimeter)
The perimeter triples.

Geometry II: Similar & Congruent Polygons

Congruent Polygons

Polygons are considered congruent if they have exactly the same size, shape, and interior angles. Congruent polygons might consist of a polygon and various combinations of translations, reflections, and rotations of itself:

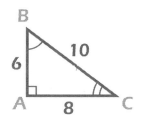 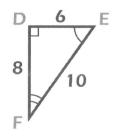

Proving Congruence

There are several ways to prove that two triangles are congruent. Here are a few:

1. Side-Angle-Side (SAS)
A pair of corresponding sides and the angle in between them are the same.

2. Side-Side-Side (SSS)
All the sides of the two triangles are the same length.

3. Angle-Side-Angle (ASA)
A pair of corresponding angles and the side in between them are the same.

Similar Polygons

Similar polygons share the same shape and angles but have different sizes. In the image on the right, the second triangle has been rotated, translated, and dilated. It is still the same shape with the same angles, so the two triangles are similar, but not congruent.

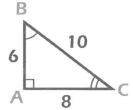 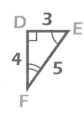

Proportional Sides

Corresponding sides in similar polygons are all proportionate. Another way to think about this is that there is a scale factor from one polygon to the other, and this scale factor is the same for every side.

In the image above, you can see that the corresponding sides have the same proportions:

AB/DE = 6/3 = 2
BC/EF = 10/5 = 2
CA/FD = 8/4 = 2

Similar & Congruent Polygons: Practice

1. **Congruent polygons have the same:** I. size
   II. orientation
   III. shape

   A. III only
   B. II and III
   C. I and III
   D. I, II, and III

2. **Similar polygons have the same** I. size
   II. orientation
   III. shape

   A. I and III
   B. III only
   C. I only
   D. I, II, and III

3. **What is the length of the missing side y in the rectangle below?**

   A. 3
   B. 7
   C. 9
   D. don't know

   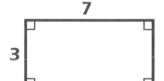 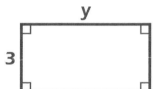

4. **Which of the following is similar to the polygon to the right?**

   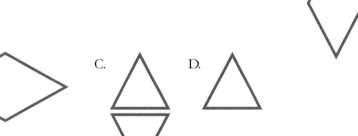

   A.  B. 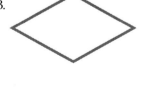 C.  D.

5. Which of the following is true?

   A. All similar polygons are also congruent.

   B. All congruent polygons are also similar.

   C. No similar polygons are also congruent.

   D. No congruent polygons are also similar.

6. What is the length of side a in the figure below if the two triangles are similar?

   A. 6
   B. 12
   C. 13
   D. don't know

7. Which of the following are methods for proving congruence for a pair of triangles?

   I. Side-Angle-Side
   II. Angle-Angle-Angle
   III. Side-Side-Side

   A. I and II

   B. I and III

   C. II and III

   D. I, II, and III

8. In two triangles, all the angles are the same when the two triangles are

   I. Similar
   II. Congruent
   III. Right triangles

   A. I only

   B. II only

   C. II and III

   D. I and II

9. Triangle ABC is similar to Triangle DEF. (Angle A = Angle D, Angle B = Angle E, Angle C = Angle F) If AB = 8, BC = 10, and DE = 12, what is the length of EF?

   A. 10
   B. 14
   C. 15
   D. 16

10. Rectangle ABCD is similar to Rectangle EFGH (AB corresponds to EF, BC corresponds to FG, etc.), and the ratio of the perimeter of ABCD to the perimeter of EFGH is 4 to 1. If BC = 16, what is the length of FG?

   A. 2
   B. 4
   C. 16
   D. 32

Similar & Congruent Polygons: Answer Explanations

1. C   The definition of congruence is that the polygons are the same size and the same shape. They can be rotated and have different orientations.

2. B   The definition of similar polygons is that they have the same shape with all the same angles. However, similar polygons can have different sizes and orientations.

3. D   Just because the two polygons are rectangles does not mean that they are congruent. Therefore, we cannot determine the length of the missing side without more information.

4. B   Similar polygons have the same shape and angles, but not necessarily the same size or orientation. Answer B is rotated and slightly larger, but it is similar to the original.

5. B   Similar polygons have the same shape. Congruent polygons have the same size and shape.

   Therefore, if polygons are congruent, then they have the same size and shape, which means that they are also similar. All congruent polygons are similar.

6. B   Since the two triangles are similar, their sides are proportional. Therefore, set up a proportion to solve for a.
   $$a/16 = 9/12$$
   Multiply both sides by 16 to isolate a.
   $$a/16 \times 16 = 9/12 \times 16$$
   $$a = 12$$

7. B Having three angles the same proves that any two triangles are similar, but it does not prove congruence because one triangle can still be a dilation of the other. For example, in the following image, the angles are the same; however, the triangles are not congruent.

If you review the tutorial, you will see that all three sides the same are enough to prove congruence. Also, two sides the same plus the angle in between are also enough for proving congruence.

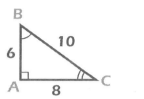

I and III prove congruence.

8. D Triangles that are similar by definition have the same shape, which means that their angles are all the same. Similar triangles can have sides of different length but angles the same. I is true.

Congruent triangles are the same size and shape. Therefore, the angles are definitely the same. Congruent triangles can have a different orientation, but the shapes and sizes are the same. II is true.

Right triangles have one 90° angle in common; however, the other two angles can be different. For instance, you can have one right triangle with the following angles: 30, 60, 90, and another with the angles 45, 45, and 90. III is false.

9. C Since the two triangles are similar, their sides are proportional.
AB/DE = BC/EF
8/12 = 10/EF

Cross-multiply and solve.
8(EF) = 12(10)
EF = 120 ÷ 8 = 15
length of EF = 15

10. B The ratio of the perimeters of two similar rectangles will be equal to the ratio of the sides of the rectangles. Therefore, set up a proportion, and solve for the missing length.

perim ABCD/perim EFGH = BC/FG
4/1 = 16/FG
4(FG) = 16
FG = 4

Geometry II: 3-Dimensional Objects & Volume

3-Dimensional Objects

There are five basic types of 3-dimensional shapes, each with its own characteristics.

Cone
A cone is a 3-dimensional object with a circle at the base converging to a point at the top.

Sphere
A sphere is a perfectly round 3-dimensional object – in effect, a 3-dimensional version of a circle.

Prisms
A prism is a 3-dimensional object of a polygon with depth. The description of a prism as triangular, rectangular, and so on indicates which type of object is repeated throughout the depth of the object.

Pyramid
A pyramid is a 3-dimensional object with a polygon at the base converging to a point at the top.

Cylinder
A cylinder is a 3-dimensional object with a circle at the base as well as depth.

Relationships between 2-D and 3-D objects

Nets
A net is a pattern in two dimensions that can be used to generate a 3-dimensional object. This example of an unfolded box is a net. It is in two dimensions but can be folded to a 3-dimensional object.

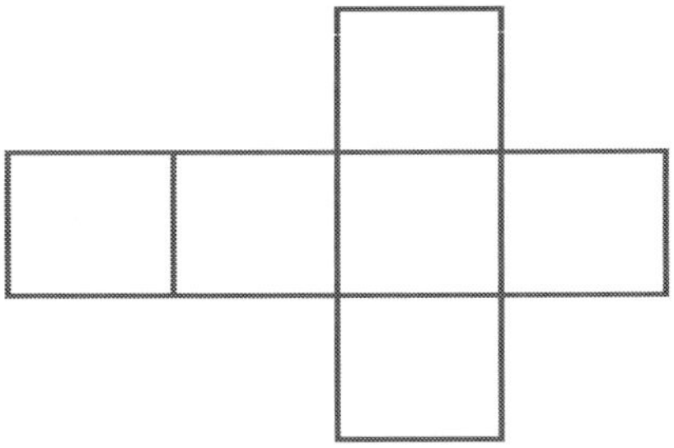

Perspective Drawings
A perspective drawing is an illustration of a 3-dimensional object on a 2-dimensional surface. An example is the representation of the cones in the diagram on the top of the next page.

Cross Sections
A cross section is the intersection of a plane through a 3-dimensional object. This creates a 2-dimensional object. For example, the intersection of a plane through a sphere creates a circle.

Conic Sections

A conic section is the shape formed by the intersection of a plane and a cone. Two cones stacked one on top of the other often represent conic sections.

The exact shape of the conic section depends on the angle and location of the intersection. Some of the more common conic sections:

Circle: Formed if the plane is parallel to the base of the cone (as in image)

Ellipse: Similar to an intersection that generates a circle, but not parallel to the base of the cone

Parabola: Intersection on either the "left" or "right" hand side of the cone at an angle to the base

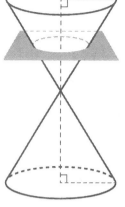

Volume

Volume is the 3-dimensional space filled by a figure. Its units are equal to a cubed length measurement. For most shapes, volume can be calculated by multiplying the area of the base times the height.

Rectangular Prism or Box

Multiply the area of the base by the height.
Volume = length x width x height.

Cube

In the case of a cube, all the dimensions are the same length.
Volume = area of base x height = side x side x side = side^3

Cylinder

In this case, the area of the base is a circle with area of π x radius^2.
Therefore, the volume = π x r^2 x height.
Note: this formula is on the formula sheet.

Triangular Prism

Volume = area of base x height = 1/2 x length x width x height.

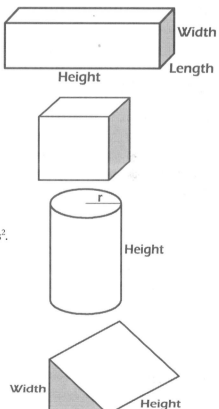

Geometry II: 3-Dimensional Objects & Volume

Exceptions to the Rule

The cone, the pyramid, and the sphere are exceptions to the standard Area of Base x Height rule because these shapes are not consistent throughout their height. Note: the formulas for calculating the volume of pyramids, cones, and spheres are on the formula sheet.

Pyramid

The volume for a pyramid is found by taking one third the area of the base times the height.
Volume = 1/3 (Area of Base) x Height

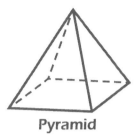
Pyramid

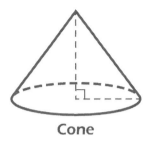
Cone

Cone

The volume for a cone is also one third the area of the base times the height, except that in this case, the base is a circle.
Volume = 1/3 (Area of Base) x Height
Volume = 1/3 (πr^2) x Height

Sphere

The volume of a sphere can be calculated by multiplying 4/3 x π x r^3.

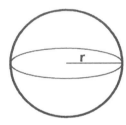

3-Dimensional Objects & Volume: Practice

1. You have a pool that is a rectangular prism. How many liters of water can fill the pool if its dimensions are 20m by 15m by 8m? (hint: 1 cubic meter = 1000 Liters)

    A. 2.4 Liters

    B. 43,000 Liters

    C. 1,200,000 Liters

    D. 2,400,000 Liters

2. Calculate the volume of a 9-foot tall cylinder with a base with a radius of 3 feet.

    A. 81π ft cubed

    B. 270 ft cubed

    C. 40.5 ft cubed

    D. 54 ft cubed

3. Which 3-dimensional object can be generated with the net below?

A. Triangular Prism

B. Triangular Pyramid

C. Square Pyramid

D. Cone

4. A cylindrical object sits on the ground as pictured below. What is the cross section of a paper through the cylinder and parallel to the ground?

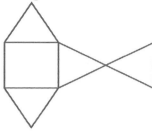

A. Sphere

B. Ellipse

C. Circle

D. Rectangle

5. Which can hold more water – a plastic cube with 2-inch sides or a plastic box that is 4 inches long, 3 inches wide, and 3/4 of an inch tall?

A. Cube

B. Box

C. Same

D. Not enough information.

6. How many times bigger is the volume of a cube with sides of length 8 m than the volume of a cube with sides of length 4 m?

A. 2

B. 4

C. 8

D. 16

7. If the width of a rectangular prism is w, the length is twice the width, and the height is 4 more than the length, what is the volume of the prism in terms of w?

A. $5w + 4$

B. w^3

C. $2w^3 + 8w^2$

D. $4w^3 + 8w^2$

8. If the volume of a right triangular prism is 400 cubic meters, and the perpendicular sides of the triangle are 8 m and 5 m, how long is the prism?

   A. 5 m
   B. 10 m
   C. 20 m
   D. 40 m

9. If the volume of a sphere is 288π, what is the diameter?

   A. 6 m
   B. 12 m
   C. 24 m
   D. 144 m

10. The three solids shown below all have the same height. The square-based pyramid has base side length equal to x. The cone has base radius equal to x. The cylinder has base diameter equal to x. Which solid has the smallest volume?

   A. pyramid
   B. cone
   C. cylinder
   D. pyramid and cone are equal and the smallest

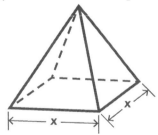
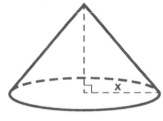

3-Dimensional Objects & Volume: Answer Explanations

1. D   Since the question asks how many liters of water can fill a pool, you must find the volume of the pool.

Volume = length x width x height
= 20 m x 15 m x 8 m = 2400 m³

Now, convert from cubic meters to Liters.
2400 cubic meters x 1000 L/1 cubic m
= 2,400,000 Liters

2. A First, find the area of the circle on the base of the cylinder. Area of circle = π x radius²
Area of Base = π x 3² = 9π ft sq

Then multiply that area by the height of the cylinder.
9π ft. sq x 9 ft. = 81π ft. cubed.

3. C When given a question involving nets, you can try to visualize how to fold it to make a three-dimensional object, or you can start by analyzing the faces.

In the net, there are 5 faces total: 1 square and 4 triangles. Now, let's go through each answer choice to see what faces those objects have.

A. Triangular prism. Remember, a triangular prism has a triangle on either end, and it is connected by three rectangles. Therefore, 2 triangles and 3 rectangles. Different faces – eliminate answer.

B. Triangular pyramid. This pyramid has a base as a triangle and connects up to a point with each of those faces as triangles. Therefore, 4 triangles total. Different faces – eliminate answer.

C. Square pyramid. This object is a pyramid that has a base as a square. A triangle off each side of the square connects up to a point. Therefore, 1 square and 4 triangles. Correct faces. Now, let's think about whether it would fold correctly. If you folded the top and bottom triangles together so they met at a point in the middle and then folded the triangles on the right to connect up to the left-hand side of the square, then it would create a square pyramid. This is your answer.

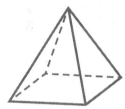

D. Cone. This object has a circle on the bottom. Different faces – eliminate answer.

4. C A cylinder is a circle extended by height. The cross section of a cylinder taken parallel to the ground is a circle. For instance, you can think of the paper parallel to the ground right at the top face of the cylinder. The top face is a circle, as would be the cross section.

5. B Find the volume of each to see how much water it can hold.
Plastic cube: 2 in x 2 in x 2 in = 8 cubic inches
Plastic box: 4 in x 3 in x 3/4 in = 9 cubic inches
Plastic box can hold more.

6. C The volume of a cube is side³.
Volume of cube with sides of length 8 m = 8³ = 512.
Volume of cube with sides of length 4 m = 4³ = 64.
512 ÷ 64 = 8

7. D The volume of a rectangular prism is the width x length x height. Let's put each dimension in terms of w.

Width = w; Length = twice the width = 2w; Height = four more than length = 2w + 4

Volume = Width x Length x Height = w x (2w) x (2w + 4) = $2w^2$(2w + 4) = $4w^3 + 8w^2$

8. C The volume of a triangular prism equals the area of the base times the length of the prism. Since we know the perpendicular sides of the triangle, we can find the area of the base and then we can solve for the length of the prism.

Area of triangular base = 1/2 x base x height = 1/2 x 8 m x 5 m = 20 sq m

Volume = Area of base x Length
400 cubic meters = 20 sq m x Length
400 ÷ 20 = Length
20 m = Length

9. B The formula for the volume of a sphere is (4/3)πradius³.

	288π = (4/3)πradius³
Divide both sides by π.	288 = 4/3 x radius³
Multiply both sides by 3/4	216 = radius³
Take the cube root of both sides.	6 = radius

If 6 m is the radius, then double that will be the diameter. Diameter = 12 m.

10. A Let's find the volume of each solid. First, since all the heights are the same, let's assign a value of 1 to the height.

Pyramid: The volume for a pyramid is 1/3 x Area of Base x Height
Vpyr = (1/3)(Area Square) (Height) = (1/3)(x^2) (1) = (1/3)x^2

Cone: The volume for a cone is 1/3 x Area of Base x Height
Vcone = (1/3)(Area Circle) (Height) = (1/3)(πx^2) (1) = (1/3)πx^2

Cylinder: The volume for a cylinder is Area of Base x Height. In this case, note that the radius is x/2.
Vcyl = (Area Circle) (Height) = π(x/2)² (1) = πx^2/4 = (1/4)πx^2

Now, let's compare the volumes.
Pyramid volume = (1/3)x^2
Cone volume = (1/3)πx^2
Cylinder volume = (1/4)πx^2
The pyramid has the smallest volume.

Geometry II: Surface Area

Surface Area

The surface area of an object is the sum of the areas of all its faces.

Rectangular Prism or Box

The surface area of a box is calculated by finding the area of each rectangle on the face of the box. There are six faces: two with an area of length x width, two with an area of length x height, and two with an area of width x height. This can be written using the formula:

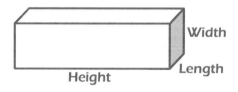

(2 x length x width) + (2 x length x height) + (2 x width x height).

Cube

A cube has six sides, all with the same area of side².
The surface area of a cube = 6 x side².

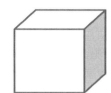

Cylinder

To find the surface area of a cylinder, you add the areas of three different faces: the top, the bottom, and the side. The top and bottom of the cylinder are circles, each with an area of π x r².

If you think about unrolling a cylinder, the side makes a rectangle with a width equal to the circumference of the base and a length equal to the height of the cylinder. Therefore, the area of the side = π x diameter x height.

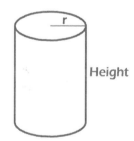

The total surface area of a cylinder = 2πr² + 2πrh.
Note: this formula is on the formula sheet.

Triangular Prism

A triangular prism has five faces. To find the total surface area, add the areas of the two base triangles along with the areas of the three rectangles that form the sides of the prism.

The length of each rectangle is equal to the height of the prism. Each side of the base triangle represents the width of one of the three rectangles. For the prism shown here, the surface area would be
(1/2)AB + (1/2)AB + A x height + B x height + C x height.

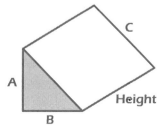

Pyramid

There is no special formula for the surface area of a pyramid – just be sure to add the areas of all the faces. For instance, if the pyramid has a square base, the surface area would be the sum of the area of the square plus the area of each of the four triangles.

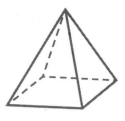

Sphere

The formula for the surface area of a sphere is 4 x π x r².
Note: this formula is on the formula sheet.

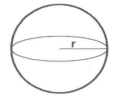

Cone

The surface area of a cone is the sum of the area of the base, which is a circle, and the area around the cone, which is called the lateral surface area. Note: this is on the formula sheet.

The area of the base is πr^2
The lateral surface area is $\pi r \sqrt{r^2 + h^2}$.
Total surface area of cone: $\pi r^2 + \pi r \sqrt{r^2 + h^2}$

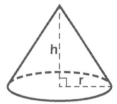

Surface Area: Practice

1. A box is 9 m tall, 7 m long, and 3 m wide. What is its surface area?

   A. 189 square meters

   B. 189 cubed meters

   C. 222 square meters

   D. 222 cubed meters

2. What is the surface area of the cylinder in the diagram?

   A. 10π

   B. 50π

   C. 70π

   D. 100π

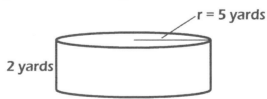

352   Geometry II: Surface Area

3. Calculate the surface area of a sphere with a radius of 6.

   A. 36π

   B. 144π

   C. 288π

   D. 864π

4. A family is wallpapering their living room. If the room is 26 ft by 19 ft with 10-ft ceilings, and they are only covering the walls, how much wallpaper will they need in square feet?

   A. 700

   B. 800

   C. 900

   D. 1000

5. What is the surface area of the triangular prism if the units are all in meters?

   A. 48 sq m

   B. 76 sq m

   C. 108 sq m

   D. 120 sq m

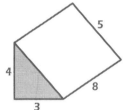

6. If the surface area of a cube is 150 square meters, what is the length of one side of the cube?

   A. 5 m

   B. 10 m

   C. 25 m

   D. 50 m

7. If a rectangular prism has a width of y, length of 2y, and height of 3y, what is its surface area?

   A. $6y^3$

   B. $12y^2$

   C. $22y^2$

   D. $36y^2$

Geometry II: Surface Area

8. If the surface area of a cylinder is 320π and the radius is 10, what is the height of the cylinder?

   A. 6
   B. 12
   C. 16
   D. 32

9. Which has a greater surface area – a cube with sides of length 8 m or a rectangular prism which is 7 m x 8 m x 9 m?

   A. Cube
   B. Rectangular Prism
   C. Equal
   D. Not enough information.

10. What is the surface area of the square-based pyramid in the figure below if the side of the square equals 6 meters, and the height of the pyramid is 4 meters?

    A. 48 m²
    B. 84 m²
    C. 96 m²
    D. 144 m²

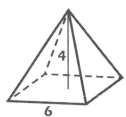

Surface Area: Answer Explanations

1. C   To find the surface area of a box, add the areas of each of the 6 faces. Plug the height, length, and width into the formula.

Surface Area of Box =
Sum of Area of 6 faces =
(2 x length x width) + (2 x length x height) + (2 x width x height) =
(2 x 9 x 7) + (2 x 9 x 3) + (2 x 3 x 7) =
126 + 54 + 42 =
222 sq meters

2. C To find the surface area of the cylinder, you must calculate the area of each face.

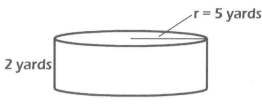

Face 1: Top – The top of the cylinder is a circle with an area of πr^2.
$\pi r^2 = \pi 5^2 = 25\pi$

Face 2: Bottom – The top and the bottom have the same area = 25π.

Face 3: Side – The side of the cylinder can be thought of as a rolled-up rectangle with one side equal to the cylinder height and the other side equal to the circumference of the base, which can be found by multiplying $2\pi r$.
height x $2\pi r = 2 \times 2\pi \times 5 = 20\pi$

Total Surface Area = $25\pi + 25\pi + 20\pi = 70\pi$

3. B Use the formula for surface area of a sphere. This formula is on the formula sheet, which you should be used to looking at, as opposed to memorizing formulas.

Surface Area of a Sphere = $4 \times \pi \times r^2 = 4 \times \pi \times 6^2 = 144\pi$

4. C The two shortest walls will be 19 feet long and 10 feet tall. Find the area by multiplying length times height, and then multiply by 2, since there are 2 walls.
19 x 10 x 2 = 380 sq ft

The two longest walls will be 26 feet long and 10 feet tall. Find the area by multiplying.
26 x 10 x 2 = 520 sq ft

Find the sum.
520 + 380 = 900 sq ft

5. C There are five surfaces on the triangular prism, so find the sum of all areas of the surfaces.

Bottom: The bottom is a rectangle with dimensions 8m by 3m. Area = 8 x 3 = 24 sq m.
Front triangle: The area of a triangle is base x height x 1/2 = 3 x 4 x 1/2 = 6 sq m.
Back triangle: This triangle has the same dimensions as the front triangle. Area = 6 sq m.
Top: This is a rectangle with dimensions of 8 m by 5 m. Area = 8 x 5 = 40 sq m.
Left side: This is a rectangle with dimensions 8 m by 4 m. Area = 8 x 4 = 32 sq m.

Sum all the sides to find the total surface area.

Surface Area
= 24 sq m + 6 sq m + 6 sq m + 40 sq m + 32 sq m = 108 sq m.

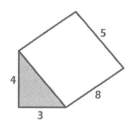

Geometry II: Surface Area

6. A A cube has 6 faces, all with the same area. The area of each face is side x side, or side^2.

So, surface area of a cube = 6 x side^2

$150 = 6 \times$ side^2

$25 =$ side^2

$5 =$ side

Length of one side = 5 m

7. C A rectangular prism has 6 faces.
Two faces with dimensions: width x length
2 x width x length = 2 x y x 2y = 4y^2

Two faces with dimensions: width x height
2 x width x height = 2 x y x 3y = 6y^2

Two faces with dimensions: length x height
2 x length x height = 2 x 2y x 3y = 12y^2

Total surface area = 4y^2 + 6y^2 + 12y^2 = 22y^2

8. A A cylinder has 3 faces.

Top Circular Base: Area = πradius^2
= π10^2
= 100π

Bottom Circular Base: Same Area as top base
= 100π

Around side of Cylinder: can be thought of as a rolled-up rectangle
Area of the rectangle = Circumference of base x height
= 2πradius x height
= 2π10 x height
= 20πheight

Total surface Area = Area of top base + Area of bottom base + Area of side
320π = 100π + 100π + 20πheight
320π = 200π + 20πheight
120π = 20πheight
120 = 20 x height
6 = height

9. A   **Cube:** A cube has six equal faces; therefore, the surface area is found by multiplying 6 by the area of one face.

Surface Area = 6 x side²
              = 6 x 8²
              = 6 x 64
              = 384

Rectangular Prism: There are six faces: two with area of length x width, two with area of width x height, two with area of length x height.

Surface Area = 2(length x width) + 2(width x height) + 2(length x height)
              = 2(7 x 8) + 2(8 x 9) + 2(7 x 9)
              = 2(56) + 2(72) + 2(63)
              = 112 + 144 + 126
              = 382

The cube's surface area is larger.

10. C   The total surface area for the pyramid is the sum of the areas of each face. Four triangles and one square make up the pyramid faces.

Area of square base: 6 m x 6 m = 36 m²

Now, the more complicated area of each triangle face. Area of a triangle is 1/2 x base x height. We know that the base of the triangles is 6 meters, but we don't know the height of each triangle. We can make a right triangle, as can be seen in the diagram below, with the height of the pyramid as one side, half the length of the base as the second side, and the height of the triangle faces as the hypotenuse. Now, using the Pythagorean Theorem, you can find the height of the triangle faces.

$3^2 + 4^2 = x^2$
$9 + 16 = x^2$
$25 = x^2$
$x = 5$

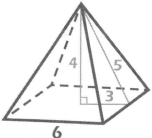

Now, to find the area of each triangular face:
1/2 x base x height = 1/2 x 6 x 5 = 15 m²

Total Surface Area = 36 m² + 4(15 m²) = 96 m²

Geometry II: Geometric Properties & Proofs

Geometric Proofs

Proofs are ways to argue logically about a certain object or angle in geometric terms with step-by-step reasoning on how the conclusion is reached. The reasoning includes definitions, axioms, postulates, and theorems.

Some basic terms in geometry are undefined, as they are self-evident in nature. Examples of undefined terms include a point, a line, and a plane. Postulates and axioms are accepted as true without proof. Quite often, the terms postulate and axiom are interchangeable; however, generally, axioms are properties of real numbers, and postulates are properties of geometric figures. Theorems are statements that can be proved from postulates or axioms. Once a theorem has been proven, it can be used in other proofs. Corollaries are statements whose truth can be easily deducted from theorems.

Axioms

The following are examples of common axioms or statements accepted as true without proof:

- The equality of an equation remains if the same number is added to both sides of the equation.
- The equality of an equation remains if the same number is subtracted from both sides of the equation.
- Substitution – Equals can be substituted for each other in any equality or inequality.
- Transitive – If two quantities are equal to a third quantity, they are equal to each other. If $A = B$ and $B = C$, then $A = C$.

Postulates

The following are examples of common postulates or statements accepted as true without proof:

- A line contains at least two points.
- Two lines can intersect at either zero or one point, but no more than one.
- Through a point not on a line, exactly one line can be drawn parallel to the first line (the parallel postulate).
- Through a point on a line, exactly one line perpendicular to the first line can be drawn.
- A segment has exactly one midpoint.
- An angle has exactly one bisector.
- The shortest distance between two points is the length of the segment joining those points.
- Every angle has a measure between 0 and 180 degrees.
- If a ray bisects two other rays, then the angles formed can be added.
- If two rays are the same, then the angle between them is 0 degrees.
- If two rays are opposite, then the angle between them is 180 degrees.
- The three methods discussed for proving the congruence of triangles are all postulates. These are the SSS, SAS, and ASA postulates.

Deductive Reasoning

A form of reasoning by which each conclusion follows from the previous conclusion and builds toward a final statement. A direct proof is a form of deductive reasoning. This type of proof begins with a premise assumed to be true based on the statement in the problem. Then, each step in the proof builds toward proving the conclusion true.

In contrast, an indirect proof does not directly demonstrate that a conclusion is true. Instead, an indirect proof shows that all alternatives to the conclusion are false.

Inductive Reasoning

A form of reasoning in which a conclusion is reached based on a pattern that can be seen in numerous observations. Just based on observations, it is not a valid method of proof on its own, since just because one observes a number of situations in a pattern doesn't mean the pattern will always be true. However, through observations, the reasoning can be turned into geometric hypotheses that can be later proved.

There are inductive proofs that start with observations. These types of proofs start with showing that the initial values make a statement hold true. Then, an assumption can be made that it holds true for a certain value k. If it can be proven that using the statement for k must hold true for k + 1, then you know it must hold true for all values. Again, first show initial values true, then show if k is true then k + 1 is true, then you know that each consecutive value will be true, and therefore, it must work for all values.

The Nature of Axiomatic Systems

Euclidean geometry is said to be an axiomatic system. In such a system, the theorems are derived from just a few axioms. Some properties of axiomatic systems are
- Consistent: Both direct and indirect versions of proofs are valid.
- Independent: The axioms are not derived from one another.
- Complete: Every statement or its negative can be derived.

Geometric Properties

Circle Theorems

Here are a few theorems associated with the properties of circles.

- A chord is a line interior to a circle that connects two points. If the chord and a radius form a right angle, then the chord bisects the radius.
- Chords that are the same distance from the center are congruent.
- If the arcs within a circle are congruent, then their corresponding angles are also congruent.

Parallelograms and Quadrilaterals

Here are some properties of these polygons that you have already covered in other lessons.

- A quadrilateral is a polygon with four sides and four corners. Parallelograms are types of quadrilaterals. However, not all quadrilaterals are parallelograms.
- A parallelogram has two pairs of parallel lines. However, none of the lines has to be perpendicular. A rectangle is a type of parallelogram with perpendicular lines.
- A trapezoid is another type of quadrilateral. In a trapezoid, only one pair of lines is parallel.

Parallel and Perpendicular Line Properties

Listed below are some line properties you have seen before.

- Parallel lines are sets of lines that never cross each other. In other words, the distance between the lines is always the same.
- Perpendicular lines cross each other at right angles (that is 90 degrees).
- Polygons are comprised of connected line segments. Some lines might be parallel; some might be perpendicular; and some are neither parallel nor perpendicular. For example, a rectangle has two pairs of parallel lines. A rectangle also has four right angles resulting from the intersection of perpendicular lines.
- In a circle, the tangent line to a circle is perpendicular to the radius at that point.
- In addition, the tangent lines at points of opposite ends of the circle are parallel.

Indirect Measurement

Indirect measurement determines a measurement value by measuring another quantity. One example is using proportions to determine the length of a side of similar triangles.

Changing Linear Dimensions

Changing the length of a particular measure of an object can affect other measurements. The particular effect is determined by the formula.

For example, a change in the radius of a circle would have a linear effect on the circle's circumference. Since $C = 2\pi r$, doubling the radius would also double the circumference. However, for the area of a circle, $A = \pi r^2$, doubling the radius would increase the area by $2^2 = 4$ times.

Effects of Measurement Error and Rounding

The measurement of the dimensions of objects is seldom without some margin of error. The margin of error is typically designated as some quantity plus or minus some rounding value.

To find the maximum possible error in measurement, compare the original measurement to the measurements at the high and low margins of error.

Non-Euclidean Geometries

In Euclidean geometry, the Parallel Postulate states that, through a point not on a particular line, only one other line is parallel to the given line. Non-Euclidean geometries are those for which the Parallel Postulate is false. Two types of non-Euclidean geometry are Hyperbolic geometry and Elliptic geometry.

Hyperbolic geometry states that, through a point not on a particular line, more than one line is parallel to the given line.

Elliptic geometry states that, through a point not on a particular line, no line is parallel to the given line.

Two parallel straight lines in Euclidean geometry would be
        Getting farther away from each other in Hyperbolic geometry.
        Curving toward each other and eventually crossing in Elliptical geometry.

If you think of drawing geometric figures on curved surfaces, this will help explain the concepts of non-Euclidean geometry.

Geometric Properties & Proofs: Practice

1. Line AB is parallel to Line CD. Another Line EF is perpendicular to Line AB. What can be said about the relationship between CD and EF?

    A. CD and EF are parallel lines.

    B. CD and EF are perpendicular lines.

    C. CD and EF are axiomatic lines.

    D. CD and EF are tangent lines.

2. The following statement is an example of what?

The shortest distance between two points is a line.

    A. Postulate

    B. Theorem

    C. Undefined Term

    D. Corollary

3. Given are two non-parallel lines, both intersected by a third line as shown in the diagram below.

   Proof: ∠b ≠ ∠c
   ∠b = ∠a
   Assume ∠a = ∠c.
   If ∠a = ∠c, then the two lines must be parallel.
   However, it is given that the two lines are not parallel. Therefore, ∠a ≠ ∠c.
   If ∠a ≠ ∠c and ∠b = ∠a, then ∠b ≠ ∠c.

What is this proof an example of?

   A. Inductive proof.
   B. Conditional proof.
   C. Indirect proof.
   D. Axiomatic proof.

4. Four line segments joined together at corners form a shape. Two line segments are parallel, but the other two are not parallel. What kind of shape is this?

   A. Pentagon
   B. Rectangle
   C. Trapezoid
   D. Parallelogram

5. Line AB is tangent to a circle at Point p. The radius is a line joining the center to Point p. What kind of angle is formed by AB and the specified radius?

   A. The lines form an acute angle.
   B. The lines form an obtuse angle.
   C. The lines form a right angle.
   D. The lines do not form an angle.

6. What is another name for a chord of maximum length?

   A. Arc
   B. Circumference
   C. Radius
   D. Diameter

7. Triangle ABC is inscribed in a semicircle with a radius of 3 units. Line segment AB has a length of 3 units. What is the length of line segment BC?

A. 3
B. 3√2
C. 3√3
D. 4√3

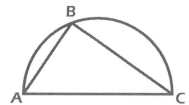

8. Which of the following is not a true statement from the angle measure postulate?

A. Every angle has a measure between 0 and 180 degrees.
B. If two rays are opposite, then the angle between them is 180 degrees.
C. If a ray bisects two other rays, then the sum of the angles is 90 degrees.
D. If two rays are the same, then the angle between them is 0 degrees.

9. A cylindrical can is measured to have a base radius of 4 cm and a height of 6 cm, both rounded plus or minus 1 cm. The volume of the can is calculated based on these measurements. What is the maximum possible error in the calculated volume of the can?

A. 51π cm³
B. 79π cm³
C. 96π cm³
D. 130π cm³

10. Using inductive reasoning, what would be the missing step, step 5, in the proof?

Prove: 1 + 2 + 3 + ... + n = n(n + 1)/2 holds for all positive integer values for n.
    1. n = 1, 1 = 1(2)/2 = 1 True.
    2. n = 2, 1 + 2 = 2(3)/2 = 3 True.
    3. n = 3, 1 + 2 + 3 = 3(4)/2 = 6 True.
    4. Assume it holds for some value k. 1 + 2 + 3 + ... + k = k(k + 1)/2
    5. MISSING STEP
    6. 1 + 2 + 3 + ... + n = n(n + 1)/2 holds for all positive integer values for n.

A. Show that statement is true for k = n.
B. Prove that statement is true for k = 4.
C. Using statement for k, prove statement holds true for k + 1.
D. Prove all alternatives to statement are false.

Geometric Properties & Proofs: Answer Explanations

1. B If two lines are parallel, then lines perpendicular to one line are also perpendicular to the other. For example, you can think of the sides of a rectangle with AB and CD as sides opposite each other and EF connecting those two sides.

2. A The statement is the distance postulate. Remember that postulates or axioms are statements that are considered self-evident and are unproven.

3. C The proof is called an indirect proof, since an alternative to the conclusion (that is $\angle a = \angle c$) is shown to be false. This indirect proof uses deductive reasoning by building step-by-step until a conclusion is reached.

4. C A shape formed with four lines is a quadrilateral. Three types of quadrilaterals are parallelograms, rectangles, and trapezoids. A pentagon has five sides.

In a rectangle, all lines are parallel and at right angles. A parallelogram also has two pairs of parallel lines. A trapezoid has four sides, but only one pair of parallel lines.

5. C The tangent line is perpendicular to the radius at that point. Perpendicular lines form a 90-degree or a right angle.

6. D A chord is a line segment that joins two points on a circle. If the two points of the chord are at opposite ends of the circle, then the chord intersects the center of the circle. A straight line through a circle passing through the center is a diameter, and this is the chord with maximum length.

7. C A triangle inscribed inside a semicircle forms a right triangle at Point B.

We also know that AC is the diameter of the circle, which is equal to twice the radius or 6 units.

Therefore, we can use the Pythagorean theorem to calculate the length of BC, called x in the following equation.

$x^2 + 3^2 = 6^2$
$x^2 + 9 = 36$
$x^2 = 27$
$x = \sqrt{27}$
$x = \sqrt{9 \times 3}$
$x = 3\sqrt{3}$

8. C Choices A, B, and D are true statements and are from the angle measure postulate.

Choice C is false. The angles can be added, but their sum is not necessarily 90 degrees.

9. B The volume of a cylinder can be found by using the formula: $V = \pi r^2 h$, as it is equal to the area of the base, which is a circle, times the height of the object.

The volume of the can based on the measurements:
$$V_{estimate} = \pi 4^2 6 = 96\pi$$

The maximum volume if the dimensions were 5cm radius and 7cm height:
$$V_{max} = \pi 5^2 7 = 175\pi$$

The minimum volume if the dimensions were 3cm radius and 5cm height:
$$V_{min} = \pi 3^2 5 = 45\pi$$

The possible errors in volume calculation are: $|V_{max} - V_{estimate}|$ or $|V_{estimate} - V_{min}|$
$$|V_{max} - V_{estimate}| = |175\pi - 96\pi| = 79\pi$$
$$|V_{estimate} - V_{min}| = |96\pi - 45\pi| = 51\pi$$

The maximum possible error then is 79π.

10. C Inductive reasoning involves starting with proving that the initial values are true. Then, assume that it works for a certain value of k. Then, prove that if it works for k, then it works for k + 1. If it holds for all the initial values and holds for each consecutive value, then it must always be true.

In this case, the proof started with showing that it works for n = 1, n = 2, and n = 3, the initial values. Then, it assumed that it holds true for n = k. The next step would be to prove that if it works for k, it must work for k + 1.

Let's review how that would be done.
1 + 2 + 3 + ... + k = k(k + 1)/2
Add k + 1 to both sides of the equation.
1 + 2 + 3 + ... + k + (k + 1) = k(k + 1)/2 + (k + 1)

Now, simplify the right-hand side of the equation. Make the denominators the same, and then add the fractions.
1 + 2 + 3 + ... + k + (k + 1) = k(k + 1)/2 + 2(k + 1)/2
1 + 2 + 3 + ... + k + (k + 1) = [k(k + 1) + 2(k + 1)]/2
1 + 2 + 3 + ... + k + (k + 1) = [(k + 1)(k + 2)]/2

The statement above shows that it is true for k + 1.

So, we know that if it works for n = k, then it must also for n = k + 1. So, it is shown that it is true for n = 1, n = 2, n = 3. Then, if it works for n = 3, it must work for n = 4. If it works for n = 4, it must work for n = 5, and so on. It must hold for all positive integers of n.

Geometry II: Module Review

1. If Triangle ABC is similar to Triangle DEF, what is the length of DE?

A. 18
B. 20
C. 21
D. 24

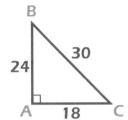

2. What is the volume of the right triangular prism below in units cubed?

A. 48
B. 60
C. 96
D. 120

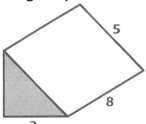

3. What is the volume and surface area of a cylinder with radius 5 m and height 8 m?

A. 200π m³, 130π m²
B. 200π m³, 105π m²
C. 80π m³, 50π m²
D. 80π m³, 130π m²

4. You have a right triangle, and you double the length of all the sides. How does the area change?

A. Increases by 2
B. Doubles
C. Triples
D. Quadruples

5. If the length of each side of a cube is doubled, what happens to the volume of the cube?

A. Doubles
B. Quadruples
C. Multiplies by 6
D. Multiplies by 8

6. If you have two similar triangles, which of the following transformations could have been performed?

   I. Translation
   II. Reflection
   III. Dilation

   A. I only

   B. II and III only

   C. I and II only

   D. I, II, and III

7. If you have two congruent triangles, which of the following could have been performed on one to generate the other?

   I. Translation
   II. Reflection
   III. Dilation

   A. I only

   B. II and III only

   C. I and II only

   D. I, II, and III

8. You have a square piece of paper, and you cut 3-inch squares off every corner, fold up, and create a box. The volume of the box is 192 cubic inches. What is the original length of one side of the square paper?

   A. 8 inches

   B. 11 inches

   C. 14 inches

   D. 64 inches

9. If Triangles ABC and DEF are similar, what is the sum of x and y?

   A. 22

   B. 24

   C. 25

   D. 26

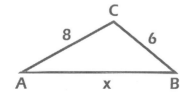
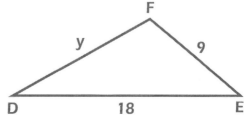

10. In the figure below, AB = AC, and Angle ABC = 55°. What is the measure of Angle ACD?

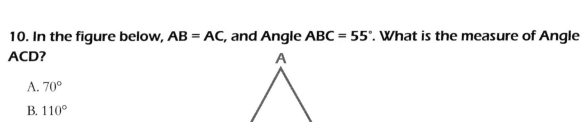

A. 70°
B. 110°
C. 125°
D. 155°

11. In Triangle ABC, Angle A = 4x, Angle B = 6x − 10, and Angle C = 2x + 10. What does x equal?

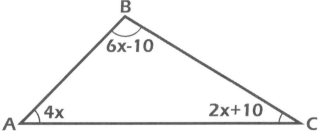

A. 10
B. 15
C. 20
D. 30

12. Choose the best answer to replace the question mark.

Surface Area of a Sphere with radius of 9 m   ?   Surface Area of a Cylinder with radius of 9 m and height of 9 m

A. <
B. >
C. =
D. Not Enough Information

13. What is the measure of each interior angle of a regular pentagon?

A. 90°
B. 108°
C. 120°
D. 540°

14. Which of the following transformations would be performed on the graph of y = (¼)x to get the graph of y = −4x?

A. translation
B. rotation
C. dilation
D. reflection

Geometry II: Module Review

15. Which of the following statements is/are true?
    I. All squares are similar.
    II. All right triangles are similar.
    III. All parallelograms are similar.

   A. I only

   B. I and II

   C. I, II, and III

   D. None of the above.

16. Which has the largest volume?

   A. Cube with sides length 6 m

   B. Sphere with diameter 6 m

   C. Cylinder with height 6 m and diameter 6 m

   D. Rectangular prism with sides length 5 m, 6 m, 7 m

17. What is the surface area of the triangular prism below?

   A. 180

   B. 336

   C. 384

   D. 720

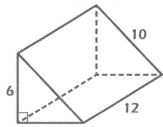

18. A cylindrical object sits on the ground as pictured below. What is the cross section of a paper, which is at a 30-degree angle to the ground, through the cylinder?

   A. sphere

   B. circle

   C. rectangle

   D. ellipse

19. A container has length x, width w, depth d, and volume V. What is the volume of a new container that has double the length, triple the width, and half the depth?

   A. V/2

   B. V

   C. 3V

   D. 6V

Geometry II: Module Review   369

20. If a student is given the following information, what can she prove about the figure?

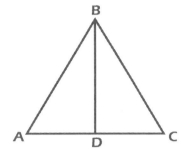

Given:
Angle ADB is 90 degrees.
Segment BD bisects Segment AC.

A. Angle ABD is congruent to Angle DCB.
B. Triangles ABD and CBD are congruent by SAS.
C. Triangle ABD is similar to Triangle ABC.
D. Not enough information for a proof.

Geometry II: Module Review Answer Explanations

1. B   Since the triangles are similar, set up a proportion.

AB/DE = AC/DF
24/DE = 18/15

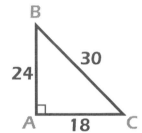

Cross-multiply and solve for DE.
(24)(15) = (DE)(18)
360 = 18(DE)
DE = 20

2. A   To find the volume of the triangular prism, you first need to find the height of the prism. Since the base makes a right triangle, and you know one side is 3 and the hypotenuse is 5, you can use the Pythagorean theorem to solve for the height.

$3^2 + height^2 = 5^2$
$9 + height^2 = 25$
$height^2 = 16$
$height = 4$

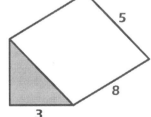

To find volume, find the area of the base and multiply it by the height. The base is a triangle, and the area of a triangle can be found by multiplying height by width and dividing by 2 (or you can think of it as multiplying height by width by ½).

Area of Base = height x width ÷ 2
= 4 x 3 ÷ 2 = 6

Volume = Area of Base x Prism Length
= 6 x 8 = 48

3. A   Volume of a cylinder can be found by multiplying the area of the base by the height of the cylinder.

Volume = Area of Base x Height
= πr^2 x height = $\pi 5^2$ x 8 = 25π x 8 = 200π
Volume = 200π m³

The surface area of a cylinder can be found by adding the areas of the top base, bottom base, and side.

Surface Area = area of top base + area of bottom base + area of side
= $\pi r^2 + \pi r^2 + \pi d h$
= $\pi 5^2 + \pi 5^2 + \pi(10)(8)$
= $25\pi + 25\pi + 80\pi = 130\pi$
Surface Area = 130π m²

Volume = 200π m³, Surface Area = 130π m²

4. D   The area of a triangle = 1/2 x base x height = 1/2bh

If you double the length of all the sides, the length of the base and the height will each double. The new area can then be found:

New Area = (1/2)(2b)(2h) = (4)(1/2)bh = 4(original area)

The area quadruples.

5. D   Let each side of the original cube = S.

Then, the volume of the original cube = S x S x S = S³

Each side of the new cube = 2S

Then, the volume of the new cube = 2S x 2S x 2S
= 8S³ = 8(volume of original cube).

Volume multiplies by 8.

6. D   Similar triangles have the same shape but can have different sizes and orientations.

I. Translation: Translation involves moving an object. Moving an object will not change its shape, so this transformation could have been performed.

II. Reflection: Reflection involves flipping an object about an axis. Flipping an object will not change its shape, just its orientation, so reflection could have been performed.

III. Dilation: Dilation involves changing an object's size. For similar triangles, the sizes can be different, just not the shapes. Therefore, dilation could have been performed.

I, II, and III

7. C Congruent triangles have the same shape and size but can have different orientations.

I. Translation: Translation involves moving an object. Moving an object will not change its shape or size, so this transformation could have been performed.

II. Reflection: Reflection involves flipping an object about an axis. Flipping an object will not change its size or shape, just its orientation, so reflection could have been performed.

III. Dilation: Dilation involves changing an object's size. For congruent triangles, the sizes cannot be different. Therefore, dilation could not have been performed.

I and II only

8. C If you cut 3-inch squares off each corner and folded up the sides, then the height of the box would be 3 inches. Therefore, the volume would be found by multiplying x by x by 3.
$3x^2 = 192$, $x^2 = 64$, $x = 8$

Therefore, the original length of a side of the square is
$x + 3 + 3 = 8 + 3 + 3 = 14$ inches

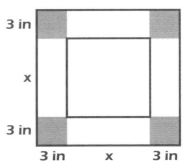

9. B Since the triangles are similar, their sides are proportional. Let's first calculate x. Side AB corresponds to Side DE. Side BC corresponds to Side EF.
AB/DE = BC/EF
x/18 = 6/9

Now, cross-multiply to solve for x.
$9x = (18)(6) = 108$
$x = 12$

To solve for y, follow similar steps.
AC/DF = BC/EF
8/y = 6/9
$6y = (8)(9) = 72$
$y = 12$

The sum of x and y = 12 + 12 = 24.

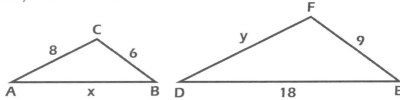

10. C If AB = AC, that means that the angles opposite the equal sides are equal. Therefore, if Angle ABC = 55°, then Angle ACB = 55°.

Angle ACB and Angle ACD form a straight line, and therefore, their angles total 180°.

Angle ACB + Angle ACD = 180°
55° + Angle ACD = 180°
Angle ACD = 125°

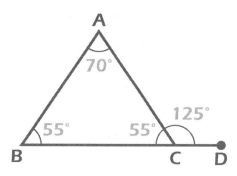

11. B In a triangle, all 3 angles add up to 180°. Set up an equation and solve for x.

Angle A + Angle B + Angle C = 180
4x + 6x − 10 + 2x + 10 = 180
12x = 180
x = 15

12. C Let's calculate the surface area of each shape.

Sphere: To calculate the surface area of a sphere, you can use the following formula: $4\pi r^2$. In this case, sphere's surface area = 4 x π x 9² = 324π

Cylinder: To calculate the surface area of a cylinder, you must find the area of all the surfaces. The top and bottom are circles with an area of πr^2. The side of a cylinder can be found by taking the circumference of the base and multiplying by the height = 2πrh.

2 x area of base + area of side =
2πr² + 2πrh =
2π9² + 2π x 9 x 9 =
162π + 162π = 324π

Their surface areas are equal.

13. B The sum of the angles in a triangle is 180°. A pentagon can be divided into 3 triangles, so the sum of the measures of a pentagon is 3 x 180° = 540°.

There are 5 interior angles in a pentagon. Since the question asks about a regular polygon, you know all angles are equal. Divide 540° by 5 to find the measure of each interior angle.

540° ÷ 5 = 108°

Pentagon = 3 Triangles
= 3 x 180°
= 540°

Geometry II: Module Review

14. B $y = (1/4)x$
$y = -4x$

Graph both equations on the coordinate plane.

As can be seen in the image to the right, to get from one graph to the other, you would rotate the line.

Translation moves objects. Dilation changes the size of objects. Reflection flips an object about an axis. None of those transformations were performed on the lines.

Rotation

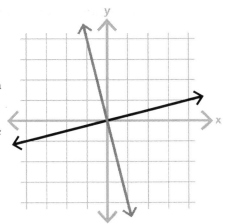

15. A   Similar polygons have the same shape and same angles. They can be different sizes and in different orientations. To be the same shape, polygons must have proportionate sides.

I. All squares are similar.
This statement is true. Squares all have the same angles and shapes. Performing the following transformations will get from one square to another: dilation, rotation, translation, or reflection. All those transformations hold true for similar polygons.

II. All right triangles are similar.
This statement is false. Similar polygons have the same angles, but not all right triangles have the same angles. For example, you can have one right triangle with angles 45°, 45°, and 90° and another with angles 30°, 60°, and 90°.

III. All parallelograms are similar.
This statement is false. Parallelograms do not necessarily have the same shape or angles. For example, a rectangle is a parallelogram and so is a rhombus, but they are not the same shape.

Only I is true.

16. A   Find the volume of each:
A: Cube with sides length 6 m
Volume = side x side x side = 6 x 6 x 6 = 216 m³

B: Sphere with diameter 6 m
Volume = $(4/3)\pi radius^3$ = $(4/3)\pi 3^3$ = 36π = approximately 110 m³

C: Cylinder with height 6 m and diameter 6 m
Volume = $\pi radius^2$ x height = $\pi 3^2$ x 6 = 54π = approximately 170 m³

D: Rectangular prism with sides length 5 m, 6 m, 7 m
Volume = length x width x height = 5 m x 6 m x 7 m = 210 m³

The cube has the largest volume.

17. B The surface area of a triangular prism is the sum of all the areas of the faces. There are five faces on a triangular prism. To find the areas of each face, we first need all the dimensions of the shape.

We know the hypotenuse and one side, so we can use the Pythagorean theorem to find the missing side.
side^2 + 6^2 = 10^2
side^2 + 36 = 100
side^2 = 64
side = 8

Now, find the area of each face.
Area of front triangle = 1/2 x 6 x 8 = 24
Area of back triangle = 1/2 x 6 x 8 = 24
Area of bottom = 12 x 8 = 96
Area of top = 12 x 10 = 120
Area of left side = 12 x 6 = 72

Surface area = 72 + 120 + 96 + 24 + 24 = 336

18. D A cylinder is a circle extended by height. The cross section of a sphere taken at an angle to the ground is an ellipse. If the cross section were taken parallel to the base, it would create a circle.

19. C The volume of the original container is V_{old} = xwd.
The volume of the new container is V_{new} = (2x)(3w)d/2 = 3xwd
And, since V_{old} = xwd, we can substitute to find the volume of the new container V_{new}.
V_{new} = 3xwd = 3V_{old}

20. B Since BD bisects AC, segment AD is congruent to segment CD.
    AD = CD

Angles ADB and CDB form a straight line, and therefore, the measures of those two angles add to 180°. It is given Angle ADB = 90°, and therefore Angle CDB = 180° − 90° = 90°.
    ∠ADB = ∠CDB

Segment BD = Segment BD. This is the reflexive property. Rather an obvious statement, but nonetheless needed in the proof.
    BD = BD

Therefore, Triangles ABD and CBD are congruent by SAS.

7. Statistics & Probability

Gathering & Visualizing Data 378
Central Tendency & Dispersion 385
Sample Space & Probability 391
Permutations & Combinations 399
Advanced Statistics 406
Module Review 414

Statistics & Probability: Gathering & Visualizing Data

Gathering Data

You can use several different methods to gather statistical data. Some are more appropriate than others in certain situations.

Experimental vs. Observational Data

One important distinction is the difference between experimental and observational data. With experimental data, the experimenter creates artificial conditions for drawing a conclusion. In an observational study, the observer gathers information without influencing the object of the study.

For example, an experiment could involve giving one set of plants one type of plant food and another set of plants a second type of plant food and then recording how the different foods affected their growth. An observational study might involve recording a plant's growth in summer and in winter and comparing the two without interfering with the plant's growth.

Census

A census involves gathering information from every person in a group. For example, to find out how many hours of sleep seniors at a high school get each night, you could conduct a census of every single senior in the school. This method is generally used for gathering information from small groups of people – the big exception being the nationwide government census conducted every 10 years.

Survey

A survey is typically used to gather information from large groups of people. In a survey, information from a representative sample of the large group is used to make inferences about the entire group. For example, if you wanted to find out how many hours of sleep seniors at a high school get each night, you could survey 50 random seniors and then infer about the entire senior class based on the answers you received.

Representative Sample/Bias

For survey results to be meaningful, the sample from which they are drawn needs to be representative of all variations within the group. A sample that represents one part of the target group more heavily than others is said to include a bias. For example, if a group conducting a survey to determine America's favorite food chose to sample only elementary school students, the results would be biased toward the opinions of younger Americans (most likely toward pizza and fast food).

A bias can also be created in the way questions are asked. For example, if the same students were surveyed immediately after a discussion on healthy eating, it's possible that the answers will show a bias toward healthy food that would not otherwise have been there.

Random Sample

The best way to ensure a representative sample is to select respondents randomly from all members of the target group. A sample for the amount of sleep that seniors get would not be representative if you only asked seniors who were on sports teams. A better approach would be to ask every fourth person based on their Student ID numbers.

Methods of Organizing Data

It is often useful to represent survey data graphically to uncover patterns in the data. There are many different ways to graph data. Some more common methods are covered here.

Bar Charts

Bar charts are typically used to compare values. In a bar chart, rectangular bars are used to proportionately represent data. The chart shows that 20 students in Ms. Jones' class chose pizza as their favorite food; 15 chose hamburgers; and 5 chose chicken nuggets.

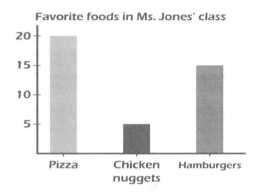

Favorite foods in Ms. Jones' class

Pie Charts

In a pie chart, the circle or pie represents the entire sample, divided up into slices to represent each set of values proportionally. Pie charts are always only used to show one data series and are particularly useful for highlighting a significant element in the data.

The diagram to the right shows the results for Ms. Jones' class in pie chart form. Since there are 40 students in the class and 20 of them chose pizza, pizza takes ½ the chart. The 5 chicken nugget responses are ⅛ the whole, and the 15 hamburger responses ⅜.

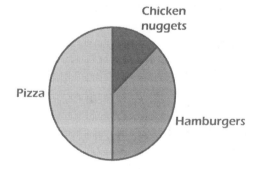

Favorite foods in Ms. Jones' class

Stem Plot

A stem plot (also called a stem and leaf plot) is useful for organizing large amounts of information. Stem plots display data by place value. Each stem is a number representing a group of ten, and it is written to the left of the line. The stems are each paired with one or more leaf digits. Each leaf shows a number in the ones place to represent different data points. For example, if a teacher gave a particularly hard test and wanted to display the results, he could use a stem plot. Below are the data points for this test, and it is clear that the majority of the students got scores in the 60s by just glancing. This plot shows 67, 67, 68, 69, and 69 in the 6-stem and 70 and 71 in the 7-stem.

Stem	Leaf	Key
6	7, 7, 8, 9, 9	Leaf unit: 1
7	0, 1	Stem unit: 10

Statistics & Probability: Gathering & Visualizing Data

Scatter Plots

Scatter plots allow you to show the relationships among numerical values graphed as coordinate pairs. Scatter plots can be used to show several series of data, making them particularly useful for scientific data. The scatter plot shows high temperatures in Menlo Park, California, for a week. Day 1 represents Sunday, Day 2 Monday, and so on.

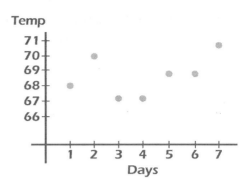

Variables and the Line of Best Fit

When using graphs with an x-axis and y-axis – such as a scatter plot – the independent variable is always graphed on the x-axis, while the y-axis is used to represent dependent variables. A line of best fit (or trend line) can be used to see if there is a trend in the relationship between the independent and dependent variables. It also helps to minimize the effect of random errors in measurements.

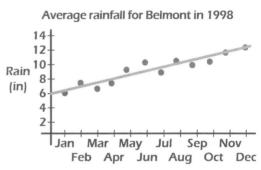

The line of best fit is as close to as many points as possible. In the graph above, the month is the independent variable, and the rainfall in inches is the dependent variable. As you can see, the line of best fit illuminates a trend of average rainfall increasing with each month.

Gathering & Visualizing Data: Practice

1. A census is the most appropriate method for collecting data about which group?

   A. 18–25 year olds in China

   B. Senior citizens worldwide

   C. Republican voters in Iowa

   D. Employees of the local supermarket

2. A representative sample is
   I. drawn from the group being analyzed
   II. random
   III. chosen by the members of the group

   A. I only

   B. II only

   C. I and II

   D. I, II, and III

3. According to the bar chart, how many more science textbooks than reading textbooks does the store have in stock?

   A. 20
   B. 30
   C. 50
   D. 80

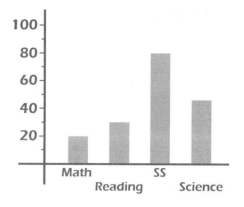

4. Which pie chart best reflects the data below?

   Monthly Finances
   Rent: $1500
   Food: $500
   Entertainment: $1000
   Car: $500

A. 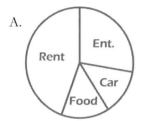   B. 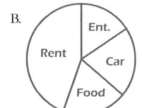   C. 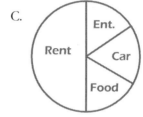   D.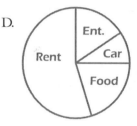

5. Which stem plot represents the following data?
Test Scores: 77, 86, 95, 62, 94, 82, 73, 70, 95, 89, 88, 82, 82

A.
Stem	Leaf
6	2
7	0, 3, 7
8	2, 2, 2, 6, 8, 9
9	4, 5, 5

B.
Stem	Leaf
6	2
7	0, 3, 7
8	2, 6, 8, 9
9	4, 5

C.
Stem	Leaf
60	2
70	0, 3, 7
80	2, 2, 2, 6, 8, 9
90	4, 5, 5

D.
Stem	Leaf
0	7
2	6, 8, 8, 8
3	7
4	9
5	9, 9
6	8
7	7
8	8
9	8

6. What trend has this company's profits followed?

   A. Sharp rise followed by sharp drop
   B. Steady rise
   C. Sharp rise, then drop, then steady rise
   D. Steady decline

Statistics & Probability: Gathering & Visualizing Data

7. Suppose you have just conducted a survey of languages spoken by college students. Your goal is to illustrate the proportion of students who speak each language. What would be the best way to visualize this data?

   A. Stem and leaf plot

   B. Table

   C. Pie chart

   D. Scatter plot

8. Which is the independent variable in the graph?

   A. Time

   B. Weight

   C. Neither

   D. Both

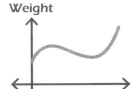

9. Bias may be introduced into a survey by:
      I. Over-representing a certain portion of the population
      II. Under-representing a certain portion of the population
      III. Phrasing of the questions used in the survey

   A. I only

   B. II only

   C. I and III

   D. I, II, and III

10. Which of the following is the line of best fit for the data?

A.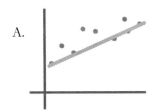

B.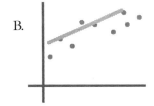

C.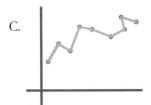

D.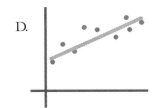

Gathering & Visualizing Data: Answer Explanations

1. D   Since a census involves collecting data from every member of a population, it is most appropriately used for small groups. In this case, the smallest group is the employees of your local supermarket.

2. C   Those conducting the experiment, not the members of the group, choose the members chosen for the representative sample. A representative sample is useful for drawing inferences about a group without surveying every member of that group.

Answer C: I and II

3. A   There are 50 science textbooks in stock and 30 reading textbooks. Subtract to find out how many more science textbooks there are. 50 – 30 = 20.

4. A   The total amount spent per month is $3,500. Rent is slightly less than half the monthly spend, so rent should take up slightly less than half the pie. This is only true in answers A and B, so eliminate C and D.

Next, we see that entertainment should have twice as large a slice of the pie as both food and car. In answer A, this is true.

5. A   To create a stem plot, take each number, represent the tens place value as the stem and take the ones place value as the leaf. For example, for the number 86, 8 would be the stem, and 6 would be the leaf. If a number occurs multiple times, such as the 82 in this sample, it should be listed multiple times in your stem plot.

Stem	Leaf
6	2
7	0, 3, 7
8	2, 2, 2, 6, 8, 9
9	4, 5, 5

6. C   The profits of this company rose from 2002–2003, dropped from 2003–2004, and then had a steady rise from 2004–2007.

7. C   To show proportionality within a single data series, the best method would be the pie chart. For each of the other plots, it would be hard to quickly see the proportion of students who speak each language.

8. A   Time is graphed on the x-axis, which is where the independent variable will always appear. Also, common sense tells us that time is not dependent on anything – it will keep going regardless. However, weight is being influenced by the amount of time that has passed.

Statistics & Probability: Gathering & Visualizing Data

9. D Bias can be introduced into a survey in many ways. If bias is introduced, then the results of the survey won't reflect the population.

I. Over-representing a certain portion of the population
If some members of a population are more likely or less likely to be included, this is a form of bias. For instance, if you wanted to find out how many high schoolers smoke and you went to the local public school to survey the students, you would have a biased sample that would not include private school or home-schooled students. In this example, public school students would be over-represented.

II. Under-representing a certain portion of the population
In the above example, private school students would be under-represented.

III. Phrasing of the questions used in the survey
If questions are not phrased appropriately, bias may be introduced. In the above example, if students were asked if they smoked and told that their parents might be made aware of their response, some students might not answer truthfully.

10. D The line of best fit minimizes the differences between the line and each of the points. You can think of the line of best fit as approximating the average of the data.

In A, the line goes through the lower points, not the average.
In B, the line goes through most of the top points, not the average.
In C, there is no line of best fit, which needs to be a single line with one slope.
In D, which can be seen to the right, the line goes through the middle of the data. It is the closest approximation of the line of best fit.

Statistics & Probability: Central Tendency & Dispersion

Describing Data Sets

There are several ways to describe a set of data. In this module, you will learn how to calculate some properties of data that are important to know for statistical analysis.

Mean

The mean (or average) value of a set of numbers is equal to the sum of those numbers divided by the number of numbers in the set. For example, the mean of 2, 3, 4, 5, and 6 is 4, that is, their sum (20) divided by 5 – (the number of numbers being averaged). The formula for mean is

> mean = sum of numbers/# of numbers

Median

Like the median on a road, the median number in a set is the one located in the middle. To find the median of 29, 113, 1, 4, and 76, order the numbers from least to greatest, and then locate the middle number:

> 1, 4, 29, 76, 113
> For this set, 29 is the median.

For a set containing an even number of numbers, take the average of the two middle numbers.

> Example: Find the median of 9, 17, 82, and 9.
> First, order the numbers: 9, 9, 17, and 82.
> Take the average of the two middle numbers: $(9 + 17)/2 = 26/2 = 13$.
> Median = 13.

Note that the median of a set of numbers can be a number not in the original set of numbers.

Mode

The mode of a set of data is the most frequently occurring number or piece of data. Take the following set: 1, 1, 1, 7, 8, 9, 9, 10, 11, 12.
The mode here is 1, since it occurs the most often.

A set can have multiple modes if several numbers occur the same number of times within the set.
> Example: Find the mode of 62, 0.9, 0.5, 3.75, 0.5, 0.9, 27.
> First, order the numbers: 0.5, 0.5, 0.9, 0.9, 3.75, 27, 62.
> 0.5 and 0.9 are the two modes, since each occurs twice.

Measures of Dispersion

Several statistical measures describe how data is dispersed within a series. Range, variance, and standard deviation are commonly used measures of dispersion.

Range

The range of a set of numbers is their spread. To find the range, subtract the smallest number from the largest number.

>Example 1: Find the range of 1, 45, 5, 9, 73.
>$73 - 1 = 72$.
>Example 2: Find the range of −27, 32, 58, 96.
>$96 - (-27) = 123$

Variance

The variance measures the amount of variation among the values of a variable. The formula for variance is

Set of numbers: $x_1, x_2, x_3, ... x_n$ with a mean of $\bar{x}$

$$\text{Variance} = v = \frac{(x_1 - \bar{x})^2 + (x_2 - \bar{x})^2 + ... + (x_n - \bar{x})^2}{n}$$

For example, if you looked at the following two sets of test scores, the second has a much higher variance, as the data deviates farther from the mean.

>Set 1: 73, 74, 74, 75, 77, 78
>Set 2: 68, 73, 84, 85, 90, 92

Standard Deviation

Standard deviation is a measure of the dispersion of a set of data from its mean. For example, if every student on an exam scored between 80 and 85, the standard deviation would be smaller than if some students got below 20, and others got perfect 100s.

>Standard deviation, σ, is calculated as the square root of the variance:
>$\sigma = \sqrt{v}$

On a graph, standard deviation can be thought of as the distances of all the data points from the line of best fit. The better the line fits the data, the smaller the standard deviation. If all the data is directly on the line of best fit (in other words, very close to the mean), the standard deviation is 0.

Central Tendency & Dispersion: Practice

1. If you have the highest score on a math test, which measure would you need to determine the lowest score on the test?

   A. Mean

   B. Median

   C. Mode

   D. Range

2. What is the median of 71, 16, 95, and 2.3?

   A. 43.5

   B. 71

   C. 46.08

   D. 95

3. Find the mode in the following set: Square, Square, Circle, Circle, Circle.

   A. Square

   B. Circle

   C. 2

   D. 3

4. For the following set, which is greater – the median or mean?
23, 75, 16, 91, 100

   A. Median.

   B. Mean.

   C. They are equal.

   D. Not enough information.

5. Find x if the range of the data set is 16.
x, 2.3, 9.8, 12.9

   A. –2.3

   B. 2.3

   C. –3.1

   D. 3.1

Statistics & Probability: Central Tendency & Dispersion

6. The following is a list of house prices for an area. What is the best way to describe the housing prices to a family interested in purchasing there?
$750,000; $595,000; $10,000,000; $800,000; $830,000; $840,000

   A. Range
   B. Median
   C. Mean
   D. Mode

7. For the data set 16, 16, 24, 96, and 3, what is 16?
   I. mean
   II. median
   III. mode

   A. I and II
   B. II and III
   C. III only
   D. I, II, and III

8. Which set of data has the largest standard deviation?

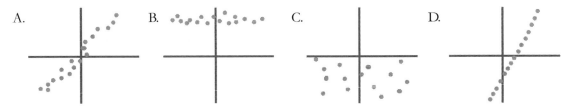

9. What is the mean of the following set: 5, −4, 0, 3, 16

   A. 3
   B. 4
   C. 5
   D. 7

10. In America, the gap between the rich and the poor is widening. What impact will that fact most likely have on data concerning average income?

   A. The line of best fit will move up.
   B. The standard deviation will increase.
   C. It will introduce bias.
   D. The range will decrease.

Central Tendency & Dispersion: Answer Explanations

1. D   Let's examine each answer choice.

A: Mean. The mean is the average of all the numbers. Only knowing the highest score and the mean would not help you find the lowest score.

B: Median. This is the middle number if you order the numbers. Therefore, knowing the median would only help you find the middle score, not the lowest score.

C: Mode. This score appears most often. This can be any score from the highest to the lowest, to any score in between, which would not help.

D: Range. This is the highest score minus the lowest score. Therefore, if you know the range and the highest score, you can find the lowest score.

2. A   First, order the numbers: 2.3, 16, 71, 95
The data set has an even number of elements, so average the two middle numbers:
$(16 + 71)/2 = 43.5$

3. B   The mode is the piece of data that occurs most often in the set. The word Circle appears three times, and the word Square occurs twice. Therefore, the mode is Circle.

4. A   To answer this question, you must calculate both the median and the mean of the set.

Median: First, order the numbers, and then find the middle number:
16, 23, 75, 91, 100. The median is the middle number, 75.

Mean: Add the numbers, and divide that sum by 5:
$23 + 75 + 16 + 91 + 100 = 305$
$305 \div 5 = 61$
Mean = 61

The median is greater than the mean for this data set.

5. C   To find the range, subtract the largest number from the smallest number:
Range = $12.9 -$ smallest $= 16$.

The smallest number that is given in the set, 2.3, is too large to give a range of 16. Therefore, x must be the smallest number:
$12.9 - x = 16$
$x = -3.1$

Statistics & Probability: Central Tendency & Dispersion

6. B Notice that the data has an outlier, or a data point whose value is very different from the rest of the sample. The outlier is the $10,000,000 home. Let's see how this affects each measure.

Range: The range does not describe the average of a set, only its spread. Therefore, this would not be useful.

Median: The median of this set is $815,000. This would give the family a good indication of the average house price.

Mean: The mean house price is $2,302,500. This is not a good description of house prices, since the outlier greatly affected it.

Mode: There is no data point occurring more than once, eliminating the usefulness of the mode as a descriptor.

7. B Let's calculate the mean, median, and mode for the data set.

I. Mean: To calculate the mean, add all the numbers and divide by 5 since there are 5 numbers in the set:
Mean = $(16 + 16 + 24 + 96 + 3) \div 5 = 155 \div 5 = 31$

II. Median: To find the median, order the set and find the middle number.
3, 16, 16, 24, 96
The middle number, or median, of the set is 16.

III. Mode: To determine the mode, find the number that appears most often in the set. 16 appears twice and is the only number appearing more than once. Therefore, 16 is the mode.

8. C The standard deviation measures how far the data varies from the line of best fit. In this case, the graph in answer C has the largest standard deviation. In the rest of the answer choices, the data is closer to following a straight line.

9. B To calculate the mean of a set, sum the elements in the set and divide by the number of elements in the set.

First, let's add the numbers in our set: $5 + -4 + 0 + 3 + 16 = 20$.
Now, divide by 5 since there are 5 numbers in the set: $20 \div 5 = 4$.

10. B Since the rich and the poor are moving in opposite directions, there is no way to determine if the line of best fit will increase or decrease overall. Introducing bias would require that the data on incomes of Americans was being misrepresented. And since the income gap is widening, the range will most likely increase.

Now, let's examine the effect on the standard deviation. If the gap is getting wider, the data points will be farther from the mean, or line of best fit. Therefore, the standard deviation will most likely increase.

Statistics & Probability: Sample Space & Probability

Sample Space

A random experiment is one for which the outcome is unknown before the experiment is performed. An example of a random experiment is flipping a coin with one side heads and the other tails. A simple event is one that relies on one independent outcome, for example, flipping the coin once. The outcome of that experiment would be whichever side lands face up – heads or tails.

To calculate the probability (likelihood of occurrence) for an event, you must first determine the sample space or total number of possible outcomes for that event. For the simple case of flipping a coin once, the sample space includes heads and tails – the only two possible outcomes. For rolling a die, the sample space includes all six possible outcomes of the die: 1, 2, 3, 4, 5, and 6.

Counting Principle

Determining sample space by listing all possible outcomes works for simple experiments, but it can be cumbersome for even slightly complex situations.

For example, suppose a woman is making a sandwich with three types of bread:
    White, Wheat, Rye

And four kinds of meat:
    Turkey, Ham, Roast Beef, Pastrami

Listing possibilities will take quite a bit of time:
    White-Turkey, White-Ham, White-Roast Beef, White-Pastrami, Wheat-Turkey, Wheat-Ham, Wheat-Roast Beef, Wheat-Pastrami, Rye-Turkey, Rye-Ham, Rye-Roast Beef, Rye-Pastrami

Notice that the number of possibilities is 12, which is equal to 3 x 4, the number of outcomes for event A (the type of bread) multiplied by the number of outcomes for event B (the type of meat). This is called the counting principle or multiplication rule. The rule states

The set of possible outcomes for n events = possible outcomes for first event x possible outcomes for second event x possible outcomes for third event x ...

The counting principle works for any number of events.

Probability

Simply put, probability is the likelihood of an event happening.

Theoretical Probability

The theoretical probability that an event will occur is the number of favorable outcomes divided by the total number of outcomes. Finding the probability of rolling a die and getting an even number would involve first finding the favorable outcomes: 2, 4, and 6.
Then, finding the total number of outcomes: 1, 2, 3, 4, 5, and 6.

There are 3 favorable outcomes and 6 total outcomes: therefore, the probability of getting an even number is $3/6 = 1/2 = 0.5$.

Experimental Probability

The experimental probability is the number of favorable outcomes divided by the number of times an experiment was performed. For example, if you rolled a die 20 times and counted that an even number came up 11 times, your experimental probability of rolling an even number would be $11/20 = 0.55$

The Law of Large Numbers

As the examples above show, there is a difference between the theoretical and experimental probabilities for an experiment. The Law of Large Numbers states that as the number of trials for an experiment approaches infinity (grows as large as possible), the experimental probability approaches the value of the theoretical probability.

For example, if you rolled the die thousands and thousands more times, the experimental probability would get closer to 0.5.

Compound Events

The probability that two or more events will occur sequentially is referred to as the probability of a compound event. For example, the probability of flipping a fair coin and having it land heads up is 1/2. But how do you calculate the probability of getting heads twice in a row?

The solution is to multiply the probability of each event. This method works when the events are independent – that is, each event does not affect the outcome of the other.

Example: Find the probability of getting 3 heads in a row.
Multiply the probability of landing heads each time: $1/2 \times 1/2 \times 1/2 = 1/8$.

Compound Events – Dependent

Dependent events are those with outcomes that affect the probability of each other. When calculating the probability of a combination of dependent events, you must consider how the sample space of the second event is affected by the first, and so on.

Example: A bag contains 8 marbles – 3 red and 5 blue. What is the probability of pulling a red marble and then a blue marble from the bag if you do not replace the marbles as you take them?

The probability of drawing a red marble from the bag is 3/8, since there are 3 red marbles and 8 marbles total. After that marble has been removed, there are 2 red marbles and 5 blue marbles remaining. Therefore, the probability of pulling out a blue marble on the second draw is 5/7.

To find the probability of drawing a red and then drawing a blue, multiply the two probabilities:
3/8 x 5/7 = 15/56.

Note that if the marbles were placed back into the bag after each round, these events would be independent and not dependent.

Compound Events with "OR"

To find the probability of one of multiple events occurring, add the probabilities of each event occurring independently and subtract any overlap (that is, double-counting situations where both events occur).

Example 1: What is the probability of rolling a 3 or a 4 on a die?
Add the probability of rolling a 3, 1/6, to the probability of rolling a 4, also 1/6. In this situation, there is no possibility of both events occurring at once, so there's no overlap.

Prob. of 3 or 4 = prob. 3 + prob. 4 – prob. (3 and 4)
= 1/6 + 1/6 – 0 = 2/6 = 1/3

Example 2: What is the probability of getting an ace or a club when pulling a card from a deck?
Add the probability of getting an ace, 4/52, to the probability of getting a club, 13/52, and subtract the overlap of getting a club and ace, 1/52.

Prob. of Ace or Club = prob. Ace + prob. Club – prob. (Ace and Club)
4/52 + 13/52 – 1/52 = 16/52 = 4/13

Sample Space & Probability: Practice

1. A man has 17 ties, 12 suits, and 3 pairs of shoes. Assuming that he wears 1 tie, 1 suit, and 1 pair of shoes each day, how many different ways can he get dressed for work?

- A. 51
- B. 204
- C. 612
- D. 1290

2. A student rolls two dice. One die has six faces marked with 1, 2, 3, 4, 5, or 6 spots. The other is a special die with eight faces marked with A, B, C, D, E, F, G, or H. How many outcomes are in the sample space for this experiment?

   A. 14
   B. 28
   C. 48
   D. 64

3. At Stacy's Ice Cream Emporium, one flavor per month is randomly selected as the "ice cream of the month." What piece of information do you need to calculate the probability that Berry Surprise will be selected this month?

   A. Number of days in the month
   B. How much of each flavor Stacy has
   C. Number of flavors Stacy carries
   D. Method of selection (drawing flavor from a hat, and so on)

4. What is the probability of drawing a red Skittle out of a bag of 100 Skittles that are 20% red, and then rolling a 2 on a fair die?

   A. 1/120
   B. 11/30
   C. 1/11
   D. 1/30

5. What is the probability of spinning purple 300 times in a row on the spinner below?

   A. 1/1200
   B. 1200
   C. 1/4
   D. $(1/4)^{300}$

6. There are 8 lockers in a school hallway, and 5 of them have star stickers on the inside. If the first locker opened does not have stars in it, what is the probability that the second won't, either?

   A. 1/4
   B. 2/7
   C. 3/8
   D. 3/7

7. A bag of marbles contains 20 red, 30 purple, and 40 yellow marbles. If marbles are drawn from the bag one at a time without replacement, how would you calculate the probability that a red will be selected on the first draw, a purple on the second, and a yellow on the third?

   A. 2/9 x 1/3 x 4/9
   B. 2/9 x 30/89 x 5/11
   C. 2/9 + 1/3 + 4/9
   D. 2/9 + 30/89 + 5/11

8. There are 5 marbles in a bag: 2 red and 3 purple. If you randomly draw 2 marbles out, what is the probability that you will draw one red and one purple?

   A. 3/5
   B. 3/10
   C. 3/20
   D. 1

9. You have a bag with 6 marbles with 3 reds. What is the ratio of the probability of picking a red on both the first 2 draws if you replace the marbles on each draw to the probability of picking two reds on the 2 draws if you don't replace the marbles on each draw?

   A. 4/5
   B. 5/4
   C. 2/1
   D. 5/6

10. A number is selected randomly from between 2 and 19 inclusive. What is the probability the number will be even or a multiple of 5?

    A. 2/3

    B. 13/18

    C. 11/18

    D. 1/2

Sample Space & Probability: Answer Explanations

1. C   Use the multiplication rule to determine the total number of ways he can get dressed.

    Total = # ties x # suits x # shoes

    = 17 x 12 x 3 = 612

    612 different ways

2. C   To find the number of possible outcomes in a sample space, multiply the number of outcomes for each part of the experiment.
    6 x 8 = 48

3. C   To calculate the simple probability, create a fraction with the number of favorable outcomes (Berry Surprise = 1 flavor) in the numerator and the number of possible outcomes in the denominator. The number of flavors carried by Stacy is the number of possible outcomes.

4. D   For independent compound events, multiply the probability of each event.

    Probability of drawing a red Skittle out of 100 Skittles that are 20% red:
    20% = 1/5

    Probability of rolling a 2 on a fair die:
    Favorable outcomes/total outcomes = 1/6

    Probability of both events happening = 1/5 x 1/6 = 1/30

5. D   The probability of multiple independent events occurring is the product of the probabilities of the individual events.

    The probability of spinning purple once is 1/4, since that is the fraction of the circle that is shaded purple.

    This question asks for the probability of spinning a purple 300 times. Therefore, you need to multiply 1/4 times itself 300 times. You can use exponents to represent this:
    $(1/4)^{300}$

6. B There were originally 5 lockers with stars and 3 lockers without stars. One locker was opened that did not have a star. Therefore, out of the remaining 7 lockers to be opened, 5 have stars, and 2 do not.

There question asks for the probability that the second locker won't have a star, either. Therefore, the number remaining without stars is 2, and there are 7 lockers still to be opened.

Probability = 2/7

7. B To find the probability of multiple events, multiply the probability of each individual event. Make sure to keep in mind how one event might affect the sample space and probability of the following events.

Probability red is selected first
   = # of red marbles divided by total marbles
   = 20/90
   = 2/9

Probability purple is selected second
   = # of purple marbles divided by total marbles remaining
   = 30/89

Probability yellow is selected third
   = # of yellow marbles divided by total marbles remaining
   = 40/88
   = 5/11

To find the probability of all three events occurring, multiply the probabilities of each event.
   = 2/9 x 30/89 x 5/11

8. A There are two possible ways that you can get a red and a purple: red first and then purple or purple first and then red. You must first figure out the probability of each occurring. Since you want the probability of either occurring, you add the two probabilities.

Probability of red then purple:
   = Prob red on first draw x Prob purple on second draw with 4 marbles remaining
   = 2/5 x 3/4 = 6/20 = 3/10

Probability of purple then red:
   = Prob purple on first draw x Prob red on second draw with 4 marbles remaining
   = 3/5 x 2/4 = 6/20 = 3/10

Now, add the probabilities:
   3/10 + 3/10 = 6/10 = 3/5

9. B To find the ratio, first find the individual probabilities.

With replacement:
On the first draw, the probability of pulling a red marble is 3/6 = 1/2. If you are replacing the marbles, that means that there is no difference between the first and second draws. Therefore, the probability of getting a red on the second draw is also 3/6 = 1/2. The probability of getting a red on the first and second is = 1/2 x 1/2 = 1/4.

Without replacement:
On the first draw, the probability of pulling a red marble is 3/6 = 1/2. If you are not replacing the marbles, that means that there are only 5 marbles left, and only 2 of them are red. Therefore, the probability of getting a red on the second draw is 2/5. The probability of getting a red on the first and second is = 1/2 x 2/5 = 1/5.

Ratio:
The ratio of replacing to not replacing is (1/4)/(1/5) = 5/4

10. C First, figure out the probability of selecting an even number, and then figure out the probability of selecting a multiple of 5. Next, subtract any overlap, that is, numbers that are both even and a multiple of 5.

Probability of getting an even number:
The even numbers in that range are 2, 4, 6, 8, 10, 12, 14, 16, and 18.
    Prob = 9/18 = 1/2

Probability of getting a 5:
The multiples of 5 in the range are 5, 10, and 15.
    Prob = 3/18 = 1/6

Probability of a number that is both even and a 5:
10 is even and a multiple of 5, so this number has been counted twice.
    Prob = 1/18

Probability of even or multiple of 5
    = Prob of even + Prob of multiple of 5 – Prob of both even and multiple of 5
    = 1/6 + 1/2 – 1/18
    = 11/18

Statistics & Probability: Permutations & Combinations

Permutation vs. Combination

Permutations and combinations deal with choosing elements from a larger set of elements. The difference is whether the order matters:

> If the order does not matter, you are counting combinations.
> If the order of the elements matters, you are dealing with permutations.

For example, suppose you are awarding 3 medals in a race to the top 3 runners from a group of 9. Figuring out how many groups of 3 could be awarded medals is an example of counting combinations. Now, let's say you want to award gold, silver, and bronze, specifically. Finding the number of ways in which 1st, 2nd, or 3rd can be awarded is an example of a permutation problem. In a problem, identify whether the arrangement or order of the chosen elements is important.

If choosing 2 letters from the alphabet in combinations, AB is the same as BA and, therefore, would only count as one combination. However, in permutations, AB and BA are different, as the order or arrangement matters, and therefore, choosing those 2 letters results in two possible permutations.

Understanding Factorials

Before we go on with permutations and combinations, it's important that you understand how to calculate factorials. The factorial of a positive integer is the product of all positive integers less than or equal to that number. An exclamation mark (!) denotes factorials. For example:

$4! = 4 \times 3 \times 2 \times 1$
$6! = 6 \times 5 \times 4 \times 3 \times 2 \times 1$

When dividing a factorial by a lesser factorial, the quotient will always be the product of the integers greater than the smaller number, up to and including the greater number. For example:

$7!/4! = (7 \times 6 \times 5 \times 4 \times 3 \times 2 \times 1)/(4 \times 3 \times 2 \times 1) = 7 \times 6 \times 5 = 210$

An exception to this rule is that $0! = 1$.

Permutations

For a set of n objects, the factorial of n (or n!) gives you the total number of possible permutations in the set. For example, take a set of three balls that are red, green, and blue. The possible permutations:

{red, green, blue}   {red, blue, green}
{green, red, blue}   {green, blue, red}
{blue, red, green}   {blue, green, red}

Note that there are 6 possible permutations, which equates to the factorial for 3. Or, $3! = 6$.

Now, suppose you are trying to figure out how many ordered sequences involving a set of numbers, r, can be made from a larger set of numbers, n. Here, you divide the factorial of n by the difference between n and r. The formula is written as

Permutations = n!/(n – r)!

For example, suppose you want to find the number of different possible selections of 10 people for 4 different lead roles in a play. The order of selection matters because choosing Bob to play Character 1 is different from choosing Bob to play Character 2.

Choosing 4 lead roles from 10 people:
= 10!/(10 – 4)! = 10!/6! = 10 x 9 x 8 x 7 = 5040
5,040 ways to select the lead roles

Combinations

A combination is also an arrangement of objects, but this time, order is not important. For example, if we wanted to find the number of combinations of pairs of the three balls, red, green, and blue, it would be 3 sets: (red, green), (green, blue), (blue, red).

When a certain number of elements are selected from a greater number of elements, various combinations of elements can be selected. The number of ways to choose r elements from n possible elements uses the formula:

Combinations = n!/r!(n – r)!

A common abbreviation for choosing r elements from n possible elements is $_nC_r$.

Example: A man chooses 8 of 12 coins in his collection to show at an exhibit. If he chooses the coins at random, how many possible combinations can he choose?
There are 12 elements, 8 of which will be selected:

12!/8!(12 – 8)! = 12!/8!4! = 495 combinations

Pascal's Triangle

A common use of combinations different from what would be expected is in algebra. Combinations are used to find the coefficients of binomial expansions, $(x + y)^n$. The calculated combinations are simplified into a counting algorithm called Pascal's Triangle.

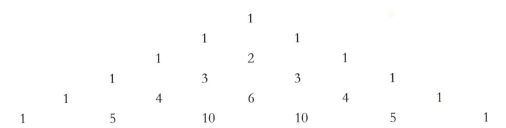

Note that each row in the triangle starts and ends with a 1, and that the numbers inside the triangle are the sum of the two numbers above it, diagonally left and right.

To find the coefficients of $(x + y)^n$, you can look at the n+1 row. For example, look at the 5th row to find the coefficients for: $(x + y)^4 = 1x^4y^0 + 4x^3y^1 + 6x^2y^2 + 4x^1y^3 + 1x^0y^4$

Pascal's Triangle and binomial expansions can also be calculated using combinations.
$(x + y)^4 = {}_4C_0\, x^4y^0 + {}_4C_1\, x^3y^1 + {}_4C_2\, x^2y^2 + {}_4C_3\, x^1y^3 + {}_4C_4\, x^0y^4$

$${}_4C_0 = 4!/(0!4!) = 1$$
$${}_4C_1 = 4!/(1!3!) = 4$$
$${}_4C_2 = 4!/(2!2!) = 6$$
$${}_4C_3 = 4!/(3!1!) = 4$$
$${}_4C_4 = 4!/(4!0!) = 1$$

$(x + y)^4 = 1x^4y^0 + 4x^3y^1 + 6x^2y^2 + 4x^1y^3 + 1x^0y^4$

Similarly, for finding the binomial expansion of $(x + y)^2$ use the 3rd row, (1 2 1).
$(x + y)^2 = {}_2C_0\, x^2y^0 + {}_2C_1\, x^1y^1 + {}_2C_2\, x^0y^2$
$= x^2 + 2xy + y^2$

Permutations & Combinations: Practice

1. You have to buy 4 gallons of ice cream for a party. The ice cream store has 20 different flavors to choose from. How many different ways can you choose the ice cream flavors?

A. 20!/4!

B. 20!/16!

C. 20!/16!4!

D. 16!/4!

2. Four hats are on a shelf. A customer is interested in buying two of the hats. How many combinations of hats might she buy?

A. 4

B. 6

C. 12

D. 24

3. There are 4 girls trying out for pitcher on a softball team and 10 girls trying out for the remaining 3 available positions: shortstop, first base, and second base. How many teams could be selected?

   A. 480
   B. 720
   C. 2880
   D. 4320

4. Based on the portion of Pascal's Triangle shown below, which of the following values is the coefficient of the xy^3 term of the expansion $(x + y)^4$?

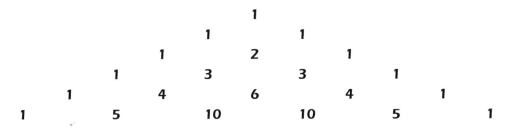

   A. 3
   B. 4
   C. 5
   D. 6

5. How many different ways can you rearrange the letters in MONKEY?

   A. 30
   B. 360
   C. 600
   D. 720

6. How many different ways are there to arrange all 26 letters of the alphabet?

   A. 26
   B. 13!
   C. 26!
   D. 26^{26}

7. If you are exhibiting 15 of the 600 pieces of art in a museum's collection, how many ways can you arrange the art?

    A. 15!

    B. 15! x 600!

    C. 600!/585!

    D. 600!/(15! 585!)

8. In how many different ways can 10 girls and 10 boys sit alternately in a row of chairs if a boy will be in the first seat? To clarify, the first three seats will be boy, girl, boy, and they will continue to alternate.

    A. 10!

    B. 20!

    C. 10! x 10!

    D. 10! + 10!

9. If a card game involves players being dealt 4 cards, how many different possible hands can you have out of a standard 52-card deck?

    A. 4!

    B. 48!

    C. 52!/4!

    D. 52!/(4! 48!)

10. How many ways can you rearrange the letters in GUPPIES if the two Ps must stay together?

    A. 6!/2

    B. 7!/2

    C. 6!

    D. 7!

Permutations & Combinations: Answer Explanations

1. C   Since the order does not matter, use the formula for combinations to find the number of ways to choose 4 ice cream flavors from 20 different flavors. The formula for combinations is $n!/(r!(n - r)!)$.

In this case, n = 20 and r = 4:
$n!/(r!(n - r)!) = 20!/(4!(20-4)!) = 20!/(4!16!)$

2. B   This question is asking you to find the number of combinations, since the order of the two hats doesn't matter.

Plugging into the formula for combination, where n = 4 and r = 2:

$$\frac{n!}{(n-r)!r!} = \frac{4!}{(4-2)!2!} = \frac{4!}{2!2!} = \frac{4(3)(2)(1)}{2(1)2(1)} = 6$$

There are 6 ways to choose 2 out of the 4 hats.

3. C   This problem has multiple steps. First, figure out the number of ways to choose the pitcher, then calculate the number of ways to choose people for the remaining positions. Finally, multiply the number of ways to choose a pitcher by the number of permutations for the remaining positions to find the number of possible teams.

Choose the pitcher:
There are 4 girls trying out for one position, so there are 4 possible ways to choose the pitcher.

Choose players to fill the 3 remaining positions out of 10 players:
The order matters for the remaining positions, since it makes a difference if someone is chosen for first base or shortstop. Therefore, use permutations:

Permutations = $n!/(n - r)!$
= $10!/(10 - 3)! = 10!/7! = 10 \times 9 \times 8 = 720$

Total number of ways to select the teams:
4 x 720 = 2880 ways

4. B   The binomial expansion has an exponent of 4: $(x + y)^4$
Therefore, you want to use the row 1 4 6 4 1.

The question asks for the xy^3 term which will be the second term, with a coefficient of 4.

Here is the full expansion to demonstrate that answer:
$(x + y)^4 = 1x^0y^4 + 4x^1y^3 + 6x^2y^2 + 4x^3y^1 + 1x^4y^0$

5. D   There are 6 letters in the word monkey, and order matters, so this is a simple permutation where you are choosing 6 elements from 6 elements.

The number of permutations is 6! = 6 x 5 x 4 x 3 x 2 x 1 = 720.

6. C   Permutations = n!/(n – r)!

In this case, n = 26 and r = 26 since you are choosing all 26 letters from 26 possible letters.

= 26!/(26 – 26)!
= 26!/0!
= 26!

Whenever a question asks for n of n permutations, the answer is always n!

7. C   The question asks for the number of ways to arrange the art, so order matters. Therefore, use the formula for permutations.

Permutations = n!/(n – r)!
n = 600, r = 15
= 600!/(600 – 15)!
= 600!/585!

8. C   Think of this problem as two sets of permutations: first, the number of permutations of the 10 girls and then the number of permutations of the 10 boys. You then multiply to find the total number of ways, since for each permutation of girls, each of the permutations for boys is possible.

Permutations of Boys: 10!
Permutations of Girls: 10!
Total = 10! x 10!

9. D   The question is asking how many ways you can select 4 cards out of the 52 cards. Since the order of the cards does not matter, use combinations.

Combinations: n!/(r!(n – r)!) where n is 52 and r is 4
= 52!/(4!(52–4)!)
= 52!/(4! 48!)

10. C   Since the two Ps must stay together, you can consider them as a single element. Therefore, you need to find the number of ways to rearrange 6 elements (G, U, PP, I, E, S).

Number of ways = 6!

Statistics & Probability: Permutations & Combinations

Statistics & Probability: Advanced Statistics

Frequency & Cumulative Distributions

A **frequency distribution** is an organization of raw data. Often, data is grouped into bins, and the frequency of occurrence is counted for each bin. The table below is an example of a frequency distribution. The third column shows the **cumulative distribution,** which indicates the total number of houses sold up to that day of the week.

Day of the Week	Number of Houses Sold	Cumulative Number of Houses Sold
Monday	2	2
Tuesday	1	3
Wednesday	2	5
Thursday	1	6
Friday	4	10

Percentile Ranks

A percentile rank is the proportion of scores in a frequency distribution that a score is less than or equal to. You calculate the percentile rank by counting the number of occurrences less than or equal to a given score. Then, divide that result by the total number of occurrences in the sample.

Day of the Week	Number of Houses Sold	Percentile Rank
Monday	2	$2/10 = 20\%$
Tuesday	1	$3/10 = 30\%$
Wednesday	2	$5/10 = 50\%$
Thursday	1	$6/10 = 60\%$
Friday	4	$10/10 = 100\%$

The median statistic is the 50th percentile value.

Another way to approach calculating percentiles is to first order all your data points. Then, multiply the percentage by the number of data points to find which data point would be equal to that percentile. For instance, use the following data points: the heights of students are 61 in, 64 in, 65 in, 65.5 in, 66 in, 66.5 in, 68 in, 68 in, 69 in, 70 in. Note, the data points are already in order, and there are 10 data points. Therefore, to find the height in the 50th percentile, multiply 10 by $50\% = 5$. So, the 5th data point, or 66 in, would be equal to the 50th percentile.

Probability Distributions

There are many probability distributions. Three of the most common are the uniform, normal, and binomial distributions. A uniform distribution means that each value in the distribution has an equal opportunity of being selected. For example, the distribution of one six-sided die would be considered uniform, since each number has an equal likelihood of occurring.

A normal distribution has a familiar bell-shape curve. In a normal distribution, the numbers in the center have a higher likelihood of occurring than those at the tails (that is, the right or left side).

A binomial distribution is based on variables that only have two possible values (for example, a coin flip). For example, if heads is a 1 and tails is a 0, the sum of the number of heads, given 10 coin flips, would be a binomial distribution.

Classifying probability distributions helps to get an idea quickly of what a distribution will be like. For instance, if you were told that choosing a lottery number in a game has a uniform distribution, you would instantly know that every value has the same likelihood of occurring, and there is no reason to choose one number over another. If you were told that test scores followed a normal distribution, you would know that the students received scores around the average, and a few students received high scores and some low scores.

Expected Value

The expected value of a probability distribution is defined as
$$E(x) = \sum xp(x)$$

Where $E(x)$ is the expected value of x, x is the value for each occurrence (for example, the value of a die from 1 to 6), and $p(x)$ is the probability of that likelihood occurring (for example, 1/6 for a die).

For example, the expected value of rolling one six-sided die is
$$E(x) = 1(1/6) + 2(1/6) + 3(1/6) + 4(1/6) + 5(1/6) + 6(1/6) = 21/6 = 3.5$$

Margin of Error

Based on the data of an observed sample, you can calculate a mean score. Depending on the sample, you can infer what the mean will be for an entire population within a certain range. This range is set by the margin of error.

For instance, the mean test score for a sample of students might be 80, but the margin of error might be 10. Then, the confidence interval will be the sample mean ± the margin of error. This margin of error has a confidence level, which is typically 95%, meaning that we are 95% certain that the true mean for all students falls within the sample mean ± the margin of error. In the above example, if all students take the exam, then the mean for all students is 95% likely to be between 70 and 90.

Correlation

Correlation is a statistic that measures how closely one variable tracks with another. The range of the correlation statistic is [–1, 1].

Correlations close to +1 indicate that variables track very closely with one another. For example, the amount of time studied and test scores are likely to be positively correlated.

Correlations close to –1 indicate that variables track inversely. For example, grades and time watching television might be negatively correlated.

A correlation close to 0 means that there is no apparent relationship between the variables.

Note that correlation does not necessarily imply causation. For example, a child's grades in school might be correlated to the number of books in her family's house, which does not mean that buying more books will directly affect a child's grades.

Regression Models and Curve Fitting

Regression attempts to model the relationship between one variable (that is, the dependent variable) and one or more other variables (that is, the independent variables). Regression is often used to attempt to predict future events based on history or an experiment.

A simple linear regression is often written in slope-intercept form, $y = mx + b$. Here, y is the dependent variable, and x is the independent variable; b is the y-intercept.

Other types of regression can be used to fit data that has a curved relationship. For this type of data, a quadratic equation can be used instead of a linear equation.

One measure of the predictive capability of a regression is the r-squared. The r-squared statistic is a measure of how well a regression line approximates real data points. Simply square the statistic r, which is the correlation coefficient, to get r-squared.

In the graphs below, you can see two examples of regression lines. In the first graph, the data points are represented by the dots, and you can see that the data matches a linear regression model. Using this regression line, you can then predict future data points. The r-squared statistic and correlation would describe how well the data matches the line.

The second graph shows that the data points are more closely modeled with a quadratic equation. If a straight line were drawn through the data points, the correlation and r-squared statistics would be low, indicating that the model doesn't fit as well.

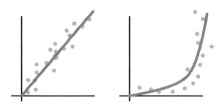

Advanced Statistics: Practice

1. What is the cumulative frequency on Wednesday?

Day of the Week	Number of Cars Sold
Monday	4
Tuesday	2
Wednesday	1
Thursday	3
Friday	5

   A. 1

   B. 4

   C. 6

   D. 7

2. A quality analyst samples products from a factory's assembly line. He notes that there is a defect rate of 20% of the sample. His supervisor asks for the range of likely defect rates for all the products on the line. What does the quality analyst need to calculate to give his supervisor an answer?

   A. Mode

   B. Median

   C. R-squared

   D. Margin of error

3. An entry level analyst calculates a series of correlations for his boss. His boss believes that one of them must be wrong. Which one is definitely incorrect?

   A. −0.98

   B. 0.00

   C. 1.02

   D. 0.54

4. A regression line is fit to a set of data. Which type of regression is most likely?

   A. Linear

   B. Quadratic

   C. Logarithmic

   D. Asymptotic

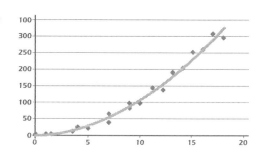

5. From the histogram, how many sick days in a year would be required to reach the 70th percentile?

A. 6
B. 7
C. 8
D. 9

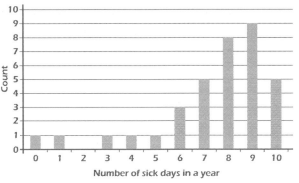

6. On the right is a histogram of the age of cars. The mean age of cars is 7 years, and the standard deviation is 2 years.

How many cars are within one standard deviation of the mean?

A. 90
B. 110
C. 260
D. 350

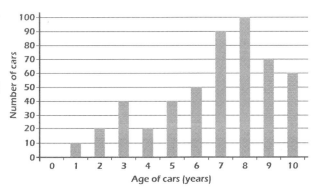

7. Ticket sales for a football team are modeled for two towns. The model relates ticket sales to the temperature.

Linear Regression Town A	Linear Regression Town B
$y = ax + b$	$y = ax + b$
$a = 0.3125$	$a = 9.5712$
$b = 121.5323$	$b = 101.4128$
$r = 0.1413$	$r = 0.9781$

Which of the following conclusions can be determined from these results?

A. The temperature in town A is higher than in town B.
B. The temperature in town B is higher than in town A.
C. The model for Town A is a better predictor of ticket sales than Town B.
D. The model for Town B is a better predictor of ticket sales than Town A.

8. A statistician performs a linear regression analysis on two variables for a small business. His client wants to know how well the model fits the variable. Which statistic should the statistician provide?

   A. Mean
   B. Median
   C. R-squared
   D. Standard Deviation

9. Each of the numbers in a normally distributed data set is added to the number 10. How does this transformation affect the mean, median, and the standard deviation of the frequency distribution curve?

   A. The mean stays the same, but the median and standard deviation increase by 10.
   B. The median stays the same, but the mean and standard deviation increase by 10.
   C. The standard deviation stays the same, but the mean and median increase by 10
   D. The mean, median, and standard deviation all increase by 10.

10. A local organization is trying to determine whether to run its annual festival outdoors or indoors. Based on data from similar regions, a simulation was run on how many days of the week it might rain in the particular month.

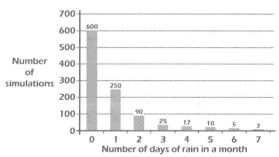

What is the likelihood that it will rain 3 or more days in the month?

   A. 0.6%
   B. 4%
   C. 6%
   D. 25%

Advanced Statistics: Answer Explanations

1. D The cumulative frequency is the frequency up to and including that bin for the frequency distribution. Therefore, the cumulative frequency on Wednesday is the total number of cars sold up to that day of the week. $4 + 2 + 1 = 7$

2. D In order to determine a confidence interval for his sample, the analyst must calculate a margin of error. The confidence interval then is the sampled mean of 20% plus or minus the margin of error.

3. C The correlation statistic can only be between –1 and +1. Sometimes, the correlation is written in terms of percents, but it must be between –100% and 100%. It is not possible to have a correlation of 1.02.

4. B Let's go through each answer choice.

A: Linear. A linear regression line would be a straight line, while this line has an increasing slope. Eliminate A.

B: Quadratic. This type of line would increase more quickly than a straight line. If you think about the graph of $y = x^2$, you can see that this graph mirrors it. This is your answer.

C: Logarithmic. This regression line increases less quickly than a straight line. The slope of the line is continually decreasing. Eliminate C.

D: Asymptotic. This regression line would be similar to the graph of $y = 1/x$, where the curve approaches a straight line, while the graph in this problem continually increases. Eliminate D.

5. D To determine the percentile, we first have to figure out the total number of people in the sample. Add the count from each bar and you will see that there are 35 total people.

The question asks for the 70th percentile, so multiply the total number of people by 70% to find out where the 70th percentile would fall.

35 x 70% = 35 x 0.70 = 24.5, or about 25 people would be needed to reach the 70th percentile. Count the number of people with less than or equal to a certain number of sick days.

Sick Days	People
0	1
1	2
2	2
3	3
4	4
5	5
6	8
7	13
8	21
9	30
10	35

The 70th percentile is reached at 9 sick days.

6. D With a mean of 7 and a standard deviation of 2 years, the range of plus or minus one standard deviation is [5, 9]. We want to total the number of cars between 5 and 9 years inclusive.

The total number of cars is 40 + 50 + 90 + 100 + 70 = 350

7. D We know nothing about the temperature inputs from the two towns. All we know is how the ticket sales will relate to the temperatures. We cannot conclude which town has higher temperatures. Eliminate A and B.

To determine whether one predictive model is better than another is, examine the r-squared. In this case, we are just given r. If we calculate r-squared for both models, the r-squared for Town B is much higher than for Town A. When a model has a higher r-squared, it is a better predictor.

8. C Knowing the mean or median will only help the client understand the average and middle values of the data, but will give no indication to whether the model fits. The standard deviation will indicate how much the data is spread, but will not be the best way to describe whether a model fits. The r-squared statistic assesses how much variance is predicted by the variables in the model. In other words, the r-squared statistic will indicate how well the model can predict future outcomes.

9. C In a normal distribution, adding a number simply shifts the mean. As the same number is added to every value, the mean will just increase by that amount.

In a normal distribution, the mean and median are identical. Therefore, if the same number is added to each data point, it will increase the median by that number.

You can think of the standard deviation as an indicator of the spread of the data – shifting every data point by the same amount will not change how much the data is spread.

10. C First, we need to determine the total number of simulations run by adding the numbers from each bar:
600 + 250 + 90 + 25 + 17 + 10 + 5 + 3 = 1000 total simulations

Since we need the probability of 3 or more days of rain, add the numbers from bins 3 and above, then divide by 1000:
(25 + 17 + 10 + 5 + 3)/1000 = 0.06 or 6%

Alternatively, add the numbers for 0, 1, and 2 days, and divide by 1000. Then, subtract this number from 100%.

(600 + 250 + 90)/1000 = 0.94 or 94%
100% − 94% = 6%

Statistics & Probability: Module Review

1. There is a bag with 5 green marbles, 2 red marbles, and 6 yellow marbles. If you reach into the bag and take out two marbles without replacing, what is the probability that both are green?

    A. 25/169

    B. 5/26

    C. 5/39

    D. 9/25

2. If a card is drawn at random from a standard 52-card deck, what is the probability that it will be a 10 or a spade?

    A. 17/52

    B. 4/13

    C. 1/13

    D. 13/52

3. At the end of a growing season, a farmer measures the amount of crop produced. He then compares that amount with amounts he has produced in past years. Then, he finds some historical information about average temperatures for each of the past growing seasons. Finally, the farmer calculates the correlation between temperature and the amount of crops produced. He calculates a correlation of –93%.

What can be said about the relationship between crop production and temperature?

    A. As the temperature increases, the crop production tends to increase.

    B. As the temperature decreases, the crop production tends to decrease.

    C. As the temperature decreases, the crop production tends to increase.

    D. The temperature has no relationship to crop production.

4. If the likelihood of a sale is the same for any day of the week, what is the expected number of sales on a day?

Day of the Week	Number of Houses Sold
Monday	6
Tuesday	5
Wednesday	1
Thursday	3
Friday	5

A. 3

B. 4

C. 5

D. 12

5. If the range of a set of test scores is 85 and median 75, which of the following could be the set of all test scores?

A. 50, 85, 75, 80, 55

B. 75, 10, 95, 55

C. 75, 15, 85, 90, 75

D. 85, 70, 20, 80, 5, 90

6. If you own a mutual fund, and the standard deviation of the return increases while the mean stays the same, what happens to the fund's risk? (A return is a measure of how much the mutual fund has increased or decreased in value over a given period.)

A. increases

B. decreases

C. stays the same

D. don't know

7. Adding a zero to a set might change which of the following:
       I. median
       II. mean
       III. range

A. I only

B. I and III

C. II and III

D. I, II, and III

8. A straight line of best fit can best represent which set of data?

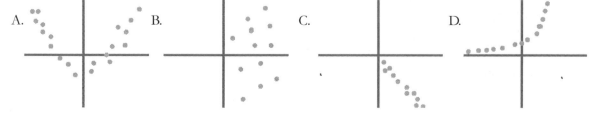

9. How many ways can you rearrange the letters of LESSON, if the two S's must remain next to each other?

   A. 24
   B. 120
   C. 360
   D. 720

10. Which of the following is/are true?
    I. The median and mean of a data set are always different.
    II. The median of a data set is always a member of the set.
    III. There can be more than one mode in a data set.

   A. I and II
   B. II and III
   C. III only
   D. None of the above

11. A woman takes her daughter to an ice cream store. The daughter has three scoops of ice cream on her banana split. The store has flavors chocolate, vanilla, strawberry, raspberry, and cookie dough. How many combinations of scoops can her daughter get on her banana split?

   A. 6
   B. 10
   C. 15
   D. 60

12. There are 3 bags and 5 different marbles. In how many ways can the marbles be put into the bags?

   A. 30
   B. 120
   C. 243
   D. 360

13. If the median of the data set is 14, which of the following could be the value of x?
    Set: 13, 92, 0, 15, 6, x

    A. –10
    B. 14
    C. 15
    D. 13

14. Which of the following sets of numbers has a higher standard deviation?
    Set A = 5, 5, 5, 5, 6, 16   Set B = 8, 9, 10, 10, 11, 12

    A. Set A
    B. Set B
    C. Equal
    D. Not enough information

15. The probability of occurrence for an event for which the number of favorable outcomes is equal to the number of possible outcomes is

    A. 0
    B. 1
    C. 1/2
    D. 100

16. Francisco is trying to guess a randomly selected letter of the alphabet. What is the probability that Francisco will guess the letter correctly on the second try?

    A. 1/26
    B. 1/25
    C. 2/26
    D. 25/26

17. There are 7 students in a club, and 3 of them need to go the next meeting. In how many ways can these 3 students be chosen?

    A. 21
    B. 35
    C. 210
    D. 840

Statistics & Probability: Module Review   417

18. There is a circular dartboard with a bull's-eye in the middle. The radius of the board is ten inches, and the radius of the bull's-eye is 2 inches. If a dart thrown randomly hits the board, what is the probability that it hits the bull's-eye?

   A. 1/25
   B. 1/5
   C. 1/8
   D. 1/96

19. What is the coefficient in front of the third term of the binomial expansion of $(x + y)^5$?

   A. 3
   B. 5
   C. 6
   D. 10

20. A dentist wants to determine whether his clients are happy, so he decides to conduct a survey. Out of the 500 patients, he wants to survey 50. Which of the following would be a simple random sample?

   A. Dentist surveys the next 50 patients who walk in his office.
   B. Dentist surveys every 10th patient.
   C. Dentist surveys the first 50 patients whose birthdays will be coming up next.
   D. None of the above.

Module Review: Answer Explanations

1. C Probability is the number of favorable outcomes over the total number of outcomes. To find the probability of multiple independent events, you multiply the probabilities of each of the individual events.

First, find the probability that the first marble drawn will be green, and then multiply that by the probability that the second marble drawn will be green.

For the first draw, there are 5 green marbles and a total of 13 marbles. The probability of drawing a green marble is 5/13.

For the second marble, there are only 12 marbles left, 4 of which are green. The probability of drawing a second green marble is 4/12, which reduces to 1/3.

The product of the two probabilities is the probability of drawing two green marbles in a row. 5/13 x 1/3 = 5/39.

2. B Use the addition rule, but be sure to account for overlap. First, find the probability of drawing a spade, and add that to the probability of drawing a 10. Then, subtract one from the sum to avoid counting the 10 of spades twice.

Probability of spade: $13/52$
Probability of 10: $4/52$
Probability of 10 and spade: $1/52$

Probability of 10 or spade = Prob of spade + Prob of 10 − Prob of 10 and spade
$= 13/52 + 4/52 − 1/52 = 16/52 = 4/13$

3. C The correlation is strongly negative at −93%, since the limits of the correlation are −100% to 100%. A negative correlation means that when one variable goes up, the other variable tends to go down (and vice versa).
Therefore, as the temperature decreases, the crop production tends to increase.

4. B The expected value is the sum of each occurrence multiplied by its probability. Since the likelihood is the same in each, the probability is always $1/5$. The expected value is
$6(1/5) + 5(1/5) + 1(1/5) + 3(1/5) + 5(1/5) = (6 + 5 + 1 + 3 + 5)/5 = 20/5 = 4$
The expected value for the number of houses sold on a day is 4.

5. D The range of a set is calculated by subtracting the lowest score from the highest score. The median is the middle number when the scores are ordered from lowest to highest. Below, the set of numbers for each answer choice is ordered from least to greatest, and the range and median are given for each.

A. 50, 55, 75, 80, 85.
Range = 85 − 50 = 35. The median is 75.

B. 10, 55, 75, 95.
Range = 95 − 10 = 85. Since there is an even number of numbers, you take the average of the middle numbers. Median = (55 + 75)/2 = 65.

C. 15, 75, 75, 85, 90.
Range = 90 − 15 = 75. Median = 75.

D. 5, 20, 70, 80, 95, 90.
Range = 90 − 5 = 85. Median = (70 + 80)/2 = 75.

Answer D has range = 85, median = 75.

6. A If the mean of the return remains the same, the average doesn't change. If the standard deviation increases, the variability in the return increases. Therefore, the risk increases.

Statistics & Probability: Module Review

7. D Let's go through each measure to see how adding a zero could affect the value.

I. median: Adding a zero could change the median since there are now more numbers in the set, and the number that used to be in the middle will no longer be there.
Example: The set 2, 4, 6 has a median of 4.
Add a zero to the set 0, 2, 4, 6. Now, the median is 3 (average of the 2 middle numbers).
Median changes.

II. mean: Adding a zero to a set could change the mean since the number of elements in the set has now changed.
Example: the set 3, 4, 5 has a mean = (3 + 4 + 5) ÷ 3 = 4
Add a zero to the set 0, 3, 4, 5. Now, mean = (0 + 3 + 4 + 5) ÷ 4 = 3.
Mean changes.

III. range: Adding a zero to the set could change the range since the smallest or largest number might change.
Example: the set 3, 4, 5 has a range = 5 − 3 = 2.
Add a zero to the set 0, 3, 4, 5. Now, the range = 5 − 0 = 5
Range changes.

I, II, and III could change if a zero is added to a set.

8. C The data in answer C roughly conforms to a straight line. The data in A is most closely parabolic in shape, and the data in D best matches an exponential function. The data in B does not have a pattern.

9. B You want to rearrange the letters of LESSON, but you must keep the two S's next to each other. Therefore, you are rearranging 5 elements: L, E, SS, O, N

The number of ways to rearrange 5 elements is 5! = 5 x 4 x 3 x 2 x 1 = 120

10. C I. The median and mean of a data set are always different.
You could have a set in which the mean and median are the same value. For example, the set 2, 3, 4 has a mean of 3 and a median of 3. I – False.

II. The median of a data set is always a member of the set.
If there is an even number of elements in a set, the median might not be a member of the set. For example, in the set 2, 4, 6, 8, the median is the average of the two middle numbers 4 and 6. The median of that set is 5, but 5 is not a member of the set. II – False.

III. There can be more than one mode in a data set.
The mode of a set is the element that appears most often. You could have multiple elements that appear the same number of times, therefore, having multiple modes. For example: the set 1, 2, 2, 3, 4, 4, 5, 6 has two modes, 2 and 4, since they both appear twice. III – true.

11. B The problem states that you want the number of combinations, implying that order does not matter. There are 5 possible flavors, and the girl wants to choose 3. Therefore, you want to find $_5C_3$.

$$\frac{n!}{(n-r)!r!} = \frac{5!}{(5-3)!3!} = \frac{5!}{2!3!} = \frac{5(4)(3)(2)(1)}{2(1) \times 3(2)(1)} = 10$$

There are 10 combinations.

12. C Let's think about each marble at a time. The first marble can be put into one of the three bags, so there are 3 ways for that marble. The second marble can also be put into one of three bags, so 3 ways for the 2nd marble. This is the same for each of the 5 marbles.

Therefore, multiply the number of ways for each marble to find the total number of ways: 3 x 3 x 3 x 3 x 3 = 243

13. C To find the median of a data set, order the elements, and then find the middle element. If there is an even number of elements in a set, then the median is the average of the two middle numbers. In this case, there are 6 elements, so the median must be the average of the two middle values.

First, order the set with the values you know: 0, 6, 13, 15, 92

If 14 is the median, it must be the average of the two middle numbers. If 13 and 15 are the two middle numbers, then 14 would be the median. X must be greater than or equal to 15, so that the middle numbers are 13 and 15.

The only answer choice that would make the median equal to 14 is 15.

14. A Let's calculate the standard deviation of each set to determine which has the higher standard deviation. Remember, the formula for finding the standard deviation is the square root of the variance that is calculated:

Set of numbers: $x_1, x_2, x_3, \ldots x_n$ with a mean of $\bar{x}$

$$\text{Variance} = v = \frac{(x_1 - \bar{x})^2 + (x_2 - \bar{x})^2 + \ldots + (x_n - \bar{x})^2}{n}$$

Set A = 5, 5, 5, 5, 6, 16

First, find the mean. Then, calculate the variance, and take the square root to find standard deviation.

Mean = (5 + 5 + 5 + 5 + 6 + 16)/6 = 42 / 6 = 7
Variance = [(5 – 7)2 + (5 – 7)2 + (5 – 7)2 + (5 – 7)2 + (6 – 7)2 + (16 – 7)2]/6
= (4 + 4 + 4 + 4 + 1 + 81)/6 = 98/6 = 49/3
Standard Deviation = √(49/3)

Set B = 8, 9, 10, 10, 11, 12

Mean = (8 + 9 + 10 + 10 + 11 + 12)/6 = 60/6 = 10
Variance = [(8 − 10)2 + (9 − 10)2 + (10 − 10)2 + (10 − 10)2 + (11 − 10)2 + (12 − 10)2]/6
= (4 + 1 + 0 + 0 + 1 + 4)/6 = 10/6 = 5/3
Standard Deviation = √(5/3)

It can clearly be seen that the standard deviation of Set A is larger. If you didn't want to calculate the standard deviation, you could still see that even though Set A had many terms that were the same, one of the terms was significantly farther away from the others, meaning the set had a lot of variance.

15. B The probability is equal to the number of favorable outcomes divided by the number of possible outcomes.

If the number of favorable outcomes is equal to the number of possible outcomes, then the probability would be a number divided by itself, which is always equal to 1.

16. A For Francisco to guess it correctly on his second try, Francisco did not guess it correctly on his first try. Therefore, we need to find the probability of these two events, which can be found by multiplying the probability of each individual event.

Probability of Francisco not guessing correctly on his first try
= Number of letters he could have guessed divided by Total number of letters
= 25/26

Probability of guessing correctly on second try
= Number of correct letters divided by Total number of letters left to guess
= 1/25

Multiply the two probabilities to find the probability that Francisco guesses the letter on his second try.
25/26 x 1/25 = 1/26

17. B The order of the students does not matter, so we are dealing with combinations.

The formula for choosing r elements from n elements in which order does not matter is
n!/(r!(n − r)!)

In this case, we are choosing 3 elements from 7 possible elements.
= 7!/3!(7 − 3)! = 7!/3!4! = 35

There are 35 ways these 3 students can be chosen.

18. A To find the probability that the dart hits the bull's-eye, find the area of the bull's-eye, and divide that by the area of the dartboard. Remember, the area of a circle is πr^2.

The bull's-eye has a radius of 2 inches; the area is $\pi 2^2 = 4\pi$.
The dartboard has a radius of 10 inches; the area is $\pi 10^2 = 100\pi$.
The probability is 4π divided by $100\pi = 4/100 = 1/25$.

19. D There are multiple ways to solve this question. You could do the entire expansion of $(x + y)^5$, but that would take much too long to do. Otherwise, you could use Pascal's Triangle or combinations.

Pascal's Triangle: Here is Pascal's Triangle, which gives the coefficients of binomial expansions. In this case, we just look at the correct row and choose the third term.

Since the exponent n = 5, we want the 6th row: 1 5 10 10 5 1. The third term is 10.

Combinations: You could also expand using combinations.
$(x + y)^5 = {}_5C_0 \, x^5y^0 + {}_5C_1 \, x^4y^1 + {}_5C_2 \, x^3y^2 + {}_5C_3 \, x^2y^3 + {}_5C_4 \, x^1y^4 + {}_5C_5 \, x^0y^5$

The third term is ${}_5C_2 \, x^3y^2$. To find the coefficient, find the number of ways to choose 2 elements from 5 possible elements.
${}_5C_2 = 5!/(2!3!) = 10$

20. D A simple random sample requires that every patient have an equal chance of being selected. In each scenario, not every patient had an equal chance of selection.

A: If he surveys the next 50 patients who walk into the office, the patients from yesterday don't have the same chance of being selected. Furthermore, bias might be introduced. For example, patients unhappy with his service might not schedule another appointment and, therefore, would not ever have a chance of being selected.

B: Again, not every patient has an equal chance of being selected. The sample has 100% determined that the 9th patient will not be selected, and the 10th patient will be selected.

C: Not every patient has an equal chance of being selected.

A simple random sample guarantees that the sample is representative of the population. One way to perform a simple random sample would be to assign every patient a number and then have a random number generator choose 50 random numbers. Those would be the patients surveyed.

8. Trig, Calculus, Discrete Math

Introduction to Trigonometry 426
Trigonometric Identities & Properties 433
Trigonometric Graphs 441
Differential Calculus 448
Integral Calculus 455
Discrete Math 461
Module Review 470

Trig, Calculus, Discrete Math: Intro to Trigonometry

Degrees and Radian Measure

Angles can be described in either degrees or radians.

Degree measure typically ranges 0 degrees $\leq \theta <$ 360 degrees.
Radian measure typically ranges 0 radians $\leq \theta < 2\pi$ radians.

To convert, note that 360 degrees = 2π radians, and 180 degrees = π radians.

To convert from degrees to radians, multiply the number of degrees by (π radians)/180°.
To convert from radians to degrees, multiply the number of radians by 180°/(π radians).

Basic Trigonometric Functions

You hear about three basic trig functions, sine, cosine, and tangent, more commonly seen in their abbreviated forms of sin, cos, and tan. In function notation, you will see them written sin(x), cos(x), and tan(x), where x is the angle.

Here is how they relate to a right triangle.

In the diagram, we will take the trig functions with x as the input angle.
sin(x) = opposite/hypotenuse
cos(x) = adjacent/hypotenuse
tan(x) = opposite/adjacent

If you take the first letter of the trig function, the numerator, and the denominator, you get the phrase: **SOH CAH TOA.** This phrase should be memorized and is a helpful way to remember the definitions of these functions.

Let's go through an example.
SOH: sin(x) = opposite/hypotenuse = 5/13
CAH: cos(x) = adjacent/hypotenuse = 12/13
TOA: tan(x) = opposite/adjacent = 5/12

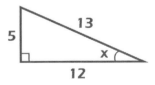

Now, you should remember from previous lessons the standard 45–45–90 and 30–60–90 triangles and the ratios of their sides. Therefore, you should know how to calculate the basic trig functions of 30, 45, and 60 degree angles.

For instance, you know that a triangle with angles of 45, 45, and 90 have two equal sides. Therefore, you can quickly calculate the tangent of 45.
tan(45) = opposite side/adjacent side = 1/1 = 1

Introduction to Trigonometry: Practice

1. How many degrees are equal to π/4 radians?

   A. 30
   B. 40
   C. 45
   D. 60

2. If sin A = 5/13, what is tan A?

   A. 5/12
   B. 12/13
   C. 5/18
   D. 12/5

3. If sin B is 3/5 and the length of side x is 12, what is length of side y?

   A. 4
   B. 16
   C. 20
   D. 7 ⅕

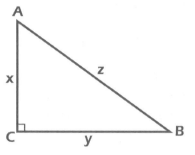

4. Which has the largest value?

   A. sin 45
   B. cos 45
   C. tan 45
   D. 0.5

5. What is cos 60°?

   A. 1/2
   B. √3
   C. √3/2
   D. √2

Trig, Calculus, Discrete Math: Introduction to Trigonometry

6. **Express the Angle 315° in radian measure.**

   A. $7\pi/2$ radians

   B. $3\pi/2$ radians

   C. $7\pi/4$ radians

   D. $3\pi/4$ radians

7. **You have a right triangle with Angles A, B, and C. If C = 90 degrees and sin A = 4/5, what is sin B?**

   A. 1/5

   B. 3/5

   C. 3/4

   D. 1/4

8. **There is a 7-foot ladder against a wall forming a 60-degree angle between the ladder and the ground, how far from the wall is the bottom of the ladder?**

   A. 14 feet

   B. 3.5 feet

   C. $7\sqrt{2}$ feet

   D. $7\sqrt{3}$ feet

9. **Which of these is the largest if the degree measures below are in radians?**

   A. $\tan(\pi/3)$

   B. $\sin(\pi/6)$

   C. $\cos(\pi/2)$

   D. $\cos(\pi/4)$

10. **Express the angle $-3\pi/4$ radians in degrees.**

    A. 270 degrees

    B. 225 degrees

    C. 135 degrees

    D. 45 degrees

Introduction to Trigonometry: Answer Explanations

1. C To convert from degrees to radians, remember that π radians are equal to 180 degrees. Therefore, π/4 radians = 180/4 degrees = 45 degrees.

2. A If sin A = 5/13, then draw a right triangle to represent this angle. The sine of an angle is equal to the opposite divided by the hypotenuse.

Therefore, make the side opposite the angle equal to 5 and the hypotenuse equal to 13. Then, use the Pythagorean theorem to find the length of the missing side.

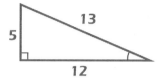

$5^2 + x^2 = 13^2$
$x = 12$

Now, the question asks for the tangent. The tangent is equal to the opposite divided by the adjacent. The opposite side is 5, and the adjacent side is 12. Therefore, the tangent = 5/12.

3. B You know that sin B = 3/5. Therefore, the ratio of the opposite of B to the hypotenuse is 3/5, or the ratio of x to z is 3/5.

x/z = 3/5
12/z = 3/5

Cross-multiply, and solve for z.
3z = 60, z = 20

Now, you know the hypotenuse and one of the sides. You can use the Pythagorean theorem to find the missing side.

$x^2 + y^2 = z^2$
$12^2 + y^2 = 20^2$
$144 + y^2 = 400$
$y^2 = 256$
$y = 16$

4. C Draw a right triangle with 45-degree angles. Since the two angles are equal, you know you have an isosceles triangle. Label the two shorter sides as 1, and you can use the Pythagorean theorem to find the longer side.

$1^2 + 1^2 = \text{hypotenuse}^2$
$1 + 1 = \text{hypotenuse}^2$
$2 = \text{hypotenuse}^2$
Hypotenuse = $\sqrt{2}$

A right triangle with 45-degree angles will always have sides in the ratio of 1:1:√2.

Now, let's go through each answer choice.

sin45 = 1/√2
cos45 = 1/√2
tan45 = 1

Since √2 is approximately 1.4, you can see that tan 45 is the largest.

5. A To calculate the cosine of 60, remember the phrase SOH CAH TOA. CAH stands for cosine is adjacent over hypotenuse.

You should know the ratio of the sides for a 30–60–90 triangle, which is shown in the diagram to the right.

The side adjacent to the 60-degree angle is x; the hypotenuse is 2x.
Therefore, cos 60° = x/2x = 1/2.

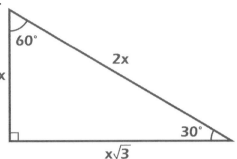

6. C To convert from degrees to radians, multiply the number of degrees by (π radians)/180°

In this problem, we convert 315° to radian measure as follows:

315° = (315 degrees)(π radians/180 degrees) = 7π/4 radians

7. B When given a problem like this, first start by sketching a right triangle.

Since C is 90 degrees, you can label that as the right angle. Next, you know that sin A = 4/5; therefore, you know that the side opposite A is 4, and the hypotenuse will be 5. Now, use the Pythagorean theorem to find the measure of the missing side.

$x^2 + 4^2 = 5^2$
$x^2 + 16 = 25$
$x^2 = 9$
$x = 3$

Now, you know the measures of all the sides, so you can find sin B. Sine is the opposite over hypotenuse, so opposite B is 3, and hypotenuse is 5.

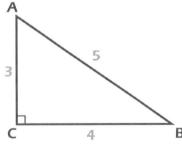

Sin B = 3/5.

8. B First, make a quick sketch of the problem. You know that the ladder will be leaning against a wall and that the ladder is 7 feet. You can see that the ladder, ground, and wall make a right triangle. Also, the problem states that a 60-degree angle is formed between the ladder and the ground.

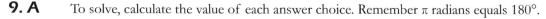

Right triangles that have angles of 30, 60, and 90 degrees are extremely common, and you should be sure to memorize the ratios of the sides. The ratio will always be

Side opposite 30: side opposite 60: hypotenuse = x: x√3 : 2x

In this case, we want how far the base of the ladder is from the wall. We want the side opposite the 30-degree angle. If the hypotenuse is 7, let's solve for x.
2x = 7, x = 3.5

Therefore, the distance from the wall to the base of the ladder is 3.5 feet.

9. A To solve, calculate the value of each answer choice. Remember π radians equals 180°.

a. tan (π/3) = tan (180°/3) = tan 60°
Tangent is opposite over adjacent. The side opposite the 60° angle is always √3 times the length of the side adjacent to the 60° angle. Therefore, tan 60° = √3.

b. sin (π/6) = sin (180°/6) = sin 30°
Sine is the opposite over hypotenuse. The side opposite the 30° angle in a 30, 60, 90 triangle is always in the ratio of 1 to 2 to the hypotenuse. Sin 30° = 1/2.

c. cos (π/2) = cos (180°/2) = cos 90°
The cosine of 90° is equal to zero. In the next few lessons, you will review the cosine graph and identities, which will make it easy to know that cos 90° = 0. However, let's just think about this in terms of right triangles. As the angle gets larger, what happens to the ratio of the sides? If you think of a triangle with a very small angle, you can see that the opposite side will be very small, while the adjacent side and hypotenuse are approaching the ratio of 1. Now, what happens as this angle grows very large? Well, the opposite side will grow, while the adjacent side will continue to get smaller. Therefore, as the angle gets closer and closer to 90 degrees, the cosine gets closer to zero. You can't calculate cosine of x using just right triangles, but you can tell that the cosine of 90 degrees will approach zero.

d. cos (π/4) = cos (180°/4) = cos 45°
Cosine is the adjacent over hypotenuse. In a 45, 45, 90 triangle, the two sides are both equal, and the ratio of the sides to the hypotenuse is 1 to √2. Therefore, cos 45° = 1/√2.

The question asks which is the largest, and as you can see, A is the largest. You can use estimation to see this quickly by noting that A is the only one with a value larger than 1.

10. B Method 1: Convert from radians to degrees, and then from a negative to a positive angle.
To convert from radians to degrees, multiply the number of radians by $180°/(\pi \text{ radians})$
$(-3\pi/4 \text{ radians}) \times (180°/\pi \text{ radians}) = -135 \text{ degrees}$

Then, convert from negative to positive degrees by adding 360 degrees.
$-135 + 360 = 225 \text{ degrees}$

Method 2: Convert from negative to positive radians, and then from radians to degrees.
To convert from negative to positive radians, add 2π radians.
$-3\pi/4 + 2\pi = 5\pi/4 \text{ radians}$

Then, convert from radians to degrees.
$(5\pi/4 \text{ radians}) \times (180°/\pi \text{ radians}) = 225 \text{ degrees}$

Trig, Calc, Discrete Math: Trig Identities & Properties

Now that you have learned the basic definitions of the trigonometric functions, let's cover some identities and properties, so you can start solving trig problems that are more complex.

Two trigonometric laws can be used when you are given problems that ask you to find the lengths of the sides and angles of triangles: Law of Sines and Law of Cosines. Conveniently, the formula sheets for MTEL47 and MTEL09 will have both of these laws listed, but be sure to understand how and when to use them.

Law of Sines

$$\frac{a}{\sin A} = \frac{b}{\sin B} = \frac{c}{\sin C}$$

where A, B, and C are the angles of the triangle; a, b, and c are the lengths of the side opposite their corresponding angles.

The Law of Sines can be used to solve problems in which either:
- Given two angles and one side opposite one of the given angles, solve for the other side.
- Given two sides and one angle opposite one of the given sides, solve for the other angle.

Example. Solve for the length x for the triangle below.

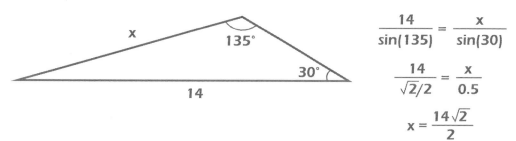

Plug the angles and sides into the Law of Sines and solve for x.

$$\frac{14}{\sin(135)} = \frac{x}{\sin(30)}$$

$$\frac{14}{\sqrt{2}/2} = \frac{x}{0.5}$$

$$x = \frac{14\sqrt{2}}{2}$$

Law of Cosines

$c^2 = a^2 + b^2 - 2ab \cos C$

where a, b, and c are the lengths of the sides, and C is the angle opposite side c.

The Law of Cosines can be used to solve problems in which either:
- Given two sides and one angle not opposite one of the given sides, solve for the third side.
- Given three sides, solve for the angles.

Trigonometric Identities

Identities are relationships that can be used to put an expression in a more convenient form. Some of the more common identities are as follows:

$$\csc \theta = \frac{1}{\sin \theta} \qquad \sec \theta = \frac{1}{\cos \theta} \qquad \cot \theta = \frac{1}{\tan \theta} \qquad \tan \theta = \frac{\sin \theta}{\cos \theta}$$

$$\sin^2 \theta + \cos^2 \theta = 1$$
$$1 + \tan^2 \theta = \sec^2 \theta$$
$$1 + \cot^2 \theta = \csc^2 \theta$$

Example: $\sec(60) = 1/\cos(60) = 1/0.5 = 2$

Unit Circle

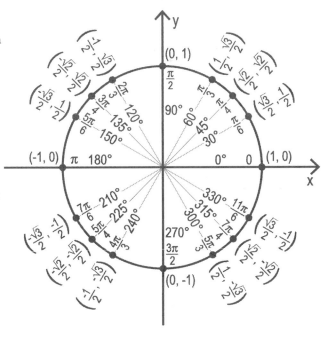

The Unit Circle is a circle centered at the origin (0, 0) with a radius of length 1. From this circle, the functions sine, cosine, tangent, as well as secant, cosecant, and cotangent, can be calculated for any angle.

In this graph, the inner set of numbers show the angles in degrees; the middle set of numbers shows angles in radians; and, the outer set of numbers shows the coordinates of the unit circle.

The x-coordinates of the unit circle are the cosine of the angle; the y-coordinates are the sine of the angle.
(Cos, Sin)

For instance, at the angle of 0 degrees, you can see that the coordinates of the unit circle are (1, 0), meaning that the cos 0 = 1, and sin 0 = 0.

If you wanted to find sin 30, you would look at the 30-degree angle and look at the y-coordinate of the unit circle. Sin 30 = 1/2.

The unit circle can look rather overwhelming. One way to handle it is to make sure you either memorize or understand how to calculate quickly all the values in the first quadrant. You can quickly calculate the sine and cosine from thinking about 30–60–90 triangles and 45–45–90 triangles and their common ratios. Then, to figure out the angles around the rest of the circle, think about whether the sine or cosine will be positive or negative based on the quadrant and what the signs of the x and y coordinates are.

For instance, let's look at the angle 150 degrees. This is 30 degrees away from the x-axis. Therefore, you should know that the coordinates of the unit circle at 30 degrees are (√3/2, 1/2), and you know that you are in the 2nd quadrant where the x-coordinate will be negative, and the y coordinate will be positive. Therefore, the coordinates for 150 degrees are (-√3/2, 1/2).

Inverse Functions

Inverse functions reverse the operations of standard functions.

The inverse sine function is described as
$$y = \sin^{-1}x, \text{ where } -\pi/2 < y < \pi/2.$$

For example, $\sin^{-1}0.5 = \pi/6$

The inverse cosine function is described as
$$y = \cos^{-1}x, \text{ where } 0 \leq y \leq \pi.$$

For example, $\cos^{-1}0.5 = \pi/3$.

Trigonometric Identities & Properties: Practice

1. Find the length of side c.

A. 7

B. √129

C. 13

D. √89

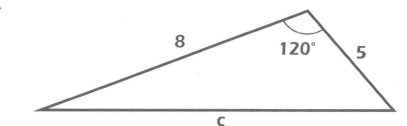

2. Which has the largest value?

A. sin 1

B. sin 30

C. sin 45

D. sin 89

3. Given the sin θ = 0.8 and cos θ = 0.6, find cot θ.

A. 4/3

B. 1/22

C. 2

D. 3/4

4. Find the value of the expression: $\tan(\sin^{-1}(\sqrt{2}/2))$.

    A. 1
    B. 1/2
    C. $\sqrt{2}/2$
    D. $\sqrt{3}/2$

5. Solve the trigonometric equation for θ. $2\sin\theta + 2 = \cos^2\theta$

    A. 270 degrees
    B. 225 degrees
    C. 90 degrees
    D. 45 degrees

6. A baseball is thrown from ground level at an initial velocity of 30 meters per second and at an angle of $\pi/12$. Gravity is approximately 10 meters per second².

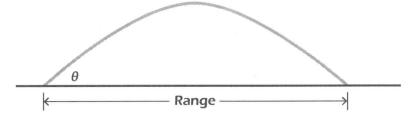

Calculate the Range R of the throw in meters using this formula: where v_0 is the initial velocity, θ is the angle from ground level, and g is gravity. $R = \dfrac{v_0^2 \sin 2\theta}{g}$

    A. 1.5
    B. 30
    C. 45
    D. 90

7. Given the equation $\tan\theta = 3/4$, find $\sec\theta$.

    A. 5/4
    B. 25/16
    C. 9/16
    D. 4/3

8. Find the length of c if A = 62°, B = 48°, b = 37, a = 41, sin 48° ≈ 0.74, sin 62° ≈ 0.82, and sin 70° ≈ 0.94?

   A. 33
   B. 39
   C. 45
   D. 47

9. For which of the following intervals of θ are the cos θ and the tan θ both negative?

   A. $0 < \theta < \pi/2$
   B. $\pi/2 < \theta < \pi$
   C. $\pi < \theta < 3\pi/2$
   D. $3\pi/2 < \theta < 2\pi$

10. Find the value of 4csc (7π/6) − 2sec (4π/3) =

    A. 2
    B. −4
    C. 8
    D. −12

Trigonometric Identities & Properties: Answer Explanations

1. B   Since you are given 2 sides and an angle, you can use the Law of Cosines to find the final side. The Law of Cosines is provided on your formula sheet:

$c^2 = a^2 + b^2 - 2ab \cos C$
$c^2 = 5^2 + 8^2 - 2(5)(8)\cos(120)$
$c^2 = 5^2 + 8^2 - 2(5)(8)(-1/2)$

NOTE: $\cos(120) = -1/2$ from the Unit Circle

$c^2 = 25 + 64 + 40 = 129$
$c = \sqrt{129}$

2. D   You should think about the unit circle to help you. Remember, on the unit circle, the coordinates are (cos Θ, sin Θ). So, if you look at the answer choices, they all are between 0 and 90 degrees and, therefore, in the first quadrant. Well, on the unit circle, the y-coordinate increases as you go from 0 to 90 degrees. Therefore, the sine value increases, and sin 89 has the largest value.

Trig, Calculus, Discrete Math: Trigonometric Identities & Properties

3. D Use a couple of trigonometric identities to solve this problem.

First, use the following identity for tangent: $\tan \Theta = \sin \Theta / \cos \Theta$

$\tan \Theta = 0.8/0.6 = 4/3$

Now, use the following identity for cotangent: $\cot \Theta = 1/\tan \Theta$

$\cot \Theta = 1/(4/3) = 3/4$

4. A When solving questions with parentheses, start with the innermost and work outward.

In this problem, start with $\sin^{-1}(\sqrt{2}/2)$.

You can think either of the unit circle or the 45–45–90 triangle. Either way, $\sin(\pi/4) = \sqrt{2}/2$.

So, $\sin^{-1}(\sqrt{2}/2) = \pi/4$ or 45 degrees.

$\tan(\sin^{-1}(\sqrt{2}/2)) = \tan(\pi/4)$

Again, think about the unit circle, and remember that $\tan \Theta = \sin \Theta / \cos \Theta$, or you could think about a 45–45–90 triangle where the sides are in the ratio of $1:1:\sqrt{2}$.

$\tan(\pi/4) = 1$

5. A $2\sin \theta + 2 = \cos^2 \theta$

Note, it will be easier to solve this equation if all the trigonometric functions are the same. Therefore, use the identity $\sin^2 \theta + \cos^2 \theta = 1$ to substitute for $\cos^2 \theta$.

$\sin^2 \theta + \cos^2 \theta = 1,\ \cos^2 \theta = 1 - \sin^2 \theta$

$2\sin \theta + 2 = \cos^2 \theta$

$2\sin \theta + 2 = 1 - \sin^2 \theta$

Now, move all the terms to one side.

$\sin^2 \theta + 2\sin \theta + 1 = 0$

Factor $\sin \theta$

$(\sin \theta + 1)^2 = 0$

Solve for $\sin \theta$

$\sin \theta + 1 = 0$

$\sin \theta = -1$

From the unit circle, $\theta = 270$ degrees.

6. C In this question, they give you the equation and the value of the following variables:

$\theta = \pi/12$ radians

$v_0 = 30$

$g = 10$

$R = \dfrac{v_0^2 \sin 2\theta}{g} = \dfrac{30^2 \sin(2 \times \pi/12)}{10} = \dfrac{900 \sin(\pi/6)}{10} = \dfrac{900 \times 0.5}{10} = 45$

438   Trig, Calculus, Discrete Math: Trigonometric Identities & Properties

7. A In this case, you want to find the secant, but the only information you have is the tangent. Hopefully, you will remember the trigonometric identity:
$1 + \tan^2 \Theta = \sec^2 \Theta$

Also, if you forget that trig identity, you can always calculate it from the following formula:
$\cos^2 \Theta + \sin^2 \Theta = 1$
Divide all the terms by $\cos^2 \Theta$, and you will get the identity relating tangent and secant.

Now, plug in 3/4 for $\tan \Theta$ and solve for $\sec \Theta$.
$1 + \tan^2 \Theta = \sec^2 \Theta$
$1 + (3/4)^2 = \sec^2 \Theta$
$1 + 9/16 = \sec^2 \Theta$
$25/16 = \sec^2 \Theta$

Take the square root of both sides. $5/4 = \sec \Theta$

8. D You are given the following information:
$A = 62°$, $B = 48°$, $b = 37$, $a = 41$, $\sin 48° \approx 0.74$, $\sin 62° \approx 0.82$, $\sin 70° \approx 0.94$

On the formula sheet, you are provided with the formula for the Law of Sines and the Law of Cosines, but based on the information provided, use the Law of Sines:

$$\frac{a}{\sin A} = \frac{b}{\sin B} = \frac{c}{\sin C}$$

First, determine all the angles. $A = 62°$ and $B = 48°$ are given. Add them, and subtract from 180 to find the measure of Angle C. Angle $C = 70°$.

$a/\sin A = c/\sin C$
$41/0.82 = c/0.94$
$c = 47$

9. B The easiest way to approach this question is to think of the unit circle. Remember that the coordinates of any point on the unit circle are $(\cos \Theta, \sin \Theta)$.

We want to find out where the cosine and tangent are negative. A quick scan of the answer choices shows that they are divided into the four quadrants of the coordinate plane. Let's start with the cosine and figure out in which quadrants it is negative. Well, we know that $\cos \Theta$ is the x-coordinate, and we know that Quadrants 2 and 3 have a negative x-coordinate.

Therefore, $\cos \Theta$ is negative in Quadrant 2: $\pi/2 < \Theta < \pi$ and Quadrant 3: $\pi < \Theta < 3\pi/2$.

Now, let's think about in which of those quadrants would the tangent also be negative. Recall that tangent is equal to $\sin \Theta / \cos \Theta$. In Quadrant 2, sine is positive, and cosine is negative; therefore, tangent is negative. In Quadrant 3, sine and cosine are negative, and therefore, the tangent is positive. So, only Quadrant 2 has a cosine and tangent that are negative.

Quadrant 2: $\pi/2 < \Theta < \pi$

10. B If you want to find the value of $4\csc(7\pi/6) - 2\sec(4\pi/3)$, you should first recall the trigonometric identities to get everything in terms of sine and cosine, which are easier to deal with and more familiar to you.

$\csc \Theta = 1/\sin \Theta$
$\sec \Theta = 1/\cos \Theta$

Now, let's simplify the first term, using the identity and the unit circle.
$4\csc(7\pi/6)$
$= 4/\sin(7\pi/6)$

Sometimes, it is easier to deal with angles in degrees instead of radians.
$7\pi/6 \times 180/\pi = 210$ degrees

210 degrees is 30 degrees more than 180 degrees and is in the 3rd quadrant, which means the sine is negative.

$4/\sin(7\pi/6)$
$= 4/\sin 120$
$= 4/-0.5$
$= -8$

Next, simplify $2\sec(4\pi/3)$ using the second identity from above and the unit circle.

$2\sec(4\pi/3)$
$= 2/\cos(4\pi/3)$
$= 2/\cos 240$
$= 2/-0.5$
$= -4$

Finally, substitute and combine the two expressions
$4\csc(7\pi/6) - 2\sec(4\pi/3) = -8 - (-4) = -4$

Trig, Calc, Discrete Math: Trigonometric Graphs

Graphs of Basic Trig Functions

You can see that these graphs are derived from the unit circle. You should understand the basic structure of the graphs and note where the maximum and minimum points are on each graph. Below are the graphs for sine and cosine.

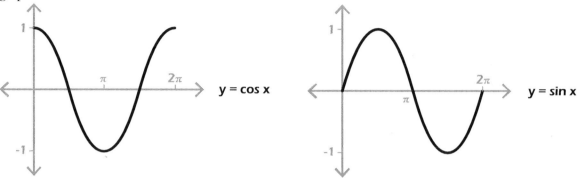

Period

The period of a graph is the interval for which the function repeats. For instance, both the cosine and sine graphs above have a period of 2π, meaning that these functions repeat at every interval of 2π on the x-axis. In other words, the y-values from $0 \leq x < 2\pi$ are the same as $2\pi \leq x < 4\pi$, $4\pi \leq x < 6\pi$, and so on. The graphs of just one period are illustrated above.

Amplitude

The amplitude of a periodic function is the absolute value of the maximum or minimum y-axis point reached. For $\sin(x)$ and $\cos(x)$, the amplitude is 1. For example, in the range of $0 \leq x < 2\pi$ for the sine graph, the amplitude is reached at $\pi/2$ and $3\pi/2$.

Phase Shift

A phase shift of a periodic function (such as sine or cosine) occurs when the periods begin at some point other than 0.

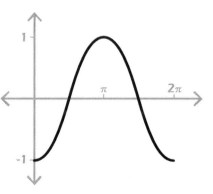

For example, the graph to the right is a phase shift of the sine function. It is of function $y = \sin(x - \pi/2)$, which has a phase shift of $\pi/2$, as that is where the period begins.

Formulas

The amplitude, period, and phase shift can be found formulaically.
$y = A \sin(\omega x - \varphi)$, $y = A \cos(\omega x - \varphi)$
Amplitude $= |A|$ Period $= 2\pi/\omega$ Phase shift $= \varphi/\omega$

Trigonometric Graphs: Practice

1. Find the amplitude of the function y = −4cos(3x + π/2).

    A. −4
    B. π/2
    C. 3
    D. 4

2. Which of the following graphs has an amplitude twice the amplitude of f(x) = sin(x)?

    A. g(x) = sin(2x)
    B. g(x) = 2sin(x)
    C. g(x) = sin(x + 2)
    D. g(x) = sin(x) + 2

3. You have a graph of a trigonometric function that passes through (0, 2), has an amplitude of 2, and has no phase shift. Which of the following could be the equation of that graph?

    A. y = 2cos(x)
    B. y = 2sin(x)
    C. y = sin(x − π/2)
    D. y = cos(2x − π)

4. What is the period of the graph?

    A. π/4
    B. π/2
    C. π
    D. 3π/2

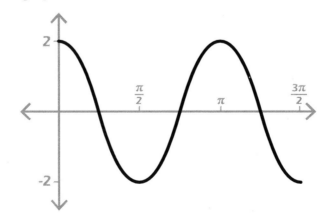

442   Trig, Calculus, Discrete Math: Trigonometric Graphs

5. What expression represents the graph:

   A. 2cosx
   B. 2cos(x − π)
   C. cos(2x)
   D. cos(2π x)

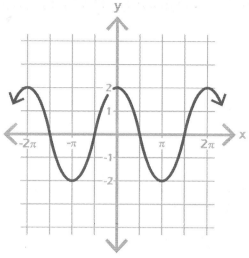

6. Find the amplitude, period, and phase shift of the function: $y = 4\sin(3x + \pi/2)$.

   A. Amplitude = –4; Period = 3; Phase Shift = π/2
   B. Amplitude = 4; Period = 2π/3; Phase Shift = π/6
   C. Amplitude = 4; Period = π/2; Phase Shift = π/6
   D. Amplitude = 4; Period = 2π/3; Phase Shift = -π/6

7. Find the period of the function $y = 3\sin(4x + \pi)$.

   A. 4
   B. π/4
   C. π/2
   D. π

8. What is the equation of the function graphed below?

   A. $f(x) = 4\cos(x - \pi/2)$
   B. $f(x) = 3\cos(2x - \pi)$
   C. $f(x) = -3\sin(x - 2\pi)$
   D. $f(x) = -3\sin(2x - \pi)$

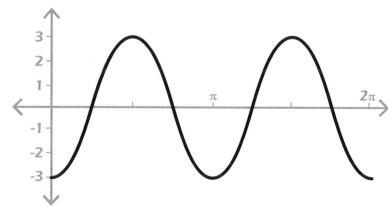

Trig, Calculus, Discrete Math: Trigonometric Graphs

9. Find the phase shift of the function y = 2cos(3x + π/6).

   A. 12

   B. π/6

   C. -π/6

   D. -π/18

10. The graph to the right represents a cosine function. What is the phase shift?

    A. π/8

    B. π/4

    C. π/2

    D. 9π/4

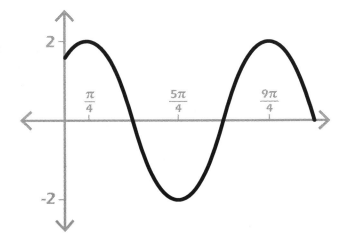

Trigonometric Graphs: Answer Explanations

1. D   There are two ways to think about this problem.

Method 1:
Let's review the standard formula for graphing trigonometric functions: $y = A \cos(\omega x - \varphi)$.
Amplitude = $|A|$
Period = $2\pi/\omega$
Phase shift = φ/ω

Therefore, looking at this equation: $y = -4\cos(3x + \pi/2)$

You see that the amplitude is $|A| = |-4| = 4$

Method 2:
Another way to think about this problem is to think that the cosine graph has an amplitude of 1. Hopefully, you have memorized the standard graphs of sine and cosine or can remember this from thinking about the unit circle.

$y = -4\cos(3x + \pi/2)$

In the above equation, you have −4 multiplied by the cosine of some angle. You can ignore everything that is going on inside the parentheses and just know that the cosine will range from −1 to 1. Therefore, multiplying those values by −4 means that y will range from −4 to 4. Therefore, the amplitude of that equation is 4.

2. B First, you need to make sure you understand what a change in amplitude does to a graph. The amplitude will change how much the graph changes vertically. In other words, the standard sine and cosine graphs will have y-values between −1 and 1. If the amplitude changes, the range of y-values will change. In this case, the amplitude is twice that of f(x) = sin(x). We know that the amplitude of sin(x) is 1, and therefore, the amplitude of the equation we want is 2.

Now, to figure out what equations have amplitudes of 2, you have to think about which equations will affect the range of y-values. If you take whatever the outcome of the original equation is and multiply each outcome by 2, you would be increasing the amplitude by 2. Therefore, we want to take f(x) and multiply each value by 2. Looking at each equation, we can see that answer B does this: g(x) = 2sin(x). The input of x is given, the sine of that is taken, and then the result is multiplied by 2.

If you have an equation of the form f(x) = a sin(bx + c), the value of a will affect the amplitude, the value of b will affect the period, and the value of c will affect the phase shift.

g(x) = 2 sin(x)

3. A If you know that the graph of the trigonometric function has an amplitude of 2, passes through (0, 2), and has no phase shift, then you know that the point (0, 2) is at a maximum on the graph.

Let's examine each answer and first eliminate any that don't have an amplitude of 2. To have an amplitude of 2, the trig function must be multiplied by 2. Answers A and B are the only ones that have an amplitude of 2. Answer C has an amplitude of 1 and a phase shift. Answer D has an amplitude of 1, a change in period, and a phase shift.

a. y = 2cos(x)
b. y = 2sin(x)
c. y = sin(x − π/2)
d. y = cos(2x − π)

Now, between answers A and B, we have to think about what happens at the value of 0. You should memorize the standard graphs of the trig functions sine, cosine, and tangent. But, in the meantime, let's think about which trig function has a value of 1 when x = 0. cos(0) = 1; sin(0) = 0.

Thinking about the sine function, which is opposite over hypotenuse, if you think about a right triangle and realize that as an angle gets smaller and smaller, the side opposite to it also gets smaller and smaller. Therefore, the sine of that angle will approach 0, which is exactly why the sin(0) = 0, and which is just the opposite for cosine, which is equal to the adjacent side over the hypotenuse. cos(0) = 1.

Therefore, your equation is y = 2 cos(x).
When x = 0, you have y = 2 cos(0) = 2, giving you the point (0, 2).

4. C The period of the graph is the horizontal distance between the start of a cycle and the end of the same cycle. You can also think of it as the horizontal distance that the cycle repeats itself.

In this graph, if you use the point at x = 0 as the start of the cycle, then the cycle ends at π, as this is the point at which the cycle will repeat. It is a maximum of the graph, and the graph will start to drop toward zero.

The period of this function is π.

5. A The graph of the cosine function has a period of 2π, as does the graph in this problem. The graph of a cosine function has an amplitude of 1; however, this graph has an amplitude of 2. In addition, the graph of the cosine function starts at 1 and goes down, and therefore, this graph does not have any phase shift. Therefore, the only transformation from the basic cosine function is an amplitude increased by a factor of 2.

2cos x.

6. D y = 4sin(3x + π/2)

For a graph that is the standard form of y = Asin(ωx − φ), ω > 0, the amplitude, period, and phase shift can be found with the following equations:

Amplitude = |A|
Period = 2π/ω
Phase Shift = φ/ω

In this case, A = 4, ω = 3, and φ = -π/2. Note that the value of φ is negative. This is a common mistake, and you must remember that the form of the equation is subtraction.

Amplitude: |4| = 4.
Period = 2π/ω = 2π/3
Phase Shift = φ/ω = (-π/2)/3 = -π/6

An alternative method of finding the phase shift is to solve for x in the equation 3x + π/2 = 0, because the unshifted sine curve starts at 0.

7. C When looking at a trigonometric function, examine how it differs from the standard equations to figure out amplitude, period, or phase shift. The standard sine function is y = sin x. In that case, the amplitude is 1, period is 2π, and there is no phase shift.

Now, let's examine this problem and think about the formula: y = A sin(ωx − φ). Since the output of the sine function is multiplied by A, the A represents the Amplitude. The input x is being multiplied by ω, which would affect the period. Finally, the phase shift is determined by φ.

$y = 3\sin(4x + \pi)$

In this problem, $A = 3$, $\omega = 4$, and $\varphi = -\pi$.

The period is determined by the ω and is equal to the period of the standard sine function, 2π divided by ω.

Period $= 2\pi/\omega = 2\pi/4 = \pi/2$

8. B   These types of problems are most easily solved by process of elimination.

When looking at a trigonometric graph, the first thing to notice is the amplitude. In this case, the maximum value on the y-axis is 3, which is the amplitude. When looking at a trigonometric equation, the coefficient in front of the trigonometric function equals the amplitude. You can eliminate answer A, as that equation has an amplitude of 4.

Then, you can proceed by plugging in points or looking at the period. I'll use a combination of both methods to eliminate the remaining answer choices.

Looking at the graph, you can see that the period is π, as the graph repeats at every interval of π. The normal period of a trig function is 2π, and therefore, if we multiply the input by 2, we would change the period to π. Answers B and D have a period of π. Eliminate answer C.

Now, let's plug in a point to eliminate another answer choice. On the graph, when $x = \pi/2$, the function equals 3. Let's plug it into each remaining answer.

B: $f(\pi/2) = 3\cos(2(\pi/2) - \pi) = 3\cos(0) = 3$. OK
D. $f(\pi/2) = -3\sin(2(\pi/2) - \pi) = -3\sin(\pi/2) = -3$. Wrong
This eliminates D, which leaves just answer B.

9. D   The easiest way to determine the phase shift is to refer to the standard formula for a trigonometric function:

$y = A\cos(\omega x - \varphi)$ where the phase shift will be equal to φ/ω.
A very common mistake is to switch the sign of φ, so be careful.

$y = 2\cos(3x + \pi/6)$
Therefore, $\varphi = -\pi/6$ and $\omega = 3$.
Phase shift $= \varphi/\omega = (-\pi/6)/3 = -\pi/18$

10. B   The function $\cos(x)$ with no phase shift has a value of 1 at $x = 0$ (that is, $\cos(0) = 1$).

Also, the cosine function starts at its peak and decreases toward the minimum point.

In the given graph, the peak occurs at $\pi/4$ and then decreases. The phase shift must be $\pi/4$ for this cosine function.

Trig, Calculus, Discrete Math: Differential Calculus

Limits

Limits convey the idea that functions approach a value as a variable grows infinitely positive or infinitely negative.

A variable growing infinitely positive is represented by x $\to \infty$.

A variable growing infinitely negative is represented by x $\to -\infty$.

For example, "the limit of g(x) as x approaches positive infinity" is expressed $\lim_{x \to \infty} g(x)$

The value that the function approaches is an asymptote.

Vertical Asymptotes

Vertical asymptotes are the values the graph approaches for x but will never equal. If you have a vertical asymptote, it means that there is a value for x that will be a restricted value. To find vertical asymptotes, determine where x is restricted. For instance, you cannot divide by 0, so if you have a value for x that will result in a division by 0, then this value is restricted, and there will be a vertical asymptote at this value for x. In addition, you can't take the square root of a negative number, so you might have a vertical asymptote at values of x that result in this.

Horizontal Asymptotes

The horizontal asymptotes will be values of y the graph approaches but never reaches. To find the horizontal asymptotes, find the limit as x approaches infinity.

For example, find the horizontal asymptote of g(x) = [4/(x – 2)] + 1.

As x approaches infinity, the denominator of that fraction will get bigger and bigger, and therefore, the fraction will get smaller and smaller and approach 0. The function will approach 0 + 1 = 1. So, as x approaches infinity, g(x) approaches 1. Therefore, you have a horizontal asymptote at y = 1.

Derivatives

Nonlinear functions have a slope that constantly changes as they move along the x-axis. A secant line is a line that connects two points along a function. A tangent line is a line that touches the function at a point. At the point where the tangent touches the curve, it has the same slope as the curve. The slope of the tangent line is called the derivative.

To calculate a derivative for x raised to an integer power,
$d/dx\,(x^n) = nx^{n-1}$

For example, the derivative of x^2 is 2x, and the derivative of x^3 is $3x^2$.

Sometimes, the notation for derivative is the apostrophe after the variable. For example, derivative y = y'.

Min/Max

You have learned other ways to find minimum and maximum of certain types of graphs (such as quadratic equations) – but using derivatives, you can find the minimum or maximum point on the graph by

1. Find the derivative of the function f(x).
2. Set the result equal to 0.
3. Solve for x.

A derivative of 0 means that the slope of the tangent line at that point is zero. Remember that a horizontal line has a slope of 0, and this would be at a minimum or maximum point.

Inflection Points & Concavity

The inflection points of a graph are the points at which it changes concavity. In other words, an inflection point is the point at which a curve changes from concave up to concave down or vice versa. Finding the inflection points is similar to finding the maximum and minimum points. However, the second derivative must be taken instead of the first. Then, set the result equal to 0, and solve for x.

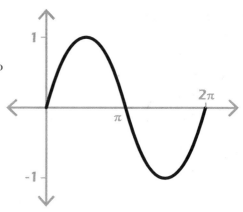

For example, the graph to the right shows a sine function. This graph is concave down from 0 to π and concave up from π to 2π, and this change at π is an inflection point.

Differential Calculus: Practice

1. $$\lim_{x \to \infty} \frac{x^3 + 3x + 5}{-2x^3 - 2x^2 + 6}$$

   A. ∞
   B. 0
   C. –1/2
   D. 5/6

2. What is the vertical asymptote of the following equation? y = 3/(x + 2)

   A. x = –2
   B. y = 3
   C. x = 2
   D. y = 0

3. A secant line of a function f(x) contains the following two points: f(−1) = 3; f(2) = −6
What is the average rate of change?

    A. −3

    B. 3

    C. −6

    D. 6

4. What is the limit of g(x) as x approaches infinity?   g(x) = (4x² − 2x + 8)/(2x² − 1)

    A. −2

    B. 8

    C. 4

    D. 2

5. Find the derivative of x⁴.

    A. 4x

    B. 4x³

    C. 3x³

    D. 4x⁵

6. At what value of x is the derivative of f(x) equal to 0?

    A. −2

    B. 0

    C. 3

    D. 4

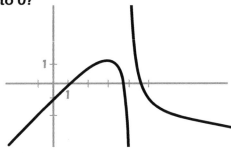

7. Describe the concavity of the cosine function:

    A. Concave up from x = 2 to x = 4;
    Concave down from x = 5 to x = 7

    B. Concave down from x = 2 to x = 4;
    Concave up from x = 5 to x = 7

    C. Concave up from x = 2 to x = 4;
    Concave up from x = 5 to x = 7

    D. Concave down from x = 2 to x = 4;
    Concave down from x = 5 to x = 7

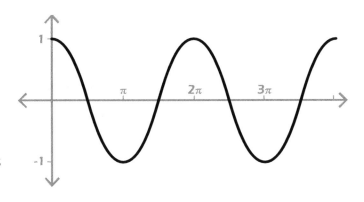

8. Find the second derivative of y = 3x⁴.

   A. 12x³

   B. 24x³

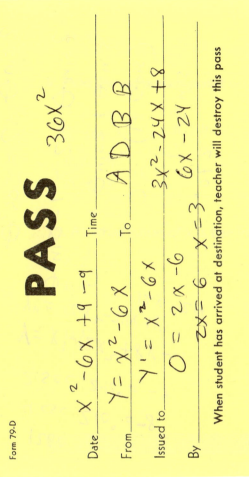

...he graph of y = (x − 3)² − 9.

...lection point of y = x³ − 12x² + 8x − 11.

Differential Calculus: Answer Explanations

1. C As x approaches infinity, the only terms you need to pay attention to on both the numerator and denominator are those with the highest powers since the other terms will not grow nearly as fast. Another way to think about it is that you are only taking the highest degree of the numerator and denominator. Therefore, you are really considering the limit as x approaches infinity of $(x^3) \div (-2x^3)$.

Now, both of those terms have the same degree or power. Since, x^3 is on both the numerator and the denominator and will always be equal, they can be cancelled out. Thus, you are left with the limit as x approaches infinity is $-\frac{1}{2}$.

2. A   Asymptotes are the values the graph approaches but will never equal. In this case, we want the vertical asymptotes. Therefore, we need to think about what values of x are restricted from the domain so that the graph can never equal that value of x. At the value of x that the graph will never equal, you will find an asymptote. So, we must find the value of x that is restricted. So, why would something be restricted in math? Well, it must break a rule, and for real numbers, the two rules in math are that you can never divide by zero, and you can't take the square root of a negative. Therefore, we must find the instances in which one of these rules is broken.

y = 3/(x + 2)

In the above equation, we are not dealing with roots, but we are dealing with division. So, we need to make sure that we are never dividing by 0. We would be dividing by zero if the denominator of the equation ever equaled 0. Therefore, set the denominator equal to zero to find the restricted value.

x + 2 = 0, x = –2

Therefore, if x equaled –2, the denominator would be 0, and this would violate a rule in math. So, we know that the vertical asymptote will be at x = –2.

3. A   This question is straightforward. The average rate of change is the slope of a secant line containing the two points.

f(–1) = 3; and f(2) = –6

The two points are (–1, 3) and (2, –6). Slope is change in y over change in x.

Average rate of change = slope = (3 – –6)/(–1 – 2) = 9/–3 = –3

4. D   When finding the limit, look at the highest orders of the polynomials in the numerator and denominator. As x approaches infinity, the highest exponent terms are more significant than the terms with exponents of 1 and 0.

g(x) = (4x^2 – 2x + 8)/(2x^2 – 1)

In the above function, the term with the highest exponent in the numerator is 4x^2. The term with the highest exponent in the denominator is 2x^2. As x approaches infinity, the terms with exponents of 0 and 1 will not have significant values.

The ratio of the coefficients for the x^2 terms will be the limit of the function.
4/2 = 2

5. B This is a simple question to test the definition of derivative. Remember that:
$d/dx\ (x^n) = nx^{n-1}$

Now, let's apply that formula to finding the derivative of x^4.

$d/dx\ (x^4) = 4x^{4-1} = 4x^3$

6. C Remember, the derivative of a function can be found by determining the slope of the line tangent to the graph at the given point. The question asks when the derivative of f(x) is equal to zero. So, you want to see at which point the slope of the tangent is zero. A line with a slope of zero is a horizontal line. Therefore, you are checking at which point the tangent is a horizontal line.

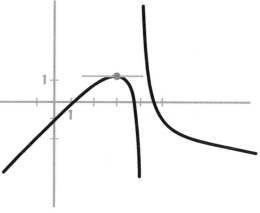

When x = 3, the tangent is a horizontal line (as can be seen by the thin line in the graph to the right).

When x = 3, the derivative of f(x) equals 0.

7. A Concavity is defined by where the graphs change direction.

In this problem, the points of interest are at pi (about 3.14) and 2pi (about 6.28).

From the first point, both sides of the curve are moving up. That section is concave up. The section is concave up between $\pi/2$ and $3\pi/2$.

From the second point, both directions of x are moving down. This section is concave down. The section is concave down between $3\pi/2$ and $5\pi/2$.

Therefore, the graph is concave up near the first point (at 3.14), and on the graph when x is between 2 and 4, the graph is concave up. The second point (at 6.28) is between 5 and 7, and the graph is concave down.

8. D To find the second derivative, simply take the first derivative and then take the derivative of the result.

Start with the first derivative:
$y = 3x^4$
$dy/dx = 3(4x^3) = 12x^3$

Now, take the derivative of the first derivative.
$d^2y/dx^2 = 12(3x^2) = 36x^2$

Trig, Calculus, Discrete Math: Differential Calculus 453

9. A There are multiply ways to approach this question. You could graph the quadratic to find the minimum. You could note that the graph is concave up and then find its vertex. Here is a method that uses derivatives.

First, expand the function.
$y = (x - 3)^2 - 9$
$y = x^2 - 6x + 9 - 9$
$y = x^2 - 6x$

Then, take the derivative.
$y = x^2 - 6x$
$dy/dx = 2x - 6$

Now, set the derivative equal to zero and solve for x.
$0 = 2x - 6, x = 3$

Now, plug 3 into the original equation and solve for y.
$y = (x - 3)^2 - 9$
$y = (3 - 3)^2 - 9 = -9$

$(3, -9)$

10. B The inflection point can be found when the second derivative of an equation is equal to zero.

So, let's start with the first derivative.
$y = x^3 - 12x^2 + 8x - 11$
$y' = 3x^2 - 24x + 8$

Now, the second derivative.
$y' = 3x^2 - 24x + 8$
$y'' = 6x - 24$

Set the second derivative to zero to find the inflection point.
$6x - 24 = 0$
$x = 4$

Trig, Calculus, Discrete Math: Integral Calculus

Approximations of Area Under Curve

The area under a curve can be approximated geometrically by taking the sum of a number of small rectangles. See the graph below for an illustration.

To find the area under the curve, we calculate the area of a number of small rectangles, which will approximate the area under the curve.

The accuracy of the approximation of this area depends on the number and width of the rectangles. A large number of narrow rectangles is more accurate than a small number of wide rectangles.

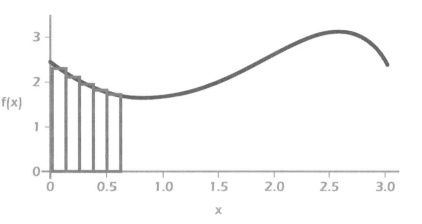

The limit as the width of these rectangles approaches zero is called an integral.

There are many methods for approximating the total area underneath a curve on a graph, one of which you may have heard of called the Riemann sum.

Integrals

Integrals can be used to calculate the area under a curve without the need for approximation. Another way to think of an integral is the reverse of a derivative, also called an anti-derivative.

$$\int x^n = \frac{x^{n+1}}{n+1} + C$$

The C stands for an unknown constant. Recall that the derivative of the right-hand side of the example to the right is equal to x^3, regardless of the value of the constant.

$$\int x^3 = \frac{x^4}{4} + C$$

We can also evaluate integrals with set boundaries. For example, the integral below is from a to b. To evaluate, take the integral result at $x = b$, and then subtract the integral result at $x = a$.

$$\int_a^b x^n = \frac{x^{n+1}}{n+1} \bigg|_a^b = \frac{b^{n+1}}{n+1} - \frac{a^{n+1}}{n+1}$$

Separation of Variables

A separate integral each for both x and y is sometimes necessary to find a general solution to a differential equation.

For instance, for the below equation, x and y can be integrated separately.
$dy/dx = x^2/y$

Cross-multiply, then integrate.
$ydy = x^2dx$
$\int ydy = \int x^2dx$
$y^2/2 = (x^3/3) + C$

Note that we only need to show one constant C.

Integral Calculus: Practice

1. $\int_1^5 (x + 3) \, dx$

   A. 4
   B. 24
   C. 27.5
   D. 32

2. Find the approximate area from the curve to the y-axis (that is, under the curve) from x = 0.5 to x = 1.0.

   A. 0.5
   B. 1.0
   C. 2.1
   D. 4.3

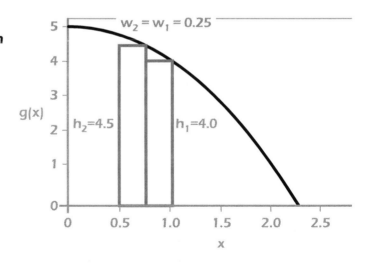

3. Evaluate the integral $\int x\,dx$.

   A. $x + C$
   B. $x/2 + C$
   C. $x^2 + C$
   D. $x^2/2 + C$

4. Evaluate the integral. $\int_0^2 x^3\, dx$

   A. 2
   B. 3
   C. 4
   D. 8

5. Evaluate the integral: $\int \sqrt{x}\, dx$.

   A. $(3x^{3/2})/2 + C$
   B. $(2x^{3/2})/3 + C$
   C. $(2x^{5/2})/3 + C$
   D. $2x^{5/2} + C$

6. Evaluate the integral $\int (-x + 1)\,dx$.

   A. $-x^2/2 + x + C$
   B. $-x^2/2 + C$
   C. $x + C$
   D. $-x^2 + x + C$

7. Acceleration is defined as the time rate of change of velocity. One way to express the acceleration due to gravity is with a differential equation: dv/dt = 10.

Find the velocity, v, as a function of t.

   A. $v = 10 + C$
   B. $v = 10t + C$
   C. $v = 50t^2 + C$
   D. $v = 100t + C$

8. Evaluate the integral. $\int_0^3 (x^2 - 2x + 1)\, dx$

   A. –6
   B. 0
   C. 3
   D. 6

9. Solve the following equation for y: dy/dx = 3x²/2y. Assume the constant C = 0.

   A. $y = x^{1/2}$
   B. $y = x$
   C. $y = x^2$
   D. $y = x^{3/2}$

10. The marginal revenue from a manufacturing plant depends on the number of widgets sold. In the equation below, c is cost and x is the number of widgets.
    dc/dx = 4x

    How much money should the company earn if 10 widgets are sold? Assume the constant C is 0.

    A. 10
    B. 100
    C. 200
    D. 400

Integral Calculus: Answer Explanations

1. B

$$\int_1^5 (x + 3)\, dx$$

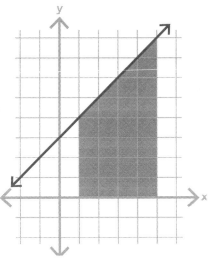

The integral is the area under the curve of the function. In this case, the graph of x + 3 is shown as a black line. Then, you want to find the area under the curve from x = 1 to x = 5. This area is shaded on the graph. You can find this area by either counting the highlighted squares or dividing the figure into 2 shapes: a square and a triangle. Either way, you will find the area is 24.

2. C The area under the curve is approximately equal to the sum of the areas of the two rectangles.

Rectangle 1: Area = (4.0)(0.25) = 1
Rectangle 2: Area = (4.5)(0.25) = 1.125

The approximate area under the curve is 1 + 1.125 = 2.125

3. D Remember the following simple formula for evaluating integrals.

$$\int x^n = \frac{x^{n+1}}{n+1} + C$$

In this case, we are evaluating: $\int x dx$. Therefore, n = 1.

$\int x dx = x^2/2 + C$

Note, if you took the derivative of that result, you would get x.

4. C $$\int_0^2 x^3 \, dx$$

First, evaluate the integral in terms of x. Then, evaluate the result at x = 0 and subtract it from the result at x = 2.

The integral equals $x^4/4 + C$.

At x = 0. $0^4/4 = 0$

At x = 2, $2^4/4 = 4$

Therefore, the integral of $x^3 dx$ from 0 to 2 is $4 - 0 = 4$.

5. B When solving integrals, since you have a clear formula for evaluating integrals when the variable is raised to a power, you should first try to put the expression in exponential form.

$$\int x^n = \frac{x^{n+1}}{n+1} + C$$

In this case, remember that $\sqrt{x} = x^{1/2}$

Now, use the formula to evaluate the integral.
In this case, n = 1/2.

$$\int x^{1/2} = \frac{x^{1/2+1}}{1/2 + 1} + C = \frac{x^{3/2}}{3/2} + C = \frac{2x^{3/2}}{3} + C$$

6. A To evaluate an integral with multiple terms, use the formula to take the antiderivative of each term and then add the results together.

$\int (-x + 1) dx$
$= \int -x \, dx + \int 1 \, dx$
$= -x^2/2 + x + C$

7. B Since you have a differential equation, your first step should be to integrate both sides.
$dv/dt = 10$
$\int(dv/dt)\,dt = \int 10\,dt$
$v + C_1 = 10t + C_2$
$v = 10t + C_1 + C_2$
$v = 10t + C$

Note, that you can combine the two constants into a different constant C.

8. C When presented with an integral problem with multiple terms, just take the antiderivative of each term and add the results.

$$\int_0^3 x^2 - 2x + 1\,dx = \left.\frac{x^3}{3} - 2\frac{x^2}{2} + x\right|_0^3 = \left.\frac{x^3}{3} - x^2 + x\right|_0^3$$

Now, evaluate the result at x = 3 and subtract the result at x = 0.
$= (3^3/3 - 3^2 + 3) - (0^3/3 - 0^2 + 0)$
$= 9 - 9 + 3 - 0 = 3$

9. D To solve the equation for y, first cross-multiply.
$dy/dx = 3x^2/2y$
$2y\,dy = 3x^2\,dx$

Then, integrate both sides.
$\int 2y\,dy = \int 3x^2\,dx$
$2y^2/2 = 3x^3/3 + C$
$y^2 = x^3 + C$
$y^2 = x^3$

Now, take the square root of both sides to solve for y.
$\sqrt{(y^2)} = \sqrt{(x^3)}$
$y = x^{3/2}$

10. C To solve this, first cross-multiply.
$dc/dx = 4x$
$dc = 4x\,dx$

Then, take the integral of both sides.
$\int dc = \int 4x\,dx$
$c = 4x^2/2 + C = 2x^2 + 0 = 2x^2$

Now, the question states that there are 10 widgets and that the variable x represents the number of widgets. Therefore, plug in x = 10 and solve for c.
$c = 2x^2 = 2(10)^2 = 200$

Trig, Calculus, Discrete Math: Discrete Math

Properties of Sets

A set is an unordered collection of distinct numbers or variables. Sets are typically expressed with braces. For example, set A = {1, 4, 5} or set B = {a, c, e}

Two sets are equal if each element in one set is uniquely present in another set.

For example, if set A = {1, 4, 5} and set C = {4, 1, 5}, then A = C; however, if set D = {4, 1, 5, 5}, this set is not equal to sets A or C.

Common operations with sets are union and intersection.
The union of two sets, often written using the U notation, contains all the unique elements of each set with no repeats. The intersection of two sets, often written using the ∩ symbol, contains all the unique elements appearing in both sets.

For example, if set A = {1, 2, 3, 4} and set B = {2, 4, 6}, then
$$A \cup B = \{1, 2, 3, 4, 6\}$$
$$A \cap B = \{2, 4\}$$

Recursive Patterns, Relationships, and Algorithms

A recursive pattern uses previous values to calculate future values.

For example, the following is a recursive relationship that increments by 2:
$$A_1 = 1$$
$$A_2 = 3$$
$$A_n = A_{n-1} + 2$$

An algorithm is a set of instructions on how to carry out computations. Algorithms are often iterative, as in the example above.

Finite Differences

The finite differences method is a way to determine whether a set of points fits a polynomial. You take the differences between the y-values. Then, take the differences between the differences, and continue until all the differences are equal. The number of differences is equal to the degree of the polynomial the data probably fits.

For example, given a set of points (1, 2), (2, 5), (3, 10), (4, 17), determine if these points fit a quadratic (degree 2) function.

Note that the first differences of all the y-coordinates are 3, 5, and 7 (that is, 5 − 2 = 3; 10 − 5 = 5; 17 − 10 = 7). The second differences are all two. Therefore, these points fit a quadratic function.

Matrices

A matrix is a rectangular array consisting of rows and columns of numbers or variables.

Example: The following is a 2 x 3 matrix with 2 rows and 3 columns. $\begin{bmatrix} 3 & -4 & 5 \\ 2 & 4 & 6 \end{bmatrix}$

Matrices can be added or subtracted element by element, as long as they have the same dimensions, and the result is a matrix with the same dimensions. Multiplication works a little differently. Matrices can be multiplied if the columns in the first matrix equal the rows in the second matrix. If you are multiplying a matrix that is m x n by a matrix that is n x k, then the resulting matrix will be m x k. For example, below shows a 2 x 3 matrix multiplied by a 3 x 4, resulting in a 2 x 4 matrix.

$$\begin{bmatrix} 1 & 2 & 3 \\ 4 & 5 & 6 \end{bmatrix} \begin{bmatrix} a & b & c & d \\ e & f & g & h \\ j & k & l & m \end{bmatrix} = \begin{bmatrix} 1a+2e+3j & 1b+2f+3k & 1c+2g+3l & 1d+2h+3m \\ 4a+5e+6j & 4b+5f+6k & 4c+5g+6l & 4d+5h+6m \end{bmatrix}$$

In the multiplication problem above, you can see that the elements in the resulting matrix are the sum of the products of each element in the row of the first matrix and the column of the second matrix.

Matrix Applications

Matrix operations can be used to calculate a number of variables efficiently. If you have multiple equations, you can use matrices to represent the equation.

For example, if plant A ordered 5 shirts and 3 work pants for its workers for $95, and plant B ordered 2 shirts and 4 work pants for its workers for $80, this can be set up as matrix multiplication. As you can see, following the rules of matrix multiplication covered above, these matrices are equivalent to the equations 5x + 3y = $95 and 2x + 4y = $80.

$\begin{bmatrix} 5 & 3 \\ 2 & 4 \end{bmatrix} \begin{bmatrix} x \\ y \end{bmatrix} = \begin{bmatrix} \$95 \\ \$80 \end{bmatrix}$

Linear Transformation of a Matrix

In a two-dimensional Cartesian coordinate system, points on the graph can be transformed with a matrix. To transform one point, multiply the transformation matrix by the coordinates of the point.

In this example, the 2 x 2 matrix transforms the coordinates (1, 2) to coordinates (1, 7).

$\begin{bmatrix} 1 & 0 \\ 1 & 3 \end{bmatrix} \begin{bmatrix} 1 \\ 2 \end{bmatrix} = \begin{bmatrix} 1 \\ 7 \end{bmatrix}$

Linear Programming

Linear programming is a mathematical technique often used to optimize a particular relationship. It involves taking various linear inequalities and finding the best value that can be obtained under those constraints.

The process for solving linear programming problems is to graph each linear inequality, or constraint, and find the feasible region, which is the overlap region. Then, find all the coordinate pairs at the corners of the feasibility region, and test each of these points in the formula or optimization equation.

For example, the graph to the right illustrates three constraints represented by dark gray lines. The light gray shaded region is the feasibility region, which is the overlap of the graphs of the three inequalities. Finally, the corners are the points that must be tested in the optimization equation to determine which yields the best results.

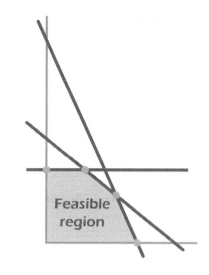

Trees

Trees can be useful diagrams for illustrating and visualizing a set of decision-making rules.

The graph to the right shows a tree diagram.

For this tree, you can see the probabilities of various decisions and combinations of decisions. For instance, the probability it rains is 80% or 0.80. If you wanted to find out the probability that the board approves and it rains, you would multiply the two probabilities together = 0.55 x 0.80 = 0.44. All the calculated probabilities are displayed in this tree, but common problems will have missing information somewhere along the decision paths.

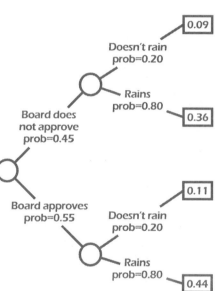

Discrete Math: Practice

1. How many 2's are there in the matrix that is the sum of A and B?

A. 0
B. 1
C. 2
D. 3

$$A = \begin{bmatrix} 1 & 3 \\ 2 & 2 \\ 4 & 5 \end{bmatrix} \quad B = \begin{bmatrix} 2 & 2 \\ 0 & 1 \\ -2 & 3 \end{bmatrix}$$

2. Use the matrix T on the right to transform the point (3, 4).

$$\begin{bmatrix} 2 & 1 \\ -1 & 3 \end{bmatrix}$$

A. $\begin{bmatrix} -3 \\ -4 \end{bmatrix}$ B. $\begin{bmatrix} 9 \\ 9 \end{bmatrix}$ C. $\begin{bmatrix} 10 \\ 9 \end{bmatrix}$ D. $\begin{bmatrix} 6 \\ 12 \end{bmatrix}$

3. The table below shows the first differences for 4 different functions, f_1, f_2, f_3, and f_4. Which function might be a quadratic function?

	f(2) – f(1)	f(3) – f(2)	f(4) – f(3)	f(5) – f(4)
$f_1(x)$	1	4	9	16
$f_2(x)$	3	3	3	3
$f_3(x)$	3	7	11	15
$f_4(x)$	2	4	8	16

A. $f_1(x)$

B. $f_2(x)$

C. $f_3(x)$

D. $f_4(x)$

4. Which algorithm applies for the series {−1, 3, −5, 7, −9, ...} starting at n = 1?

A. $a_n = (-1)^n(2n - 1)$

B. $a_n = n - 2$

C. $a_n = (-1)^n(n + 2)$

D. $a_n = (-1)^n(n)$

5. A flight will only take off if there are enough customers and if the weather is good. Based on the tree diagram, calculate the probability that the flight will take off.

A. 45%

B. 56%

C. 70%

D. 80%

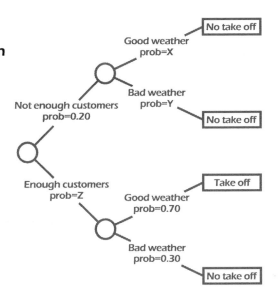

6. Find the intersection of sets A and B.
$$A = \{1, 3, 5, 7\}$$
$$B = \{5, 2, 7, 9\}$$

A. $\{1, 3, 5, 7\}$

B. $\{1, 2, 3, 5, 7, 9\}$

C. $\{5, 7\}$

D. $\{1, 2, 3, 5, 5, 7, 7, 9\}$

7. Find the value of a_5 given the following information.
$$a_1 = 0$$
$$a_2 = 1$$
$$a_n = 2a_{n-1} + a_{n-2}$$

A. 12

B. 5

C. 2

D. 1

8. Which is the matrix representation of the following three equations?
$$x + 2y - z = 4$$
$$2x = z$$
$$y = -x + 8$$

A. $\begin{bmatrix} 1 & 2 & 1 \\ 2 & 0 & 1 \\ -1 & -1 & 0 \end{bmatrix} \begin{bmatrix} x \\ y \\ z \end{bmatrix} = \begin{bmatrix} 4 \\ 0 \\ 8 \end{bmatrix}$

C. $\begin{bmatrix} 1 & 2 & -1 \\ 2 & 0 & 0 \\ 1 & 1 & 0 \end{bmatrix} \begin{bmatrix} x \\ y \\ z \end{bmatrix} = \begin{bmatrix} 4 \\ 1 \\ 8 \end{bmatrix}$

B. $\begin{bmatrix} 1 & 2 & -1 \\ 2 & 1 & 0 \\ 1 & -1 & 8 \end{bmatrix} \begin{bmatrix} x \\ y \\ z \end{bmatrix} = \begin{bmatrix} 4 \\ 0 \\ 0 \end{bmatrix}$

D. $\begin{bmatrix} 1 & 2 & -1 \\ 2 & 0 & -1 \\ 1 & 1 & 0 \end{bmatrix} \begin{bmatrix} x \\ y \\ z \end{bmatrix} = \begin{bmatrix} 4 \\ 0 \\ 8 \end{bmatrix}$

9. Which commutative properties hold true for matrices?

A. Commutative Addition only.

B. Commutative Multiplication only.

C. Commutative Addition and Multiplication.

D. Commutative properties do not hold for matrices.

10. You have $100 to buy fruit for the team. Bunches of 20 bananas cost $10 each, and bags of 15 apples cost $7 each. You know that 20 students are allergic to apples, so you must buy them bananas. If you want to solve this question using linear programming, what set of equations would you use?

A. $10b + 7a \leq 100$
    $a \geq 0$
    $b \geq 0$
    max $f(a, b) = a + b$

C. $15a + 20b \leq 100$
    $a \geq 0$
    $b \geq 1$
    max $f(a, b) = 10b + 7a$

B. $10b + 7a \leq 100$
    $a \geq 0$
    $b \geq 20$
    max $f(a, b) = 15a + 20b$

D. $10b + 7a \leq 100$
    $a \geq 0$
    $b \geq 1$
    max $f(a, b) = 15a + 20b$

Discrete Math: Answer Explanations

1. C To sum matrices, first make sure they are the same dimensions to ensure that the operation is possible. Matrices A and B both have 3 rows and 2 columns. Then, to add the matrices, sum each pair of the terms in their respective locations.

There are two 2's in the resulting matrix.

$$A+B = \begin{bmatrix} 1 & 3 \\ 2 & 2 \\ 4 & 5 \end{bmatrix} + \begin{bmatrix} 2 & 2 \\ 0 & 1 \\ -2 & 3 \end{bmatrix}$$

$$= \begin{bmatrix} 1+2 & 3+2 \\ 2+0 & 2+1 \\ 4+-2 & 5+3 \end{bmatrix}$$

$$= \begin{bmatrix} 3 & 5 \\ 2 & 3 \\ 2 & 8 \end{bmatrix}$$

2. C To transform a point, multiply the matrix T by that point. Set up with the matrix on the left and the point on the right:

$$\begin{bmatrix} 2 & 1 \\ -1 & 3 \end{bmatrix} \begin{bmatrix} 3 \\ 4 \end{bmatrix} = \begin{bmatrix} 2 \times 3 + 1 \times 4 \\ -1 \times 3 + 3 \times 4 \end{bmatrix} = \begin{bmatrix} 10 \\ 9 \end{bmatrix}$$

3. C A function is potentially quadratic if the second differences are identical but nonzero. Calculate the second differences for each given function.

$f_1(x)$: $4 - 1 = 3$; $9 - 4 = 5$; $16 - 9 = 7$
$f_2(x)$: $3 - 3 = 0$; $3 - 3 = 0$; $3 - 3 = 0$
$f_3(x)$: $7 - 3 = 4$; $11 - 7 = 4$; $15 - 11 = 4$
$f_4(x)$: $4 - 2 = 2$; $8 - 4 = 4$; $16 - 8 = 8$

The only possible candidates for a quadratic equation are $f_2(x)$ and $f_3(x)$. However, $f_2(x)$ has zeros for the second difference, which indicates that this is a linear function (and not quadratic). Therefore, only $f_3(x)$ can possibly be quadratic.

4. A The definitions describe a recursive process, as each term refers to previous terms. Try each answer choice to see if any of them fit the values in the series.

A: $a_n = (-1)^n(2n - 1)$
$a_1 = (-1)^1(2(1) - 1) = -1$
$a_2 = (-1)^2(2(2) - 1) = 3$
$a_3 = (-1)^3(2(3) - 1) = -5$
$a_4 = (-1)^4(2(4) - 1) = 7$
$a_5 = (-1)^5(2(5) - 1) = -9$
The definition works for all the values in the series.

B: $a_n = n - 2$
$a_2 = 2 - 2 = 0$
Does not work.

C: $a_n = (-1)^n(n + 2)$
$a_1 = (-1)^1(1 + 2) = -3$
Does not work.

D: $a_n = (-1)^n(n)$
$a_2 = (-1)^2(2) = 2$
Does not work.

5. B Based on the tree diagram, the flight will take off only if there are enough customers, and the weather is good.

The probability of enough customers is $1 - \text{prob(not enough)} = 1 - 0.20 = 0.80$. This is prob = Z on the diagram.

To find the probability of having enough customers and good weather, multiply the individual probabilities.

$0.80 \times 0.70 = 0.56$.

Multiply 0.56 times 100% to get a percentage of 56%.

6. C The intersection of A and B (sometimes noted A ∩ B) contains all the unique elements appearing in both sets A and B.

In this case, the only elements appearing in both sets are {5, 7}.

7. A $a_1 = 0, a_2 = 1, a_n = 2a_{n-1} + a_{n-2}$

The definition describes a recursive process. The value of a_5 must be found iteratively.

$a_3 = 2a_2 + a_1 = 2(1) + 0 = 2$
$a_4 = 2a_3 + a_2 = 2(2) + 1 = 5$
$a_5 = 2a_4 + a_3 = 2(5) + 2 = 12$

8. D The first equation is in the form we need to represent as a matrix. The other two equations must be rearranged so that all the terms are on the left-hand side. It is also sometimes easier to visualize if you include all the variables, even if you have to include them with zero as a coefficient.

$x + 2y - z = 4$

$2x = z$
$2x - z = 0$
$2x + 0y - z = 0$

$y = -x + 8$
$y + x = 8$
$x + y + 0z = 8$

Now, the three rearranged equations are
$x + 2y - z = 4$
$2x + 0y - z = 0$
$x + y + 0z = 8$

To represent these equations as matrices, take the coefficients of the variables for the first matrix, and then complete the equation with the remaining matrices.

$$\begin{bmatrix} 1 & 2 & -1 \\ 2 & 0 & -1 \\ 1 & 1 & 0 \end{bmatrix} \begin{bmatrix} x \\ y \\ z \end{bmatrix} = \begin{bmatrix} 4 \\ 0 \\ 8 \end{bmatrix}$$

9. A The Commutative Property of Addition states that you can add A and B in any order and still get the same answer.
A + B = B + A

When adding two matrices, the corresponding elements are added for each matrix. Since addition is commutative, matrix addition is also commutative.

The Commutative Property of Multiplication states that you can multiply A and B in any order and still get the same answer.
A x B = B x A

The multiplication of matrices is not as straightforward as addition or subtraction.

For example, if A is a 4 x 3 matrix and B is a 3 x 2 matrix, then A x B is a 4 x 2 matrix. However, you cannot multiply B x A since the number of columns in B does not equal the number of rows in A. Therefore, A x B ≠ B x A.

Commutative Property of Multiplication does not hold for matrices.

10. D The first step in any problem with unknowns is to define your variables. With a quick glance at the answer choices, you can see that they are using a and b as the variables.

Let a = number of bags of apples purchased and b = number of bunches of bananas purchased.

Let's go through each constraint of the problem.
20 students need bananas. There are 20 bananas in each bunch. Therefore, at least one bunch of bananas must be purchased.
$b \geq 1$

The only restriction on the minimum number of bags of apples is that it cannot be negative, as that would not make sense in the real world.
$a \geq 0$

We know the prices on the fruit, and we know the total amount of money that can be spent; therefore, a new constraint can be written.
$10b + 7a \leq 100$

Finally, in a linear programming problem, there is always a function you are trying to optimize, either minimize or maximize. In this case, you are trying to maximize the amount of fruit that can be purchased. Remember, the variables represent the number of bags or bunches; therefore, you must multiply that variable by the number of pieces of fruit in each group to get the total number of pieces of fruit.
max $f(a, b) = 15a + 20b$

Trig, Calculus, Discrete Math: Module Review

1. A triangle has one angle of 120 degrees and a second angle of 30 degrees. The longest side has a length of 8. What is the length of the shortest side?

    A. $4\sqrt{2}$
    B. $8\sqrt{3}/2$
    C. $4\sqrt{3}$
    D. $8\sqrt{3}/3$

2. What is the horizontal asymptote of the following equation? $y = 3/(x + 2)$

    A. $x = -2$
    B. $y = 3$
    C. $x = 2$
    D. $y = 0$

3. If the length of side y is 15 and angle B is π/3 radians, what is the length of side x?

    A. $15\sqrt{3}$
    B. $15\sqrt{3}/2$
    C. $15/2$
    D. $15\sqrt{2}/2$

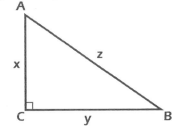

4. You have an isosceles right triangle with the longest side equal to 12. What is the length of the shortest side?

    A. $3\sqrt{2}$
    B. $6\sqrt{2}$
    C. $4\sqrt{3}$
    D. 6

5. What is the limit as x approaches negative infinity? $f(x) = -3 + \dfrac{4}{x+1}$

    A. 3
    B. –3
    C. –7
    D. 1

6. Find the length of segment x.

A. 200
B. 400√3
C. 400
D. 200√3

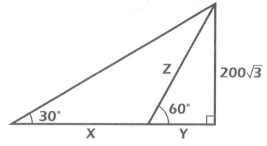

7. Find the value of $a_4 + a_5$ given the following information.

$$a_1 = 1$$
$$a_2 = 1$$
$$a_n = 3a_{n-1} - a_{n-2} - 2n$$

A. −90
B. −69
C. −21
D. −20

8. Solve the following equation on the interval $0 \leq \theta \leq \pi$: $\cos\theta = \sqrt{2}/2$.

A. 3π/4
B. π/2
C. π/4
D. 3π/2

9. For the function, y = sin(x), what are the inflection points in the graph below.

A. π, 2π, 3π
B. π/2, 3π/2, 5π/2, 7π/2
C. π/2, π, 3π/2, 2π, 5π/2, 3π, 7π/2
D. No inflection points

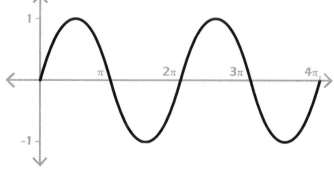

10. Find the value of the expression $\sin(\cos^{-1}(\sqrt{3}/2))$.

A. √3/2
B. 1/2
C. π/2
D. 2

11. Evaluate the integral. $\int_{1}^{3} (x-1)^2 \, dx$

   A. 8/3
   B. 10/3
   C. 3
   D. 9

12. The current, I, is defined as I = 230 sin 60πt. What is the current at time 1/80 second?

   A. 115√2
   B. 230
   C. 115
   D. 230√3/2

13. In the graph of y = sin(x) plotted below, at what values of x is the derivative of y equal to zero?

   A. $x = 0$; $x = \pi$; $x = 2\pi$
   B. Only at $x = 0$
   C. $x = \pi/2$; $x = 3\pi/2$
   D. Only at $x = \pi$

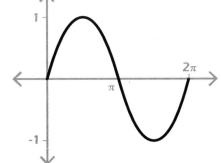

14. Find the derivative of y = x² + 5x − 8.

   A. 5
   B. 2x
   C. −8
   D. 2x + 5

15. Find the union of sets A and B.
$$A = \{1, 3, 5, 7\}$$
$$B = \{5, 2, 7, 9\}$$

   A. {1, 3, 5, 7}
   B. {1, 2, 3, 5, 7, 9}
   C. {5, 7}
   D. {1, 2, 3, 5, 5, 7, 7, 9}

16. Find the product AB. $A = \begin{bmatrix} 1 & 2 & 3 \\ 0 & 2 & 4 \end{bmatrix}$ $B = \begin{bmatrix} 2 & 1 \\ 0 & 3 \\ -1 & 2 \end{bmatrix}$

A. $AB = \begin{bmatrix} -1 & 13 \\ -4 & 14 \end{bmatrix}$ B. $AB = \begin{bmatrix} 2 & 2 \\ 0 & 6 \end{bmatrix}$ C. $AB = \begin{bmatrix} 4 & 3 \\ 0 & 12 \end{bmatrix}$ D. $AB = \begin{bmatrix} 3 & 4 \\ -1 & 5 \end{bmatrix}$

17. Maximize the sum of x and y based on the following constraints.

$$2x + y \leq 8$$
$$x \geq 0$$
$$0 \leq y \leq 4$$

A. $x = 3, y = 2$

B. $x = 4, y = 4$

C. $x = 2, y = 4$

D. $x = 4, y = 0$

18. What is the equation of the graph?

A. $y = 3\cos(x - 2\pi)$

B. $y = 3\cos(0.5x)$

C. $y = \cos(3x - \pi)$

D. $y = 3\cos(2\pi x)$

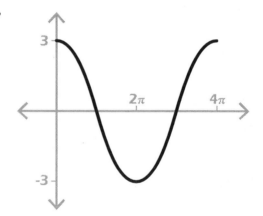

19. Find the approximate integral of the curve below between x = 0 and 5.

A. 21

B. 25

C. 26.5

D. 30

20. If the probability of getting the ball in is 0.2 and if the probability of rolling an even number is 0.5 as it is a standard die, what is the probability of winning this game?

A. 0.1

B. 0.2

C. 0.5

D. 0.7

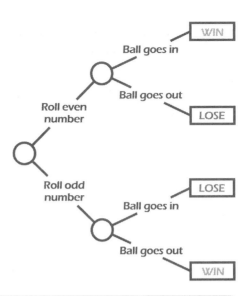

Module Review: Answer Explanations

1. D For any given triangle, the sum of the angles is equal to 180 degrees. As such, the undefined third angle is 30 degrees $(180 - 120 - 30 = 30)$. We now see that this is an isosceles triangle with two equal angles of 30 degrees with two equal sides opposite the 30-degree angles. The longest side of length 8 is opposite the 120-degree angle, while the shortest sides are opposite the 30-degree angles.

Now, you can either use the Law of Sines or the Pythagorean theorem to calculate the length of the shortest sides (that is, opposite the 30-degree angles).

Method 1: Law of Sines

The formula for the Law of Sines, which is provided on the formula sheet, is

$$\frac{a}{\sin A} = \frac{b}{\sin B} = \frac{c}{\sin C}$$

Applying the formula to this problem, where b is the length of the shortest side:
$8/\sin(120) = b/\sin(30)$

Cross-multiplying yields an equation for b: $\quad b = \dfrac{8\sin 30}{\sin 120} = \dfrac{8(1/2)}{\sqrt{3}/2} = \dfrac{8}{\sqrt{3}}$

Finally, rationalize the denominator: $\quad b = \dfrac{8}{\sqrt{3}} \times \dfrac{\sqrt{3}}{\sqrt{3}} = \dfrac{8\sqrt{3}}{3}$

Method 2: Pythagorean Theorem

The isosceles triangle can be split into 2 right triangles, as shown below (not to scale).

You know the cosine of an angle is the adjacent leg divided by the hypotenuse.

$\cos 30 = 4/b$

Rearrange: $b = 4/\cos 30$

$b = 4/\cos 30 = 4/(\sqrt{3}/2) = 8/\sqrt{3} = 8\sqrt{3}/3$

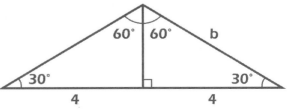

2. D Asymptotes are the values that the graph approaches but will never equal. In this case, we want the horizontal asymptote. These are the values of y that the graph will never equal. To find this, you have to think about what these y-values in the graph approach as x gets closer to infinity. In other words, we want to find the limit of the equation as x approaches infinity.
y = 3/(x + 2)

As x approaches infinity, the denominator of that fraction will get bigger and bigger, and therefore the fraction will get smaller and smaller and approach 0. However, the equation will never equal zero, since a positive number divided by a positive number will never equal to 0. Try some very high values of x to help you visualize what is happening.

For instance, try x = 2,999,998. Then, y = 3/(2,999,998+2) = 3/3,000,000 = 1/1,000,000.

As you can see, the larger the value of x, the smaller y will become. So, the equation will approach 0 as x gets larger, but y will never equal 0. Thus, the horizontal asymptote is at y = 0.

3. A Remembering, SOH CAH TOA, you know that the tangent of a given angle is the opposite side divided by adjacent leg.

In this case, tan B = x/y. Then x = y tan B.
Now, we must solve for tan B, where B = π/3 radians.
So, we must find tan(π/3).

To solve for tangent, remember that one identity is tangent = sine/cosine.
tan(π/3) = sin(π/3)/cos(π/3)
= (√3/2)/(1/2) = √3

Now, substitute the value of tan B back into the equation to solve for x.
x = y tan B = 15√3

4. B First, let's recall the definition of an isosceles triangle. An isosceles triangle has two equal sides and two equal angles. In this case, we are dealing with a right triangle. You know that means one of the angles is equal to 90 degrees, and we need two angles to be equal since it is isosceles. Since you can't have two 90-degree angles in a triangle, then we know the other angles must be equal, and they must total 90 degrees. Therefore, each is 45 degrees.

Now, you can either remember the ratio of the length of the sides of all right triangles with 45-degree angles, or you can use the Pythagorean theorem to find the ratio of the sides.

Method 1: Pythagorean theorem
Set both the equal sides to y, and we know that the hypotenuse is given as 12.
y² + y² = 12²
2y² = 144
y² = 72
y = √72 – √(36 * 2) = √36 √2 = 6√2

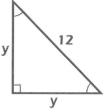

Method 2: Using ratios of all 45, 45, 90 triangles.

You should be able to recall that all 45, 45, 90 triangles or right isosceles triangles have sides that are in the ratio of y:y:y√2.

In this case, we know that the hypotenuse is 12, and therefore, we need to solve for y.

y√2 = 12   Divide both sides by √2.
y = 12/√2   Do not leave a square root in the denominator; therefore, multiply the numerator and denominator by √2 to rationalize it.
y = 12√2/2   There is no longer a root in the denominator.
y = 6√2   Simplify.

5. B $f(x) = -3 + \dfrac{4}{x+1}$ Even though we are talking about x approaching negative infinity versus more common questions that ask what happens when x approaches positive infinity, the fraction 4/(x+1) will still approach zero. As the absolute value of the denominator increases, the fraction will get closer to zero. Therefore, as x approaches negative infinity, the function will approach –3 + 0 = –3.

6. C   For the small triangle on the right, since we have one angle that is 60 degrees and a second that is 90 degrees, the third angle must be 180 – 90 – 60 = 30 degrees. Then, you know that the angle supplementary to 60 degrees is 120 degrees (180 – 60 = 120 degrees). Finally, you can figure out the last missing angle since you know the two angles of that triangle, 180 – 120 – 30 = 30 degrees. All the angles are now filled into the diagram.

Now, we see that the triangle on the right is a 30–60–90 triangle, which means the sides are in proportion 1:√3:2. Therefore, side Y is 200, and side Z is 400.

An alternate way of finding sides Y and Z is to use the Law of Sines.
200√3/sin 60 = Y/sin 30 = Z/sin 90
200√3/(√3/2) = Y/0.5 = Z/1
400 = 2Y = Z
Y = 200; Z = 400

Next, you can find the length of side X.
You can use the Law of Sines again.
X/sin30 = Z/sin30
X = Z = 400

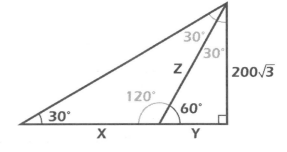

You also could note that the triangle on the left is an isosceles triangle, and therefore, the two sides opposite the equal angles would be equal. X = Z = 400.

7. A $a_1 = 1; a_2 = 1; a_n = 3a_{n-2} - a_{n-1} - 2n$

The definition describes a recursive process. The values of a_4 and a_5 are found iteratively.
$$a_3 = 3a_2 - a_1 - 2(3) = 3(1) - (1) - 2(3) = -4$$
$$a_4 = 3a_3 - a_2 - 2(4) = 3(-4) - (1) - 2(4) = -21$$
$$a_5 = 3a_4 - a_3 - 2(5) = 3(-21) - (-4) - 2(5) = -69$$

Now, take the sum of $a_4 + a_5 = -21 + -69 = -90$

8. C   The question asks you to solve the equation on the interval $0 \leq \theta \leq \pi$: $\cos\theta = \sqrt{2}/2$.

The cosine function has a period of 2π. However, the given interval only allows for the first two quadrants. Therefore, there is only possible solution to this equation.

From the unit circle, remember that cosine is the x-coordinate of the angle. We want to find the angle that gives a cosine value that is positive; therefore, we know the angle will be in the first quadrant. From the unit circle, or from memory of a 45–45–90 triangle, $\cos(\pi/4) = \sqrt{2}/2$.

9. A   Inflection points indicate where concavity changes.

The inflection points are indicated by the dashed vertical lines in the graph.

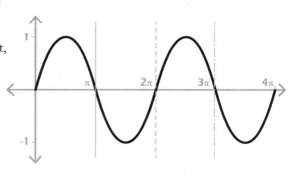

Between 0 and π, the first inflection point, the graph is concave down. Between the 1st and 2nd inflection points at π and 2π, the graph is concave up. At 2π, the concavity changes to concave down. Finally, at 3π, the concavity changes to concave up.

There are three inflections points in the graph: at π, 2π, and 3π.

10. B   To solve the following equation, start with the inner parentheses.
$\sin(\cos^{-1}(\sqrt{3}/2))$

The inverse cosine function, $y = \cos^{-1}x$, has a range between $0 \leq y \leq \pi$. Within this range, you can think of the unit circle or 30–60–90 triangles, and $\cos^{-1}(\sqrt{3}/2) = \pi/6$.

Now, substitute $\pi/6$ into the expression.
$\sin(\cos^{-1}(\sqrt{3}/2)) = \sin(\pi/6) = 1/2$

11. A Here are two methods that could be used to evaluate this integral.

Method 1: Expand using FOIL and then integrate.

$$\int_1^3 (x-1)^2\, dx = \int_1^3 (x^2 - 2x + 1)\, dx$$

$$= \left. \frac{x^3}{3} - 2\frac{x^2}{2} + x \right|_1^3$$

$$= \frac{3^3}{3} - 3^2 + 3 - \left(\frac{1^3}{3} - 1^2 + 1\right)$$

$$= 9 - 9 + 3 - \frac{1}{3} + 1 - 1$$

$$= 3 - \frac{1}{3} = \frac{9}{3} - \frac{1}{3} = \frac{8}{3}$$

Method 2: Substitute $u = x - 1$

You could also evaluate this integral for substituting u for x–1. Note, however that this will involve quite a few other changes.

Substitute: $u = x - 1$, $du = dx$, and integral is evaluated from x = 1 or u = 1 – 1 = 0 to x = 3 or u = 3 – 1 = 2.

$$\int_1^3 (x-1)^2\, dx = \int_0^2 u^2\, du$$

$$= \left. \frac{u^3}{3} \right|_0^2$$

$$= \frac{8}{3}$$

12. A This is a straightforward question where you only have to plug in the value of time and solve. Then, think about the unit circle or 45–45–90 triangles to find the value of the sine function.

$I = 230 \sin 60\pi t$
$= 230 \sin[60\pi(1/80)]$
$= 230 \sin[3\pi/4]$
$= 230(\sqrt{2}/2)$
$= 115\sqrt{2}$

13. C The derivative is the slope of the tangent line at a particular point of x.

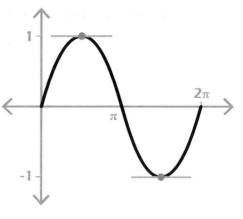

The slope is zero at the local maximum and minimum points on this graph, as shown in the graph. Remember, a slope of zero is a horizontal line; therefore, we want to find the tangent lines that are horizontal.

In the graph, the light gray lines are tangents at points x = π/2 and x = 3π/2. At these two points, you can see that the tangent is a horizontal line with a slope of zero. Therefore, the derivative at these two points is zero.

Answer C: x = π/2; x = 3π/2.

14. D To take the derivative of an algebraic expression, first take the derivatives of each of the terms in the function. Remember the following formula for finding derivatives:
d/dx (x^n) = nx^{n-1}

d/dx (x^2) = 2x
d/dx (5x) = 5
d/dx (–8) = 0

The derivative of the function will be the sum of the derivative of the terms.
d/dx (x^2 + 5x – 8) = 2x + 5 + 0 = 2x + 5

15. B The union of A and B (sometimes noted A U B) contains all the unique elements appearing in set A, plus the unique elements appearing in set B. The union does not repeat any elements. In this case, the union of these two sets is {1, 2, 3, 5, 7, 9}.

16. A First, note that A is a 2 x 3 matrix, and B is a 3 x 2 matrix; therefore, the product will be a 2 x 2 matrix.

$$AB = \begin{bmatrix} 1 & 2 & 3 \\ 0 & 2 & 4 \end{bmatrix} \begin{bmatrix} 2 & 1 \\ 0 & 3 \\ -1 & 2 \end{bmatrix}$$

$$= \begin{bmatrix} row1(A) \times col1(B) & row1(A) \times col2(B) \\ row2(A) \times col1(B) & row2(A) \times col2(B) \end{bmatrix}$$

$$= \begin{bmatrix} 1 \times 2 + 2 \times 0 + 3 \times -1 & 1 \times 1 + 2 \times 3 + 3 \times 2 \\ 0 \times 2 + 2 \times 0 + 4 \times -1 & 0 \times 1 + 2 \times 3 + 4 \times 2 \end{bmatrix}$$

$$= \begin{bmatrix} -1 & 13 \\ -4 & 14 \end{bmatrix}$$

17. C This is a classic linear programming question. First, graph each of the inequalities or constraints. Find the feasible region, which is the area for which the graphs overlap. Then, take the coordinates of each corner of the feasible region and plug them into the equation to be maximized.

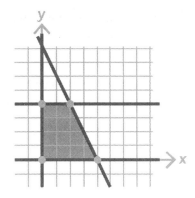

The graphs of each constraint are shown in the diagram to the left. The feasible region has been marked off by shading, and the corners of the feasible region are marked with dots.

The coordinate pairs for each of the corners are: (0, 0), (4, 0), (0, 4), and (2, 4).

The function to be maximized is the sum of x and y = x + y.
The point that maximizes this is (2, 4).

18. B When determining the trigonometric equation that represents a graph, you should identify the trigonometric function, amplitude, period, and phase shift.

Amplitude: This is the easiest part to determine. Look at the range, and determine the maximum value that y reaches. In this case, it is 3. The amplitude is 3.

Period: The period can be identified by looking at where the graph will start repeating. In this graph, only one period is shown, and it spans 4π. The period is 4π.

Trigonometric Function: This graph could be a sine or cosine graph, as the two graphs are the same with just a shift. By glancing at the answer choices, you can see that all the equations use cosine. Therefore, we will examine the graph, assuming it is a cosine function.

Phase Shift: Now that we know that we are dealing with a cosine function, we know that the graph should start at its maximum value and then drop down to its lowest value. This graph does that, and thus, there is no phase shift.

Now, use the above pieces of information to determine the equation.

$y = A \cos(\omega x - \varphi)$
Amplitude = A, Period = $2\pi/\omega$, Phase shift = φ/ω

Phase shift = $0 = \varphi/\omega$
$\varphi = 0$

Amplitude = 3
A = 3

Period = 4π
$2\pi/\omega = 4\pi$
$\omega = 1/2 = 0.5$

$y = 3 \cos(0.5x)$

19. B The integral of a function is the area under the curve. It can be approximated by taking the sum of the area of small rectangles underneath the curve. Conveniently, the rectangles were drawn on the graph.

Find the sum of the areas of each rectangle from x = 0 to 5. There are 5 rectangles, each with a width of 1. Therefore, you can just sum the number of squares between x = 0 and 5. There are 25 squares total.

20. C There are two ways to win this game: the first is rolling an even number and ball goes in, and the second is rolling an odd number and ball goes out. To calculate the total probability of winning the game, add the probabilities of each individual option.

Rolling even number and ball goes in:
To find this probability, multiply the probabilities of each event since you need both to occur to win. The probability of rolling an even number is 0.5, and the probability of the ball going in is 0.2.
0.5 x 0.2 = 0.1

Rolling odd number and ball goes out:
Multiply the probabilities of each event. The probability of rolling an odd number on a die is 0.5. Probability of the ball going out is 1 – the probability of ball going in. Prob of ball going out = 1 – 0.2 = 0.8.
0.5 x 0.8 = 0.4

Probability of winning:
0.1 + 0.4 = 0.5

9. Open Response

Open Response Strategies	484
Open Response Sample 1	486
Open Response Sample 2	489
Open Response Sample 3	492
Open Response Sample 4	495
Open Response Sample 5	498

Open Response: Strategies

About the Open Response Section

The open response section of the MTEL 47 includes two questions that account for up to 20% of the entire test score. These questions are designed to evaluate the breadth of your math knowledge as well as your ability to integrate concepts from different areas of math. You should allow for 20 to 30 minutes to complete each open response question on exam day.

Evaluation Criteria

Open response questions are scored according to a set of standard performance characteristics.

Performance Characteristic	Definition
Purpose	The extent to which the response achieves the purpose of the assignment
Subject Matter Knowledge	Accuracy and appropriateness in the application of subject matter knowledge
Support	Quality and relevance of supporting details
Rationale	Soundness of argument and degree of understanding of the subject matter

Scoring Scale

Score	Description
4	**Reflects a thorough knowledge and understanding of the subject matter.** • Purpose of the assignment is fully achieved. Substantial and accurate use of subject matter knowledge. • Supporting evidence is sound with high quality and relevant examples. • Response reflects an ably reasoned and comprehensive understanding of topic
3	**Reflects an adequate knowledge and understanding of the subject matter.** • Purpose of the assignment is largely achieved. • Generally accurate and appropriate use of subject matter knowledge. • Supporting evidence is adequate with some acceptable, relevant examples. • Response reflects an adequately reasoned understanding of topic.
2	**Reflects a limited knowledge and understanding of the subject matter.** • Purpose of the assignment is partially achieved. • Limited, possibly inaccurate or inappropriate use of subject matter knowledge. • Supporting evidence is limited with few relevant examples. • Response reflects a limited, poorly reasoned understanding of topic.
1	**Reflects a weak knowledge and understanding of the subject matter.** • Purpose of the assignment is not achieved. • Little or no appropriate or accurate use of subject matter knowledge. • Supporting evidence, if present, is weak; there are few or no relevant examples. • Response reflects little or no reasoning about or understanding of topic.

Constructing a Strong Response

1. **Identify the Skills Required**

   After reading through the problem, identify the specific skills and concepts you will need to complete it. An open response question consists of a number of tasks. Look for keywords in each part of the problem to help you quickly figure out the methods required. Typically, the question prompt will include some wording to give you guidance (for example, "Use your knowledge of quadratic equations to...").

2. **Address All Tasks**

   The first criterion you will be scored on is the extent to which you completed the assignment. Your first step when answering a question should be to identify your tasks. Your last step should be to ensure that you have completed all of them.

3. **Demonstrate Your Understanding**

   Much of your score will be based on your ability to show understanding of the subject matter. Explain the reasoning behind your approach to each part of the problem. Include relevant information from the problem to support your reasoning, and use charts or visual aids where appropriate. In the same way, discuss the significance of the results of your calculations. This is important, since even if the final calculation is incorrect, you might still be awarded marks for your methods and reasoning.

4. **Write Your Answer Clearly**

   Two scorers will review your answer, so it needs to be clear and easy to read. Use the free space on your test booklet to work out calculations, make notes, and structure your response. When you are happy with your approach, write it on your answer sheet as a clear and cohesive solution. The response should be structured to match the order of the tasks.

5. **Check Your Work**

   It is crucial that you check your work completely before moving on to the next question. Checking for calculation errors is important, but it's not the only thing you should look for. Check for errors in your logic; reappraise your approach; and make sure you have fully explained each step.

Open Response: Sample 1

A manufacturing company discharges waste in a local river as a byproduct of its operations. The cost of removing the waste is modeled by the following function:

$R(p) = 100000p/(1 - p)$

In this function, R(p) is the cost of removing a proportion p of the pollution.

Use your knowledge of functions and limits to develop a response in which you analyze the costs for removing different proportions of pollution.

A. What percentage of the pollution could be removed for $800,000?

B. What would be the cost of removing 90% of the pollution from the river?

C. Based on the given model, can 100% of the pollution be removed? Why or why not?

D. Does this function have an asymptote? If so, where?

E. Based on the practical application of this model, what are the domain and range of this function?

Open Response: Sample 1 Explanation

Write your reasoning, show your units, and demonstrate your approach. Here is a sample strong response.

A. How much of the pollution could be removed for $800,000?

The input of the function is the proportion of the pollution you want to remove, and the output is the cost of removal. In this case, we are told the output, and therefore, if we substitute this for the output, we can find the proportion. Therefore, replace R(p), the cost of the removal, with $800,000, and then solve for p, the proportion of pollution that can be removed for that cost.

$R(p) = 100000p/(1 - p)$
$800000 = 100000p/(1 - p)$

Cross-multiply as the first step in solving this equation.
$800000(1 - p) = 100000p$

Then, use the distributive property to simplify the left-hand side of the equation.
$800000 - 800000p = 100000p$

Finally, move all the terms with the variable p to one side. Then, you can isolate the variable by dividing, and then solve for the proportion.

$800000 = 900000p$
$p = 800000/900000 \approx 0.889$

Finally, to convert from a decimal to a percentage, multiply by 100%.
$0.889 \times 100\% = 88.9\%$

For $800,000, 88.9% of the pollution can be removed.

B. What would be the cost of removing 90% of the pollution from the river?

I just calculated that for $800,000, 88.9% of the pollution can be removed. This question is asking to remove an even higher percentage of the pollution. Therefore, I know that the cost will be slightly greater than $800,000. Now, I will plug in the input, 0.90, for p, which is the proportion of pollution I want to remove. The output of the function will be the cost of removing 90% = 0.90.

$R(0.90) = 100000(0.90)/(1 - 0.90)$
$= 90000/0.10 = 900,000$
$R(0.90) = \$900,000$

My estimation based on the answer to part A was that the cost would be slightly higher than $800,000, which is the result of the calculations.
It would cost $900,000 to remove 90% of the pollution from the river.

C: Based on the given model, can 100% of the pollution be removed? Why or why not?

Again, this part is giving you the proportion of the pollution to be removed, and the question is asking for the cost. Following the same procedure as in part B, plug in p = 100% = 1 and solve.
$R(1) = 100000(1)/(1 - 1) = 100000/0 =$ undefined (You can't divide by zero)
In the given model, 100% of the pollution can't be removed.

D. Does this function have an asymptote? If so, where?

In part C, it was just determined that 100% of the pollution cannot be removed. Therefore, it is known that the function has a limitation on its domain. An asymptote is the point at which a function will approach a certain value, but never reach it. It won't reach a certain value if there is a limitation on the domain or range.

A vertical asymptote signifies that the domain will approach a certain value, but never reach it. Vertical asymptotes take the form x = constant (or input = constant). Looking at the equation, we know that we can never divide by zero. Therefore, this restricts the domain. We have already determined in part C that when p = 1, there is no valid value for the function. There are no other restrictions on the domain. So, there is one vertical asymptote at p = 1.

A horizontal asymptote means that there is a restriction on the range – the graph will have a horizontal line the function will approach, but never reach. A horizontal asymptote takes the form of y = constant (or output = constant), as this defines a horizontal line. Let's set R(p) = y to make it easier to manipulate the equation and find a restriction on y. Solve for p.

R(p) = 100000p/(1 – p)
y = 100000p/(1 – p)
y(1 – p) = 100000p
y – yp = 100000p
y = yp + 100000p
y = p(y + 100000)
p = y/(y + 100000)

You can't divide by 0; thus, y + 100000 ≠ 0. So, y ≠ – 100000. Since this is a restriction on the range, it would create a horizontal asymptote when graphed. R(p) = –100000 is a horizontal asymptote.

E. Based on the practical application of this model, what are the domain and range of this function?

The domain is all valid values of the first coordinate (the input), which is p in this case. Since we are dealing with proportions or percentages, the domain is restricted to 0% to 100%. In addition, we found out that when p = 1 or 100%, there is a divide-by-zero error, so the domain cannot reach 100%. So, the domain is greater than or equal to 0 and less than 1. The domain, which is the proportion of pollution to be removed, is 0 ≤ p < 1 or can be written [0.00, 1.00).

The range is all valid values of the second-coordinate (the output), which is R(p) or the cost of removing pollution. We know that the cost will never be negative. So, the range starts at $0. Then, we know that as the proportion of pollution to be removed approaches 100%, the cost keeps increasing to infinity. Therefore, the range can be any real number greater than or equal to zero. The range, which is the cost of removing the pollution, is 0 ≤ R(p) < ∞ or can be written [0.00, ∞).

Open Response: Sample 2

A man needs to repair siding that blew off his house during a storm. The height from the ground to the point of repair on the side of the house is 21 feet. The man has a 24-foot ladder he plans to use for the project. Safety guidelines dictate that the base of the ladder must be at least 8 feet away from the building to prevent it from tipping over.

Using your knowledge of geometry and trigonometry, analyze what repairs the man can make while meeting the safety guidelines.

A. Is the man's ladder long enough to make the repair safely? Demonstrate why or why not. Assume that the side of the house and the ground form a 90-degree angle. (Hint: the square root of 2 is approximately 1.4.)

B. What is the farthest distance the base of the ladder can be from the side of the house to allow a safe repair?

C. What is the range of heights on the house at which the man can make repairs with this ladder?

D. A friend needs to make a similar repair on his house. The friend's house is built on a steep hill, where the angle between the ground and the side of the house is 60 degrees (instead of 90 degrees). How long a ladder will he need to make a repair at a height of 26 feet from the ground? Assume the requirement to keep the ladder at least 8 feet from the base of the house is the same.

Open Response: Sample 2 Explanation

A. Is the man's ladder long enough to make the repair safely?

For geometry problems, it is helpful to draw a diagram of the problem. In this case, the angle is 90 degrees between the house and the ground and forms a right triangle. If you know two sides of a right triangle, the third side can be found with the Pythagorean theorem.

The ladder is 24 feet long and forms the hypotenuse of the right triangle. The ladder must be 8 feet from the base of the house to meet the minimum safety guidelines. The missing side of the triangle is the height up the side of the house. We want to check if the maximum height h is less than or equal to the necessary height, which is 21 feet. In other words, we are checking if $h \geq 21$ with a 24-foot ladder.

The Pythagorean theorem states that the sum of the squares of the sides of a right triangle is equal to the square of the hypotenuse of the triangle. Plugging in the known numbers and h for the unknown, we can solve for h.

$h^2 + 8^2 = 24^2$
$h^2 + 64 = 576$
$h^2 = 512$
$h = \sqrt{512} = \sqrt{(16 \times 16 \times 2)} = 16\sqrt{2}$

Using the hint that the square root of 2 is approximately 1.4,
$h \approx 16(1.4) \approx 22.4$

The ladder can reach over 22 feet and still meet the safety guidelines. The answer is greater than 21, so the ladder is long enough to make the repair.

B. What is the farthest distance the base of the ladder can be from the side of the house to allow a safe repair?

This is another application of the Pythagorean theorem. This time, we know the height of the triangle, but the other side is unknown. Following a similar procedure, solve for d.

$d^2 + 21^2 = 24^2$
$d^2 + 441 = 576$
$d^2 = 135$
$d = \sqrt{135}$

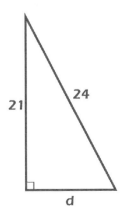

The factors of 135 are 3, 3, 3, and 5.
$d = \sqrt{135} = \sqrt{(3 \times 3 \times 3 \times 5)} = 3\sqrt{15}$
$3\sqrt{15}$ is approximately 11.6.
The farthest distance the base of the ladder can be from the side of the house is $3\sqrt{15}$ feet, or approximately 11.6 feet.

C. What is the range of heights on the house at which the man can make repairs with this ladder?

To determine the range, we must find the maximum and minimum and see if there are any restrictions in between. There's no reason to assume from the problem that there would be a restriction on the range in between the minimum and maximum heights.

First, let's think about the minimum. Since we are dealing with height on a building, a negative number would not make sense. The problem did not place any constraints on the lowest point at which repairs can be made, so we can assume that it can be any height greater than or equal to 0 feet.

Now, to find the maximum value. In part A, we calculated the height at which the man can make repairs if the ladder is 8 feet away from the house. The ladder must be at least 8 feet away from the base of the house. Placing it farther away would lower the working height of the ladder. Therefore, the height calculated in part A is the maximum height that can be reached.

The range of heights the man can make repairs is $[0, 16\sqrt{2}]$.

D. A friend needs to make a similar repair on his house. The friend's house is built on a steep hill, where the angle between the ground and the side of the house is 60 degrees (instead of 90 degrees). How long a ladder will he need to make a repair at a distance of 26 feet from the ground? Assume the requirement to keep the ladder at least 8 feet from the base of the house is the same.

Since we do not have a right angle, we cannot use the Pythagorean theorem. However, when you know two sides of a triangle and the angle opposite the missing side is also known, and then you can use the Law of Cosines to solve for c. The Law of Cosines is provided on the formula sheet but is repeated below.
$c^2 = a^2 + b^2 - 2ab \cos C$

Plug in, and solve for c:
$c^2 = 8^2 + 26^2 - 2(8)(26) \cos 60°$
$c^2 = 64 + 676 - 416 \cos 60°$

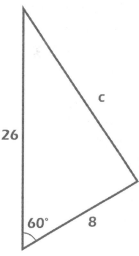

Using either the unit circle or from a 30–60–90 triangle, the cosine of 60 degrees can be found. In a 30–60–90 triangle, the sides of the triangle are always in the ratio of $1:\sqrt{3}:2$. The cosine of 60 degrees is 0.5.

$c^2 = 740 - 416(0.5)$
$c^2 = 532$
$c = \sqrt{532} = \sqrt{(4 \times 133)} = \sqrt{4} \times \sqrt{133} = 2\sqrt{133}$
Note that c is approximately 23 feet.
To make a repair at 26 feet, the friend needs a ladder $2\sqrt{133}$ feet long.

Open Response: Sample 3

You are in a school hallway, and the wall is lined with 100 closed lockers numbered 1 through 100. A student passes by and opens all of them. A second student comes by and closes all the even numbered ones. A third student passes by and "toggles" every third locker (that is, if a locker is closed, she opens it, but if it is open, she closes it).

Student number 4 toggles every fourth locker, student number 5 toggles every fifth one, and so on until 100 students have passed through the hallway opening and closing lockers.

Using your knowledge of number sense, analyze how the students' behavior will affect which lockers are open or closed.

    A. Which students will toggle locker number 15? Which students will toggle locker number 16? Are they open or closed at the end?

    B. Which of the first 10 lockers will remain open after all the students have passed?

    C. Which of the 100 lockers will remain open at the end? Why?

Open Response: Sample 3 Explanation

A. Which students will toggle locker number 15? Which students will toggle locker number 16? Are they open or closed at the end?

To understand how the students toggle lockers and to determine what will happen with locker number 15, first follow the students' process one student at a time. The first student opens all lockers. Therefore, he will toggle locker number 15. The second student only toggles those lockers that are multiples of 2, so he will not touch locker 15. The third student toggles every 3rd locker, so he will toggle 15. The fourth student only toggles those lockers that are multiples of 4, so he will not touch locker 15. The fifth student toggles every 5th locker, so he will toggle 15.

After going through the first five students, it is clear how the students' process will affect which lockers are toggled. We can see that only students whose position is a factor of 15 will toggle 15. The students who will toggle 15 are 1, 3, 5, 15, as those are the four factors of 15. It starts closed, then student 1 opens it; student 3 closes it; student 5 opens it; and student 15 closes it. It will be closed at the end.

We can quickly analyze locker number 16 by finding the factors of 16: 1, 2, 4, 8, and 16. Therefore, the students who will toggle 16 are 1, 2, 4, 8, and 16. It starts closed, then student 1 opens it; student 2 closes it; student 4 opens it; student 8 closes it; and student 16 opens it. It will be open at the end.

Locker 15: students 1, 3, 5, 15; Closed
Locker 16: students 1, 2, 4, 8, 16; Open

B. Which of the first 10 lockers will remain open after all the students have passed?

This question asks which of the first 10 lockers will remain open. Let's examine each locker. We know that students who are factors of the locker number will toggle it. If there is an odd number of toggles, it will be open. If there is an even number of toggles, it will be closed.

Locker 1: the only student who will toggle it is student 1, who will open it.
Locker 2: students 1 & 2 will toggle it. Two students touch it; therefore, it will be closed.
Locker 3: students 1 & 3 will toggle it. Two students touch it; therefore, it will be closed.
Locker 4: students 1, 2, & 4. Three students touch it. Open.
Locker 5: students 1 & 5. Two students touch it; therefore, it will be closed.
Locker 6: students 1, 2, 3, 6. Four students touch it; therefore, it will be closed.
Locker 7: students 1 & 7. Two students touch it; therefore, closed.
Locker 8: students 1, 2, 4, & 8. Four students touch it; therefore, closed.
Locker 9: students 1, 3, & 9. Three students touch it. Open.
Locker 10: students 1, 2, 5, 10. Four students touch it; therefore, closed.

To look for a pattern, it is helpful to organize the information in a chart

Locker Number	Number of Toggles	Open or Closed?
1	1	Open
2	2	Closed
3	2	Closed
4	3	Open
5	2	Closed
6	4	Closed
7	2	Closed
8	4	Closed
9	3	Open
10	4	Closed

Lockers 1, 4, and 9 will be open. The rest of the first ten lockers will be closed.

C. Which of the 100 lockers will remain open at the end? Why?

The open lockers will be the ones with an odd number of factors. Those with an even number of factors will be closed.

Now, we need to determine which numbers have an odd number of factors. As can be seen with the lockers we already solved, those that are open are 1, 4, 9, and 16. These numbers follow a pattern – they are all perfect squares.

Factors generally come in pairs. Given any number n, if a is a factor of n, n/a will also be a factor. For instance, since 3 is a factor of 15, 5 is also a factor.

If a number is a perfect square, such as 16, a and n/a will equal each other. In the example of 16, 4 is obviously counted as only one factor. Perfect squares are the only numbers that have an odd number of factors.

The lockers open at the end are the perfect squares - those numbered 1, 4, 9, 16, 25, 36, 49, 64, 81, and 100. There are 10 open lockers.

Open Response: Sample 4

A costume designer is creating a top hat for an actor playing Abe Lincoln in an upcoming play. The hat is constructed as a cylinder with a brim attached. The diagram shows the top hat upside down.

The cylindrical part of the hat (that is, not including the brim) has a diameter of 8 inches. The area of the brim of the hat is 33π in².

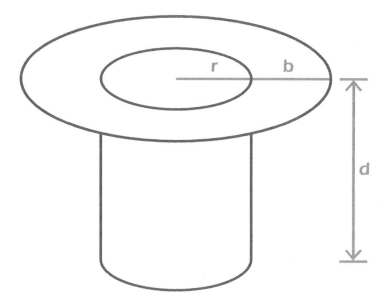

Using your knowledge of geometry, analyze the top hat.

   A. What is the area of the top of the hat (the part of the hat without the brim)?

   B. What is the width of the brim of the hat, b?

   C. The depth of the hat d = 18 inches. Stuffing is sewn into the cylindrical portion of the hat to fill a volume of 240π in³. How many inches of depth are left for the actor's head?

Open Response: Sample 4 Explanation

A. **What is the area of the top of the hat?**

The top of the hat is a circle. The formula for the area of a circle is π times radius squared. The diameter of the cylindrical portion of the hat is 8 inches. The radius is half the diameter, or 4 inches. We, therefore, have all the information we need to find the area.

Area of a circle = π radius²
$A = \pi r^2$
$A = \pi 4^2$
$A = 16\pi$

The units of area are always unit squared. Area of the top of the hat is $16\pi \text{ in}^2$.

B. **What is the width of the brim of the hat, b?**

We know that the area of a circle is $A = \pi r^2$. If we include the brim as part of a wider circle, then the radius is now the radius of the top of the hat plus the length of the brim. The new radius is r + b. Plug this into the formula, and solve.

$A_{total} = \pi(r + b)^2$
$A_{total} = \pi(4 + b)^2$

We calculated in part A that the area of the top of the hat was 16π. We are given the area of the brim of the hat as 33π. The total area must be the sum of the areas of the brim and the area of the top of the hat. Place these values into an equation, and then we can solve for b, the width of the brim.

$A_{total} = A_{cylinder} + A_{brim}$
$\pi(4 + b)^2 = 16\pi + 33\pi$
$\pi(4 + b)^2 = 49\pi$

Divide all terms on both sides by π:
$(4 + b)^2 = 49$

Use FOIL to expand the binomial:
$16 + 8b + b^2 = 49$

Move everything to the left-hand side to factor:
$b^2 + 8b + 16 - 49 = 0$
$b^2 + 8b - 33 = 0$

Factor by finding two numbers that multiply to give –33 and add to give 8. The numbers are 11 and –3.
$(b + 11)(b – 3) = 0$

If two terms multiplied by each other equal zero, one of the terms must be zero. Set each term equal to zero, and solve for b:
$b + 11 = 0, b = –11$
$b – 3 = 0, b = 3$

Since b cannot be negative, $b = 3$.
The width of the brim of the top hat, b, equals 3 inches.

C. The depth of the hat d = 18 inches. Stuffing is sewn into cylindrical portion of the top hat to fill a volume of 240π in³. How many inches of depth are left for the actor's head?

The volume of a cylinder is the area of the base of the cylinder times the height of the cylinder. Since the base of a cylinder is a circle, the formula for the volume of a cylinder is
$V = \pi r^2 h$

We know that the radius is 4 inches, and the depth is 18 inches. Plug in to find the volume:
$V = \pi 4^2 (18)$
$V = 288\pi$

Next, subtract the volume of the stuffing from this volume:
$V_{actor} = V_{total} - V_{fabric}$
$V_{actor} = 288\pi - 240\pi$
$V_{actor} = 48\pi$

Use the formula for the volume of a cylinder again to find the depth left for the actor's head:
$48\pi = \pi r^2 h$
$48\pi = \pi 4^2 h$

Solve for h. Divide both sides by π, and simplify:
$48 = 16h$
$h = 3$

There are 3 inches left for the actor's head.

Open Response: Sample 5

A clothing manufacturing company makes a profit of $250 on a box of shirts. The same company makes a profit of $400 on a box of coats.

Using your knowledge of linear programming, analyze what the clothing manufacturing company should produce to maximize profits.

   A. If x is the number of boxes of shirts and y is the number of boxes of coats, write a function representing total profit z.

   B. The company can manufacture, at most, 300 boxes of clothes in a day. The stores demand a minimum of 75 boxes of shirts and 25 boxes of coats every day. Write a set of inequalities representing these constraints.

   C. Graph the equations from part B.

   D. Determine what is the most profitable combination of production.

Open Response: Sample 5 Explanation

A. If x is the number of boxes of shirts and y is the number of boxes of coats, write a function that represents total profit z.

The total profit is the product of the boxes of each type multiplied by the profit per box for each type.

Total profit = Profit on Box of Shirts x Number of Boxes of Shirts + Profit on Box of Coats x Number of Boxes of Coats
$z = 250x + 400y$

B. The company can manufacture at most 300 boxes of clothes in a day. The stores demand a minimum of 75 boxes of shirts and 25 boxes of coats every day. Write a set of inequalities representing these constraints.

First, represent the total number of boxes that can be manufactured in one day. The total number of boxes will be the sum of the boxes of shirts and the boxes of coats. The company can produce, at most, 300 boxes a day. In other words, the company can produce less than or equal to 300 boxes a day. Using the above two pieces of information, an inequality can be written.

Boxes of Shirts + Boxes of Coats $\leq$ Maximum Boxes of Clothes in one day:
$x + y \leq 300$

Next, represent the minimum of 75 boxes of shirts. Since we want the minimum number of boxes, we must have greater than or equal to 75 boxes:
$x \geq 75$

Finally, represent the minimum of 25 boxes of coats:
$y \geq 25$

The constraints are written as linear inequalities in terms of the variables:
$x + y \leq 300$
$x \geq 75$
$y \geq 25$

C. Graph the equations from part B.

There are three inequalities to be graphed. When graphing an inequality, first graph the line, then determine whether it is solid or dashed, and then shade in the appropriate side of the line. All three inequalities will be solid lines, as they use the inequality signs $\geq$ and $\leq$, meaning that we want to include the lines that are the equalities, in addition to shading above or below the lines.

x ≥ 75: This will be a vertical line passing through x = 75 and shaded to the right for all values of x greater than 75.

y ≥ 25: This will be a horizontal line passing through y = 25 and shaded above the line for all values of y greater than 25.

x + y ≤ 300: This is a diagonal line with a y-intercept of 300 and a slope of −1.

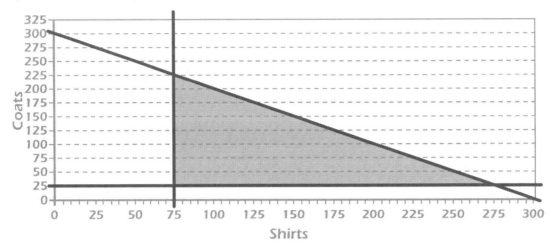

The area of optimization is the triangle formed by the three boundaries.

D. Determine what is the most profitable combination of production.

To find the most profitable combination, first find the coordinates of the feasible region in the graph above. The feasible region is the shaded triangle in the graph in part C. The vertices of the triangle will be at the intersection of the lines. Two lines will intersect at the coordinate pair that makes both equations true.

Let's take pairs of two of the three inequalities and find the point at which the lines intersect:
x + y ≤ 300
x ≥ 75
y ≥ 25

x + y = 300 and x = 75
Plug x = 75 into the first equation and solve for y:
75 + y = 300, y = 225
(75, 225)

x + y = 300 and y = 25

Plug y = 25 into the first equation and solve for x:

x + 25 = 300, x = 275

(275, 25)

x = 75 and y = 25

(75, 25)

Vertices of feasible region: (75, 25), (275, 25), and (75, 225).

Now that the vertices are determined, calculate the profit at each of the points.
Plug each coordinate pair into the profit equation and solve. The profit equation is z = 250x + 400y.

(75, 25)
z = 250(75) + 400(25) = 18750 + 10000 = 28750

(275, 25)
z = 250(275) + 400(25) = 68750 + 10000 = 78750

(75, 225)
z = 250(75) + 400(225) = 18750 + 90000 = 108750

Profit at three vertices: $28,750, $78,750, and $108,750.

The most profitable combination will always be at one of the vertices of the feasible region. We calculated the profit at each vertex. The coordinate pair with the greatest profit was (75, 225).

The most profitable combination is 75 shirts and 225 coats, which yields a profit of $108,750.

10. Diagnostic Exam

Diagnostic Questions..504
Answers & Explanations...514

Diagnostic Exam

1. Two positive odd integers and one negative even integer are multiplied together. Which of the following could be their product?

    A. −60.5

    B. −15

    C. 100

    D. −100

2. You take the square root of a number, multiply it by 3, add 4, and then divide by 2 to get 26. What was the original number?

    A. 4

    B. 32

    C. 256

    D. 2601

3. An electronics store owner buys products from the manufacturer and then marks them up 20%. For the Labor Day weekend, the store owner has a 10% off sale. What is the percent change from the manufacturer's price to the sales price?

    A. 8% increase

    B. 10% increase

    C. 12% increase

    D. 18% increase

4. If the area of a circle is A and the circumference is C, what happens to the area and circumference when you triple the diameter of the circle?

    A. 3A, 3C

    B. 9A, 3C

    C. 9A, 9C

    D. A + 3, C + 3

5. What is the area of the square with the coordinates (2, 2), (2, −1), (−1, 2), (−1, −1)?

    A. 2

    B. 4

    C. 8

    D. 9

6. In the following problem, what properties were used from step 2 to 3 and step 3 to 4, respectively?

$$1.\ 73 \times 101 + 200 =$$
$$2.\ 73(100 + 1) + 200 =$$
$$3.\ 7300 + 73 + 200 =$$
$$4.\ 7300 + 200 + 73 =$$
$$5.\ 7500 + 73 = 7573$$

A. Distributive, Associative

B. Associative, Commutative

C. Commutative, Distributive

D. Distributive, Commutative

7. A farmer is checking on his animals. He passes by the chickens, counts their feet, and then passes by the pigs and counts their feet. He counts 100 feet. Since he has 8 more chickens than pigs, he knows that none of the animals are missing. How many chickens does he have?

A. 14

B. 22

C. 23

D. 44

8. For the following set, which statistical measure is the largest?
$$7, -3, 11, -4, 8, 2, 9, 2$$

A. Mean

B. Median

C. Mode

D. All of the above are equal.

9. You have 10L of a 40% saline solution. Which equation would help you calculate how much pure (100%) saline you need to add to create a 60% solution?

A. $40\%(10) + X = 60\%(10 + X)$

B. $40\%(10 + X) = 60\%(X)$

C. $40\%X = 60\%(10 + X)$

D. $40\%(10 + X) = 60\%$

10. Two cards are drawn at random from a standard 52-card deck containing four suits of 13 cards each. What is the probability they will both be hearts?

   A. 1/16
   B. 1/8
   C. 1/4
   D. 1/17

11. The average number of points you scored in the first 9 basketball games of the season was 23. What do you need in the 10th game to get your average to n?

   A. n – 23
   B. 10n – 207
   C. 9n – 23
   D. 207 – 9n

12. Find the limit of f(x) as x approaches infinity: $f(x) = 1 + \dfrac{2}{x^2}$

   A. 1
   B. 2
   C. 1/2
   D. 0

13. What values does the number line represent?

   A. Whole numbers
   B. Real numbers greater than –1
   C. Positive integers
   D. Integers greater than –2

14. Which of the following is true?
   I. There are no even prime numbers.
   II. The greatest common factor of two numbers will always be smaller than both.
   III. The least common multiple of two numbers will always be greater than both.

   A. I only
   B. II and III
   C. I, II, and III
   D. None of the above

15. The expression $(2^3 \times 4^{-7})$ is equal to which of the following?

    A. 2^{-11}

    B. 2^{-2}

    C. 4^{-11}

    D. 8^{-4}

16. What is the distance between A and B on the number line?

    A. 0.14

    B. 0.15

    C. 1.2

    D. 7

17. The temperature in degrees Celsius is $(5/9)(F - 32)$, where F is the temperature in degrees Fahrenheit. If the temperature increases from 50° to 68° degrees Fahrenheit, what is the increase in degrees Celsius?

    A. 8°

    B. 10°

    C. 18°

    D. 20°

18. What is the volume of this right triangular prism if the units are in meters?

    A. 300 m³

    B. 325 m³

    C. 600 m³

    D. 650 m³

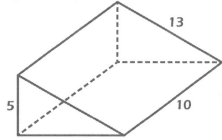

19. If AB = AC and Angle BAC = 80°, what is the measure of Angle ACD?

    A. 50°

    B. 100°

    C. 130°

    D. 180°

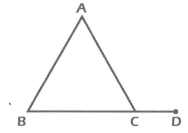

20. Which of the following best represents the area of an isosceles right triangle as a function of the length of the sides?

A.   B.   C.   D.

21. The figure below shows a quarter of a circle. What is the perimeter if the entire circle has a diameter of 10 m?

A. 2.5π meters

B. 10π meters

C. 10 + 6.25π meters

D. 10 + 2.5π meters

22. Identify the pattern shown by the following numbers: −2.1, −3.2, −4.3, −5.4, −6.5.

A. $y = 0.1x - 2$

B. $y = -2.1x + 1$

C. $y = -x^2 - 1.1$

D. $y = -1.1x - 1$

23. Given the function f(x), find $f^{-1}(2)$.
$$f(x) = (x + 3)/(2x + 4)$$

A. ½

B. −⅔

C. −¾

D. Undefined

24. Find the y-intercept and x-intercept of the following equation: $-2x + 7y = 14$.

A. y-int: −2, x-int: −7

B. y-int: 2, x-int: −7

C. y-int: 7, x-int: −2

D. y-int: −7, x-int: 2

25. Solve for x in the following equation. −4 ≤ −3x + 2 < 11.

A. −3 < x ≤ 2
B. −3 ≤ x < 2
C. −2 < x ≤ 3
D. 2 ≤ x < −3

26. What equations represent the graph below?

A. y ≤ x or y ≥ −x
B. y ≥ x or y ≤ −x
C. y ≤ x and y ≥ −x
D. y ≥ x and y ≤ −x

27. The diagram shows two non-parallel lines, both intersected by a third line.

Which of the following properties justifies statement 1 in the proof below?

Proof: ∠b ≠ ∠c

1. ∠b = ∠a.
2. Assume ∠a = ∠c.
3. If ∠a = ∠c, then the two lines must be parallel.
4. However, it is given that the two lines are not parallel. Therefore, ∠a ≠ ∠c.
5. If ∠a ≠ ∠c and ∠b = ∠a, then ∠b ≠ ∠c.

A. The vertical angles are the same.

B. The corresponding angles of two lines cut by a transversal are the same.

C. The interior angles on the same side of two lines cut by a transversal are the same.

D. The interior angles on the same side of two lines sum to 180 degrees.

28. What is the slope of the line between the points (−6, 4) and (8, −12)?

A. ¼
B. −8/7
C. 4
D. −7/8

29. You are making oatmeal raisin cookies and the recipe calls for ¾ cup of raisins and ⅔ cup of brown sugar. You have 2 cups of brown sugar and decide to increase the recipe to use all your sugar. How many cups of raisins should you use to keep the ratio the same as the original recipe?

  A. 1 ⁷⁄₉
  B. 2 ¼
  C. 2 ⅚
  D. 3

30. The function h(x) is defined as h(x) = f(x) − g(x).
    f(x) = 3x + 1
    g(x) = −x² − 2x + 6
    Find h(2).

  A. 0
  B. 2
  C. 9
  D. 14

31. If the remainder of a number when divided by 7 is 2, what is the remainder when 4 times that number is divided by 7?

  A. 1
  B. 2
  C. 4
  D. 6

32. A softball league has 8 teams. Only 4 teams will make the single elimination playoff. What is the ratio of the number of permutations of playoff teams over the number of combinations of playoff teams?

  A. 6
  B. 10
  C. 24
  D. 60

33. What is the linear transformation T of the point (1, 2)? $T = \begin{bmatrix} 2 & 0 \\ 0 & 1 \end{bmatrix}$

   A. (1, 1)
   B. (2, 2)
   C. (2, 1)
   D. (3, 2)

34. Suppose you have a number with a 3 in the tens place and you want to move the 3 to the thousandths place. How much do you need to divide the original number by?

   A. 100
   B. 1000
   C. 10,000
   D. 100,000

35. What is the solution to the following equation? $x^2 + 10x + 30 = 0$

   A. $-5 \pm i\sqrt{5}$
   B. $(-5 \pm i\sqrt{5})/2$
   C. $-5 \pm i\sqrt{10}$
   D. $-10 \pm \sqrt{20}$

36. What is the sum of the following series? $\sum_{k=1}^{50} \frac{2}{5}k$

   A. 510
   B. 530
   C. 1020
   D. 1326

37. The height of Plant A is always 4/3 the height of Plant B. How tall is Plant A when Plant B is 9 feet tall?

   A. 27/4 feet
   B. 9 feet
   C. 10 feet
   D. 12 feet

38. What is the axis of symmetry in the graph of the following quadratic equation?
$$3x^2 + 12x - 3 = y$$

A. $x = -2$

B. $x = -3$

C. $y = -3$

D. $y = -15$

39. Which of the following trigonometric equations is graphed?

A. $y = \sin(4x - \pi)$

B. $y = 2\sin(\pi x - \pi/4)$

C. $y = 2\sin(2x - \pi/2)$

D. $y = 2\sin(2x - \pi)$

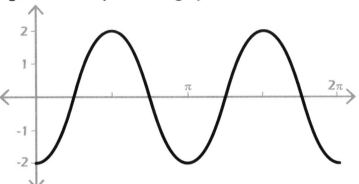

40. If Triangle ABC is similar to Triangle DEF, what is the sum of their perimeters?

A. 36

B. 48

C. 50

D. 52

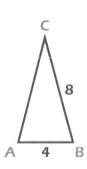
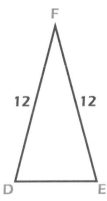

41. What is the surface area of a square pyramid with a base length of 12 and a height from the center of the base to the vertex of 8?

A. 336

B. 384

C. 624

D. 1152

42. What transformations would be performed to the graph of f(x) = −3x to get to the graph of g(x) = 3x + 4 ?

A. Reflection and Dilation

B. Rotation and Reflection

C. Rotation and Dilation

D. Reflection and Translation

43. Evaluate the integral. $\int \sqrt{x}$

A. x + C

B. (½)x + C

C. (½)x√x + C

D. (⅔)x√x + C

44. What is the length of y, the missing side in the triangle below?

A. 2√19

B. 5√2

C. 6√3

D. 8

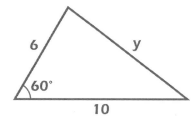

45. The following are students' test scores. Which student is at the 60th percentile?

George = 73	Brad = 59	Michael = 63
Steve = 71	Sandra = 52	William = 86
Patricia = 89	Sophie = 90	Marissa = 78
Joseph = 62	Chris = 69	Cyndi = 51
Richard = 91	Terry = 94	Kate = 82

A. Chris

B. Marissa

C. George

D. Kate

Diagnostic Exam: Answers & Explanations

1. D   Let's examine each answer choice.

A: The product of integers is always an integer (no fractions or decimals), so eliminate A.

B: The rules of multiplying odd and even integers are as follows:
Even x Even = Even
Even x Odd = Even
Odd x Odd = Odd
In this case, we have Odd x Odd x Even = Odd x Even = Even
Eliminate answer B.

C: The rules of multiplying positive and negative integers are
Positive x Positive = Positive
Positive x Negative = Negative
In this case, we have Positive x Positive x Negative = Negative.
Eliminate answer C.

D: This is the only answer remaining, so it must be correct.
Here is one possible option:
Positive Odd x Positive Odd x Negative Even = 25 x 1 x –4 = –100

2. C   **Method 1: Work backward to find the original number.**
The last step was to divide by 2 to get 26.
Therefore, perform the inverse operation – multiply by 2:
26 x 2 = 52.

The step before that was to add 4.
Perform the inverse operation – subtract 4:
52 – 4 = 48.

The step before that was to multiply by 3.
Perform the inverse operation – divide by 3:
48 ÷ 3 = 16

The first step was to take the square root of the number.
Perform the inverse operation – square the number:
$16^2 = 256$

Method 2: Set up an equation and solve for the original number.
In this case, there is an unknown, the original number. Therefore, you could assign a variable to that unknown. In this case, I will choose n. Then, set up an equation in terms of this variable and solve for n.

Take the words in the problem and translate them into an equation.

"the square root of a number, multiply it by 3, add 4, and then divide by 2 to get 26"

$[(\sqrt{n}) \times 3 + 4]/2 = 26$

Multiply both sides by 2.	$(\sqrt{n}) \times 3 + 4 = 52$
Subtract 4 from both sides.	$(\sqrt{n}) \times 3 = 48$
Divide by 3 on both sides.	$\sqrt{n} = 16$
Square both sides.	$n = 256$

3. A The easiest way to solve percent problems is to set the original price of the product to $100 and see how the price changes.

The manufacturer sells the product for $100, and the store owner marks it up 20%: $100 × 20% = $100 × 0.20 = $20.

The store sells it for $100 + $20 = $120.

The store has a 10% off sale: $120 × 10% = $120 × 0.10 = $12.

The sale price is $120 − $12 = $108.

The sale price of $108 is an 8% increase from the manufacturer's price of $100.

4. B Let's first examine the area.

The formula for the area of a circle is π × radius².

If the diameter triples, the radius also triples.
Therefore, the new area of the circle is π(3 × radius)²
= π × 9 × radius²
= 9πradius²
= 9A

The formula for the circumference of a circle is π × diameter.
Therefore, the new circumference = π(3 × diameter)
= 3 × π × diameter = 3C.

5. D The easiest way to solve this problem is by first graphing the coordinate pairs and then finding the dimensions of the square. The coordinate pairs are graphed on the right.

As can be seen in the graph, the square is 3 x 3. Therefore, the area is 9.

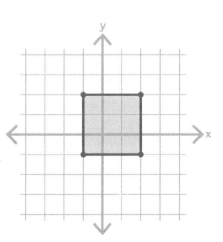

6. D   The distributive property states that a(b + c) = ab + ac. In the above problem, the distributive property was used to help calculate 73 x 101.

From steps 3 to 4, the order of the addition problem was changed. The commutative property states that for addition, order does not matter.

7. B   For algebra word problems, you should assign variables to the unknowns. In this case, there are two unknowns: the number of chickens and the number of pigs.
Let c = number of chickens; let p = number of pigs

Then, set up equations by using information in the problem.
We know that the farmer had 8 more chickens than pigs: c = p + 8
We know that the total number of feet is 100 and that each chicken has 2 feet and each pig has 4: 2c + 4p = 100.

Now, solve this system of equations:
c = p + 8
2c + 4p = 100

You can use the substitution method by substituting for c in the second equation what c equals in the first equation:

2c + 4p = 100	Second Equation
2(p + 8) + 4p = 100	Substitute first equation for c
2p + 16 + 4p = 100	Distribute
6p + 16 = 100	Combine like terms
6p = 84	Subtract 16 from both sides
p = 14	Divide both sides by 6 to solve for p
c = p + 8	Use first equation to solve for c
c = 14 + 8 = 22	Plug in value for p, and solve for c

8. B   Let's calculate each of the statistical measures of the following set: 7, –3, 11, –4, 8, 2, 9, 2

A: Mean: Mean is the average of the data. It is found by adding all the elements and dividing by the number of elements.
Mean = (7 + –3 + 11 + –4 + 8 + 2 + 9 + 2) ÷ 8 = 4

B: Median: The median is the middle value when the numbers are in order. First, order the numbers from smallest to largest: –4, –3, 2, 2, 7, 8, 9, 11
Since this data set has an even number of elements, you must find the average of the two middle numbers, 2 and 7:
Median = (2 + 7) ÷ 2 = 4.5

C: Mode: The mode is the element that appears most often. In this case, 2 is the only number that appears more than once.
Mode = 2

9. A Let X represent the unknown, which is the amount of pure saline that must be added.

Now, set up an equation relating the amount of saline in the solutions. Remember, the amount of saline will be the percentage of saline in each solution multiplied by the total amount of that solution. For example, the amount of saline in the 40% solution is equal to 40% x the total amount of that solution = 40%(10L)

Amount of saline in 40% solution + amount of added saline = amount of saline in 60% solution
40%(10) + 100%(X) = 60%(10 + X)
40%(10) + X = 60%(10 + X)

10. D You want to find the probability that both cards will be hearts. To find the probability of compound events, multiply their individual probabilities.

The probability of the first card being a heart is $13/52 = 1/4$.
For the second card, there are only 51 cards left and only 12 hearts left. Probability = $12/51$.
Multiply the probabilities: $1/4 \times 12/51 = 3/51 = 1/17$

11. B If the average for the first 9 games was 23, the total number of points you scored in those games was 9 x 23 = 207.

If the average on all 10 games is n, the total number of points scored in all 10 games must be 10 x n = 10n.

To find what you need to get in the 10th game, subtract the total number of points in the first 9 games from the total number of points in all 10 games:
10n – 207

12. A $f(x) = 1 + \dfrac{2}{x^2}$

Let's think about what happens when x gets extremely large. As x grows, the fraction $2/x^2$ will get closer and closer to zero as the denominator grows. Therefore, as x approaches infinity, $2/x^2$ approaches 0. Therefore, the function: f(x) will approach 1 + 0 = 1.

13. D

As you can see in the number line, only the values greater than –2 are marked. In addition, only the integers are marked – the fractions or decimals in between are not highlighted. Therefore, the number line only represents integers greater than –2.

14. D Let's examine each option.

I. There are no even prime numbers.
There is one even prime number, 2. The only factors of 2 are 2 and 1, and a prime number is a number whose only factors are itself and 1.

II. The greatest common factor of two numbers will always be smaller than both numbers.
The greatest common factor (GCF) is not always smaller since it can equal one of the numbers. For instance, the GCF of 6 and 12 is 6, since 6 is a factor of both 12 and 6.

III. The least common multiple of two numbers will always be greater than both numbers.
The least common multiple can equal one of the numbers. For instance, the LCM of 6 and 12 is 12, since 12 is a multiple of both 12 and 6.

15. A All answer choices are a single number raised to an exponent. Therefore, we need to combine the terms in the expression to something that will match one of the answer choices.

There is not much that can be done with 2^3. Therefore, let's focus on 4^{-7}.
You can see that 4 can be turned into an expression with an exponential base of 2:
$4 = 2^2$
$4^{-7} = (2^2)^{-7} = 2^{-14}$
Now, multiply. $2^3 \times 4^{-7} = 2^3 \times 2^{-14} = 2^{-11}$.

16. A First, determine the value of each space.

Between 3.4 and 3.5, there are 5 spaces:
$3.5 - 3.4 = 0.1$
$0.1/5 = 0.02$
Each space is worth 0.02.

Now, let's determine the values of A and B.
A is one space, or 0.02, below 3.4:
$A = 3.4 - 0.02 = 3.38$.

B is one space above 3.5:
$B = 3.5 + 0.02 = 3.52$.

The distance between A and B:
$B - A = 3.52 - 3.38 = 0.14$

17. B To solve this problem, find the corresponding Celsius temperatures, and then subtract.

50° Fahrenheit: $C = (5/9)(50 - 32) = (5/9)(18) = 10$
68° Fahrenheit: $C = (5/9)(68 - 32) = (5/9)(36) = 20$

$20 - 10 = 10°$ C

18. A To find the volume of a triangular prism, multiply the area of the base by the height of the prism.

First, find the area of the base. In this case, you need to know the dimensions of the right triangle, and we only know the hypotenuse and the length of one side. Use the Pythagorean theorem to find the length of the missing side.

Find length of missing side:
$5^2 + side^2 = 13^2$
$25 + side^2 = 169$
$side^2 = 144$
$side = 12$

Find area of base:
Area of the triangular base = ½ x length x width
= ½ x 12 x 5
= 30

Find volume of prism:
Volume = Area of base x height
= 30 x 10 = 300

19. C Since AB = AC, the triangle is isosceles. Therefore, Angle ABC = Angle ACB.

Let Angle ACB = y.
The angles in a triangle add to 180.
Angle ABC + Angle ACB + Angle BAC = 180
y + y + 80 = 180
2y = 100
y = 50

The angles on a straight line add to 180. Angle ACB and Angle ACD are along the straight line; therefore,
50 + Angle ACD = 180
Angle ACD = 130 degrees

20. B The area of a triangle is found by multiplying ½ x base x height. For an isosceles triangle, the base and the height are equal.

Therefore, the area = ½ x side x side = ½ $side^2$.

Thus, as the length of the side increases, the area will increase as the length is squared.

The graph must show that the increase in the y-direction is exponential – answer B is the only graph that shows this.

Diagnostic Exam: Answers & Explanations

21. D If the circle had a diameter of 10 m, its radius must be 5 m. Therefore, fill in the lengths of two of the sides of the figure:

To figure out the length around the curve, realize it is ¼ the circumference of the entire circle. The circumference of a circle is found by multiplying π by the diameter.

Length of the Curve = ¼ x π x 10 = ¹⁰⁄₄ π = 2.5π

The total perimeter is found by adding the lengths of all the sides:

5 m + 5 m + 2.5π m = 10 + 2.5π meters

22. D Plug in values for each answer choice, and see which exhibits the pattern −2.1, −3.2, −4.3, −5.4, −6.5.

(For x = 1, y = −2.1; for x = 2, y = −3.2; and so on.)

A: $y = 0.1x - 2$
$x = 1, y = 0.1(1) - 2 = -1.9$ False.

B: $y = -2.1x + 1$
$x = 1, y = -2.1(1) + 1 = -1.1$ False.

C: $y = -x^2 - 1.1$
$x = 1, y = -1^2 - 1.1 = -2.1$
$x = 2, y = -2^2 - 1.1 = -5.1$ False.

D: $y = -1.1x - 1$
$x = 1, y = -1.1(1) - 1 = -2.1$

You can try more values for x, but since it is the only answer remaining, there is no need.

23. B When finding the inverse of a function, first let f(x) = y. Then, switch the x's and y's and rearrange the equation to solve for y.

Replace f(x) with y: $y = (x + 3)/(2x + 4)$

Switch all the x's and y's to find inverse: $x = (y + 3)/(2y + 4)$

Now, rearrange and solve for y. Cross-multiply: $x(2y + 4) = y + 3$

Distribute: $2xy + 4x = y + 3$

Bring all y's to one side: $2xy - y = -4x + 3$
$y(2x - 1) = -4x + 3$
$y = (-4x + 3)/(2x - 1)$

Therefore, $f^{-1}(x) = (-4x + 3)/(2x - 1)$
Plug in 2 and solve:
$f^{-1}(x) = (-4x + 3)/(2x - 1)$
$f^{-1}(2) = (-4(2) + 3)/(2(2) - 1)$
$f^{-1}(2) = -5/3$

24. B   The y-intercept is the point on the graph that crosses the y-axis. A point that crosses the y-axis has an x-value of 0. Therefore, plug in x = 0 and solve for y:

−2x + 7y = 14
−2(0) + 7y = 14
7y = 14
y = 2
y-intercept = 2

The x-intercept is the point on the graph that crosses the x-axis. A point that crosses the x-axis has a y-value of 0. Therefore, plug in y = 0 and solve for x:
−2x + 7y = 14
−2x + 7(0) = 14
−2x = 14
x = −7
x-intercept = −7

25. A   Isolate the variable. Ensure that what you do to one side of the inequality, you do to all sides of the inequality.

Subtract 2:
−4 − 2 ≤ −3x + 2 − 2 < 11 − 2
−6 ≤ −3x < 9

Divide by −3. When dividing by a negative number, flip the inequality signs:
−6 ÷ −3 ≥ −3x ÷ −3 > 9 ÷ −3
2 ≥ x > −3

Rearrange the inequality statement:
−3 < x ≤ 2

26. C   First, you can tell that the graph represents an AND statement since only the overlapped portion is shaded. An OR statement would mean all areas that represent either statement are shaded.

Let's look at the line y = x, which has the positive slope. All the points below that are shaded. Therefore, y ≤ x has been shaded.

Now, let's look at the line y = −x, which has the negative slope. All the points greater than that are shaded. Therefore, y ≥ −x has been shaded.

27. A   Although all the statements are true in and of themselves, statement 1 is about angles a and b, which are vertical angles. Vertical angles always have the same measure.

28. B The slope of a line is the rise over the run. This can also be thought of as the change in y over the change in x.

(−6, 4) and (8, −12)

Slope = change in y/change in x
= 4 − (−12)/−6 − 8 = 16/−14 = −8/7

29. B Set this problem up as a ratio. The variable y represents the number of cups of raisins needed.

$$\frac{\text{Raisins}}{\text{Brown sugar}} = \frac{\frac{3}{4} \text{ cups}}{\frac{2}{3} \text{ cups}} = \frac{y \text{ cups}}{2 \text{ cups}}$$

You can solve for the variable y by cross-multiplying:
¾ cups x 2 cups = ⅔ cups x y cups
¾ x 2 = (⅔) y
3⁄2 = (⅔) y

Multiply both sides by 3⁄2 to get y by itself.
3⁄2 x 3⁄2 = (⅔) y x 3⁄2
9⁄4 = y
2 ¼ = y

2 ¼ cups of raisins

30. C Let's first simplify the function h(x):

h(x) = f(x) − g(x)
= (3x + 1) − (−x^2 − 2x + 6)
= 3x + 1 + x^2 + 2x − 6
= x^2 + 5x − 5

Now, find the result when 2 is the input to the function h:
h(x) = x^2 + 5x − 5
h(2) = 2^2 + 5(2) − 5 = 4 + 10 − 5 = 9

31. A To solve this problem, first pick a number that has a remainder of 2 when divided by 7. There are an infinite number of possible numbers to choose from, including 2, 9, 16, and 23. Let's choose 9.

The problem asks what is the remainder when 4 times that number is divided by 7. Multiply 9 by 4 and divide by 7 to find the remainder: 9 x 4 = 36
36 ÷ 7 = 5 remainder 1

The remainder is 1.

32. C To find the ratio of permutations to combinations, first solve for each.

Permutations
= 8!/(8–4)! = 8!/4! = (8 x 7 x 6 x 5 x 4 x 3 x 2)/(4 x 3 x 2) = 8 x 7 x 6 x 5 = 1680

Combinations
= $_8C_4$ = 8!/[4!(8–4)!] = 8!/[4!4!] = (8x7x6x5x4x3x2)/[(4x3x2)(4x3x2)]
= (8 x 7 x 6 x 5)/(4 x 3 x 2) = 70

Ratio: The ratio of permutations to combinations = 1680/70 = 24

33. B To transform a point, multiply the matrix T by the point. The result will be the coordinates of the new point.

When multiplying two matrices, find the sum of products of each element in the row of the first matrix and each column of the second matrix.

$$\begin{bmatrix} 2 & 0 \\ 0 & 1 \end{bmatrix} \begin{bmatrix} 1 \\ 2 \end{bmatrix} = \begin{bmatrix} 2x1 + 0x2 \\ 0x1 + 1x2 \end{bmatrix} = \begin{bmatrix} 2 \\ 2 \end{bmatrix}$$

34. C Let's first write two numbers: the original number with a 3 in the tens place and the new number with a 3 in the thousandths place.

Original: 3 in the tens place = 30
New: 3 in the thousandths place = 0.003

To move one place value to the right, you must divide by 10. In this case, you must move the 3 by 4 places. First divide by 10 to move from the tens place to the ones place. Then, divide by another 10, or divide by 100 total, to move to the tenths place. Then, divide by another 10, or divide by 1000 total, to move to the hundredths place. Finally, divide by another 10, or divide by 10,000 total, to move to the thousandths place.

35. A When solving a quadratic equation, it is often easiest to first check if you can factor the equation. In this case, that means finding two integers that add to 10 and multiply to 30. If you go through each pair of factors for 30, you will notice that none of them satisfy this condition. Thus, your next step should be to use the quadratic equation.

$x^2 + 10x + 30 = 0$
$a = 1, b = 10, c = 30$

$$x = \frac{-b \pm \sqrt{b^2 - 4ac}}{2a}$$

$x = [-10 \pm \sqrt{(10^2 - 120)}]/2$
$x = [-10 \pm \sqrt{-20}]/2$

Notice that you are taking a square root of a negative number. Therefore, the roots to this quadratic equation will be complex:

$x = [-10 \pm 2i\sqrt{5}]/2$
$x = -5 \pm i\sqrt{5}$

36. A When asked to find the sum of a series, the first step is always to determine what type of series it is: arithmetic or geometric. From sigma notation, you can quickly determine the type of series by looking at where the variable is. If it is in the exponent, then the series is geometric. Otherwise, it is an arithmetic series. In this case, we are just multiplying a constant by the variable and there are no powers, and thus it is an arithmetic series.

Conveniently, the formula for finding the sum of an arithmetic series is included on your formula sheet.

$$S_n = \frac{n}{2}[2a + (n-1)d] = n\left(\frac{a + a_n}{2}\right)$$

For this problem, you can either factor out the 2/5 since it is being multiplied by each term and then find the sum and multiply the result by 2/5. Or, you can solve the summation as is. I will just show the steps keeping it as is.

First, find the value of each of the variables.
n = number of terms = 50
a = first term = 2/5
a_n = fiftieth term = (2/5)(50) = 20
S_{50} = 50(2/5 + 20)/2 = 50(102/5)/2 = 1020/2 = 510

37. D Since we are given the height of Plant B, and we know that Plant A is directly proportionate to Plant B, all you have to do is multiply to find the height of Plant A.

Plant A's height = 4/3 x Plant B's height.
Plant A = 4/3 x 9 = 4/3 x 9/1 = 12

12 feet

38. A The axis of symmetry is the vertical line that divides the parabola in half. Therefore, it takes the form x = x-coordinate of vertex.

The x-coordinate of the vertex of a quadratic equation can be found by solving -b/2a.

$3x^2 + 12x - 3 = y$
a = 3, b = 12, c = −3

x-coordinate of vertex = -b/2a = −12/6 = −2
Axis of Symmetry: x = −2

39. C To determine which equation matches the graph, first determine the amplitude of the function. You can do this by looking at the maximum y-value reached. In this case, the graph goes up to 2. Thus, amplitude = 2.

Next, look at the period, which indicates the intervals at which the graph will repeat. The period of this graph is π, since at that x-value, you can see that the graph is again at its minimum and rising up toward the maximum.

Now, note that all answer choices are in terms of sine. The sine graphs and cosine graphs are equivalent but shifted. Therefore, this graph could have represented either trig function but with different phase shifts. However, the answer choices tell us we are dealing with a sine function.

The graph of a sine function starts at zero and then rises to the maximum. Thus, this graph has a phase shift of $\pi/4$ as that it is where the period of a sine function starts.

Amplitude = 2, Period = π, Phase Shift = $\pi/4$

Plug in the calculated values into the standard formula for a trigonometric function:
$y = A \sin(\omega x - \varphi)$
Amplitude = A, Period = $2\pi/\omega$, Phase Shift = φ/ω

Amplitude = A = 2

Period = $\pi = 2\pi/\omega$
$\omega = 2$

Phase Shift = $\pi/4 = \varphi/\omega = \varphi/2$
$\varphi = \pi/2$

$y = 2\sin(2x - \pi/2)$

40. C To find the sum of the perimeters of the two triangles, you must first figure out the length of each missing side. Since the triangles are similar, the lengths of the sides of the triangles are proportional.

AC/DF = BC/EF
AC/12 = 8/12
AC = 8

AB/DE = BC/EF
4/DE = 8/12
DE = 6

Now, add the lengths of their sides to find the perimeters:
Sum of perimeters = Perimeter of Triangle ABC + Perimeter of Triangle DEF
= (4 + 8 + 8) + (6 + 12 + 12)
= 20 + 30 = 50

41. B It is often easiest to start with a sketch when solving geometry problems. Draw a pyramid with a square base. The base should have a side of length 12, and the height of the pyramid should equal 8.

To find the surface area, you must find the sum of the areas of each surface. However, since you do not know the height of any of the triangles, you must first calculate that.

Draw a right triangle using the height of the pyramid as one side, half of the base as the second side, and the height of the triangular face as the hypotenuse. You know the sides of the right triangle are 6 and 8, so you can use the Pythagorean theorem to find the hypotenuse:

$6^2 + 8^2 = hyp^2$
$36 + 64 = hyp^2$
$100 = hyp^2$
$hyp = 10$

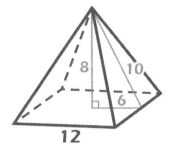

Now, find the surface area:
Area of square base = 12 x 12 = 144
Area of each triangular face = ½ x base x height = ½ x 12 x 10 = 60
Surface Area = Area of square base + 4 (Area of Triangular Face) = 144 + 4(60) = 384

42. D There are two transformations required to go from the graph of f(x) to g(x). The first transformation is due to the change of the x term from –3 to 3 by multiplying by –1. The second transformation is due to the addition of 4.

–3x to 3x:
In the function f, every input x is multiplied by –3. In the new function g, every input x is multiplied by 3. Therefore, the outputs for function g will be equal to –1 times the output from function f. In other words, for an input x, the outputs of f and g will be on opposite sides of the x-axis. Thus, to get from the graph of one of these functions to the other, each point is reflected over the x-axis.

+ 4:
Adding 4 to every output moves the graph up by 4 units in the y-direction. This is a translation transformation by 4 units in the positive y-direction.

43. D Evaluating an integral requires the following formula:
$$\int x^n = \frac{x^{n+1}}{n+1} + C$$

In this case, you must first convert $\sqrt{x}$ to the form x^n. Remember that the square root of x is the same as $x^{1/2}$. Now that you know what n equals, you can use the formula.

$$\int \sqrt{x} = \int x^{1/2} = \frac{x^{3/2}}{3/2} + C$$

$$= \frac{2x^{3/2}}{3} + C$$

$$= \frac{2(x)x^{1/2}}{3} + C$$

$$= \frac{2x\sqrt{x}}{3} + C$$

44. A If asked to find the length of the missing side of a triangle, first determine whether there is a right triangle – if so, you can use the Pythagorean theorem. Since there's no right angle here, you should use one of the Trigonometric Laws. As you know the length of two sides and one angle, use the Law of Cosines.

Law of Cosines: $c^2 = a^2 + b^2 - 2ab \cos C$
a and b are the lengths of the sides that are known: a = 6, b = 10
C is the measure of the angle opposite the missing side = 60°

$c^2 = 6^2 + 10^2 - 2(6)(10) \cos 60°$
$= 36 + 100 - 120 \cos 60°$
$= 136 - 120 \cos 60°$

If you recall the unit circle or the measurements of the sides of a 30–60–90 triangle, the cos 60° = 1/2.

$c^2 = 136 - 120(1/2)$
$c^2 = 136 - 60 = 76$
$c = \sqrt{76} = \sqrt{(4)(19)} = \sqrt{4}\sqrt{19} = 2\sqrt{19}$
$y = 2\sqrt{19}$

45. B First, put the scores in order: Cyndi = 51, Sandra = 52, Brad = 59, Joseph = 62, Michael = 63, Chris = 69, Steve = 71, George = 73, Marissa = 78, Kate = 82, William = 86, Patricia = 89, Sophie = 90, Richard = 91, Terry = 94

To find the 60th percentile, multiply the number of scores by 60%.
15 x 60% = 15 x 0.60 = 9

Thus, the student at the 60th percentile is the student with the 9th highest score, Marissa.

11. Final Exam

Final Exam Questions..530
Answers & Explanations...551

Final Exam

1. Which of the following CANNOT be true of the triangle?

A. The hypotenuse equals 1000.
B. The side lengths add to 20.
C. Two angles are equal.
D. One angle measures 60 degrees.

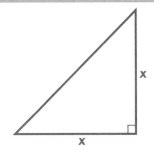

2. f(x − 3) + 4 will shift a graph of f(x):

A. 4 up and 3 to the right
B. 4 up and 3 to the left
C. 4 right and 3 down
D. 4 right and 3 up

3. Which of the following problems could be solved by using the equation: 3.5 ÷ 0.5 ?

A. A concert lasts three and a half hours, and you missed a half hour. How much of the concert did you see?
B. The base of a triangle is 0.5 cm and the height is 3.5 cm, what is the triangle's area?
C. The length of the wooden plank is three and a half feet, and you need pieces that are half a foot long, how many pieces can you get from the plank?
D. Jimmy's house is 5 miles from Susie's house. If Jimmy can run 3.5 miles per hour, how long will it take him to reach Susie's house?

4. If 4 of the letters of ABCDEFGH are arranged in a row, what is the probability that A will be first?

A. 1/8
B. 1680
C. 1/4
D. 1/16

5. A lab assistant has 9 ounces of a 5% acid solution but needs a 10% acid solution. How much pure acid should he add?

A. 0.5 ounces
B. 1 ounce
C. 4.5 ounces
D. 9 ounces

6. If you roll two dice, what is the probability that the sum on them will be 6?

   A. 1/6

   B. 1/36

   C. 5/36

   D. 5/6

7. If a scale is off by 5 lbs, what measure changes?

   I. mean
   II. median
   III. mode

   A. I and II

   B. I only

   C. II and III

   D. I, II, and III

8. Which graph best represents the perimeter of an equilateral triangle as a function of the length of one side?

A.   B.  C.   D.

9. Twenty people are playing in a chess tournament, and 3 prizes will be awarded. Which of the following has more possible outcomes?

   A. 3 prizes are different: 1st, 2nd, 3rd place.

   B. 3 prizes are the same: order does not matter among winners.

   C. Same number of outcomes.

   D. Not enough information.

10. How many integers between 1 and 1000, inclusive, are divisible by both 5 and 8?

    A. 25

    B. 76

    C. 125

    D. 200

11. The mean of your five test scores for the semester is 82, and you know your scores for the first four tests were 84, 72, 98, and 86. What did you score on that last test?

   A. 68

   B. 70

   C. 82

   D. 85

12. Use the student work sample below to answer the question that follows.

   1. $4(16 + 23) + 36 = 64 + 23 + 36$
   2. $64 + 23 + 36 = 64 + 36 + 23$
   3. $64 + 36 + 23 = 100 + 23$
   4. $100 + 23 = 123$

What property does the student use incorrectly, and in which step?

   A. Associative, Step 1

   B. Distributive, Step 1

   C. Distributive, Step 3

   D. Commutative, Step 3

13. If n is an odd, prime integer and 10 < n < 19, which is true about the mean of all possible values of n?

   A. It is greater than the median and greater than the mode.

   B. It is greater than the median.

   C. It is equal to the median.

   D. It is less than the median.

14. Which of the following equations has a slope of ⅗ and y-intercept of 2?

   A. $-3x + 5y = 10$

   B. $3x + 5y = 2$

   C. $5x + 3y = 2$

   D. $-5x - 3y = 10$

15. What is the slope of the line between the origin and (−3, 2)?

   A. ⅔

   B. −⅔

   C. 3/2

   D. −3/2

16. Find the zeros of the following function. $y = 2x^2 + x - 6$.

   A. (3/2, 0); (–2, 0)

   B. (–3, 0); (2, 0)

   C. (0, 3/2); (0, –2)

   D. (3, 0); (–2, 0)

17. A man leaves on a business trip, and at the same time, his wife takes their children to visit their grandparents. The cars, traveling in opposite directions, are 360 miles apart at the end of 3 hours. If the man's average speed is 10 mph faster than his wife's speed, what is her average speed?

   A. 50 mph

   B. 55 mph

   C. 60 mph

   D. 65 mph

18. If a student wanted to find the equation of a line with a known y-intercept, which of the following would independently provide enough information?

   A. A coordinate pair on the line

   B. The slope

   C. The x-intercept

   D. All of the above

19. Figure ABCDE is a regular pentagon with BD parallel to AE. What is the sum of the measure of ∠ EDB and the measure of ∠ BCD?

   A. 72°

   B. 108°

   C. 150°

   D. 180°

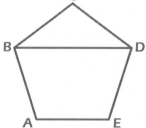

20. For which equation y, is the following equation true? $y + y'' = 0$

   A. 5

   B. x

   C. x^2

   D. None of the above.

Final Exam   533

21. If the prime factorization of a number Y is n^2p^3, and the prime factorization of Z is n^3p^2, what is the prime factorization of the least common multiple of Z and Y?

   A. np
   B. n^2p^2
   C. n^3p^3
   D. n^5p^5

22. At an amusement park, there is a circular dartboard with radius of 20 cm. In the middle of the dartboard, there is a small circle with radius of 4 cm. If you have an equal probability of hitting any spot on the dartboard, what is the probability that you will hit the small circle?

   A. 1/5
   B. 1/10
   C. 1/25
   D. 1/80

23. The age of Sonia's brother is 5 years less than twice her age. Five years ago, he was 11 years less than 3 times her age then. How old is she now?

   A. 6 yrs old
   B. 11 yrs old
   C. 16 yrs old
   D. 27 yrs old

24. Which of the following is the largest?

   A. 8 square yards
   B. 70 square feet
   C. 10,000 square inches
   D. 5 square yards, 20 square feet, and 500 square inches

25. The formula for converting temperatures in Celsius (°C) to Fahrenheit (°F) is $C = \frac{5}{9}(F - 32)$. If the temperature at the beginning of a day was 68°F, and it increased by 50% on the Celsius scale, what was the temperature at the end of the day?

   A. 30° F
   B. 86° F
   C. 98° F
   D. 102° F

26. A school is putting on a production of *A Midsummer Night's Dream*. There are 5 students trying out for Puck and 10 students trying out for the two roles of Lysander and Demetrius. How many different ways can students be selected?

   A. 95
   B. 225
   C. 230
   D. 450

27. Choose the best answer to replace the question mark.

   surface area of a sphere of radius y   surface area of a cylinder of radius y and height y

   A. >
   B. <
   C. =
   D. Not enough information.

28. Which is a possible ratio of the numbers represented by the 5's in 532.385?

   A. One hundred thousand to one
   B. One hundred to one hundredth
   C. One hundred to one
   D. One to one thousandth

29. What is the volume of the triangular prism?

   A. 288
   B. 360
   C. 576
   D. 720

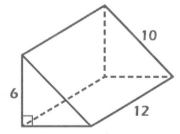

30. Order the following from least to greatest:
   I. the number of fourths in $1\frac{1}{2}$
   II. $5 \times \frac{1}{2}$
   III. $\frac{3}{2} \div 3$

   A. I, II, III
   B. III, II, I
   C. III, I, II
   D. II, III, I

Final Exam

31. The graph can be represented by the equation y = Zx – 2. What is the value of Z?

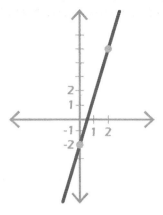

A. –2
B. 2
C. 3 ½
D. 4 ½

32. If the volume of a cube is 216 m³, what is its surface area?

A. 108 m²
B. 144 m²
C. 216 m²
D. 432 m²

33. A game starts by flipping a coin. If you get a heads, then you get to roll a die, and if you roll a 4, you win the jackpot. If you get a tails, then you must pick a card from a deck, and if you get a heart, then you win the jackpot. What is the probability of winning the jackpot in this game?

A. 5/12
B. 1/8
C. 5/24
D. 1/96

34. If the length of one living room is 1.2 x 10¹ meters and the length of a bacteria is 2 x 10⁻⁶ meters, how many times longer is the room?

A. 6 x 10⁶
B. 6 x 10⁸
C. 2.4 x 10⁻⁵
D. 2.4 x 10⁷

35. A researcher lost one piece of data from his set. He knows that the median is 83. Which could be the missing element if the rest of the set is 81, 92, 85, 76, 80?

   A. 78
   B. 82
   C. 84
   D. 90

36. Beth can type 40 words per minute, and Vanessa can type 3 words for every 2 that Beth types. If they both start typing at the same time, how many words has Beth typed when Vanessa has finished 4200 words?

   A. 157.5 words
   B. 2800 words
   C. 6300 words
   D. 7000 words

37. You have a circle centered at (−2, −2) with a diameter of 8. What are the coordinates of the point that is on the circle and with the largest x-coordinate?

   A. (2, −2)
   B. (6, −2)
   C. (8, −2)
   D. (2, 2)

38. If N is a positive integer, which of the following products could be a negative number?

   A. (N + 1)(N − 1)
   B. (N + 1)(N + 2)
   C. N(N − 2)
   D. N(N)

39. Which of the following is the farthest from 1?

   A. 7/8
   B. 1.12
   C. 0.9^2
   D. 7/6

Final Exam   537

40. Use the following incorrect work sample below from a student who was asked to calculate the distance between (5, 5) and (−5, −5) to answer the question.

    Vertical distance: 5- −5 = 10
    Horizontal distance: 5- −5 =10
    Total distance: 10 + 10 = 20

Which of the following strategies would help this student visualize the correct solution to the problem above?

   A. Drawing a square with corners at (0, 0), (0, 5), (5, 0), and (5, 5), then rotating the square until it has corners at (0, 0), (0, −5), (−5, 0), and (−5, −5).

   B. Drawing a circle with the two points placed along the circumference

   C. Drawing a right triangle with the hypotenuse connecting the two points

   D. Drawing two parallel lines that each have a length of 5 units

41. Which of the following is/are true?
I. The greatest common factor of two numbers can be equal to one of the numbers.
II. The least common multiple of two numbers can be equal to one of the numbers.
III. The product of two numbers can equal the product of their LCM and GCF.

   A. I only

   B. I and II

   C. I, II, and III

   D. None of the above

42. Everyone in a group is being assigned a secret code of 3 characters. The first character must be a letter, and the second and third are numbers which cannot be the same. How many possible codes can be made?

   A. 46

   B. 126

   C. 2340

   D. 2600

43. The price of a camera was first increased by $17 and then decreased by 38%. If the final price of the camera was y, what was the original price?

   A. y/0.62 − 17

   B. 0.62(y + 17)

   C. 17 + (1.38)y

   D. 0.38(y + 17)

44. Which of the following transformation or series of transformations best describes the change from Figure 1 to Figure 2?

A. Flip across y-axis, then flip across x-axis
B. Flip across y-axis, then translation
C. Flip across x-axis, then translation
D. Rotation

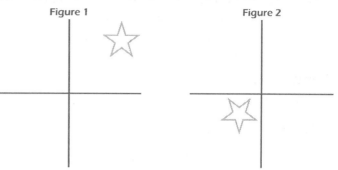

45. If 5|y − 2| ≤ 10, which of the following inequalities describes all of the possible values of y and only those values?

A. y ≥ 0
B. 0 ≤ y ≤ 4
C. y ≤ 4
D. −2 ≤ y ≤ 0

46. You have a piece of paper shaped like the diagram. If you fold along the dotted line, what shape have you created?

A. Pyramid
B. Tetrahedron
C. Right triangular prism
D. Prism with equilateral triangle base

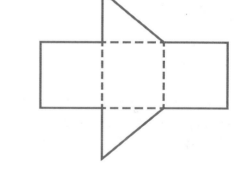

47. The graph represents the growth of a student's plant over the course of his 7-day science experiment. Which of the following equations best models the relationship between days, d, and plant height in centimeters, h, as shown in the graph?

A. d = (½)h + 5
B. d = 5h + ½
C. h = (½)d + 5
D. h = 5d + ½

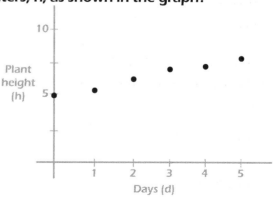

48. Assuming that every order includes one sandwich, one bag of chips, and one drink, how many different combinations of lunch orders are possible for 5 types of sandwiches, 4 types of chips, and 6 different drinks?

   A. 15
   B. 26
   C. 60
   D. 120

49. In the figure, the distance from B to C is twice the distance from A to B, and the distance from C to D is equal to half the distance from A to C. If the distance from B to C is x, what is the distance from A to D?

   A. (½)x
   B. (¾)x
   C. (2 ¼)x
   D. (2 ½)x

50. If you start with an even number, add it to an odd number, multiply it by a different odd number, and then subtract the original even number, the result will be

   A. Even
   B. Odd
   C. Zero
   D. Not enough information

51. $|11 - 5| + 12 \div 3^2 \times 6 - 10 =$

   A. –9
   B. 2
   C. 4
   D. 206

52. Which answer choice is the largest?

   A. $(-2)^0$
   B. $(-2)^7$
   C. $(-2)^8$
   D. -2^{10}

53. Ralph has been offered a job, and he can choose from the three earnings plans. If he sells $200,000 worth of merchandise, which plan will give him the highest salary for his first year?

Earnings Plan	Payment Structure
1	$55,000 base salary
2	$25,000 base salary + 15% of sales
3	$35,000 base salary + 1/8 of sales

A. Plan 1.

B. Plan 2.

C. Plan 3.

D. All three plans allow Ralph to earn the same amount in his first year.

54. What is the limit of the function g(x) as x approaches infinity?
$g(x) = (4x^2 - 2x + 8)/(2x^2 - 1)$

A. –2

B. 8

C. 4

D. 2

55. What is the ratio of the area of Triangle T to the area of Triangle S?

A. 2

B. 4y

C. 3/2

D. 4

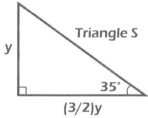
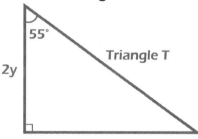

56. A blacktop has a circle painted inside it as shown in the diagram. If a raindrop falls randomly from the sky and lands on the blacktop, what is the probability that it will land inside the circle?

A. $1/\pi$

B. $\pi/16$

C. $\pi/8$

D. 16π

57. A student looks at a circle with a circumference of 24 and estimates that the radius is 8. Which of the following most accurately describes the estimate?

    A. The estimate is too low by a factor of 2.

    B. The estimate is too low by a factor of 3.

    C. The estimate is too high by a factor of 2.

    D. The estimate is correct.

58. A jogging track is made up of two half-circles on either end with a straight line of 50 m connecting them. Joaquin jogs at 5 km per hour. If his coach estimates that it will take Joaquin a half-hour to jog around the track, her estimate is

    A. Too high by a factor of 15

    B. Too low by a factor of 15

    C. Too high by a factor of 6

    D. Too low by a factor of 6

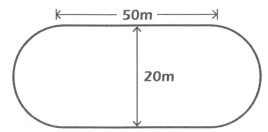

59. Noah is papering one of the walls in his bedroom. He uses 3 rolls of paper to cover 20 square yards of wall space. If the wall is 15 feet high and 18 feet long, how many rolls of paper will he need to purchase?

    A. 2

    B. 3

    C. 4

    D. 5

60. In the figure below, Angle DCB = 50°, and Angle BDC = 60°. If AB = BD, find the measure of Angle DAB.

    A. 35°

    B. 50°

    C. 55°

    D. 70°

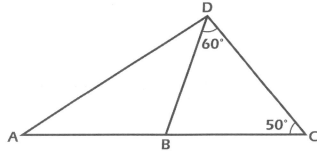

61. What is the perimeter of the shape?

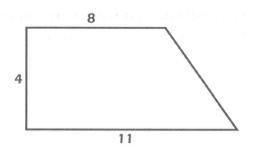

A. 23
B. 26
C. 28
D. 32

62. A cylindrical can is measured to have a base radius of 4 cm ± 1 cm and a height of 7 cm ± 2 cm. The volume of the can is calculated based on these measurements. What is the difference between the maximum and minimum possible volumes?

A. 45π
B. 60π
C. 90π
D. 180π

63. How many solutions does the following system of equations have?
$$4x - 6y = -10$$
$$3y = 5 + 2x$$

A. 0
B. 1
C. 2
D. Infinite

64. What is the range of the function?

A. $-\infty < x < \infty$
B. $-\infty < x < -1$ and $1 \leq x < \infty$
C. $-\infty < y < \infty$
D. $-\infty < y < 1$ and $1 < y < \infty$

65. In the equation, $y = x^3 - x^2$, what is the change in the y-value when x increases from 4 to 5?

A. 0
B. 52
C. 70
D. 148

66. The length of a rectangle is 5 feet less than 3 times the width. If the perimeter must be less than 86 feet, and the dimensions of the rectangle are all whole numbers of feet, what is the largest possible width for the rectangle?

   A. 10 ft
   B. 11 ft
   C. 12 ft
   D. 13 ft

67. The ratio of the number of marbles Mike has to the number David has is 5 to 8. If David has 12 more marbles than Mike, how many marbles does Mike have?

   A. 7 marbles
   B. 9 marbles
   C. 20 marbles
   D. 28 marbles

68. If the pattern repeats, what is the shape of the 61st object?

   A. Circle
   B. Triangle
   C. Square
   D. Hexagon

69. In a family, the oldest child is $7/3$ times the sum of the younger children's ages. If the two younger children are twins with an age greater than s and less than t, which inequality most accurately gives the range of possibilities for the oldest child's age, c?

   A. $s < c < t$
   B. $2s < c < 2t$
   C. $(7/3)s < c < (7/3)t$
   D. $(14/3)s < c < (14/3)t$

70. Y varies directly with x and inversely with z. If y = 20, when x = 10 and z = 2, what does y equal when x = 15 and z = 5?

   A. 3
   B. 12
   C. 75
   D. 300

71. Find three consecutive odd integers, such that three times the second is 9 more than twice the third. What is the smallest number?

A. 9
B. 11
C. 12
D. 15

72. Which of the following is an inverse of f(x)? $f(x) = x^2 + 5$

A. $g(x) = -x^2 - 5$
B. $g(x) = x^2 - 5$
C. $g(x) = \sqrt{(x - 5)}$
D. $g(x) = \sqrt{(x + 5)}$

73. Which of the following statements is true about the function below?

$$f(x) = 3x \quad \text{if } x < -1$$
$$f(x) = 5 \quad \text{if } -1 \leq x < 1$$
$$f(x) = 2(x + 1)^2 \quad \text{if } x \geq 1$$

A. Domain is from −1 to 1.
B. Range is from −1 to 1.
C. Function has discontinuities at −1 and 1.
D. Function has a maximum at x = 0.

74. What is the y-intercept of the graph of the equation? $y = 3x^2 - 8x + 9$

A. −8
B. 3
C. 4
D. 9

75. In a uniform distribution with 6 unique elements, if each element is multiplied by 3, which of the following statements are true?

I. Mean is multiplied by 3.
II. Median is multiplied by 3.
III. Probability of lowest element being chosen is multiplied by 3.

A. I only
B. I and II only
C. I, II, and III
D. Not enough information

76. The shaded region represents what set of inequalities?

A. $y \leq -1$ or $y \leq -\frac{1}{2}x$

B. $y \leq -1$ and $y \leq \frac{1}{2}x$

C. $x \leq -1$ and $y \leq -\frac{1}{2}x$

D. $x \leq -1$ and $y \leq -2x$

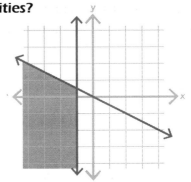

77. You are graphing the number of employees of a startup company versus the year. The graph follows a straight line, where the company started in 2004 (thus had 0 employees at the start of the year) and then in 2006 had 250 employees. Assuming the slope of the line stays the same, how many employees will there be in 2009?

A. 500

B. 625

C. 750

D. 975

78. It takes a painter 2 hours to paint a wall that is 10 m x 10 m. How long would it take 2 painters working at the same rate to paint a wall that is 40 m x 40 m?

A. 2 hours

B. 4 hours

C. 8 hours

D. 16 hours

79. The graph shows the distance that a car traveled over time. Which of the following graphs shows the same car's speed over time?

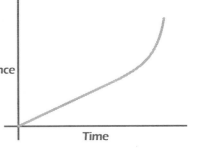

A.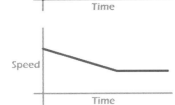

B.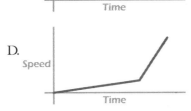

C.

D.

546   Final Exam

80. There are 60 marbles in a bag. The probability of a marble being green or red is 5/12, and there are 5 green marbles. How many red marbles are in the bag?

A. 5
B. 12
C. 20
D. 25

81. Plant A ordered 4 shirts and 5 work pants for their workers for $115, and plant B ordered 2 shirts and 3 work pants for their workers for $65. What is the correct matrix setup of this problem?

A. $\begin{bmatrix} x \\ y \end{bmatrix} \begin{bmatrix} 4 & 5 \\ 2 & 3 \end{bmatrix} = \begin{bmatrix} \$115 \\ \$65 \end{bmatrix}$

B. $\begin{bmatrix} 4 & 5 & 2 & 3 \end{bmatrix} \begin{bmatrix} x \\ y \end{bmatrix} = \begin{bmatrix} \$115 \\ \$65 \end{bmatrix}$

C. $\begin{bmatrix} 4 & 2 \\ 5 & 3 \end{bmatrix} \begin{bmatrix} x \\ y \end{bmatrix} = \begin{bmatrix} \$115 \\ \$65 \end{bmatrix}$

D. $\begin{bmatrix} 4 & 5 \\ 2 & 3 \end{bmatrix} \begin{bmatrix} x \\ y \end{bmatrix} = \begin{bmatrix} \$115 \\ \$65 \end{bmatrix}$

82. Which of the following equations would have a graph that passes through the points (0, −3) and (π, 0)?

A. y = −3cos(x)
B. y = −3sin(x + π)
C. y = −sin(3x + π)
D. y = −3cos(x/2)

83. How many more members are in the union of sets A and B than the intersection of A and B?

A = {−6, −3, 0, 3, 6}   B = {−4, −3, −2, −1, 0, 1, 2, 3, 4}

A. 3
B. 8
C. 11
D. 14

84. What is 531 in base 10 as a base 2 number?

A. 1000010011
B. 10101
C. 201200
D. 1001010101

85. Find the value of n that makes the equation true.

$$\sum_{k=1}^{n}\left(\tfrac{1}{2}k+1\right)=26$$

A. 8
B. 10
C. 12
D. 13

86. What quadratic equation is represented in the graph?

A. $2x^2 - 3x + 5$
B. $x^2 + 4x - 15$
C. $-x^2 + 4x + 5$
D. $2x^2 - 8x + 5$

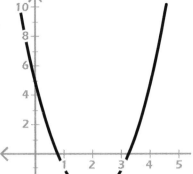

87. What is the sum of the missing numbers in the lattice multiplication problem?

A. 6
B. 14
C. 16
D. 27

88. Which of the following lines is perpendicular to: $3x + y = 6$?

A. $-3x + y = 6$
B. $-6x - y = -3$
C. $-x/3 + y = 10$
D. $x + 3y = 6$

89. What is the 85th percentile out of the test scores below?
82, 75, 62, 80, 91, 86, 71, 54, 61, 92, 78, 68, 89, 85, 88, 100, 94, 76, 72, 76

A. 85
B. 88
C. 89
D. 91

90. Which of the following quadratic equations has two complex roots?

A. $y = -3x^2 + 4x + 2$

B. $y = 2x^2 - 7x + 9$

C. $y = x^2 - 29$

D. $y = 4x^2 + 13x + 2$

91. In the triangle below, tan Θ = 5/12. Find the measure of AC.

A. 10

B. 12

C. 20

D. 24

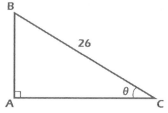

92. If f(x) = sin(2x) and g(x) = cos(2x), which transformation relates the two functions?

A. $g(x) = f(x + \pi/4)$

B. $g(x) = f(x - \pi/4)$

C. $g(x) = f(x) + \pi/2$

D. $g(x) = f(x + \pi)$

93. Evaluate the integral. $\int_{2}^{11} \left(\frac{x}{2} + 3\right) dx$

A. 4.5

B. 12.5

C. 56.25

D. 58.5

94. How many of the following are valid methods for proving triangles are congruent?   SSS, SAS, SSA, AAA, ASA, AAS

A. 3

B. 4

C. 5

D. 6

95. What is the ratio of the result of the series if n = ∞ to the result if n = 4?

$$\sum_{k=0}^{n} 2\left(\frac{1}{4}\right)^k$$

A. 4

B. 8/3

C. 32/3

D. 256/255

Final Exam

96. The graph represents the constraints from a linear programming problem. The shaded area is the feasible region. If the following function is to be maximized, what is the optimal combination? Maximize: −3x + 2y

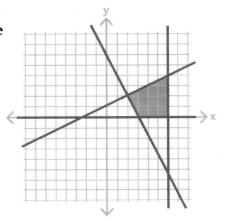

A. (0, 1)

B. (2, 2)

C. (3, 0)

D. (6, 4)

97. The Triangle ABC has angles measuring 15°, 135°, and 30°. If the measure of AC = 12, what is the measure of AB?

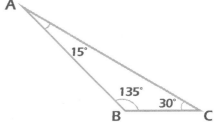

A. 6

B. $6\sqrt{2}$

C. $6\sqrt{3}$

D. $12\sqrt{2}$

98. Which of the following statements are true?

A. Taking the derivative of an integral of a function will equal the original function.

B. The integral is equal to the rate of change at any given point along a curve.

C. The area under a curve from 0 to ∞ is called the integral.

D. All of the above.

99. A person invests $2000 in a CD at an interest rate of 4% compounded quarterly. How much will the individual have in the account after 10 years?

A. $2000(1.01^{10})$

B. $2000(1.01^{40})$

C. $2000(1.04^{10})$

D. $2000(1.04^{40})$

100. How many points on the graph of y = sin x from 0 ≤ x ≤ 2π have a derivative of 0?

A. 0

B. 2

C. 4

D. Infinite

Final Exam: Answers & Explanations

1. D Let's examine each answer choice to see if it can be true.

Answer A: The hypotenuse equals 1000. This can be true. We know nothing about the lengths of the sides.

Answer B: The side lengths add to 20. There is no reason why this could not be true.

Answer C: Two angles are equal. This is definitely true. The triangle has two sides that are the same size; therefore, the angles opposite those sides must also be equal.

Answer D: One angle measures 60 degrees. This is false. Since there are two sides that each equal x and one right angle, the triangle is a 45–45–90, or right isosceles triangle. None of the angles can equal 60 degrees.

2. A The "+ 4" will shift all the y-values up by 4. Therefore, if you had f(x) and instead had f(x) + 4, then you would plug x into the function to get an output and then add 4 more to that output. Therefore, the output is shifted up by 4.

f(x – 3) versus f(x)

If you originally plugged x into f(x) to get your output, you would have to plug in a value of 3 more than x to get the same output. Therefore, any original input will have to be shifted 3 units to the right to get the same output.

f(x – 3) + 4 will shift a graph of f(x): 4 up and 3 to the right.

3. C Let's examine each answer to see how you would solve it.

A: A concert lasts three and a half hours, and you missed a half hour. How much of the concert did you see?
This problem would be solved by using the following equation: 3.5 – .5 = 3

B: The base of a triangle is 0.5 cm and the height is 3.5 cm, what is the triangle's area?
The area of a triangle is found by multiplying ½ x base x height.
Area = ½ x 0.5 x 3.5

C: The length of the wooden plank is three and a half feet, and you need pieces that are half a foot long, how many pieces can you get from the plank?
In this case, you want to divide the total plank into pieces. The total plank is 3.5 feet, and each piece is 0.5 feet. You must divide to find the total number of pieces.
3.5 ÷ 0.5 = 7 Correct Answer

D: Jimmy's house is 5 miles from Susie's house. If Jimmy can run 3.5 miles per hour, how long will it take him to reach Susie's house?
Distance = rate x time. Therefore, to figure out the time, you divide the distance by the rate.
time = 5 miles ÷ 3.5 mph

4. A   There are a few ways to solve this problem.

Method 1: The question asks what the probability is that A will be first. Well, each letter has an equal probability of being selected first, and there are 8 possible letters to choose from; therefore, the probability is 1/8.

Method 2: You could also first calculate all the possible permutations. Then, find all the possible permutations where A is first, and divide to find the probability that A is first.

All possible permutations: $8!/(8 - 4)! = 8!/4! = 1680$

Number of possible permutations with A in front = number of ways you can choose 3 from 7 for the remaining 3 spots = $7!/(7 - 3)! = 7!/4! = 210$

Probability = $210/1680 = 1/8$

5. A   The unknown in this problem is how many ounces of acid the assistant should add. Let's call that a.

The total amount of solution will then be the 9 ounces plus the additional a ounces.
Total amount of final solution = 9 + a.

We can set up an equation for the amount of acid in the solutions.
  The amount of acid in the 5% solution = 5% x 9 ounces = .05 x 9 = .45
  The amount of acid in the pure acid = 100% x a = 1 x a = a
  The amount of acid in the final solution = (9 + a) x 10% = 0.1(9 + a)

0.45 + a = 0.1 (9 + a)
0.45 + a = 0.9 + 0.1a
0.45 + 0.9a = 0.9
0.9a = 0.45
a = .5
0.5 ounces of pure acid

6. C   Probability is the number of favorable outcomes divided by the total number of outcomes. We must calculate how many favorable outcomes and how many total outcomes.

The number of favorable outcomes is how many ways you can get a sum of 6 if you roll 2 dice. Let's list the possible ways:
1 and 5, 2 and 4, 3 and 3, 4 and 2, 5 and 1
5 possible ways

The number of total outcomes can be found by multiplying how many possible outcomes on the first die multiplied by how many outcomes for the 2nd die.

6 x 6 = 36
Probability = 5/36

7. D   Let's go through each measure and see what would happen.

I. mean : The mean is the average of the numbers. If each number changes by 5 lbs, the average will also change by 5 lbs.

II. median: The median is the middle value. If each value changes by 5, so does the middle value. Therefore, the median changes.

III. mode: The mode is the value that appears most often. If all values change by 5, so will that value. Therefore, the mode changes.

8. A   In this case, the x-axis represents the length of one side of the triangle, and the y-axis represents the perimeter. As the length of the side of a triangle increases, the perimeter also increases at a linear rate.

Let's try a few values to see this.
length = 2, perimeter = 6
length = 4, perimeter = 12
length = 6, perimeter = 18

As can be seen by those values, as x increases, y also increases. As x goes up by 2, y increases by 6. Therefore, the slope of the line is 3, and the equation of the line is y = 3x.

Examining the answer choices, you see that answers B and C do not show straight lines, eliminate both of those answers. Answer D's slope is too low, and therefore, answer A is the correct answer.

9. A   We have to figure out how many possible outcomes there are if the prizes are different and how many possible outcomes there are if the prizes are the same.

Different Prizes: 1st, 2nd, 3rd place. In this case, the order of the prizes matters. Therefore, to find the number of outcomes, you would be finding the number of permutations.
Permutations = n!/(n – r)!, where in this case n = 20 and r = 3.
= 20!/(20 – 3)! = 20!/17!

Same prizes, order does not matter. In this case, figure the number of combinations that 3 prizes can be chosen from the 20 people.
Combinations: n!/(r!(n – r)!) = 20!/(3!(20 – 3)!) = 20!/(3!17!)

Compare: 20!/17! and 20!/(3!17!)
The first number is bigger, and therefore, more permutations are possible. Answer A.

In addition, you could have solved this problem by using common sense. For both situations, you have to choose 3 people from the 20. But if order matters, then for each group of 3 you choose, there are many possible outcomes for how the prizes are awarded. Therefore, there are more ways to choose winners for different prizes.

10. A If a number is divisible by both 5 and 8, then it must be divisible by 40. Now, we need to find out how many integers between 1 and 1000 are divisible by 40.

$1000/40 = 25$. Therefore, there are 25 numbers that are evenly divisible by 1000.

11. B If the mean or average of the five tests is 82, then you can calculate the total number of points you got on all five tests by multiplying.

Total number of points on five tests = $5 \times 82 = 410$

You remember the scores on four of your tests, so find the total of those four tests.
Total number of points on four tests = $84 + 72 + 98 + 86 = 340$

Find the score on the last test by subtracting your total points on four tests from your total points on all the tests.
Last test = $410 - 340 = 70$.

12. B From Step 1 to Step 2, the student attempted to use the distributive property. The distributive property states that $a(b + c) = ab + ac$.

In this case, the correct use of distributive property is:
$4(16 + 23) + 36 = 4(16) + 4(23) + 36 = 64 + 92 + 36$

The student forgot to multiply the 4 by the 23.
Answer B. Student incorrectly used distributive property in first step.

13. B The possible values of n are 11, 13, and 17 (15 is not prime).

To find the median, put the numbers in order and take the middle number. 11, 13, 17. Median = 13.

Mean is found by adding the numbers and dividing by 3. $(11 + 13 + 17)/3 = 41/3 = 13\ 2/3$.

Mode is the number that appears the most frequently. However, each number is used exactly once.

Mean is greater than the median.

14. A There are two methods to solving this problem. The first method involves rewriting the answer choices in slope-intercept form ($y = mx + b$). The second method involves writing the problem in slope-intercept form and then rearranging that equation to match the form of the answer choices.

Method 1: Rearrange each answer choice so that the equations are in slope-intercept form.

A: $-3x + 5y = 10$
$5y = 3x + 10$
$y = 3/5\ x + 2$ Slope = $3/5$, y-intercept = 2

Final Exam: Answers & Explanations

B: $3x + 5y = 2$
$5y = -3x + 2$
$y = -3/5\, x + 2/5$ Slope $= -3/5$, y-intercept $= 2/5$

C: $5x + 3y = 2$
$3y = -5x + 2$
$y = -5/3\, x + 2/3$ Slope $= -5/3$, y-intercept $= 2/3$

D: $-5x - 3y = 10$
$-3y = 5x + 10$
$y = -5/3\, x - 10/3$ Slope $= -5/3$, y-intercept $= -10/3$

Method 2: First, write the equation in slope-intercept form: $y = mx + b$. Then, you can rearrange the equation to standard form: $ax + by = c$.

In this case, the problem states both the slope and y-intercept. Therefore, immediately plug them into the equation, $y = mx + b$.
$y = 3/5\, x + 2$

Now, rearrange the equation. First, multiply everything by 5 to get rid of the fraction.
$5y = 3x + 10$
Now, bring the x's and y's to the same side of the equation.
$-3x + 5y = 10$

15. B   The slope between two points is the rise over run, or the change in y over the change in x.

(0, 0) and (–3, 2)
From the first point to the second, y goes up by 2.
From the first point to the second, x goes down by 3.
Slope $= 2/-3 = -2/3$

16. A   There are numerous methods to solving quadratic equations. You can factor the expression; you can complete the square; you can use the quadratic formula; or you can plug in the answers to see which make the expression true. I will demonstrate two methods.

Factoring: Generally, this is the first method people will try when solving quadratic equations. In this case, it is more difficult than your normal equation, as the coefficient of the x^2 term is not 1. However, I will still go through the steps to solve it.

$y = 2x^2 + x - 6$: In this case, we can try the ac method of factoring. Find two numbers that multiply to ac, –12, and add to b, 1. The two integers are 4 and –3.
$y = 2x^2 + 4x - 3x - 6$

Now, factor by grouping.
$y = 2x(x + 2) - 3(x + 2)$
$y = (2x - 3)(x + 2)$

Final Exam: Answers & Explanations

Since the expression is now factored, you can solve for the zeros. First set y to zero. Then, set each term to zero to solve for x.

$0 = (2x - 3)(x + 2)$
$2x - 3 = 0, x = 3/2$
$x + 2 = 0, x = -2$

The two zeros are: $(3/2, 0)$ and $(-2, 0)$

Quadratic Equation:
When factoring is difficult, the quadratic equation is generally the next easiest method.

$y = 2x^2 + x - 6$
$a = 2, b = 1, c = -6$

$$x = \frac{-b \pm \sqrt{b^2 - 4ac}}{2a}$$

$x = [-1 \pm \sqrt{(1 - (-48))}]/4$
$x = [-1 \pm 7]/4$
$x = (-1 + 7)/4 = 3/2$
$x = (-1 - 7)/4 = -2$

$(3/2, 0)$ and $(-2, 0)$

17. B There are two unknowns in this problem. The man's average speed and his wife's average speed. Create variables to represent the two unknowns.
m = man's average speed
w = wife's average speed

Now, let's create two equations.
"the man's average speed is 10 mph faster than his wife's speed"
m = w + 10

"The cars, traveling in opposite directions, are 360 miles apart at the end of 3 hours"
The man's car travels 3m, The wife's car 3w
3m + 3w = 360

Now, solve the system of equations using any method you like, substitution, elimination, and so on.
m = w + 10
3m + 3w = 360

In this case, let's try substitution. Substitute w + 10 for m in the second equation.
3m + 3w = 360
3(w + 10) + 3w = 360
3w + 30 + 3w = 360
6w = 330
w = 55
The wife's average speed is 55 mph.

18. D There are various ways to find the equation of a line. The y-intercept is one point. Any other point on the line would provide enough information for the student to write the equation of the line. Therefore, answer A, which says a coordinate pair would be enough. In addition, the x-intercept is just another point, so answer C would be enough.

Also, using the slope-intercept form of the equation, y = mx + b, the slope and y-intercept are the two pieces needed to find the equation. Answer B is enough.

Therefore, all would independently provide enough info.

19. D In a regular pentagon, all 5 of the angles have the same angle measure. The sum of the interior angles of just the pentagon is
180(n − 2) = 180(5 − 2) = 540 degrees

Dividing this sum by the number of angles gives the measure per interior angle.
540/5 = 108 degrees

All interior angles of the pentagon are thus 108 degrees, including ∠ BCD.

The object BDAE forms a trapezoid, with one pair of parallel lines BD and AE. This creates two parallel lines cut by a transversal, which makes
∠ AED + ∠ EDB = 180°

∠ AED is an interior angle of the pentagon and equals 108°.
108° + ∠ EDB = 180°
∠ EDB = 72°

∠ BCD + ∠ EDB = 108° + 72° = 180°

20. D To approach this question, you should go through each answer choice, find the second derivative, and check if it satisfies the equation: y + y″ = 0.
A. 5
y = 5   y′ = 0   y″ = 0
5 + 0 ≠ 0
Does not satisfy equation.

B. x
y = x   y′ = 1   y″ = 0
x + 0 ≠ 0, since we don't know what x is, we cannot say that this satisfies the equation.

C. x^2
y = x^2 y′ = 2x   y″ = 2
x^2 + 2 ≠ 0
We don't know x, so we cannot say that this satisfies the equation.

Final Exam: Answers & Explanations

21. C To find the least common multiple of Y and Z, you know you want the smallest possible number that both divide evenly into.

Y must divide evenly into the least common multiple. Therefore, n^2p^3 must divide into the least common multiple.

So far, the least common multiple has a factor of n^2p^3.

Next, let's look at Z.
$Z = n^3p^2$, which does not divide evenly into n^2p^3. There are not enough multiples of n in the least common multiple, so you must add another n.

Now, the least common multiple is n^3p^3.

22. C To find the probability, find the area of the small circle and divide that by the area of the total dartboard.

Area of small circle = $\pi \text{radius}^2 = \pi 4^2 = 16\pi$

Area of dartboard = $\pi \text{radius}^2 = \pi 20^2 = 400\pi$

Probability of getting in the small circle
= Small Circle Area ÷ Dartboard Area
= $16\pi \div 400\pi = 16/400 = 1/25$

23. C There are two unknowns: Sonia's age and her brother's age. Choose variables to represent each of the unknowns.
Let s represent Sonia's age. Let b represent her brother's age.

Now, set up equations.
The age of Sonia's brother is 5 less than twice her age.
$b = 2s - 5$

Five years ago, he was 11 years less than 3 times her age then.
$b - 5 = 3(s - 5) - 11$
$b - 5 = 3s - 15 - 11$
$b - 5 = 3s - 26$
$b = 3s - 21$

Now, solve the system of equations.
You can use substitution since they are both solved for b.
$b = 2s - 5$
$b = 3s - 21$
$2s - 5 = 3s - 21$
$-5 = s - 21$
$16 = s$
Sonia is 16 years old.

24. A Let's convert each answer to square inches, so that you can easily compare the quantities.

A: 8 square yards
8 sq yd x 36 in/1 yd x 36 in/1 yd = 10368 sq. in.

B: 70 square feet
70 sq ft x 12 in/1 ft x 12 in/1 ft = 10080 sq. in.

C: 10,000 square inches

D: 5 square yards, 20 square feet, and 500 square inches
5 sq yd x 36 in/1 yd x 36 in/1 yd = 6480 sq. in.
20 sq ft x 12 in/1 ft x 12 in/1 ft = 2880 sq in.
6480 + 2880 + 500 = 9860 sq in.

25. B This problem involves many steps. First, convert the temperature from Fahrenheit to Celsius. Then, increase the temperature by 50% on the Celsius scale. Finally, convert the temperature back to Fahrenheit.

Convert from 68° Fahrenheit to Celsius
C = $5/9$(F – 32) = $5/9$(68 – 32) = $5/9$(36) = 20° C

Increase by 50%
20 x 50% = 20 x 0.50 = 10
20 + 10 = 30
30° C

Convert from Celsius back to Fahrenheit. C = $5/9$(F – 32)
30 = $5/9$(F – 32)
30($9/5$) = F – 32
54 = F – 32
F = 86
86° F

26. D This problem has multiple steps. First, figure out the number of ways to choose the role of Puck. Then, calculate the number of ways to choose students for the remaining roles. Finally, multiply the number of ways to choose Puck by the number of ways to choose for the remaining roles to find the total number of ways students can be selected.

Choose Puck: There are 5 students trying out for Puck, so there are 5 ways to choose Puck.

Choose students for the 2 roles out of the 10 students: The order matters for the remaining roles, since it makes a difference if someone is chosen for Lysander or Demetrius. Therefore, use permutations.
Permutations = $n!/(n - r)! = 10!/(10 - 2)! = 10!/8! = 10 \times 9 = 90$

Total number of ways to select the actors: 5 x 90 = 450 ways

27. C Solve algebraically by plugging in y for the radius and the height of each of the formulas.

Surface area of a sphere:
$= 4\pi \times radius^2$
$= 4\pi y^2$

Surface area of a cylinder:
$= 2\pi \times radius^2 + 2\pi \times radius \times height$
$= 2\pi \times y^2 + 2\pi \, y \times y$
$= 2\pi y^2 + 2\pi y^2$
$= 4\pi y^2$

The surface areas are equivalent for all values of y.

28. A The 5's in 532.385 represent 500 and 0.005.

The possible ratios are 500/0.005, which equals 100,000/1 and 0.005/500, which equals 1/100,000.

29. A The volume of a triangular prism is the area of the base x height.

To find the area of the base, you must know the dimensions of the triangle, but unfortunately, not all the dimensions are stated. We know the hypotenuse and one of the sides, so we can use the Pythagorean theorem to find the missing side.

$side^2 + 6^2 = 10^2$
$side^2 + 36 = 100$
$side^2 = 64$
$side = 8$

Now, find the area of the base.
Area of triangular base $= \frac{1}{2} \times 6 \times 8 = 24$

Volume = Area of base x height of prism = 24 x 12 = 288

30. B Let's examine each answer choice.

I. The number of fourths in 1½. To calculate this, you want to divide 1½ by ¼ to see how many there are.
$1\frac{1}{2} \div \frac{1}{4} = \frac{3}{2} \div \frac{1}{4} = \frac{3}{2} \times 4 = 6$

II. $5 \times \frac{1}{2} = \frac{5}{2}$

III. $\frac{3}{2} \div 3 = \frac{3}{2} \times \frac{1}{3} = \frac{1}{2}$

$\frac{1}{2} < \frac{5}{2} < 6$
III, II, I.

31. C In the equation y = Zx – 2, Z is the slope of the line. You are given two points on the line: (0, –2) and (2, 5). You can calculate the slope either by plugging one of the points into the equation of the line and solving for Z or by using the formula for calculating slope.

Method 1: Plugging into the equation.
Use the point (2, 5) to plug into the equation so that Z does not get multiplied by 0.
y = Zx – 2
5 = Z(2) – 2
2Z = 7
Z = 7/2 = 3½

Method 2: Using both points in the slope formula. (0, –2) & (2, 5)
Slope formula: $(y_2 - y_1)/(x_2 - x_1)$
(5 – –2)/(2 – 0) = 7/2 = 3½

32. C The volume of a cube is found by cubing the length of the side. Volume = side³
216 = side³
6 = side

The surface area of a cube is found by multiplying the area of each face by the 6 faces.
Surface Area = 6 x Area of each face = 6 x side² = 6 x 6² = 216
Surface Area = 216 m²

33. C You must figure out the probability of winning the jackpot if you flip a heads and then add that to the probability of winning the jackpot if you flip a tails.

Jackpot with Heads: Multiply the probability of getting a heads by probability of rolling a 4.
= 1/2 x 1/6 = 1/12

Jackpot with Tails: Multiply the probability of tails by the probability of picking a heart.
= 1/2 x 13/52 = 13/104 = 1/8

Now, add the two probabilities.
1/12 + 1/8 = 2/24 + 3/24 = 5/24

34. A To determine how many times longer the room is, divide the length of the room by the length of the bacteria.

$(1.2 \times 10^1) \div (2 \times 10^{-6})$
First, divide the numbers. Then, divide the powers of ten by subtracting the exponents.
1.2 ÷ 2 = 0.6
$10^1 \div 10^{-6} = 10^{1-(-6)} = 10^7$
0.6×10^7

0.6×10^7 -- Convert into proper scientific notation.
$0.6 \times 10^7 = 6 \times 10^{-1} \times 10^7 = 6 \times 10^6$

Final Exam: Answers & Explanations

35. D   The data set is missing an element; let's call it n.

Place the rest of the elements in order: 76, 80, 81, 85, 92.

The median is the middle element in a list. If there is an even number of elements in your set, the median is the average of the two middle elements. In this case, when the missing element is included, there will be 6 elements, and the median must be the average of the two middle terms.

The median is 83, which is the average of 81 and 85. Therefore, 81 and 85 must remain the middle elements. The only way this can happen is if the missing element is greater than or equal to 85.

Answer D, 90, is the only answer that fits this requirement.

36. B   First, figure out Vanessa's typing rate.
"Vanessa can type 3 words for every 2 that Beth types."
Therefore, Vanessa can type 3/2 times faster than Beth.
Vanessa's rate = 3/2 x Beth's rate = 3/2 x 40 words per minute = 60 words per minute

Next, determine the amount of time that Vanessa typed.
Vanessa typed 4200 words, and she can type 60 words per minute.
If you divide the number of words by her rate, you will determine the time it takes.
Time Vanessa typed = Number of words ÷ Typing rate = 4200 ÷ 60 = 70 minutes

Finally, determine how many words Beth can type in 70 minutes.
Number of words Beth types = Beth's rate x Beth's time
= 40 words per minute x 70 minutes = 2800 words

37. A   The easiest way to visualize this problem is on a graph. If the diameter is 8, then the radius is 4. From the center at (–2, –2), go out 4 in each direction, and then draw the circle.

The point on the circle with the largest x-coordinate is 4 points from the center in the positive direction and with the same y-coordinate. 4 points away is at (–2 + 4, –2) = (2, –2)

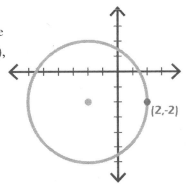

38. C   Let's examine each answer choice.

A. The smallest positive number for N is 1. Therefore, the smallest that N – 1 can be is 0; it can never be negative. N + 1 is positive if N is positive, therefore, this answer choice will never be negative.

B. N + 1 and N + 2 are both positive, and a positive times a positive is positive. Eliminate B.

C. The smallest positive is 1. If N = 1, then N(N – 2) = 1(1 – 2) = 1(–1) = –1. Answer C.

D. N is positive; positive times positive = positive. Eliminate D.

39. C A: 7/8
Convert the fraction to a decimal by dividing. $7/8 = 0.875$.
Now, subtract from 1. $1 - 0.875 = 0.125$

B: 1.12
Already in decimal form, so subtract 1. $1.12 - 1 = 0.12$

C: 0.9^2
Compute exponent. $0.9^2 = 0.9 \times 0.9 = 0.81$
Subtract from 1. $1 - 0.81 = 0.19$

D: 7/6
Convert to a decimal by dividing 7 by 6. $7 \div 6 = 1.1666...$
Subtract from 1. $1.1666... - 1 = 0.1666...$

Answer C is 0.19 from 1, which is the largest distance from 1.

40. C The student incorrectly assumed that to find the distance between two points you should add the vertical distance to the horizontal distance. However, the shortest distance between two points is the straight line that connects the two points. In this case, as can be seen in the diagram, it is the diagonal line between them.

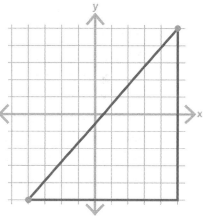

From looking at the diagram, a common way to calculate the distance between two points is to draw a right triangle with the hypotenuse connecting the points. The sides of the right triangle will be the horizontal distance (10 in this problem) and the vertical distance (10 in this problem), and then the hypotenuse or distance between the points can be calculated with the Pythagorean theorem.

41. C I. The greatest common factor of two numbers can be equal to one of the numbers. This is true. If one number divides evenly into the second number, then it would be the greatest common factor of the numbers. Example: the GCF of 8 and 16 is 8.

II. The least common multiple of two numbers can be equal to one of the numbers. This is true. If one number divides evenly into the second number, then the second number would be the least common multiple of the numbers. Example: the LCM of 6 and 24 is 24.

III. The product of two numbers can equal the product of their LCM and GCF. This is true. If one number divides evenly into the second number, then the smaller is the GCF, and the larger is the LCM. Therefore, the product of the two numbers would be equal to the product of the LCM and GCF.
Example: 5 and 10. GCF = 5; LCM = 10; product = 50.

Final Exam: Answers & Explanations

42. C To find the total number of possibilities, multiply the number of possible characters for each space in the code.

The first character must be a letter; therefore, there are 26 possibilities.
The second character must be a number; therefore, there are 10 possibilities.
The third character must be a distinct number; therefore, there are 9 possibilities (since one number was already used).

Total possibilities = 26 x 10 x 9 = 2340.

43. A Let the original price equal p.   p
The price was first increased by $17.   p + 17
This was decreased by 38%.   (100% – 38%)(p + 17)

Now, set this price equal to y and rearrange to isolate the original price p.
(100% – 38%)(p + 17) = y
(62%)(p + 17) = y
p + 17 = y/0.62
p = y/0.62 – 17

44. C The star in figure 1 has one point facing exactly up, while the star in figure 2 has one point facing exactly down. Either rotation or a flip about the x-axis would be necessary to reorient the star in that way, so eliminate answer B. The star in figure 2 is much closer to the axes than the star in figure one, so it must have been translated as well. Eliminate A and D.

45. B Simplify the inequality by dividing both sides by 5.
$5|y-2| \leq 10$
$|y-2| \leq 2$

Separate the inequality containing an absolute value into two statements joined by "and" as the absolute value or distance from zero is less than a certain value.
$y - 2 \leq 2$ and $y - 2 \geq -2$

Simplify both statements: $y \leq 4$ and $y \geq 0$
Combine the two statements joined by "and" into one statement. $0 \leq y \leq 4$

46. C A. Pyramid. All sides other than the base of a pyramid must be triangles. Therefore, you can have one side that is different, but all the rest must be triangles. This is not the case here.

B. Tetrahedron: A tetrahedron has 4 triangular faces. This diagram shows 5 sides. Eliminate.

C. A right triangular prism would have 2 faces that are right triangles, and the remaining faces would be rectangles. In addition, you can see that you can fold up each of the sides, and they would connect to form a prism. Answer C is correct.

D. Prism with equilateral triangle base. Not answer, as no equilateral triangles in this diagram.

47. C The data on the graph is close to a straight line, so it can best be represented by an equation of the form h = md + b, where h is the dependent variable, and d is the independent. The y-intercept is 5, so substitute 5 for b.

None of the points is an obvious outlier, so you can use any one of them to calculate an approximate slope. The final point appears to be (5, 7.5). Plug that point into the equation.
7.5 = m(5)+5
2.5 = 5m
m = 0.5

Slope of ½ and y-intercept of 5 gives the following equation: h = (½)d + 5

48. D The counting principle states that to determine the total number of possible outcomes, multiply the number of ways each event can occur. In this problem, there are 5 types of sandwiches, 4 types of chips, and 6 different drinks.

To find the number of possible outcomes, multiply 5 x 4 x 6 = 120.
There are 120 different lunch combinations.

49. C Distance from B to C = x
Distance from A to B = (½)x
Distance from A to C = A to B + B to C = x + (½)x = (3/2)x
Distance from C to D = (½)(3/2)x = (¾)x
Distance from A to D = A to B + B to C + C to D = x + (½)x + (¾)x = (2 ¼)x

50. B You start with an even number. Even.
You add it to an odd number. Even + Odd = Odd
Multiply it by an odd number. Odd x Odd = Odd
Subtract an even number. Odd – Even = Odd

Result is odd. You can also solve by picking numbers and plugging them in each step.

51. C |11 – 5| + 12 ÷ 3² x 6 – 10 =

Order of Operations is PEMDAS. Parentheses come first. The terms inside an absolute value sign are considered to be in parentheses.
|6| + 12 ÷ 3² x 6 – 10 = 6 + 12 ÷ 3² x 6 – 10 =

Next, Exponents.
6 + 12 ÷ 9 x 6 – 10 =

Next, Multiplication and Division from left to right.
6 + 12/9 x 6 – 10 = 6 + 4/3 x 6 – 10 = 6 + 8 – 10 =

Finally, Addition and Subtraction from left to right.
14 – 10 = 4

52. C A: $(-2)^0$: Anything to the zero power is equal to 1. Therefore, $(-2)^0 = 1$.

B: $(-2)^7$: This equals –2 times itself 7 times. Since we are multiplying 7 negatives, the answer will be negative. Therefore, this answer is smaller than A. Eliminate B.

C: $(-2)^8$: This equals –2 times itself 8 times. Since we are multiplying 8 negatives, the answer will be positive. Therefore, this equals 2^8.

D: -2^{10} : This equals $-(2^{10})$. Only the 2 is being raised to the power, so the answer is negative.

Answer C is the largest.

53. C Calculate the amount Ralph will make under each plan, then compare.

Plan 1: $55,000 base salary

Plan 2: $25,000 base salary + 15% of sales
First, convert the percent to a decimal. 15% = 0.15.
$25,000 + 0.15($200,000) = $25,000 + $30,000 = $55,000

Plan 3: $35,000 base salary + 1/8 of sales
First, convert the fraction to a decimal. 1/8 = 0.125.
$35,000 + 0.125($200,000) = $35,000 + $25,000 = $60,000

54. D When finding the limit, look at the highest orders of the polynomials in the numerator and denominator. As x approaches infinity, the highest exponent terms are more significant than the terms with exponents of 1 and 0.

$g(x) = (4x^2 - 2x + 8)/(2x^2 - 1)$

In the above function, the term with the highest exponent in the numerator is $4x^2$. The term with the highest exponent in the denominator is $2x^2$. As x approaches infinity, the terms with exponents of 0 and 1 will not have significant values.

The ratio of the coefficients for the x^2 terms will be the limit of the function. $4/2 = 2$

55. D Here are two ways to solve this problem.
Method 1: Find the length of the missing sides, find the areas of the triangle, and find the ratio. Since the triangles have the same angles, they are similar. Therefore, their sides are proportional.
The length of the side of Triangle T (2y) is twice as much as the corresponding side of Triangle S (y). So, the missing base of Triangle T is twice as much as the corresponding side. Missing side = 2(3/2 y) = 3y.

Area of a triangle = 1/2 x base x height
Area of Triangle S = (1/2)(y)(3/2 y) = 3/4 y^2
Area of Triangle T = (1/2)(2y)(3y) = 3y^2
Triangle T is 4 times as large as Triangle S.

Method 2: If you know the proportionality of the sides in one dimension, you can square that to find the proportionality of the area in 2-dimensions. The sides of Triangle T are twice as much as the lengths of Triangle S.

Therefore, square that to find the ratio of the areas. $2^2 = 4$.

56. C   Probability = favorable outcomes/total outcomes

The raindrop has an equal probability of landing on any one point, so the favorable outcomes are represented by the area of the circle, and the total outcomes are represented by the area of the blacktop.

Area of the circle: $\pi r^2 = 16\pi$

Area of the blacktop: length x width
Width is equal to the diameter of the circle = 4 x 2 = 8
Area blacktop = 16 x 8 = 128

Area of Circle/Area of blacktop: $(16\pi)/(128) = \pi/8$

57. C   Estimate the radius, and then compare your estimate to the student's estimate.

Circumference = 2π x radius = 24
π is approximately 3
Substitute that into the formula

2π x radius = 24
2(3) x radius ≈ 24
6 x radius ≈ 24
radius ≈ 4

The radius is approximately 4, and the student said the radius was approximately 8. The estimate is too high by a factor of 2.

58. A   Rate x time = distance

The distance around the track is 50 m + 50 m + the total circumference of the two half circles. The two semicircles make one whole circle. The circumference of the circle is π x diameter = 20π.

If you use 3 as an approximation for π, then the circumference is $20\pi \approx 20(3) = 60$. Distance is approximately 50 + 50 + 60 = 160 m

Joaquin jogs at 5 km per hour = 5000 m per hour
Rate x time = distance
5000 m per hour x time = 160 m
Time ≈ 0.03 hour
The coach estimated 0.5 hours. His estimate is 0.5/0.03, approximately 16 times too high.

59. D First, convert from feet to yards. Then, find the area of the wall. Finally, determine the number of rolls of paper that are needed.

15 ft x (1 yd/3 ft) = 5 yd

18 ft x (1 yd/3 ft) = 6 yd

Area = 5 yards x 6 yards = 30 square yards

30 square yards x 3 rolls/20 square yards = 90/20 rolls= 4 ½ rolls

The question asks how many rolls Noah will purchase. If he cannot purchase a part of a roll, then round up. 5 rolls.

60. A First, let's find the measure of Angle CBD. In a triangle, the measures of the angles must sum to 180°. In Triangle CBD, you know the measure of two of the angles, so add them up and subtract the sum from 180 to determine the measure of the third angle.
180° − (50° + 60°) = 180° − 110° = 70°. Angle CBD=70°

Now, let's find the measure of Angle ABD. You know that Angle ABD and Angle CBD form a straight angle, which must total 180°.
Angle ABD = 180° − Angle CBD = 180° − 70° = 110°. Angle ABD = 110°.

The problem stated that AB = BD. That makes Triangle ABD an isosceles triangle. The angles opposite equal sides are equal, so Angle ADB and Angle DAB are equal. We know the third angle in Triangle ABD is 110°, so we know the other two angles must sum to 70° so that the total of all three angles is 180°.

Therefore, we know that Angle ADB + Angle DAB = 70°. We also know that Angle ADB = Angle DAB, so each of the angles must equal 35°.

61. C The perimeter of a shape is the distance around its edges. The last side must be found.

Draw a vertical line through the middle of the shape to create a rectangle and a right triangle. The rectangle has dimensions of 4 by 8. The right triangle's sides are 4 and 3.

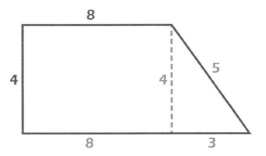

To find the missing side, use the Pythagorean theorem.

$3^2 + 4^2 = \text{hypotenuse}^2$

$9 + 16 = \text{hypotenuse}^2$

$25 = \text{hypotenuse}^2$

$5 = \text{hypotenuse}$

To find perimeter, sum the length of all the sides. Perimeter = 8 + 5 + 11 + 4 = 28

62. D The volume for a cylinder can be found with this formula: Volume = πr²h.
Note that the above formula is on the formula sheet.

Let's calculate the volumes of a cylinder with the minimum dimensions and the maximum dimensions and then subtract.

On the smaller end, the base radius would be 3 cm and the height would be 5 cm.
$V_{min} = πr^2h = π3^25 = 45π$

On the larger end, the base radius would be 5 cm and the height would be 9 cm.
$V_{max} = πr^2h = π5^29 = 225π$

The difference is 225π − 45π = 180π.

63. D Rearrange so the x's and y's are on the same side of the equations in the same order.
4x − 6y = −10, keep 1st equation in same order
3y = 5 + 2x; −2x + 3y = 5

Now, solve using elimination.
4x − 6y = −10
−2x + 3y = 5

Keep the first equation as is. Multiply the second equation by 2 to eliminate a variable. Then, add the two equations.
4x − 6y = −10 (1st eq)
−4x + 6y = 10 (2nd eq)
0 + 0 = 0 (sum of equations)

Since you get a true statement, that 0 = 0, it means that any solution to the first equation will be a solution to the second equation. The two equations are the same, just rearranged.

Infinite number of solutions to the system of equations. This can also be seen if you graphed the two equations. You would realize that you are graphing the exact same line.

64. C The range of a function is all the possible y-values. This graph shows that the function is continuous for all y-values. Therefore, the range is all real numbers from −∞ to ∞.

−∞ < y < ∞

65. B Plug x = 4 and x = 5 into the equation and calculate the difference in the outputs.

x = 4: $y = x^3 − x^2 = 4^3 − 4^2 = 64 − 16 = 48$
x = 5: $y = x^3 − x^2 = 5^3 − 5^2 = 125 − 25 = 100$

Difference in y-values: 100 − 48 = 52

66. B Let the width of the rectangle be w. Then, set up an equation for the length.

"The length of a rectangle is 5 feet less than 3 times the width"
length = 3w − 5

The perimeter is the length + length + width + width
Perimeter = 3w − 5 + 3w − 5 + w + w
Perimeter = 8w − 10

The perimeter must be less than 86 feet
8w − 10 < 86
8w < 96
w < 12

If the width must be a whole number and is less than 12 ft, the largest possible width is 11 ft.

67. C **Method 1**: The ratio of marbles Mike has to marbles David has is 5 to 8. Therefore, the ratio of the difference in the number of marbles to the marbles Mike has is 3 to 5.

Set up a proportion knowing that the difference in the number of marbles is 12. Also, let m represent the number of marbles Mike has.

Difference in number of marbles to marbles Mike has
= 3 to 5 = 12 to m
= 3/5 = 12/m

Cross-multiply, and solve.
3m = 60
m = 20

Mike has 20 marbles.

Method 2: Another way to solve this problem is to write the possible numbers of marbles each person has until you find a set of values with a difference of twelve. Assuming that each person can only have a whole number of marbles, the first few possibilities are
5/8, 10/16, 15/24, and 20/32

When David has 32 marbles, and Mike has 20, David will have 12 more marbles than Mike.

68. A Extrapolate from the pattern that is given. The pattern is 4 elements (shapes) long.

You are asked to predict the 61st element. The closest multiple of 4 to 61 is 60 (15 x 4). Since the 60th element would complete a repetition of the pattern, the 61st element is the first element of a new repetition—the first element in the pattern.

Therefore, the 61st object will be a circle.

69. D   The lowest possible sum of the two younger children's ages is 2s, and the highest possible sum is 2t.

If the oldest child is 7/3 times the sum of the younger children's ages, then the oldest child is older than (7/3)(2s) and younger than (7/3)(2t).

(7/3)(2s) < c < (7/3)(2t)
(14/3)s < c < (14/3)t

70. B   First, set up an equation to represent the relationship between the variables. Let k represent the constant of variation between the variables.

y varies directly with x and varies inversely with z.   y = kx/z

Now, plug in the values of the variables to find k.
y = kx/z
20 = 10k/2
20 = 5k
4 = k
y = 4x/z

Now, determine what y equals when x = 15 and z = 5.
y = 4x/z
y = (4)(15)/5
y = 60/5
y = 12

71. B   Use variables to represent the unknown quantities. Let the smallest number = n. Then, the second number would be n + 2. The next number would be n + 4.
Variables: n, n + 2, and n + 4. Now, set up an equation and solve for n.

Three times the second is 9 more than twice the third.
3(n + 2) = 9 + 2(n + 4)
3n + 6 = 9 + 2n + 8
3n + 6 = 2n + 17
n + 6 = 17
n = 11

72. C   **Method 1: Solve by switching x and y.** A method for solving for inverses is to switch the variables for x and y. Then, rearrange the equation to solve for y.

To find the inverse, switch the y and x in the original equation (y = x^2 + 5). Then, solve for y.
x = y^2 + 5
y^2 = x − 5
y = $\sqrt{x - 5}$

Final Exam: Answers & Explanations   571

Method 2: Check each solution to see which satisfies f(g(x)) = x and g(f(x)) = x.

If two functions are inverses of each other, then they must satisfy the following two rules: $f(g(x)) = x$ and $g(f(x)) = x$. Therefore, let's check each answer choice to see which satisfies both rules. Remember that $f(x) = x^2 + 5$.

A. $g(x) = -x^2 - 5$
$f(g(x)) = (-x^2 - 5)^2 + 5$
$f(g(x)) \neq x$ Eliminate A.

B. $g(x) = x^2 - 5$
$f(g(x)) = (x^2 - 5)^2 + 5$
$f(g(x)) \neq x$ Eliminate B.

C. $g(x) = \sqrt{(x - 5)}$
$f(g(x)) = (\sqrt{(x - 5)})^2 + 5$
$f(g(x)) = x - 5 + 5$
$f(g(x)) = x$

$g(f(x)) = \sqrt{(x^2 + 5 - 5)}$
$g(f(x)) = \sqrt{(x^2)}$
$g(f(x)) = x$

Inverse of f(x) is g(x). Answer C.

D. $g(x) = \sqrt{(x + 5)}$
$f(g(x)) = (\sqrt{(x + 5)})^2 + 5$
$f(g(x)) = x + 5 + 5$
$f(g(x)) = x + 10$
$f(g(x)) \neq x$ Eliminate D.

73. C   A. Domain is from –1 to 1.

The domain is all the possible input values for a function. In this case, the domain is all values from $-\infty$ to ∞. As you can see, the function is defined for all values of x, less than –1, from –1 to 1, and greater than 1. Eliminate A.

B. Range is from –1 to 1.

The range represents all possible outputs. It is clear that the range is not restricted to just values between –1 and 1. For instance, when x = 0, the output, f(x) = 5. Eliminate B.

C. Function has discontinuities at –1 and 1.

This function is a piecewise function. The discontinuities are at the transition points of the function. In this case, the discontinuities are at x = –1 and x = 1. Answer C is correct.

D. Function has a maximum at x = 0.

First, let's find the value at x = 0. When x = 0, f(x) = 5. Therefore, we have to examine this function and see if there are any outputs greater than 5. As can be seen, when x > 1, the function keeps growing. For instance, when x = 19, $f(19) = 2(19+1)^2 = 800$. Eliminate D.

74. D The y-intercept of a graph is the point on the graph that crosses the y-axis. If a point is on the y-axis, then its x-value is 0. Therefore, plug in x = 0 to find the y-intercept.

$y = 3x^2 - 8x + 9$
$y = 3(0^2) - 8(0) + 9$
$y = 9$

75. B Let's first analyze the problem.

Uniform distribution: This is a distribution where each element has the same likelihood of occurring. For instance, flipping a coin has a uniform distribution since it is the same probability that you will get heads or tails. In addition, rolling a standard dice has a uniform distribution, since it is equally likely that each number will be rolled. This does not affect the mean, median, or probability of elements being chosen, but it is worth noting.

I: The mean is found by taking the sum of all the elements and then dividing by the total number of elements. If you multiply each element by 3, their sum will also be multiplied by 3. Since the number of elements stays the same at 6, the mean will be multiplied by 3. I is true.

II: The median is found by listing all the elements from smallest to largest and taking the middle element. Since there is an even number of elements, 6 in this case, the median is the average of the two middle values. However, multiplying each element by 3 will just be the same as multiplying the two middle values by 3 and, therefore, increasing their average by a factor of 3. II is true.

III: The probability each element is chosen is not at all affected by changing its value. The probability of the lowest element being chosen will stay the same. III is false.

76. C Let's first determine the equation of each line.

The vertical line.
The equation for the vertical line is x = −1. In this case, the values that are less than −1 are shaded. Therefore, the inequality that represents this is x ≤ −1.

The diagonal line.
The diagonal line has a y-intercept of 0 and a slope of −½. Therefore, the equation of the line is y = −½ x. The region below this line is shaded. The inequality that represents this is y ≤ −½ x.

Only the overlapped region of the two inequalities is shaded, which is only the areas that make both inequalities true. "AND" is used to represent only areas that satisfy the first inequality and the second inequality.

x ≤ −1 and y ≤ −½ x

77. B This problem has given you the coordinate pairs of two points on the line and is asking you to find a third point. Using the first two points, find the equation of the line, then plug in the year 2009 to find the number of employees.

x = year; y = number of employees
Two points: (2004, 0) and (2006, 250)

Slope is change in y divided by change in x
Slope = (250 − 0)/(2006 − 2004) = 250/2 = 125

Equation: y = mx + b. We have m, so plug in a point to find b.
y = 125x + b
0 = 125(2004) + b
b = −250,500

y = 125x − 250,500

Now, plug in x = 2009 to find the number of employees in that year.
y = 125(2009) − 250,500
y = 625

There will be 625 employees in 2009.

78. D Let's figure out the rate of each painter. The painter can paint a wall 10 m x 10 m in 2 hours. Therefore, he can paint 100 sq m in 2 hours, or to reduce that, 50 sq m in 1 hour.

Now, we have 2 painters. The rate of one painter is 50 sq m in 1 hour. If you have 2 painters working at the same rate, then they can paint 100 sq m in 1 hour.

The wall is 40 m x 40 m.
The area of the new wall is 40 m x 40 m = 1600 sq m.
The two painters rate is 100 sq m in 1 hour; thus, to paint 1600 sq m, it will take 16 hours.

79. B As can be seen in the graph, the distance that the car travels increases steadily during the first part of the car's trip. If the distance increases at a steady rate, that means the speed is staying the same over that period.

During the second part of the trip, the car's distance increases exponentially. Therefore, the car is accelerating, and the speed is increasing.

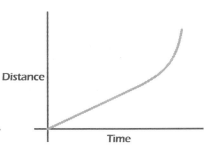

80. C If there are 60 marbles in a bag and the probability of being green or red is 5/12, then you can multiply the probability by the total number to find the number of red or green marbles.

Red or Green marbles = 60 x 5/12 = 25
We know there are 5 green marbles. So, the number of red marbles is 25 − 5 = 20 marbles.

81. D Let's assign the variable x to represent the number of shirts and y to represent the number of work pants. Then, the equations would be

4x + 5y = $115
2x + 3y = $65

Here are the matrices that represent these equations. You can perform matrix multiplication to confirm.

$$\begin{bmatrix} 4 & 5 \\ 2 & 3 \end{bmatrix} \begin{bmatrix} x \\ y \end{bmatrix} = \begin{bmatrix} \$115 \\ \$65 \end{bmatrix}$$

82. D First, note that all answer choices are of trigonometric functions. Therefore, if we know that a trigonometric function passes through the point (0, –3), then it must have an amplitude of 3. If we look at the coefficient in front of the trigonometric function, we see that answer C has an amplitude of only 1 and can be eliminated. Now, let's review the other choices.

A: y = –3cos(x)
From the graph of a cosine function or the unit circle, cos(0) = 1 and cos(π) = –1.
(0, –3): –3cos(0) = –3(1) = –3 True
(π, 0): –3 cos(π) = –3(–1) = 3 False

B: y = –3sin(x + π)
From the graph of a sine function or the unit circle, you know that sin(π) = 0.
(0, –3): –3sin(0 + π) = –3sin(π) = –3(0) = 0 False

C: y = -sin(3x + π)
Eliminated as amplitude was 1 and not 3.

D: y = –3 cos(x/2)
First, let's plug in both coordinate pairs.
(0, –3): –3cos(0/2) = –3cos(0) = –3 True
(π, 0): –3cos(π/2) = –3(0) = 0 True

The graph of this equation would have an amplitude of 3. In addition, since the coefficient is negative, the entire graph would be reflected across the x-axis. Finally, the period of the graph is 4π.

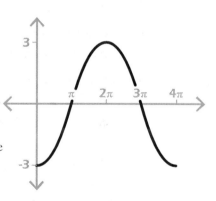

83. B The union of two sets includes all the unique elements that appear in either set with no repeats. The intersection of two sets includes all the unique elements that appear in both sets.

A = {–6, –3, 0, 3, 6}, B = {–4, –3, –2, –1, 0, 1, 2, 3, 4}

Union: A U B = {–6, –4, –3, –2, –1, 0, 1, 2, 3, 4, 6}: 11 elements in the union
To find the union, list out all members in each set, and don't include repeats.

Intersection: A ∩ B = {–3, 0, 3}: 3 elements in the intersection
To find the intersection, find all the elements that appear in both sets.

There are 8 more elements in the union than the intersection.

84. A Base 10 is the number system that we are used to. We want to move to a base 2 number. The value of each number in a base 2 number is multiplied by consecutive powers of 2. Let's first list out a few powers of 2.

$2^0 = 1$	$2^3 = 8$	$2^6 = 64$	$2^9 = 512$
$2^1 = 2$	$2^4 = 16$	$2^7 = 128$	$2^{10} = 1024$
$2^2 = 4$	$2^5 = 32$	$2^8 = 256$	

Now, start with the largest possible power of 2 that goes into 531. That is 2 to the 9th power. That is equal to 512. Thus, you have $531 - 512 = 19$ left.

Now, looking at the next highest power of 2 that goes into 19 is 2 to the 4th power, which is equal to 16. This gives you $19 - 16 = 3$ left.

Then, you have 2 to the power of 1 that goes into 3, leaving you with $3 - 2 = 1$ left.

Finally, 2 to the power of 0 is 1.

As a summary, we will have 1 for 2^9, 1 for 2^4, 1 for 2^1, and 1 for 2^0. Remember the 0th power is in the first place, 1st power in the 2nd place, and so on. So, the 9th power will be the 10th place. Thus, write out the number with a 1 in the 10th, 5th, 2nd, and 1st place. 1000010011

85. A Since the variable k does not have an exponent, you can tell this is an arithmetic series. You could also find the first few numbers in the sequence to confirm.

Now, we want to use the formula for the sum of an arithmetic series, which is included on the formula sheet.

$$S_n = \frac{n}{2}[2a + (n-1)d] = n\left(\frac{a + a_n}{2}\right)$$

We will use the first part of the equation as the second part would have too many unknowns.

Find the value of the variables that can be calculated.

a, the first term is when $k = 1$, $a_1 = \frac{1}{2} + 1 = \frac{3}{2} = 1.5$.

d, the difference between terms, is $\frac{1}{2} = 0.5$. You could either find the second term, $a_2 = 2$, or you could realize that $\frac{1}{2}$ is multiplied by k, so each term will be increased by $\frac{1}{2}$.

$S_n = (n/2)[2(1.5) + (n-1)(0.5)]$
$26 = (n/2)[3 + 0.5n - 0.5]$
$26 = (n/2)[2.5 + 0.5n]$

$52 = n[2.5 + 0.5n]$	Multiply both sides by 2 to remove fraction.
$52 = 2.5n + 0.5n^2$	
$104 = 5n + n^2$	Multiply all terms by 2 to remove decimals.
$n^2 + 5n - 104 = 0$	Move all terms to one side to solve quadratic.
$(n + 13)(n - 8) = 0$	Set both terms equal to zero to find possible values of n.
$n = -13; n = 8$	

Since n cannot be negative, $n = 8$.

86. D When analyzing the graphs of quadratic equations, there are a few key pieces to look at:
1 – Does the graph open up or down? In this case, the graph opens up. So, the variable a, the coefficient in front of the x^2 term, will be positive. Eliminate C, which has a negative a.

2 – What is the y-intercept? This graph intercepts the y-axis at y = 5. So, you know that when x = 0, y = 5. Plug x = 0 into the remaining equations to solve for y. Since each quadratic equation is in standard form, $y = ax^2 + bx + c$, you can see that when you plug in x = 0, you will get y = c. Therefore, check each equation to see which has c = 5. Eliminate answer B.

3 – What is the vertex? The x-coordinate of the vertex can be found by calculating –b/2a. In this case, the x-coordinate of the vertex is 2. Let's check the remaining choices, A and D.

A. $2x^2 - 3x + 5$: x-coordinate of vertex = –b/2a = 3/4
D. $2x^2 - 8x + 5$: x-coordinate of vertex = –b/2a = 8/4 = 2

87. B Using the lattice multiplication method, each square is the product of the numbers in its row and column. The four missing numbers each represent the digit in the tens place.
The multiplication problem has been completed to the right. But, let's go through each step.

In the square in the upper right, 8 x 3 = 24. The 2 is missing.
In the square in the upper left, 5 x 3 = 15. The 1 is missing.
In the square in the lower right, 8 x 9 = 72. The 7 is missing.
In the square in the lower left, 5 x 9 = 45. The 4 is missing.

After all the numbers in the squares are completed, the diagonals are summed. Starting in the lower right, the first diagonal has just a 2, so the sum is 2. The next diagonal: 5 + 7 + 4 = 16. Put the 6 at the end of the diagonal and carry the 1. Then, the next: 1 + 2 + 5 + 4 = 12. Put the 2 down, and carry the 1. Finally, 1 + 1 = 2.

58 x 39 = 2262. The question asks for the sum of the missing numbers. 1 + 2 + 4 + 7 = 14

88. C Perpendicular lines have slopes that are negative reciprocals. Or, you can think of it as the slopes of perpendicular lines have slopes that multiply to –1.

Therefore, first find the slope of the original equation and then check each answer choice.
3x + y = 6   Rearrange equation to put in slope-intercept form.
y = –3x + 6   In this form, the slope is the coefficient in front of the x. Slope = –3.

A line perpendicular to that equation will have a slope of ⅓, as that is the negative reciprocal of –3. (⅓)(–3) = –1. Now, let's go through each answer to find which has a slope of ⅓.

A: –3x + y = 6   y = 3x + 6   Slope = 3
B: –6x – y = –3   –6x + 3 = y   Slope = –6
C: –x/3 + y = 10   y = x/3 + 10   Slope = ⅓
D: x + 3y = 6   3y = –x + 6   y = –x/3 + 6   Slope = –⅓

89. D When solving a question involving finding the percentiles, first order your data points.
54, 61, 62, 68, 71, 72, 75, 76, 76, 78, 80, 82, 85, 86, 88, 89, 91, 92, 94, 100

Next, figure out how many data points you are dealing with. In this case, we have 20 scores.

Finally, simply multiply the percentile as a percent by the number of data points. This will give you the data point that is at that percentile.
85% x 20 = 0.85 x 20 = 17

Thus, the 17th data point will be at the 85th percentile. The score 91 is the 85th percentile.

90. B You can use the discriminant to determine the types of roots that a quadratic equation will have. Remember, the discriminant equals $b^2 - 4ac$ and is derived from the quadratic formula.

Note that the discriminant is the part of the quadratic formula under the radical sign. If the discriminant is negative, you can tell that the roots will be complex, because you would be taking the square root of a negative number. Therefore, since you want the quadratic equation with two complex roots, find the quadratic that has a negative discriminant.

$$x = \frac{-b \pm \sqrt{b^2 - 4ac}}{2a}$$

A: $y = -3x^2 + 4x + 2$, $a = -3$, $b = 4$, $c = 2$
discriminant = $4^2 - 4(-3)(2) = 16 + 24 = 40$, Two real roots

B: $y = 2x^2 - 7x + 9$, $a = 2$, $b = -7$, $c = 9$
discriminant = $(-7)^2 - 4(2)(9) = 49 - 72 = -23$, Two complex roots

C: $y = x^2 - 29$, $a = 1$, $b = 0$, $c = -29$
discriminant = $0 - 4(1)(-29) = 116$, Two real roots

D: $y = 4x^2 + 13x + 2$, $a = 4$, $b = 13$, $c = 2$
discriminant = $13^2 - 4(4)(2) = 169 - 32 = 137$, Two real roots

91. D You can use the handy phrase SOH CAH TOA and remember that the tangent of an angle is equal to the opposite side over the adjacent side.
tan Θ = 5/12 = AB/AC

Since we want to solve for AC, let's put each unknown in terms of AC.
AB = (5/12)AC

Next, since we are dealing with a right triangle, we can use the Pythagorean theorem.
$AB^2 + AC^2 = 26^2$

$[(5/12)AC]^2 + AC^2 = 26^2$	Substitute value for AB into equation.
$(25/144)AC^2 + AC^2 = 26^2$	
$25AC^2 + 144AC^2 = 144(26^2)$	Multiply both sides by 144 to remove fraction.
$169AC^2 = 144(26^2)$	
$AC^2 = 144(26^2)/169 = 144(4) = 576$	
$AC = \sqrt{576} = 24$	

Final Exam: Answers & Explanations

92. A You could analyze the equations or the graphs. Let's review the graphs.

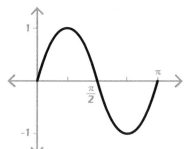

$f(x) = \sin(2x)$
Amplitude = 1
Period = π
Phase Shift = 0

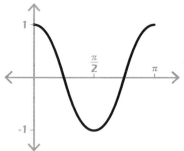

$g(x) = \cos(2x)$
Amplitude = 1
Period = π
Phase Shift = 0

You can see that they are the same graphs with just a shift in the x-direction. The function $g(x)$ is the same as $f(x)$ but shifted by $\pi/4$ in the negative x-direction.

$g(x) = f(x + \pi/4)$. You can plug in a few points from the functions to confirm.

93. C You could evaluate this question by using the formula for finding integrals, or you could find the area under the curve, or line in this case. Let's find the area. First, graph the line and then find the area under the line from 2 to 11.

To find the area, first find the vertices. You can plug x = 2 and x = 11 into the equation for the line to find the y-coordinates of the vertices.

(2, 0), (11, 0), (2, 4), (11, 8.5)

To find the area, you can separate the trapezoid into a rectangle and a triangle, and then find the sum of their areas.

Rectangle: 4 x 9 = 36
Triangle: (1/2) x 9 x 4.5 = 20.25

Total Area = 36 + 20.25 = 56.25
Integral = 56.25

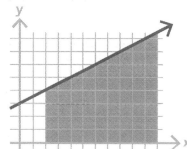

Final Exam: Answers & Explanations   579

94. B

Remember that S stands for Side, A stands for Angle. Also, remember that if two triangles are congruent, then all the sides and all the angles are equal.

There were three postulates that you learned to prove triangles are congruent. Postulates are statements that are accepted as true without proof. The three postulates for proving triangles congruent were

SSS: Side-Side-Side: If three sides of one triangle are congruent to three sides of another triangle, then the two triangles are congruent.

SAS: Side-Angle-Side: If two sides and the angle in between in one triangle are congruent to two sides and the included angle in a second triangle, then the two triangles are congruent.

ASA: Angle-Side-Angle: If two angles and the side in between in one triangle are congruent to two angles and the included side in a second triangle, then the two triangles are congruent.

Now, we know the above are all valid postulates for proving triangles congruent, let's examine the other suggested methods.

SSA: Side-Side-Angle: This is not a valid method of proving triangles congruent. Just because two sides and one angle are equal does not mean the triangles are congruent. See the diagram below for an example.

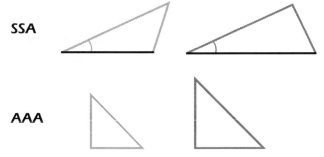

AAA: Angle-Angle-Angle: This is used for proving two triangles are similar, but not congruent. For instance, you can easily think of two 45–45–90 degree triangles that have the same angles, but are not the same size. See diagram for a counterexample showing two triangles with the same angles, but not congruent.

AAS: Angle-Angle-Side: If we know two angles of a triangle, we can find the third angle by subtracting the sum of the first two angles from 180 degrees. So, if two angles of triangles are congruent, then all angles of the triangle are congruent. Thus, we know two angles and the side in between the angles is congruent to another triangle. We know that ASA is a postulate that holds true, and therefore, AAS is also true. Therefore, this can be used to prove congruent triangles.

Four methods for proving triangles are congruent: SSS, SAS, ASA, AAS.

95. D First, note that the series is a geometric series as the variable is in the exponent; thus having the same quotient between consecutive numbers in the sequence: a quotient of 1/4. You are asked to find the ratio for two different sums. Calculate each and then find ratio.

n = ∞. If n equals infinity, this is an infinite geometric series, and we can use the formula on the formula sheet to solve.

$$\sum_{n=0}^{\infty} ar^n = \frac{a}{1-r}, |r| < 1$$

In this case, r = 1/4 = 0.25, a = 2.
Sum = 2/(1 − 0.25) = 2/(0.75) = 2/(3/4) = 8/3

n = 4. You can use the formula for the sum of a geometric series, also on the formula sheet.

$$S_n = \frac{a(1-r^n)}{1-r}$$

In this case, r = 1/4 = 0.25, a = 2, and n = 4.
S_{20} = 2(1 − 0.25^4)/(1 − 0.25) = 2(1−(1/256))/0.75 = 2(255/256)/(3/4) = (8/3)(255/256)

Now, find the ratio.
(8/3)/[(8/3)(255/256)] = 256/255

96. B The optimal result for a linear programming problem will be equal to one of the vertices of the feasible region. To find the result, plug each coordinate pair into the function to be maximized.

Maximize: −3x + 2y
Vertices: (2, 2), (3, 0), (6, 0), and (6, 4)

(2, 2): −3(2) + 2(2) = −2
(3, 0): −3(3) + 2(0) = −9
(6, 0): −3(6) + 2(0) = −18
(6, 4): −3(6) + 2(4) = −10

Optimal combination: (2, 2)

97. B   Since we are not dealing with a right triangle, we are going to have to use trigonometry to solve this question. In this case, we know all the angles, and we know the measure of one side. Therefore, we can use the Law of Sines to calculate the missing sides. The Law of Sines is given on your formula sheet. $$\frac{a}{\sin A} = \frac{b}{\sin B} = \frac{c}{\sin C}$$

The problem is asking for AB, the side opposite Angle C, which equals 30°. We are given that AC, the side opposite Angle B, is 12. Therefore, we can set up the following equation.
b/sin B = c/sin C
12/sin 135 = c/sin 30

Next, we must find the sines of those angles. From a 30–60–90 triangle, you should remember that sin 30° = 1/2. In addition, from the unit circle or the graph of a sine function, you should note that sin 135 = sin 45 = √2/2.

Now, plug those back in, and solve for the missing side.
12/(√2/2) = c/(1/2)
12/√2 = c

Multiply numerator and denominator by √2.
12√2/2 = c
6√2 = c
AB = 6√2

98. A   A: Taking the derivative of an integral of a function will equal the original function.
This is true. Remember the integral is also called the anti-derivative. Let's try an example to illustrate this property. Let's use the function x^m. Now, plug into the formula for integrals:

So, the integral of $x^m = x^{m+1}/(m + 1) + C$. $$\int x^n = \frac{x^{n+1}}{n+1} + C$$

Next, we will take the derivative of the result.
Remember the definition of the derivative: $d/dx\ (x^n) = nx^{n-1}$

$d/dx\ (x^{m+1}/(m + 1) + C)$
Note that the derivative of a constant is equal to zero, as a constant would be a horizontal line, and therefore, the slope of the line tangent to that constant would be zero.
$d/dx(x^{m+1}/(m + 1)) = (m + 1)x^m/(m + 1) = x^m$
Therefore, if we take the derivative of the integral of x^m, the result is x^m.

B: The integral is equal to the rate of change at any given point along a curve.
This is the definition of a derivative, not an integral. The derivative is equal to the rate of change or slope at any given point along a curve. The integral equals the area under a curve.

C: The area under a curve from 0 to ∞ is called the integral.
This one is close to a true statement. The area under a curve is equal to the integral. However, it does not have to be from 0 to ∞. Refer to the lesson to see many examples of integrals that were from various intervals along the axis.

99. B This is a simple application of the formula for exponential growth, and in particular, for compound interest. The formula is

$A = P(1 + r/n)^{nt}$
A = accumulated amount
P = principal (amount invested)
r = interest rate
n = number of times amount compounds
t = time of investment

Thus, in this case, we are trying to solve for A.
P = $2000
r = 4% = 0.04
n = 4 as interest compounds quarterly or four times a year
t = 10 years

$A = 2000(1 + 0.04/4)^{4(10)}$
$A = 2000(1 + 0.01)^{40}$
$A = 2000(1.01)^{40}$

This is impossible to calculate without a calculator, and you wouldn't be required to on the test, but in case you were curious, the amount in this case is $2977.73.

100. B The derivative of the sine function is the cosine function, but you wouldn't have learned that yet or need to know that. However, you can still solve this question quite easily. The derivative of a function at a point is the slope of the tangent line at that point. Therefore, you can examine the graph of the sine function and find the points whose tangents will have a slope of 0. Remember, horizontal lines have a zero slope, and therefore, if the tangent is horizontal, that point will have a derivative of zero.

As you can see in the graph, two points have tangents that are horizontal lines.

This occurs when $x = \pi/2$ and $x = 3\pi/2$.

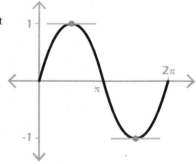

Final Exam: Answers & Explanations

12. Appendix

Formula Sheet 586
Glossary 588

Appendix: Formula Sheet

The following formulas will be provided to you on the day of the test. This list is taken from the latest version published by www.mtel.nesinc.com.

Description	Formula
Sum of the measures of the interior angles in a polygon	$S = (n-2) \times 180$
Circumference of a circle	$C = 2\pi r$
Area of a circle	$A = \pi r^2$
Area of a triangle	$A = \frac{1}{2}bh$
Surface area of a sphere	$A = 4\pi r^2$
Lateral surface area of a right circular cone	$A = \pi r \sqrt{r^2 + h^2}$
Surface area of a cylinder	$A = 2\pi rh + 2\pi r^2$
Volume of a sphere	$V = \frac{4}{3}\pi r^3$
Volume of a right cone and a pyramid	$V = \frac{1}{3}Bh$
Volume of a cylinder	$V = \pi r^2 h$
Sum of an arithmetic series	$S_n = \frac{n}{2}[2a + (n-1)d] = n\left(\frac{a + a_n}{2}\right)$
Sum of a geometric series	$S_n = \frac{a(1 - r^n)}{1 - r}$
Sum of an infinite geometric series	$\sum_{n=0}^{\infty} ar^n = \frac{a}{1-r}, \ |r| < 1$
Distance formula	$d = \sqrt{(x_2 - x_1)^2 + (y_2 - y_1)^2}$
Midpoint formula	$\left(\frac{x_1 + x_2}{2}, \frac{y_1 + y_2}{2}\right)$
Slope	$m = \frac{\Delta y}{\Delta x} = \frac{y_2 - y_1}{x_2 - x_1}$
Law of sines	$\frac{a}{\sin A} = \frac{b}{\sin B} = \frac{c}{\sin C}$
Law of cosines	$c^2 = a^2 + b^2 - 2ab \cos C$
Arc length	$s = r\theta$
Density of an object	$D = \frac{m}{V}$
Quadratic formula	$x = \frac{-b \pm \sqrt{b^2 - 4ac}}{2a}$

Appendix: Glossary

Absolute Value: The magnitude or distance a number is from zero. It is always expressed as a positive number. Example: The absolute value of 7, written as $|7|$ is 7. $|-3| = 3$.

Acute angle: An angle that has a measure between 0 and 90 degrees.

Amplitude: The amplitude of a periodic function is the absolute value of the maximum or minimum y-axis point that is reached.

Area: The two-dimensional space inside an object.

Arithmetic Series: A series that has a constant difference between each pair of consecutive terms.

Associative: Property that states for problems containing just addition or just multiplication, grouping of numbers does not affect the result.

Asymptote: Lines that graphs will approach but never reach. These include vertical and horizontal lines.

Axioms: Statements that are accepted as true without proof.

Axis of Symmetry: The line along which the graph of a quadratic equation is symmetric.

Base: The number of digits in a number system. The decimal number system is the one we use standardly, and it has 10 digits and is thus base 10.

Bisector: A line that cuts an angle in half.

Census: A method of gathering data for which information is gathered from every item in a group.

Chord: A line that begins at one point on the circle and ends at another, but does not necessarily pass through the center.

Circumference: The perimeter of a circle, which is equal to the product of π and the diameter of the circle.

Closure: A set is said to be closed under an operation if the operation is performed to members of the set, and the result is also in the set.

Combination: The number of ways a group of elements can be chosen from a larger set of elements when the order of the chosen elements does not matter.

Commutative: Property that states for problems containing only multiplication or only addition, order does not matter.

Complementary: Angles that add up to 90 degrees.

Complex Numbers: Numbers that include an imaginary part. The imaginary part is represented by i, which is equal to the square root of negative 1.

Composition of Functions: A process of combining two functions where one function is performed first and then the result of which is the input to the other function.

Concavity: The curve of a graph. Either concave up or concave down.

Congruent: Two polygons that are congruent have the same size and shape. All the sides and angles of the shapes will be equal.

Conic-Section: The intersection of a plane through one or two cones.

Coordinate Plane: Shows relationship between two variables with a horizontal number line called the x-axis and a vertical number line called the y-axis.

Correlation: A statistic that measures how closely one variable tracks with another. The range of the correlation statistic is [–1, 1].

Cosine: A trigonometric function, abbreviated cos. For a right triangle, the cosine of an angle is equal to the length of the adjacent side divided by the hypotenuse.

Counting Numbers: Positive numbers: 1, 2, 3, 4... Also called natural numbers.

Cross-Section: The intersection of a plane through a 3-dimensional object, which creates a 2-dimensional object.

Deductive Reasoning: A form of reasoning by which each conclusion follows from the previous conclusion, and it builds toward a final statement.

Denominator: The part of a fraction that lies below the line. It serves as the divisor of the numerator.

Dependent Variable: The observed result of the changes in the independent variable.

Derivative: Slope of tangent line at a point where it touches a graph.

Diameter: Any line that begins at one point on a circle, passes through the center, and ends at another point on the circle.

Difference: The result of a subtraction problem.

Dilation: A transformation for which an object's coordinates are all increased proportionately.

Direct Variation: When the value of a variable is equal to a constant multiplied by another variable. $y = kx$

Distributive: A property indicating a way in which multiplication is applied to addition of two or more numbers. Each term inside a set of parentheses can be multiplied by a factor outside the parentheses. $a(b + c) = ab + ac$

Dividend: A number to be divided. For example, in the division problem $16 \div 8 = 2$, 16 is the dividend.

Divisor: The number by which a dividend is divided. For example, in the division problem $16 \div 8 = 2$, 8 is the divisor.

Divisible: Whether a number is capable of being divided. In other words, if a number is divisible by 3, then 3 is a factor of that number.

Domain: A description of all the inputs or x-values for which a function has a valid output.

Equilateral: An equilateral polygon has sides of equal length.

Even Number: Any integer that is divisible by 2.

Expanded Form: Writing a number as the sum of the value of each of its digits. Example: 321 in expanded form = 300 + 20 + 1.

Exponent: The exponent represents how many times a number is to be multiplied by itself. Exponent is also called power.

Exponential Function: A function where the rate of change continually increases or decreases along the graph.

Factor: An integer that divides evenly into a number with no remainder. Example: 4 is a factor of 12.

Factorial: The factorial of a positive integer is equal to the product of all positive integers less than or equal to that number.

Fibonacci Sequence: A famous sequence where each successive number is equal to the sum of the two previous numbers. The Fibonacci sequence is 1, 1, 2, 3, 5, 8, 13, 21...

Finite Differences: A method for determining whether a set of points fits a polynomial.

FOIL: An acronym standing for First Outer Inner Last. It is a method for multiplying two binomials.

Frequency Distribution: An organization of raw data where the data is grouped into bins, and the frequency of occurrence is counted for each bin.

Function: A specific type of relation for which each independent variable produces exactly one dependent variable.

Fundamental Theorem of Arithmetic: The Fundamental Theorem of Arithmetic states that every positive integer can be expressed as a product of prime numbers.

Geometric Series: A series that has a constant ratio between each pair of consecutive terms.

Greatest Common Factor (GCF): The GCF of two numbers is the largest factor that they share. Example: GCF of 18 and 24 is 6.

Identity: The identity of addition is 0. Therefore, any number plus zero will equal itself. The identity of multiplication is 1. Therefore, any number times 1 will equal itself.

Improper Fractions: Fractions with numerators that are greater than or equal to the denominator.

Independent Variable: The variable that is being manipulated or changed.

Inductive Reasoning: A form of reasoning in which a conclusion is reached based on a pattern that can be seen in numerous observations.

Infinity: The idea that something never ends. The symbol for infinity looks like a sideways 8 and is used in math to represent a number that is endlessly large.

Inflection Point: Points on a graph where the graph changes concavity.

Integers: ...–3, –2, –1, 0, 1, 2, 3... Integers include negative, zero, and positive numbers. Any number that must be expressed as a fraction or decimal is not an integer.

Integral: Area under a curve.

Indirect Variation: When the value of a variable is equal to a constant divided by another variable. y = k/x. If two variables vary indirectly, then they are inversely proportional.

Inequality: A statement about the relationship between two values that are not equal.

Intersection: The intersection of two sets contains all the unique elements that appear in both sets.

Irrational Number: Any number that cannot be expressed as a fraction, such as decimals that do not terminate or repeat. The square root of 2 and pi are examples of irrational numbers.

Isosceles Triangle: A triangle that has exactly two equal sides and exactly two equal angles.

Lattice Method: A method for multiplying large numbers using a visual representation of a lattice. More on this method can be seen in Computation Methods in the Numbers & Operations chapter.

Law of Cosines: A trigonometric law used to find missing lengths and angles on triangles. The law is provided on the formula sheet. $c^2 = a^2 + b^2 - 2ab \cos C$.

Law of Sines: A trigonometric law used to find missing lengths and angles on triangles. The law is provided on the formula sheet. $a/\sin A = b/\sin B = c/\sin C$.

Least Common Denominator: The least common multiple of all the denominators in an addition or subtraction problem involving fractions.

Least Common Multiple (LCM): The LCM of two numbers is the smallest non-zero multiple that they both share. Example: LCM of 15 and 20 is 60.

Limit: The value a function approaches as a variable grows infinitely positive or infinitely negative.

Linear Programming: A mathematical technique used to optimize a particular relationship.

Matrix: A rectangular array consisting of rows and columns of numbers or variables.

Mean: The average of a set of numbers, which is equal to the sum of the numbers divided by the number of numbers.

Median: The middle number in a set of numbers.

Mixed Number: A number containing both a fraction and an integer. For example, $3\frac{4}{5}$ is a mixed number.

Mode: The most frequently occurring number or piece of data in a set of data.

Multiple: A multiple of a number is equal to that number times an integer. Example: Multiples of 12 include 12, 24, 36, and 48.

Natural Numbers: Positive numbers: 1, 2, 3, 4... Also called counting numbers.

Net: A pattern in two dimensions that can be used to generate a 3-dimensional object.

Number Line: A straight line used for representing positive and negative numbers.

Numerator: The part of a fraction that is above the line. The numerator signifies the number to be divided by the denominator.

Obtuse Angle: An angle that is greater than 90 degrees but less than 180 degrees.

Odd Number: Any integer that is not divisible by 2.

Order of Operations: Often called PEMDAS. For problems with multiple operations, this is the standardized order in which operations must be carried out. The order is Parentheses, Exponents, Multiplication and Division from left to right, and Addition and Subtraction from left to right.

Origin: The point at which the x-axis and the y-axis intersect. Coordinates of origin are (0, 0).

Parallel Lines: Lines that never intersect and have the same slope.

Partial Products Method: A method for multiplying large numbers. It involves taking the base ten factors of each number, multiplying all pairs of the resulting terms, and then finding their sum.

Pascal's Triangle: A counting algorithm that can be used to find the coefficients of the binomial expansion $(x + y)^n$.

Perimeter: The distance around the edge of an object.

Period: The period of a graph is the interval for which the function repeats.

Permutation: The number of ways a group of elements can be chosen from a larger set of elements when the order of the chosen elements matters.

Perpendicular Lines: Lines that intersect to form four 90-degree angles. The slopes of perpendicular lines are negative reciprocals of each other.

Perspective Drawing: An illustration of a 3-dimensional object on a 2-dimensional surface.

Phase Shift: A phase shift of a periodic function (such as sine or cosine) occurs when the periods begin at some point other than 0.

Pi: Constant that is equal to the ratio of any circle's circumference to its diameter. It is an irrational number but can be approximated as 3.14. It is written as π.

Piecewise Defined Function: A function that is continuous over certain defined intervals of x.

Place Value: The value of where the digit is in a number. Examples: units, tens, hundreds, hundredths.

Postulates: Statements that are accepted as true without proof.

Power: The power represents how many times a number is to be multiplied by itself. Power is also called exponent.

Prime Number: Any number that has only itself and 1 as its factors. Examples: 2, 7, 23.

Probability: The number of favorable outcomes divided by the number of possible outcomes.

Product: The result of a multiplication problem.

Proof: A way to logically make an argument about a certain object or angle in geometric terms with step-by-step reasoning on how the conclusion is reached.

Pythagorean Theorem: A relation among the three sides of a right triangle that states that the square of the hypotenuse of a right triangle is equal to the sum of the squares of the other two sides.

Quadrant: The four areas of the coordinate plane. The quadrant in the upper right is called Quadrant I and the quadrants are counted counterclockwise.

Quotient: The result of a division problem.

R-Squared: A statistic that measures how well a regression line approximates real data points.

Radian: A unit for measuring angles. 2 pi radians = 360 degrees.

Radical: An expression with a square root, cube root, or other root sign.

Radius: The distance between the center of a circle and any point on the circle itself.

Range: Set of y-values or outputs of a function.

Ratio: A means of comparing one expression containing numbers or variables to another.

Rational Number: Any number that can be expressed as a fraction. This includes decimals that terminate or repeat. Examples: –3.451, 7/3.

Real Numbers: All rational and irrational numbers.

Recursive Pattern: A pattern that uses previous values to calculate future values.

Reflection: A transformation that involves flipping an object around an axis, creating a mirror image of an object.

Relation: A patterned relationship between two variables.

Remainder: The portion of the dividend that is not evenly divisible by the divisor. For example, when 13 is divided by 5, the remainder is 3.

Right angle: An angle that equals 90 degrees.

Root: The root of an equation is where it equals zero. Sometimes, root is used as an abbreviation for square root (see definition of square root).

Rotation: A transformation that involves turning an object about a pivot point.

Sample Space: The set of all possible outcomes.

Scalene Triangle: A triangle with sides of different lengths. In addition, all angles of a scalene triangle will be different.

Scatter Plots: Scatter plots allow you to show the relationships between numerical values, and they are graphed as coordinate pairs.

Scientific Notation: A way of writing numbers as products consisting of a number between 1 and 10 multiplied by a power of 10.

Sequence: A list of numbers or objects that are in a special order. The list is the result of a function at each consecutive input starting at x = 1.

Series: The result when the terms of a sequence are summed.

Similar: Figures that have the same shape are similar. They can be different sizes and positions as the result of uniform scaling (enlarging or shrinking) or transformations (rotation, reflection, or translation). When two figures are similar, the ratios of the lengths of their corresponding sides are equal.

Sine: A trigonometric function, abbreviated sin. For a right triangle, the sine of an angle is equal to the length of the opposite side divided by the hypotenuse.

Slope: The change in the y-coordinate divided by the change in the x-coordinate for a line. This is often referred to as "rise over run."

Square Root: The square root of a number is the value that when multiplied by itself gives you the number.

Standard Deviation: A measure of the dispersion of a set of data from its mean.

Stemplot: Stemplots, also called Steam and Leaf Plots, display data by place value.

Sum: The result of an addition problem.

Supplementary: Angles that add to 180 degrees.

Surface Area: The sum of the areas of all the faces of an object.

Survey: A method of gathering data for which information is gathered from a representative sample, and inferences are made about the entire group.

Tangent Line: A line on the outside of a circle that touches the circle at only one point.

Tangent Function: A trigonometric function, abbreviated tan. For a right triangle, the tangent of an angle is equal to the length of the opposite side divided by the adjacent side.

Tesselation: Also known as tiling, it is a collection of figures that completely fills a plane with no overlaps and no gaps.

Theorems: Statements that can be proven using postulates and axioms.

Translation: A transformation that involves the movement of an object without changing it in any other way.

Tree: Diagram for illustrating and visualizing a set of decision-making rules.

Union: The union of two sets contains all the unique elements of each set with no repeats.

Unit Circle: A circle centered at the origin (0, 0) with a radius of length 1 that is used to calculate the trigonometric functions for angles.

Variable: A letter that represents a value in an algebraic expression.

Variance: Variance measures the amount of variation among the values of a variable.

Volume: The three-dimensional space filled by an object.

Whole Numbers: 0, 1, 2, 3, 4, ... Includes zero and the counting numbers.

X-axis: The horizontal axis of a two-dimensional coordinate plane.

X-intercept: The point at which a line crosses the x-axis. This will happen when $y = 0$.

Y-axis: The vertical axis of a two-dimensional coordinate plane.

Y-intercept: The point at which a line crosses the y-axis. This will happen when $x = 0$.

Made in the USA
Lexington, KY
29 August 2014